Arkansas Democratic Politics, 1896–1920

Arkansas Democratic Politics, 1896–1920

Richard L. Niswonger

The University of Arkansas Press
Fayetteville 1990 London

Copyright © 1990 by Richard L. Niswonger
All rights reserved
Manufactured in the United States of America
94 93 92 91 90   5 4 3 2 1

DESIGNER: *Dixon Boyles*
TYPEFACE: *Linotron 202 Bembo*
TYPESETTER: *G & S Typesetters, Inc.*
PRINTER: *Braun-Brumfield, Inc.*
BINDER: *Braun-Brumfield, Inc.*

The paper used in this publication meets the minimum requirements
of the American National Standard for Permanence of Paper for
Printed Library Materials
Z39.48-1984. ⊗

Library of Congress Cataloging-in-Publication Data

Niswonger, Richard L.
    Arkansas Democratic politics, 1896–1920 / Richard L.
Niswonger.
        p.   cm.
    Includes bibliographical references.
    ISBN 1-55728-116-5 (alk. paper)
    1. Democratic Party (Ark.)—History.   2. Arkansas—Politics
and government—To 1950.   I. Title.
JK2318.A8N57   1990
324.2767'06—dc20   89-5195
                                                     CIP

for five loyal razorbacks, my children:

Rick Niswonger, Allan Mesko, John Mesko,
Kathryn Niswonger Bandas, Joseph Mesko

Contents

Preface

    This book represents an attempt to describe the operation of the one-party system in Arkansas. The study begins with the election of 1896 because that event saw an upheaval in the Democratic Party over the silver issue. In Arkansas the frenetic career of the "Popocratic" Governor Jeff Davis kept the party in that state embattled for more than a decade after the joust between silver and sound money men. Davis's bombastic reformism gave way to the more business-like progressivism of Governors George Donaghey and Charles Brough. The study ends with the final year of Brough's administration in 1920. In Brough, the state had its scholar in politics, the Woodrow Wilson of Arkansas. Although the focus is upon the Democratic Party, one chapter is devoted to the examination of the Republican Party and its special role in a one-party state.

    With gratitude I express my indebtedness to many friends and associates who have helped to bring this work to completion. I am especially in debt to Lewis L. Gould of the University of Texas at Austin for his counsel and guidance during my initial foray into Arkansas politics. Barnes F. Lathrop, Norman Brown, and Thomas McCraw, also of the University of Texas, read the manuscript and suggested improvements. Samuel Sizer of the University of Arkansas and James Walker of the National Archives gave expert advice on the use of manuscript and archival sources. A number of institutions gave special aid: the University of Arkansas Library and its Special Collections division, the Library of Congress Manuscripts Division, and the Arkansas History Commission.

The *Arkansas Historical Quarterly* has not only been a treasure house of information but has also kindly granted permission to use materials which I had previously published in that journal. Chapter two of this work is a revision of the article "Arkansas and the Election of 1896" published in the Spring of 1975. Also some portions of my articles on Jeff Davis (Summer, 1980) and on William F. Kirby (Autumn, 1978) have been used in this work. Publication of this book is supported in part by a grant from the Arkansas Endowment for the Humanities and the National Endowment for the Humanities.

Most of all I acknowledge the generous contribution made by my wife, Grace Niswonger, who typed my hen scratchings on many long evenings. Finally, I hope no one will hold any of these good people culpable for errors of mine.

Arkansas Democratic Politics, 1896–1920

1

The Rise of the Arkansas Democracy

For politicians seeking to understand the state's political behavior and writers searching for safe generalizations, Arkansas politics has defied analysis. Many observers comment on the state's diversity and its enigmatic, idiosyncratic character. A survey of the state's geographic, economic, and social patterns should contribute toward lifting the shroud of mystery. The most arresting characteristic of Arkansas at the turn of the century was the continued prevalence of frontier conditions in the midst of attempts to modernize and industrialize society. In education, cultural pursuits, urbanization, communications, transportation, credit facilities, and industrialization Arkansas followed in the wake of other states.

The mountainous terrain of much of Arkansas accounts in part for the state's parochialism and retarded development. The Ozark and Ouachita mountains, rising almost three thousand feet, are far from being the nation's tallest, but they lie astride the vast plains between the Appalachian and Rocky mountains.[1] The hills and mountains interrupted the movement of settlers into Arkansas in large numbers, and the existence of Indian Territory on the western border, legally closed to white settlement until 1889, tended to divert westward movement around the state.

Remote mountain strongholds secluded the hill people from rapid communication of ideas and exchange of goods. During early twentieth-century elections, primary returns slowly filtered into Little Rock because of poor telephone and wire communications with isolated areas. Usually *The Arkansas Gazette* never did get around to printing the complete official primary returns. Hill folk regarded political or social innovation with suspicion. The rejection by the voters of the innocuous work of the 1918, and again of the 1970 constitutional conventions, suggests that a spirit of negativism lingers on.

The redneck's distrust of politicians and the "high-collared" Little Rock crowd provided an easy road to political success for a skillful politician like Jeff Davis of Pope County. In his first campaign for governor, Davis told a Conway audience he was not "trying to array the prejudices of the country against Little Rock . . . it is a fine city, but they have got a few things there that I am going to tell the people of Arkansas about in no uncertain sound, either." *The Helena Weekly World* called him "a red-faced, loud-lunged deep-voiced, ox-driving mountaineer." Davis happily agreed to the assessment and admitted he was "a friend of the fellow that brews the forty-rod bug juice." In the same speech, Davis accused the Little Rock press of raking him "fore and aft," and he castigated the Little Rock banks for their alleged refusal to cash his checks. "I never said the people of Little Rock were corrupt," he explained, "but they live in an atmosphere of trusts. They just breathe trusts; they inhale it; their surroundings and their environments have poisoned their judgment."[2]

Little Rock has not only occupied a place at the geographical center of Arkansas, it has also been the political, social, intellectual, and cultural heart of the state. The city is located on the Arkansas River and also lies on the boundary between the hilly and the lowland regions of the state. With a population of 38,307 in 1900, it had more than three times the population of its nearest rival, Fort Smith. Most of the industries, wholesale businesses, and financial institutions of Arkansas established headquarters at Little Rock. Politically, the city represented the more conservative elements in the Democratic Party. It harbored the state's most prominent goldbug leaders and frequently elected legislators who opposed antitrust legislation and restrictive railroad measures. In 1898 Charles Collins, a leading Bryan man in Arkansas, lost his bid for selection as a delegate from Little Rock to the State Democratic Convention while gold men easily won positions in the city and Pulaski County central committees. During a state senate debate on a proposed revision of the fellow-servant rule, one senator lashed out at the legislator from Pulaski County and his cohorts, "I have got my first time to see any of them vote for a measure that truly had the interests of the people at heart." Yet, during the second decade of the twentieth century, Little Rock also served as a focal point for reform groups. Prohibitionists and woman suffrage advocates established headquarters in the capital and then moved out to organize in other areas. The city frequently vied with Hot Springs as the site for conventions and gatherings of all kinds.[3]

Politicians often spoke of the Little Rock machine, and while the city did exercise a large influence, it did not actually dominate the state government at the turn of the century. The Delta region was a more powerful factor in state politics. Eastern Arkansas counties juggled election returns more frequently than other areas and generally maintained a more tightly disciplined party organization at the county level. Arkansas politicians had to reckon with sectional considerations when seeking statewide offices. Usually the south, east, or north supported their own favorites, but many popular Democrats succeded in scattering their support across the state. Jeff Davis spent much of his first three years as governor in an effort to ally the Delta chieftains with his hill Democracy. Governor Charles H. Brough (1917–21) discovered in the "swamp Democrats" his chief political hurdle and made defiance of the eastern establishment one of the leading themes of his administration.

A diagonal line drawn across Arkansas from the northeastern to the southwestern corner approximates the division between hill and lowland country. The triangular area south of this line comprises the plains area which further divides into the Mississippi Alluvial Plain on the east and the Gulf Coastal Plain in the south. Planters found the black soils of the east suitable for large farms while smaller farms and timberlands predominated in the south.[4] A large number of river valleys providing fertile bottom lands extend out of the southern triangle up into the hilly section of the state. Since much of the lowland area along the great waterways lay under water during part or all of the year, levee construction and drainage became a frequent concern of Arkansas politics. At the turn of the century, Arkansas politicians sought federal aid in establishing a system of levees to reclaim a vast fertile floodland area in the northeastern section of the state, and by 1902, a 3,500 square mile area (part of it in Missouri but mostly in Arkansas) was free from flooding. The federal government aided the construction of a 212 mile levee along the St. Francis

River from New Madrid, Missouri, to its mouth at Helena, Arkansas. The Arkansas General Assembly established the St. Francis Levee Board to administer and maintain the levee system along the St. Francis river and also authorized the creation of many smaller drainage boards.[5]

The same diagonal line running between hilly and lowland areas also separated the black belt from predominantly white areas. Although blacks made up 28 percent out of a total population of 1,311,564 in Arkansas in 1900, the hill counties had so few blacks that in one of them, Marion County, the 1920 census reported no Negro population at all. Of the eight counties having 62.5 percent black population or more in the 1920 census, five of them, Crittenden, Lee, Phillips, Desha, and Chicot, border the Mississippi River. The border of one of the three remaining counties, St. Francis, is within a few miles of the river, and the other two, Jefferson and Lincoln, lie along the Arkansas River just before it empties into the Mississippi.[6]

The prairie lands in the central section of the state form a third division within the southern triangle. This rice belt area consists of Arkansas, Desha, Jefferson, Lonoke, Monroe, Phillips, Prairie, and St. Francis counties. In the early twentieth century, this area between Little Rock and Memphis produced the nation's third largest rice crop and the country's largest rice yield per acre. The prairie lands lie west of one of Arkansas's most unusual geographical features, Crowley's Ridge. This ridge, from one to ten miles wide, up to 150 feet high, and about 150 miles long, extends from the northeastern corner of the state to the vicinity of Helena on the Mississippi. Because the area afforded an escape from the flood plains, settlers sometimes dubbed it "God's Levee." The ridge rises abruptly from the lowlands and marks the division between the valleys of the St. Francis River and the Mississippi River and the prairie lands. The prairie area also produced cotton, corn, and potatoes in the early twentieth century.[7]

Only four states supplied bauxite for the manufacture of aluminum in the early 1900s. Most of this ore, 85 percent of all bauxite mined in the world, came from Arkansas. The Aluminum Company of America controlled almost all of the bauxite supply in the southern states. Arkansas's semi-anthracite coal mines near Fort Smith in Sebastian County provided coal for the United States Navy. The Iron Mountain and Southern Railroad, Arkansas's largest rail line, owned many of the coal mines. The state ranked first in the production of ash, cottonwood, and red gum, with hickory, oak, and yellow pine not far behind. The railroads built lines into the timber areas in the southern triangle but often abandoned the tracks after the trees were cut.[8]

Arkansas industries of all kinds employed only twenty-six thousand five hundred laborers by 1900. Miners, lumber workers, railroaders, and factory workers received low pay and slight protection from the state government.[9] The coal companies of western Arkansas paid the miners $2.50 daily on the average, although wages might range from $1.50 up to $4.00 a day. In 1899 Sebastian County coal miners went on strike to secure pay increases and recognition of their union. The mine owners retaliated by transporting Negro replacements into the state and by stockpiling pistols, rifles, and shotguns in anticipation of violence. Although a Sebastian County Court restrained the mine owners from further importation of strike breakers, a federal court dissolved the injunction. In 1901 the United States Supreme Court reversed the decision of the federal court and remanded the case to the state court. The stance of the state government revealed an increased concern for the miners although its actions also smacked of racism.[10] Governor Daniel W. Jones (1897–1901) denounced "Government by Injunction" and supported the decision to take the case to the nation's highest court, where he received vindication.[11] Also vocal on the miners' behalf was gubernatorial candidate, Jeff Davis. "The miners of this state," said Davis in an 1899 speech, "have as much right to organize and protect themselves from the greedy grasp of mine owners as have the mine owners to organize and cut down the wages of miners, and sell them goods from company stores at extortionate prices."[12]

The lumber worker in Arkansas did not fare much better than the miner. Before 1890, timber operations in Arkansas were primarily local ventures by farmers who supplied lumber only to their immediate area. But by the turn of the century, the availability of capital for further development and the extension of railroad lines into previously isolated areas made further exploitation possible. Many railroad workers lived in tents in temporary camps that sprang up near the rail lines. Others found shelter at boarding houses in newly built towns.[13] Ormond H. Twiford, a southeastern Arkansas logger, tells in his diary of carrying his revolver with him, living in a boarding house, visiting the "scarlet women" at the hotel, and getting drunk frequently. When an area had been

cut over, he helped rip up the old mill and move on to virgin timber land. His pay for one month amounted to $16.50.[14] Although
most of the loggers worked in the southeastern counties, a few
served in the cedar forests of northern Arkansas. Daniel B.
Lackey, an Arkansas cedar logger, recounted how for a day's work
he received a dollar plus room and board. His bed was a straw-
filled bunk in a tent and his food was simple but adequate. The
floaters who took the logs down river in the spring received
double pay, two dollars a day, because of the great hazards involved in their work.[15]

The timber depredators victimized Arkansas and left much of
its cutover forest land naked to the soil blasting attacks of wind
and water. Thomas C. McRae, later a Woodrow Wilson progressive and governor of Arkansas (1921–25), aided the northern
timber companies during his tenure in Congress (1885–1903).
As a member of the House Committee on Public Lands he was in
a favorable position to acquire information about cheap government forest land. In 1902 he boasted to Samuel S. Barney, a potential client, that timber men had made a huge profit in Arkansas
during the previous five years. He had the right connections to
locate valuable timber areas and would provide the information
at fifty cents per acre. Private acreages could not be purchased as
cheaply, he explained, because such owners knew "timber values" were rising. McRae explained that his fee was for "professional services in purchasing of scrip." Many of his letters offer to
locate "Military Bounty Land Warrants" and "Surveyor General
scrip" lands. McRae promised to secure the yellow pine forest
land for five dollars an acre plus a fee.[16] In his later years, he called
for "protection and replacement of our forests" and condemned
"wasteful methods of logging."[17]

As in many other states, the railroads of Arkansas received
credit for the economic ills of the state. Politicians frequently
charged the railroads with corrupting the legislature and stran-
gling native commerce. Governor Jeff Davis told the general assembly of 1907 that the railroads continually "dish out small favors to the members of the legislature, and large ones" if needed
to defeat measures like the proposed abolition of the fellow-
servant rule. *The Arkansas Gazette* expressed a common opinion
when it accused the Goulds of deliberately draining the state of
raw materials to enrich eastern manufacturers. "The Iron Mountain does not want any factories in Arkansas." The Goulds, ac-

cording to the newspaper, preferred to get two hauls instead of one by carrying cotton to the east and returning the finished cloth to Arkansas.[18]

Jay Gould's St. Louis, Iron Mountain and Southern Railroad ranked as the largest line and the one most frequently denounced. In 1881, Gould purchased the Cairo and Fulton Railroad, made famous by its connection with James G. Blaine. This line became the nucleus of a larger system which he named the Iron Mountain. By 1900 the road had a little over three hundred miles of track on its main line which cut across the state not far from the diagonal line dividing hill country from lowlands. A lengthy section of the railroad followed the path of Crowley's Ridge. Spur lines enabled it to tap the coal and timber resources of Arkansas as well as cotton and other agricultural goods. The Iron Mountain became a part of Gould's Missouri Pacific system.[19]

The Arkansas Gazette accused the Goulds of discriminating in favor of the Coal Hill, Jenny Lind, and Denning mines which were operated by their own Western Coal Mining Company. Independent operators found it difficult to compete with Gould's company. Because the Missouri Pacific carried coal mined by convicts in Alabama at a lower rate than Arkansas coal could be transported within the state, investors avoided risking development of Arkansas mines. The line charged a rate of $1.50 per ton for coal brought from Birmingham to Little Rock over two different lines for a distance of 325 miles. The railroad charged $1.75 per ton for a 195 mile haul within the state. In December of 1896, Fort Smith hosted a conference urging development of the Arkansas River as a waterway to deliver the state from the hands of the railroad monopolists.[20]

Little Rock merchants and businessmen gave their support to the movement to create a railroad commission. The agrarian protest movement in Arkansas demanded regulation of rates and curtailment of railroad monopolies but made little headway against the railroad lobby until after the 1896 election. The voice of Arkansas wholesalers and merchants joined in the chorus with agrarian dissidents to demand a commission. In 1896 and 1898, the state Democratic plaforms and the gubernatorial candidate, Dan Jones, took positions in favor of the commission concept. With *The Arkansas Gazette* echoing the call, the legislature finally acceded to demands by establishing a commission in 1899.[21]

The Arkansas Railroad Commissioners reflected the general

disgust with the railroad corporations. "By their system of rate making," said the commission's first report, "they reversed natural laws. They abrogated distance as an element of transportation, and made Arkansas tributary to the great cities of the border states." For goods shipped from Memphis into Arkansas, the railroads charged a rate as low as or lower than for goods shipped over the same line within the state. Sugar, molasses, and other products came from Memphis to points along the Little Rock to Fort Smith line at a rate of twenty-five cents per one hundred pounds. The same goods originating at Little Rock to a point on the road between Little Rock and Fort Smith paid a higher rate, twenty-seven and one-half cents per one hundred pounds. Flour and corn meal traveled from Memphis to Fort Smith for fifteen cents per one hundred pounds while from Little Rock to Fort Smith the price rose to seventeen and one-half cents. Since wholesalers in Little Rock could not compete with Memphis businessmen, they joined ranks with those favoring railroad regulation. Such practices, the commission reasoned, drove capital which might have been invested in Arkansas to Memphis or St. Louis.[22]

The commission recognized the same sinister influences at work to depress cottonseed prices. The planter seeking a fair return found the railroads agreeing with favored mills to hold prices at a fixed level. Freight rates kept interstate mills from competing with the prices charged in Arkansas. Each mill controlled the market in its own district of the state and did not compete with other mills in their districts.[23]

The Railroad Commission initially enforced the published rates of the railroads but soon discovered these rates to be excessive. Before the commission made its first annual report, it responded to criticism by establishing the "Standard Freight Distance Tariff." The new rate system significantly lowered freight rates in Arkansas and ended discrimination in favor of certain localities within the state. The rates could not affect discrimination in favor of out-of-state cities, but they did provide for greater competition within the state. The commission also broke up the cottonseed monopolies, which had established control over their own districts. Because of the new standard freight rate for cottonseed, the farmer could sell his cottonseed to mills other than the one formerly controlling his district.[24]

Although the general assembly gave broad regulatory powers to the commission, it retained the practice of establishing maxi-

mum rates. In 1907, the legislature lowered the maximum passenger rates to two cents per mile on lines extending eighty-five
miles or more. In 1908, the railroads secured an injunction from
the United States Circuit Court at St. Paul to restrain the legislature's passenger rates and the commission's freight tariff that
had been in effect eight years. In 1917, the United States Supreme
Court upheld the railroads in their contention that Arkansas's rates
were confiscatory. Despite setbacks in the courts, the Arkansas
Railroad Commission had a modicum of success in reducing
rates and increasing competition within the state. The railroads
fought the commission concept initially and continued their assault during the early decades of the twentieth century.[25]

The railroads promoted migration to the state but had less success in Arkansas compared to their record in other states. G. A.
Deane, Jr., son of the land commissioner for the Iron Mountain
Railroad, told a reporter in 1896 that the New York office was
sending large numbers of Germans to White County to engage in
farming. Hungarians, he said, were moving into Jackson County.
But *The Arkansas Gazette,* in the same year, reported the state's
foreign-born population to be only 14,264, or 1.26 percent of the
whole population.[26] The Germans, as evidenced by place-names
like Stuttgart, were the largest foreign group. But the foreign
element, though it was vocal in opposition to prohibition, was a
minor element in Arkansas politics. According to the 1900 census, Arkansas's foreign-born population amount to only 1.1 percent of the total population, and by 1920 the figure had declined
to 0.8 percent. In absolute figures the foreign-born population
dropped from 14,186 in 1900 to 13,975 in 1920.[27] Arkansans had
mixed attitudes toward the new immigrants. On the one hand
they viewed the foreigners as a valuable source of needed labor.
But nativism also manifested itself. The *Baptist Advance* warned
in 1913 that the "sturdy Anglo-Saxon citizenship of America
faces a grave threat to American institutions in the unchecked
flood of ignorant Europeans, mostly Roman Catholics or anar-
chists, which continue to pour into this country. . . ."[28] Arkansas, like many other Southern states, had an extremely homogeneous white population. Before the Civil War, Tennessee ranked
as the major source of white migration into Arkansas. Close behind were Mississippi, Alabama, and Georgia. After the war
settlers from the trans-Mississippi area came to the state in increasing numbers, especially from Missouri and Texas. Black mi-

gration came chiefly from Tennessee and Mississippi during the middle decades of the nineteenth century.[29]

Arkansas's population ranked as one of the nation's most rural and agricultural. Out of a total population of 1,311,564 inhabitants, the 1900 census classified 1,199,831 as rural. Stated another way, fewer than one person in twelve lived in a town of 2,500 people or more. By 1890, only nine towns had reached the 2,500 mark. By 1920, there were forty-one towns of this size. The largest urban area in the state, Little Rock, reached a population of 65,142 in 1920, but no other city in that year had even half as many inhabitants. Fort Smith climbed to 28,870. Hot Springs and Pine Bluff boasted about 20,000 each.[30]

Rural Arkansas provided a fertile field for the agrarian protest movement. Cotton planters saw profits dwindle as cotton prices fell in the 1890s, and the hill farmers awakened in the same period to the evils of monopoly and a government dominated by city people with money. No state illustrated more graphically the struggle and upheaval within the one-party system as the agrarian tide swept against the Democratic dike. Only a gradual and continuing capitulation to the agrarian spirit prevented the Populist Party from gaining a stronger foothold in the state. The rural society also offered the demagogue a receptive audience because of its narrow outlook, suspicious mentality, and limited access to outside information. In 1910, George A. Cole, president of the Arkansas Farmers' Union, admitted to a St. Louis audience that the farmer had been "'easy money' for the barnstorming candidate." The admission contained a sly reference to the silver crusaders, but the farm leader castigated political demagogues of various molds. He warned that "the farmer is no longer the plaything of the demagogue politician, who sought to prey upon his prejudices for the sole purpose of riding into office."[31]

A large percentage of the state's farmers were tenants, and the percentage of tenants increased without respite from 1880 to 1930. The proportion of farms operated by tenants rose from 32.1 percent in 1890 to 51.3 percent in 1920. Most of this increase came in the 1890s when tenancy increased by 13.3 percent. But in the fifteen counties in the Ozark region, which comprises northwestern and north central Arkansas, the tenancy rate steadily declined from 30.9 percent to 25.2 percent in the 1890 to 1920 period. In the Ozarks, farmers were white and operated family farms with few or no hired hands, while in the plains areas share cropping was common.[32]

The discontent of those sharecroppers living in virtual peonage sometimes exploded into violent clashes. In 1919 Governor Charles H. Brough explained to the legislature that he had requested the aid of five hundred federal troops because "a very serious insurrection of negroes [sic] occurred at Elaine, Phillips County, Arkansas, involving the loss of six whites and nineteen negroes." Except for the aid of the soldiers, the governor envisioned "an orgy of lawlessness and a saturnalia of human and economic loss."[33] The riot occurred because Negro sharecroppers failed in an attempt to secure a "settlement" (a settling of accounts at the end of a year's service). The sharecroppers had established the "Progressive Farmers and Household Union of America" to press for a higher price for their cotton.[34] Although the Ozark farmers suffered from want during the depression years, they did not express their discontent through mass violence. James W. Moore, an Ozark farmer, wrote a letter to William Jennings Bryan on the back side of a sheet of newsprint and told him of the depressed conditions in Boone County. The family was "poverty stricken and times being so awful hard and no work to do, we will be almost bound to suffer for bread."[35]

The political culture of Arkansas reflected the state's frontier heritage, retarded economic development, and agrarian cast. Politicians appealed to the prejudices of the Anglo-Saxon hill people and approached the problems of the era with solutions acceptable to suspicious mountaineers. Since Arkansas was an agricultural state, the needs of miners, loggers, and industrial workers generally received less attention than farm problems, although some progressive labor measures did become law; Arkansas was one of the first states to ratify an abortive child labor amendment to the federal constitution in the 1920s.

The rural people expressed strong anti-corporation sentiments, and by 1900 most politicians repeated the familiar denunciations of the combinations and interests. The country folk also turned to negativistic and iconoclastic political leaders. Sectionalism affected the state's political cast. The hill country often ranged itself against the "Swamp Democracy," and the rural areas were often in conflict with the few urban centers. Since the state moved lazily out of the frontier stage, it resented the advantages of the northeastern United States but also of closer centers like Memphis and St. Louis. Citizens of underdeveloped Arkansas vented their wrath upon the colonial masters of the East and the railroad monopolies. The economic, geographic, and agrarian characteristics of Arkansas had a major impact on the state's political style. But the most important single factor affecting the political development of the state was the development of a single dominant political institution—the Democratic Party.

Looking back upon a long life of leadership in the Republican Party, Reconstruction governor Powell Clayton vented his frustration with the Democratic Party's continued domination of Arkansas politics. "It is plain," he complained in 1915, "that the basic principle of good government, which depends on two parties, . . . is completely destroyed." *The Arkansas Gazette* seldom found any point of agreement with Clayton, but it saw the same pattern of dominance, though in a different light. "The people generally are so well pleased with Democratic rule," claimed the *Gazette,* "that opposition is minimized. With only one ticket to be voted for, a great number of voters do not feel that it is necessary to go to the polls."[36] By the 1896 election, the Democratic Party had solidified its control over the state.[37] Not until the 1960s could an opposition party breach the Democratic fortress.

On the basis of presidential elections, Arkansas maintained, at least through 1968, a more consistent Democratic record than any other state. In 1928 and again in 1964, when five former Confederate states bolted the Democratic presidential ticket, Arkansas remained in the Democratic column.[38] Before the 1970s the state failed to vote Democratic only twice. In 1868 Arkansas's electoral votes went to Republican U. S. Grant, and one century later, in 1968, the state cast its votes for George Wallace. Between 1896 and 1920, only Searcy County in northern Arkansas voted consistently Republican in presidential elections. Newton County, in the northwest, almost met this standard by casting its votes for the Republican candidate in every year except 1912. The closest rivals to Newton and Searcy counties were Pike and Madison counties which voted Republican in three of the seven presidential elections between 1896 and 1920. Fifty-two of Arkansas's seventy-five counties never deviated from the Democratic side in the seven elections.[39]

Democratic strength was a fact of life as early as 1836 when the territory gained statehood. During Arkansas's territorial period powerful family groupings dominated Arkansas politics. Factions centered about family combinations or personalities. Toward the end of the territorial phase, the two major factions joined forces with either the supporters of Andrew Jackson or Henry Clay. By the time Arkansas became a state, the Sevier family, which supported Andrew Jackson, had gained control of the new state's politics.[40] Civil War and Reconstruction brought only a brief interruption of Democratic dominance, and in 1874 the redeemers ushered in another long era of Democratic rule. During the decades of agrarian agitation, the Republicans and the independents raised fears but never succeeded in forming a combination of interests powerful enough to unseat the Democrats. Yet the Republicans and third-party movements could not be shrugged off without concern. The rising agrarian protest gained political strength during the 1880s and early 1890s, and the threat of fusion with the Republicans was more than a specter haunting Democratic dreams. At times, it became a fearsome reality.

In 1880 the Greenback Party challenged Democratic control of the state by nominating W. P. "Buck" Parks, a Lafayette County attorney, for governor and enlisting the support of the Republican Party. The Republicans did not put up a slate of candidates but decided to back the Greenback slate for statewide offices. Rufus K. Garland announced in 1879 that he was deserting the Democratic Party to support the Greenback ticket because the Democrats had not lived up to promised concessions to the agrarian rebels. With no Republican nominee in the field, the Greenback candidate polled 31,284 votes to Democrat Thomas Churchill's 84,088. Even with the support of small-scale businessmen and farmers, Parks carried only six counties.[41]

Despite the failure of 1880, the agrarians persisted. In 1882 mortgage-plagued farmers in the vicinity of Des Arc in Prairie County gathered at an old school building to establish an agricultural protest organization. The symbolism of Ezekiel's wheels within wheels suggested a name, the Agricultural Wheel. As agrarian leader Winfield Scott Morgan saw it, if the politician could have his rings, the farmer could establish wheels. Founded in the same year as the Wheel, the Brothers of Freedom served a similar purpose for the farmers in western Arkansas. The organization originated in Johnson County and enlisted support in other counties bordering the Arkansas River valley, where voters traditionally opposed the "ring" rule in Little Rock. The Johnson

County organization grew rapidly, but its membership did not reach beyond Arkansas. In 1885 when the Brothers of Freedom counted forty-three thousand members, they merged with the Wheel, which was a much smaller body but had established itself in other states as well as in Arkansas. In 1889 the national Wheel became a part of the Farmers' Alliance, but in Arkansas this merger was not actually consummated until 1891. The linking of these organizations created a national body with seven hundred fifty thousand members. The newly merged Farmers' Alliance reached into every state in the South.[42]

During the 1880s, a controversy between Democrats favoring full payment of the state's Reconstruction obligations and those supporting repudiation nearly disrupted the party. The strong "state credit" faction wished to protect Arkansas's reputation with those in the East who provided capital. Some of those who led the fight for financial integrity held state bonds themselves. *The Arkansas Gazette* and *The Arkansas Democrat* lent their voices to the demand for protection of credit sources. William Fishback led the drive for passage of an amendment to repudiate the Reconstruction levee and railroad bonds while Senator Augustus H. Garland bitterly opposed the move. The repudiationists gained the victory in 1884 when the "Fishback Amendment" became the first amendment to the state constitution by a vote of 63,703 to 16,940. During the decade, repudiationism became orthodox Democratic doctrine, and in 1888 Fishback made a serious bid for the gubernatorial nomination. He failed in 1888, but in 1892 the Democrats sent him forth as their standard-bearer against the Populist hosts.[43]

Another serious threat to the one-party system came in the 1888 election. The Wheelers bolted the Democratic Party to aid the Union Labor ticket, and the Republicans joined hands with them to support former state Senator C. M. Norwood of Prescott, who was the Union Labor nominee for governor. The Democratic candidate, James P. Eagle of Lonoke, defeated his opponent by a surprisingly small margin for an Arkansas election, 99,229 to 84,223. In the same year, an Arkansan, C. E. Cunningham, ran as vice presidential nominee of the Union Labor Party, and Arkansas's first congressional district sent an agrarian leader, Lewis P. Featherston of Forrest City, to the house of representatives as the victor in a contested election. The composition of the Arkansas General Assembly also reflected the mood of the state. Two Republicans and two Union Labor Party men served in the state senate while twelve Republicans and four Union Labor men went to the state house of representatives. In the presidential election, Benjamin Harrison won in fifteen counties and polled 58,752 votes to Grover Cleveland's 85,962. The Republicans combined with the agrarians again in 1890 and polled 85,181 votes to the Democrats' 106,267 in the gubernatorial election. Despite the overtures made to the Republicans, Winfield Scott Morgan held little hope that the lower economic classes could get a hearing from one of the two major parties. He believed it was only "barely possible" that one of them "would accede to our demands and carry them out in good faith. . . ." If the major parties refused such aims as nationalization of the railroads and the telegraph, their rejection "Would hasten the disruption of the existing parties. . . ." Morgan warned that the laboring classes would form a new political party if cooperation with existing parties proved unfruitful.[44]

Although the Populist Party in Arkansas captured its largest vote in 1892, it did so without joining forces with the Republican organization. The People's Party nominated a mathematics teacher from the little red brick college at Cane Hill, Arkansas. Dressed in farmer's garb, Professor J. P. Carnahan campaigned along the rocky Ozark roads, stopping his buggy occasionally to wash his clothes in a creek. Resuming his journey, Carnahan would fly his clothes out of the buggy to dry them. Traveling with him in the joint canvass was a more dignified and genteel figure, William Fishback, the Democratic nominee of repudiationist fame.[45]

Dissension within the Democratic ranks over the Fishback nomination further endangered the party's hold on the state. But Joseph W. House, chairman of the Democratic State Central Committee, ably harmonized the Fishback and anti-Fishback forces. His role as peacemaker won for him the position of United States District Attorney for eastern Arkansas.[46] In the gubernatorial contest the voters gave the Populist nominee barely more than one-third the number of votes they gave Fishback. The Republican vote also exceeded the Populist vote by a small margin.[47]

The Populist Party in Arkansas peaked in strength almost as soon as the party entered the state. In 1892 J. P. Carnahan polled 31,117 votes for governor, but in each succeeding bienniel election the Populists lost about 30 percent of their total votes in the preceding election. In 1892, 1894, and 1896, the Populists sent either seven or eight members to the Arkansas House of Representatives in each election. During the same years they elected only one of their nominees to the state senate.[48] Clearly the People's Party did not attain the influence it had in other states.

The Democratic response to the challenge of the Republicans and Populists was twofold. The party gradually accommodated itself to Populist ideology to entice dissidents to remain. The other tactic involved manipulating the electoral machinery to favor the dominant party. Through the latter decades of the nineteeth and into the early twentieth century, the Democratic party in Arkansas responded to pressure from the hill farmers, small businessmen, and rural folk. At least one reason for the failure of Populism to secure a firm foothold in rural Arkansas was the ability of the Democratic Party to adjust its ideology and rhetoric to suit the increasingly dissident farmer. The victory of repudiation, the drafting of a silver plank in the 1894 Democratic state platform, the creation of a railroad assessment board and of a regulatory railroad commission, the almost total victory of the silver forces in 1896, and the capture of the party machinery by redneck leader Jeff Davis in 1901 demonstrated the flexibility of the Democratic Party. In Texas, Governor James S. Hogg cut the ground from under the Populists by shifting the Democratic Party toward agrarian positions.[49] The Arkansas pattern parallels that of Texas except that Arkansas had fewer non-anglo and non-evangelical groups within its boundaries.

Before the 1896 election, the Democratic Party strengthened its grip on the state by changing the election process. The party developed legal means to supplement less appealing methods, such as stuffing ballot boxes or theft of the boxes. Fraud might lead to complications. John M. Clayton, Republican candidate for Congress from the second district, charged fraud after the election of 1888. When an over-zealous Democrat gunned down the contestant, Sheriff Shelby of Conway County refused at first to even begin an investigation.[50] Such scandals offended even loyal Democrats, and the state experimented with more refined methods of vote manipulation.

The decade of the 1890s became an era of black disfranchisement. Democrats after 1890 came to view black voting as a dangerous threat to their control of the political system, and they took measures to restrict black voting and office holding. Contrary to a commonly held opinion, blacks voted in significant numbers during the late 1870s and 1880s. Whites had approved and even encouraged black voting in this era. This can be understood when one considers the background of the former Confederate military leaders who came to political power after Reconstruction in the 1870s and 1880s. These Redeemers encouraged the growth of business and industry. But since their economic interests ran contrary to that of many whites, they looked to blacks for support at the ballot box. The former planters among the Redeemers found it easy to have contact with blacks since they had done so since childhood. Up until 1894 they had permitted blacks to hold office in the Delta counties. In those areas, Republicans and Democrats entered into a fusion arrangement whereby a slate of both blacks and whites would be on the ticket.[51]

During the late 1870s, the Redeemers used black votes to maintain themselves in power. White agrarian rebels had joined the Greenback Party in an attempt to displace one-party Democratic rule. The conservative business-oriented leadership, often referred to as the "Bourbons," found the blacks a valuable ally. But when the agrarians gained greater strength in 1888 and 1890, the threatened Bourbons began to reconsider their alliance with blacks. The Union Labor candidates for governor had come perilously close to equaling the number of Democratic votes. With agrarians and Republicans joining hands, the one-party system seemed to be in jeopardy. But the most decisive event leading the Redeemers to abandon the blacks was the development of the Populist movement in Arkansas. Eleven of the 170 delegates to the Populist convention in Little Rock in 1892 were blacks. Agrarians at the conference made a conscious effort to woo black support by including several planks representing their interests in the platform. One plank called for due process and condemned lynchings.[52] These events encouraged the Redeemers to raise the specter of "Negro domination." In desperation Democrats turned to racial demagoguery as a means of retaining control of Arkansas state politics.

Arkansas had gained a reputation for being relatively moderate in its racist tendencies, at least when compared to most other Southern states. But early in the 1890s, the situation abruptly changed. Willard Gatewood discovered that between 1888 and 1891 there developed "a substantial increase in anti-Negro prejudice." Segregation also was much more rigidly enforced in the

1890s. The passage of a separate coach law in 1891 helped terminate Arkansas's earlier reputation as a haven for blacks.[53]

One of the means used to end black participation was the abandonment of the fusion system. During the elections of 1892 and 1894, the Democrats began to run straight tickets in most of the eastern counties of Arkansas. By the time of the 1896 election, the Democrats had discovered that they no longer needed to make any pre-election arrangements with Republicans and blacks for the dividing of offices among themselves. There were no fusion tickets after 1894. The election of 1894 was also the first since the beginning of black voting rights that did not send a single black to the state legislature. But the straight Democratic tickets could not have been so successful in the old plantation counties of the east without some kind of specific devices to disfranchise blacks.[54]

One of the devices used to disfranchise blacks and weaken Republican influence was the adoption of changes in the election machinery. The general assembly passed a new election law in 1891. Legislators viewed the measure as a praiseworthy reform effort. Public outrage over fraud at the polls had called attention to the need for a change in the system. The new law prohibited moving the location of polling places without sufficient prior notice and provided for a standard ballot.[55] The control of election machinery now passed from the hands of county judges to the State Board of Election Commissioners. This meant that the governor, secretary of state, and the auditor, who were consistently Democrats, would be supervising the electoral process. Republicans quickly saw the new system as one to be used to weaken their influence. In 1915 Powell Clayton complained that no Republican had ever served on the state board. The commissioners appointed the three-member county election boards, usually consisting of two Democrats and one Republican. The county board, in turn, appointed clerks and judges of election for each polling place with the same two-to-one representation. Sometimes a Populist might serve instead of a Republican.[56]

In 1896 Secretary of State C. B. Mills reported the new election law to be "entirely satisfactory to a large majority of the taxpayers of the state." The Australian ballot had "minimized the pernicious and demoralizing effects of the Fifteenth Amendment to the United States Constitution." But he did recommend the minority party's member on the county board be permitted to choose one of the judges in each precinct.[57] From Republican complaints it is clear that the minority judges and clerks were not always those persons the minority party would have chosen to safeguard its own interests. In practice the Democrats chose whomever they wished from the minority party. Usually a Republican county committee insisted on at least one Republican judge of election in each township. But in 1896, Sid B. Redding, secretary of the Arkansas Republican State League, castigated the Sebastian County Democratic Committee for its alleged plan to choose only Democrats to the three judgeships in each township. *The Arkansas Gazette* denied any violation of the election law and claimed that in some precincts the Populists were given the minority representation claimed by Republicans.[58]

In the 1896 election, some counties had not a single Republican judge of election. To Henry M. Cooper, chairman of the Republican State Central Committee, it was "perfectly apparent" that the Democratic election judges in Woodruff County placed a large number of Republican votes in the Democratic column. The county had 1,147 qualified white voters by Republican count and about 1,400 according to *The Arkansas Gazette.* The newspaper counted as qualified those who had reached voting age after the 1895 poll tax assessment or who had a receipt from another county. The 1,859 votes for the Democratic candidate for governor meant either that a large number of blacks cast their ballots for the Democrat or that the election judges had manipulated the returns. Another black-belt county, Phillips, had one Republican on the county board of election commissioners but had no minority judges or clerks at polling places. The lopsided gubernatorial vote (1,181 to 156 for the Democratic and Republican gubernatorial candidates, respectively) again raised the cry of fraud. Henry Cooper estimated that twenty counties engaged in practices similar to those in Woodruff and Phillips counties.[59]

Whatever the degree of truth to the Republican and Populist charges, and surely they were partially true, the Arkansas election law operated to the disadvantage of minority parties. The first year of the law's operation saw Desha County vote its first straight Democratic ticket in the post–Civil War era. Most counties did comply with the letter of the law. In Pulaski County a list of election judges for the city of Little Rock shows one Republican appointee for each ward.[60]

One of the most devastating sections in the 1891 law struck at illiterate people. Approximately 26.6 percent of the population of Arkansas was illiterate in the 1890s. A little less than half of them were white. Thus the restrictions on illiterate voting injured almost as many poor whites as blacks. The 1891 law made it illegal for an illiterate voter to choose a friend to aid in marking the ballot. The law stipulated that an illiterate voter must rely upon two precinct judges to cast his vote properly. Although it might be argued that such a system guaranteed secrecy for an illiterate person's ballot, it also opened the door to the possibility of fraud. Blacks naturally came to distrust the system and to think of voting as a futile enterprise.[61]

Arkansas never adopted literacy tests or the grandfather clause, but in 1892 the voters ratified a poll tax amendment. The poll tax became a significant device for reducing black voting. It became even more effective in 1895 when the general assembly provided that poll taxes be paid during the period between the first Monday in January up to the Saturday preceding the first Monday in July in order to qualify to vote at any election in the following year that came before the first Monday in July. Simply stated, this meant that voters would have to hold on to poll tax receipts for months or forfeit their voting right. Since blacks tended to be more mobile and have poorer facilities for storing papers, they found it difficult to comply with this provision.[62]

United States Circuit Court Judge for the Eastern District of Arkansas Jacob Trieber, a Republican appointee, expressed the view in an *obiter dictum* that the poll tax amendment had not been legally approved at the 1892 election. Some debate and confusion persisted in Arkansas from the 1880s until the 1920s over whether the state constitution required a majority of all votes cast in an election or simply a majority of all votes cast on the question to ratify an amendment to the constitution. The Arkansas Supreme Court, in 1906, indicated its agreement with the Trieber opinion without actually invalidating the amendment. Before a test case could invalidate the poll tax, the voters approved an identical amendment in 1908.[63] Voting records in Arkansas indicate a substantial decline in participation following enactment of the new restrictive measures.

The white primary was another effective device to limit black participation in the political system. Primaries at the county level had appeared as early as the 1870s in Arkansas, and in 1898 the Democratic Central Committee mandated the primary for all counties. The older system had used township conventions to instruct delegates who would attend the county convention. These gatherings were actually controlled by political bosses and were not essentially democratic. The primary broadened the participation of party members in choosing nominees. In January 1906, the State Democratic Central Committee established the white primary for the whole state.[64] The election law of 1891, the poll tax, and the white primary combined to seriously diminish black voting in Arkansas. The Fifteenth Amendment to the United States Constitution had been in effect nullified.

John W. Graves has estimated that the effect of the election law alone reduced voter participation 17 percent. The reduction for blacks was higher, 21 percent, and for whites, 7 percent. The poll tax further contracted the voting population by 10 percent (15 percent for blacks, and 9 to 12 percent for whites).[65] The returns for gubernatorial races show that a voter turnout of approximately one hundred eighty-three thousand in 1888 declined to one hundred forty-one thousand in 1896 and to one hundred thirty-three thousand in 1900. The decrease in voting numbers came at the same time that the 1900 census indicated Arkansas's population increase entitled her to another seat in the United States House of Representatives. An eastern Arkansas newspaper, in 1898, rejoiced over the elimination of blacks from Phillips County politics and announced that white rule was proving beneficial for both races. Joseph T. Robinson, later a prominent United States senator from Arkansas, defended the poll tax because it affected white as well as black voters without creating any "hardships." Like many other Arkansans, he believed the tax a proper way to support the common school and a good test of a man's genuine interest in voting.[66]

The poll tax amendment and the new election machinery were probably not the only factors causing a decline in voter participation. Texas experienced a similar decline at the turn of the century before it had adopted the poll tax. While a national decline in voting after the election of 1896 did not equal that of Southern states, it did reveal a lessening of interest nationwide. Perhaps agrarian disillusionment, absorption of Populist concepts by the Democrats, and the general resistance against black voting had almost as much effect in the South as formal techniques for restricting voting.[67]

Dewey W. Grantham has seen the transformation of Southern

politics as an important element in the development of the Southern brand of progressivism. The disfranchising of blacks and poor whites and the strengthening of the one-party system helped middle-class whites to exercise greater influence over government decisions. From the viewpoint of the rising entrepreneurial class, the changes would promote order, unity, and predictability. Grantham sees a paradox in the fact that the South appeared to be moving toward greater political democracy at the very time that political power was increasingly exercised by elites. The direct primary, the "rhetorical emphasis on the common man," and the factionalism in the one party seemed to offer democracy. The major effect of these changes was to increase the influence of a wider range of interest groups and professionals. The political changes along with industrialization and a humanitarian impulse that gained strength in Southern churches were the key elements shaping Southern progressivism.[68]

Another historian, Jack Temple Kirby, has forthrightly argued that "black disfranchisement and segregation—was itself the seminal 'progressive' reform of the era." For many whites the removal of blacks from the political context was the necessary prerequisite for further reforms.[69]

The movement to make segregation a matter of law gained momentum at the same time as the disfranchisement crusade was under way. Before 1891, segregation had been customary but had not been institutionalized by means of legalization.[70] There appears to be a link between disfranchisement and segregation. The Redeemers believed that by emphasizing black social inferiority, they could exploit the racial prejudices of poorer whites and woo them away from political alignment with blacks. Impoverished whites who might link with their black brethren in Republican or third-party movements to achieve economic aims could be discouraged by increased racial segregation. Thus segregation could be a means of aiding white Democratic political power. As Joe T. Segraves has put it, "If the white non-Democrat could be convinced that the Negro was unfit to participate in white society, then it would be easy to persuade them that the Negro was unfit for participation in government."[71]

An 1891 separate railway coach law provided that all major rail lines in Arkansas must provide both separate passenger cars and waiting rooms for the two races. The so-called Tillman Act even

attempted a definition of the black race. All those would be considered Negroes who had "a visible and distinct admixture of Af-
rican blood."[72] Governor James P. Eagle, who earlier in life had
been a Baptist minister and who would in 1902 begin serving
three terms as president of the Southern Baptist Convention, refused to ask the state legislature to approve a separate coach law.
Still, Eagle did not offer any opposition to the proposal.[73] The
protest of individual black legislators and of a mass meeting in
Little Rock failed to persuade the Arkansas General Assembly to
reject the measure. The only black member of the senate, George
W. Bell, delivered a passionate denunciation of the Tillman Act.[74]
Despite these protests, the measure passed by votes of twenty-six
to two in the senate and seventy-two to twelve in the lower assembly. Only three whites joined with black legislators to vote
against the bill. Senator J. N. Tillman of Washington County defended his bill as a progressive measure that would lessen racial
tensions.[75] But racial prejudices did not diminish. The rhetoric of
race-baiters like Jeff Davis would assure that.

With the agrarian rebels neutralized, Republican strength viti-
ated, and blacks disfranchised and segregated, the Arkansas Democracy in 1896 stood at the threshold of an era of unthreatened
supremacy. The "Solid South" had finally crystallized in Arkansas. The state was not alone in its disfranchisement policy. Segraves has described the pattern of disfranchisement in the Southern states as one of gradual development. The South did not
disfranchise blacks immediately upon the end of Reconstruction.
Almost all of the devices employed to restrict voting were set in
place during the years 1888 to 1902.[76]

To many, Southern politics after the Civil War seems the very
antithesis of democracy. Yet in spite of the disfranchisement of
blacks and some poor whites, the weakening of all opposition
parties, the control of election machinery, and voting fraud in the
Mississippi valley counties, some elements of democracy remained. Factions, while often fluctuating and centering on personalities, exhibited sufficient permanence and issue-consciousness to afford white voters a choice in the Democratic primary
elections.[77] It would be a mistake to picture the one-party system
as offering a full-blown democratic choice to voters. The Davis
faction did not crystallize immediately when the redneck messiah
appeared on the scene. Alignments were often temporary, and

patterns of political alliances frequently lacked any ideological rationale. Personalities and rhetoric often obscured any genuine differences between candidates and factions.

After Jeff Davis's death in 1913, his supporters did not succeed in maintaining his organization more than a few years. Arkansas politics reverted to an earlier pattern of fluid factionalism and issueless campaigns. Sectional divisions became less important as politicians no longer set the hill country against the plains and city. Agrarianism as a political force succumbed to the dominance of conservative business interests. But the Davis era demonstrated that even in a state with a classic one-party system, a measure of democracy could exist.[78]

During the early twentieth century, the "Old Guard," Jeff Davis's organization, attained sufficient cohesiveness, issue orientation, and durability to present a choice to voters. In 1899 Davis used his office as attorney general to launch an all-out assault upon the monopolies. He continued his warfare during his three terms as governor from 1901 to 1907 and then in the United States Senate from 1907 until his death in 1913. Small town and rural folk saw in Davis a tribune of the people, one whose heart, soul, and mind was dedicated to the one-gallus fellow who lived up the forks of the creek. To such people, Davis represented an alternative to boodling, bribery, and chicanery in high places. And Davis's opponents viewed their cause as a crusade against cheap demagoguery, misrepresentation, pandering to class interests, and disrespect for honorable party leaders.

The divergence in the party, in a rough way, represented socioeconomic differences in the state. But political concerns, the vagaries of personality, and geographical differences also joined to confuse any simple division of the Davis and anti-Davis factions. Davis often said he would never support any politician who was not a Democrat, white, and a Jeff Davis man. Despite Davis's rhetoric, one did not need to be a one-gallus Ozark farmer to be a Davis man. For histrionic effect he might assault some of the mightiest political dynasties of the state. But he was also enough of a pragmatist to garner support where it could be found. Raymond Arsenault suggests that although Davis "relied heavily on class rhetoric," he did so only in a vague manner. He was more concerned with the "cultural and social gap between town and country, or the gap between North and South, than on the distribution of wealth per se." Davis's rhetoric was aimed, he believes, at the lower middle class rather than the "low-down poor whites." Over 55 percent of the state's population belonged to the yeoman class, a group that struggled to maintain land ownership.[79] Arsenault's analysis of election returns indicates that Davis's rhetoric could be misleading. A study of 1900 precinct returns in five counties for the election of 1900 led him to conclude that "in 1900 Davis was as popular among the landowning yeomanry as he was among poor whites." Affluent precincts voted for Davis in numbers at least as large as poorer precincts.[80] After Davis's death in 1913, the "Old Guard" continued to function as an element to be reckoned with in state politics. But it increasingly became a disorganized bloc of voters within the state and almost more of a sentiment than an organization.[81]

The Arkansas Democratic Party at the turn of the century consisted of a coalition of diverse economic and sectional groups. The yeoman hill farmers, cotton planters, timberland speculators, railroad promoters, urban business and professional men, and a few industrial workers and miners gave support to the Democracy. The drama of conflicting groups seeking to wrest control of the national party had its counterpart at the state level as the Democratic Party became a battleground for resolving the conflicts of the new industrial age. Some of the more prosperous conservative Democrats in Arkansas chafed at the party's radical turn in 1896, and a few of them flirted with the Republican Party. George E. Dodge, general attorney for the Iron Mountain Railroad and a gold Democrat, informed William McKinley in 1900 that a large number of Democrats were "heartily in harmony with your administration."[82] In Massachusetts, old-stock Yankees, Irish Catholics, and independent-minded Mugwumps sought their own narrow community interests and contributed toward the sudden eclipse of the party during the 1896 upheaval.[83] Even in a Southern state like Texas, the party depended upon Mexican Catholics, other Catholic ethnic groups, German Lutherans, and blacks in addition to its primary reliance upon the Anglo-evangelical community.[84] But Arkansas Democrats relied upon the homogeneous Anglo-Saxon Protestant constituency. Only a few Germans and other European groups in the eastern plains area and the Sebastian County coal mining centers looked to the Democracy for support of their non-moralistic or non-pietistic outlook. Factionalism in the Arkansas Democratic Party represented economic and sectional interests or personalities more than ethnic differences, although it has been argued that the Davis movement with its country-versus-town emphasis could be compared to the Northern ethnocultural effect on political party identification.[85]

Arsenault has argued that Arkansas Democratic factionalism grew out of "a form of cultural conflict" similar to the ethnocultural conflict that historians have seen as the force determining party loyalty in the Northeastern and Midwestern states. He believes the ethnocultural model should be applied to the South. The division between town and country in the early twentieth century, in his opinion, determined whether one would support Jeff Davisism or oppose it. Davis did not merely represent the poor whites. His faction cannot be explained simply as the "poor vs. the rich" movement. Thus Jeff Davis was not a "Karl Marx for Hill Billies." Davis garnered support from all who opposed the "quasi-colonial relationship between town-dwelling merchants and farmers," and who opposed Northern capitalism's colonial domination of the South. According to this view, the Davis movement was more culturally based than economic. Rural folk of various categories and ranks alike were seeking respect. Davis offered them a symbolic crusade more than a struggle for specific economic goals. A clear-cut appeal for substantial economic reforms would have cost Davis the support of planters residing in towns and of other middle-class groups. In order to succeed politically, Davis needed the prosperous yeomen and better-off villagers. Thus Davis made his appeal to all who identified with the Southern rural outlook. To do this he developed not only the "Old Guard" but also a "shadow movement." The latter term, derived from Laurence Goodwyn's description of Populist fellow travelers, suggests that better-off rural folk supported much of the symbolic crusade of Davis without giving full credence to his more drastic economic reform ideas.[86] Although the shadow movement constituted a minority element, it did supply much of the leadership for the Davis faction.[87] Arsenault's method of analyzing the Davis faction seems to provide useful insights.

Although Arkansas Democrats did not need to mollify varied ethnic groups, they did experience the factionalization and ideological conflict characteristic of the national party. Before 1896, Arkansas Democrats began taking an agrarian and silver stance on the one hand or a conservative and sound money position on the other. The election of 1896 helped consolidate divisions apparent during the years preceding Bryan's campaign. Divisiveness and a lack of leadership capable of compromising the divergent interests brought down the national Democratic Party from its pinnacle of 1892. In that year the Democrats won control of the presidency and both houses of congress. But depression and inept political leadership reduced the national party's Northern outposts to a minimum. Grover Cleveland and William Jennings Bryan, whatever the merits of their points of view, did not represent a mediating or mainstream position.[88] Arkansas contributed to this destructive situation. Its own party found no middle path but surrendered to the control of the William Jennings Bryan men. The Arkansas silver men sent the goldbugs scurrying for cover, and the state's Democratic Party became a center of agrarian agitation. Arkansas Senator James K. Jones, as chairman of the National Democratic Committee, sought to promote healing in the national party. He himself represented an older era of moderation and conservatism, but he increasingly yielded to the high tempo of agrarian agitation in his own state. He did not succeed in conciliating the dissident elements nationally, because, in part, he never found a way to unite his own divided constituency, and in 1902 the more agrarian-minded Democrats joined with Jones's other enemies to remove him from the United States Senate.

Arkansas Democrats espoused an essentially negative view of government. They distrusted their state and national leaders. In 1912 the voters overwhelmingly approved an amendment to limit the length of legislative sessions to a sixty-day biennial session, believing that the less time the politicians spent in Little Rock the less damage would be done to the state. Governor Jeff Davis continually played upon the redneck's suspicions of government. Davis opposed building a new state capitol, the building of a state railroad, and purchasing a convict farm. He preferred driving the corporations from Arkansas to finding constructive methods of regulation to protect the consumer and stimulate the state's productivity. Although Davis abounded with energy, he preferred smashing shrines to erecting temples. He developed his own "stewardship theory" of the state executive office. A governor must do more than pardon criminals and appoint notaries. He should "constitute himself a department of publicity in a community." The governor should take responsibility for shaping and directing "the policies of the people of the state and of the party."[89] But Davis conceived of the executive role as that of a watchdog or chief obstructor. The governor must prevent others in the government from carrying out wasteful or dangerous programs. Arkansas Democrats continued to praise the Jeffersonian ideal of limited government and states rights in an age that demanded positive action at state and national levels to meet the problems of an industrial age. But Davis believed government had a responsibility to curb corporate interests. Eventually a more positive conception of the role of government emerged.[90]

Although the national party failed to find a consensus on major issues, the Arkansas Democrats agreed on a few basic doctrines. All factions supported white supremacy, and more than any other ideal it became the cement holding various economic and sectional interests together.[91] Increasingly during the 1890s and early 1900s, Arkansas Democrats championed more democratic procedures in government. In 1901 the Arkansas State Senate by an eighteen to four vote called upon the congressional delegation to give support to the movement for popular election of senators.[92] Both United States Senators James K. Jones and James H. Berry supported the proposal with enthusiasm. Jeff Davis gave impetus to the development of the primary election system in Arkansas.

To be a Democrat in Arkansas usually meant to advocate tariff reform. But the tendency toward localism afflicting the party on a national level also divided Arkansas Democrats. Some Arkansas senators and congressmen set an example of loyalty to the low tariff principle that almost elevated the position to the level of official Democratic dogma. James K. Jones praised the Arkansas delegation in 1897 for its pronounced low tariff stance in contrast to the weakened position of some Texas Democrats. The Arkansans had "taken the genuine Democratic ground." But he feared the continuing pressure from lumber men of the northwestern United States who had "been very busily inculcating the idea that our people should have some of the benefits of this system of plunder as long as it was going on," and he feared that such pressure might cause a breach in the ranks.[93] In the 1896 Senate primary, Senator Jones defeated Governor James P. Clarke who condemned Jones's failure to protect Arkansas lumber interests. In the second decade of the twentieth century, Senator Joseph T. Robinson ignored the shrill cries of the cotton farmers as he dedicated himself to Wilson's moderate tariff policy. H. S. Mobley, president of the Arkansas Farmers Union, promised Robinson he would seek the aid of "every man who puts a seed in the ground or plow in the furrow," to raise a protest against lowering duties on cotton fabric and yarn. In a reply to the farm leader Robinson said, "as a Democrat I feel that I am in every way honorably bound to support the fundamental principles of tariff reduction and I believe the cotton schedule quite as bad as any of them." Robinson sent the correspondence to President Woodrow Wilson to demonstrate the kind of pressure placed upon him and the way in which he had supported Wilson in the fight for the Underwood tariff.[94]

Agrarian unrest forced a testing and reshaping of Democratic ideology. The Populist threat encouraged reassertion of white supremacy lest blacks become the focal point of some future alignment against the Democrats. The agrarians also contributed more directly to the democratic and iconoclastic tendencies in the Democratic Party. The ideology and spirit of progressive Democrats, especially during Davis's governorship, was closely akin to Populism. Arkansas agrarians began the crusade for direct election of senators, the initiative and referendum, railroad regulation, antitrust legislation, and revision of the currency and banking system, but Democratic progressives took up the same causes and wrote Populist concepts into the law books. But a catalogue of crusades cannot adequately express the indebtedness of the progressives to the agrarians. The Davis phenomenon appealed to the same anti-establishment, conspiracy-oriented mentality. Like the Populists, Davis's followers oversimplified complex economic problems and viewed politics as a moral crusade against the malignant forces of evil.

In 1905 Jeff Davis paused in a campaign speech to reflect on the virtures of the People's Party he once maligned. He had spoken, he thought, with less reason in his early days when he lashed out at the hated Populists. "Ah, . . . this old Populist Party advocated some of the grandest doctrines that the world ever knew." One of the Populist concepts he had considered a "fool idea" was the belief "that you could legislate prosperity into a country." Now he believed, with the right kind of men in government, a nation could legislate its way to prosperity.[95]

The progressives coming to the fore after Davis's zenith found the Populist platforms no less inspiring than did Davis. Governors George W. Donaghey (1909–13) and Charles H. Brough 1917–21) espoused reforms once championed by agrarian leaders. During Woodrow Wilson's era, the radical agrarian element in the Democratic Party in the Southern states urged the president toward progressive change. Representative Otis Wingo and Senator William F. Kirby, vigorous Arkansas progressives, had their counterparts at Washington from Texas and other Southern states. The agrarian impulse fostered a genuine Southern progressivism, and the movement had a significant impact upon the Wilsonian reforms.[96]

Arkansas progressivism, after Davis's administration, displayed the same zest for reform, but it became less bombastic. The Donaghey and Brough administrations emphasized orderliness, efficiency, scientific planning, budgeting, and regulation without iconoclasm. Their progressivism became a compound of agrarian reformism as moderated by an increased respect for business ideals and methods. They also adopted a less negative view of the role of government in social and economic affairs than had characterized agrarians and Democrats in the past. Progressives in the South believed the state should take positive action to provide better social services and to regulate business activity in the interest of the general welfare.[97]

If the Progressives's program in Arkansas resembled the Populists', can the same carry-over be found in personnel? A few of the agrarian leaders did return to the Democratic Party and reached places of power. But not very many of them continued to have political influence. At least their names seem to disappear from the newspaper columns after 1900, and only a few won election to the Arkansas General Assembly after that date. The Populists of the 1890s did not constitute a major element of Progressive support in the 1900s.[98] Although not many Populist leaders managed to secure leadership positions in the Democratic Party, the agrarian movement did influence the reform programs of the majority party. The Arkansas Democratic Party during the 1890s continually shifted ground to ease the seething agrarian discontent. The state party's shift toward the silver camp culminating in its support for Bryan's nomination in 1896 illustrated the impact of the agrarian movement on the Democrats. As Charles Collins, one of Bryan's Arkansas friends, put it, the state was one of those "storm centers which resulted in Chicago" and Bryan's nomination.[99]

2

The Election of 1896

As the 1896 election approached, the Democratic Party suffered the debilitating effects of an unpopular and stubborn leader in the presidency, the divisiveness of a constituency too diverse to agree on a single ideology or plan of action, and the devastation of a lengthening depression. Since the Civil War, the party had never managed to forge its diverse national following into a cohesive coalition. Eastern machine Democrats whose immigrant constituency focused on local interests had little in common with Southern agrarians who looked to the national government for changes in economic policy. In 1890 and 1892, the Democratic Party apparently emerged from the doldrums as it strengthened its position in the Congress and captured the presidency. But the victory did not long obscure the chronic weakness of the party. During Grover Cleveland's second administration (1893–97), Democrats across the nation failed to agree on any consistent program to combat economic ills. Some thought the party had a commitment to lower tariffs, but others—like Arthur Pue Gorman of Maryland—gave support to local interests and the protection concept. Many believed the party's chief doctrine was dedication to state's rights and local solutions rather than federal action to correct economic and social ills. While Southerners denounced attempts to regulate elections by federal law, they sought the national government's aid to construct levees and to produce inflation for debtor relief.

President Cleveland failed to unify his party. He disliked politicians and isolated himself from the legitimate demands of state leaders who sought to achieve compromises on the differences disrupting the party. Rather than serve as a harmonizer of discordant elements, the corpulent president obstinately clung to sound money principles. His refusal to give any ground to those who differed on the currency issue became, to the disaffected, the symbol of his unwillingness to take positive government action on behalf of the economically depressed classes in the West and South. Cleveland earned not only a reputation as a stodgy and unbending conservative but also as an isolated and uncaring president. He demanded repeal of the Sherman Silver Purchase Bill as the solution to economic ills, and when Southerners and Westerners demanded the coinage of the seigniorage, the president refused to give ground even to a modest silver act.

During Grover Cleveland's second term, the silver forces gained strength and created tensions in their struggle for control of the Democratic Party in the Southern and Western states. Free silver had become established doctrine in the states west of the prairies in the early 1890s. Not only silver-producing areas, like Nevada and Colorado, but also Western states, like Wyoming, accepted silver as an economic panacea. Although he was a Republican, Senator Francis E. Warren of Wyoming announced his conversion to the silver cause in 1893. He managed to retain allegiance with the regular Republican organization nationally while aligning the state party with the silver forces. In other Western states, Republicans bolted their party rather than make compromises with the sound money leaders.[1] During the fall of 1891, Nebraska Democrats in convention endorsed a moderate silver plank, but they divided into a free silver and a gold faction. William Jennings Bryan and the silver men failed to prevent the Nebraska Democrats from endorsing Grover Cleveland in their 1892 convention. The struggle between the two factions became intense during the early 1890s as both sides sought control of the party machinery. Nebraska silver forces finally managed to dominate the Democratic state convention in 1894. In the same year, Alabama Democrats averted a party split by adopting a straddling plank which favored both free silver and sound money.[2]

The divisions within the party and the failure of the administration to take positive action to redress economic grievances brought disastrous defeat in the 1894 congressional elections. Although the party could still rely generally upon the support of the Southern states, the challenge of the agrarians and a Republican Party—a challenge which was far from extinct—threatened Democratic power even in the South. Within the Southern Democratic Party during the middle 1890s, the rift widened; silver men became more vocal and gained control in state after state.[3] Arkansas illustrated the tensions occurring in the Southern Democracy. Goldbugs in the state lost places of authority in the party. During Cleveland's second administration, depression, discontent, and agrarian agitation provoked turmoil in the Arkansas Democratic Party. Silver became the symbol of resistance to Cleveland and the Eastern establishment, and in Arkansas the dissenters moved into places of power at an early date. The state party shifted its stance during the 1890s to accommodate some of the demands of the agrarian protest movement, and by 1896 the party aligned itself with those states demanding an anti-Cleveland candidate for president.

The Helena Weekly World, voice of the "Swamp Democracy," bemoaned the surrender of the Arkansas Democratic Party to Populist principles. The state party, the paper complained, "is cutting the dirt from under the Pops by granting much of what they have contended for." Later, in the same election year of 1896, a more sympathetic newspaper, The Arkansas Gazette, declared that the victorious gubernational nominee of the Democrats, Daniel Jones, "represents all the essential ideas of government which Populists hold dear." Hard times and years of agrarian rebellion were forcing the party to make some concessions to the small town merchants and hill farmers.[4] In the early 1890s, under the leadership of Governor James Stephen Hogg, the Texas Democracy followed a similar pattern when it wooed agrarian support by creating a railroad commission and improving the antitrust laws. In Alabama Joseph F. Johnston successfully sought the governship on a silver platform and as governor continued to make overtures to the Alabama Populists. Johnston used rhetoric, patronage, and promises of reform to attract defecting Populists in the late 1890s.[5]

In Arkansas the sound money champions were in full retreat by 1896. In the Democratic platform of two years earlier, the state convention declared for the silver standard. Those who remained loyal to gold tended to live in the larger towns and in the eastern portion of the state. George B. Rose, a prominent gold Democrat, found many kindred souls in the towns but admitted the country people were "practically solid for free silver." Little

Rock ranked as the strongest sound money bastion. When the gold Democrats held their convention at the Little Rock Board of Trade in late August 1896, scarcely a dozen men from outside the city attended. *The Brinkley Argus* rebuked the gold men in the eastern lowlands for raising the cry of "party unity" as a cover for maintaining their power. No longer, announced the *Argus,* will Arkansas people vote for a "yellow dog" just because he wears a collar with the word "Democrat" on it. Jerry South, a Baxter County politician, claimed he could find only one gold man in his central Ozark hills region. "Its two to one," sniffed *The Helena Weekly World,* "that the fellow who is an advocate of free mountain dew will go in for anything." The Helena newspaper convinced itself that in its own lowland area, Phillips County, the party did not harbor Populists.[6]

Men who had been prominent in state politics either surrendered to silver doctrines or suffered at least temporary political eclipse. One of Arkansas's most distinguished congressmen, Clifton Rodes Breckinridge, a goldbug, failed to retain his seat in Congress when he lost in the 1894 Democratic primary election over the silver issue. Breckinridge came from a notable family. His great-grandfather, John Breckinridge, had been President Thomas Jefferson's attorney general. His father, John Cabell Breckinridge, had served as a senator and vice president of the United States. Clifton Breckinridge also had a distinguished career of his own. He entered Congress in 1882 and continued to serve until his 1894 defeat. During his twelve years in office, he became one of the most powerful figures in the House of Representatives. But as the depression came on in 1893, he took a firm stand with President Cleveland and the Bourbons, and he played a role in the battle to repeal the Sherman Silver Purchase Act in 1893. Despite his lineage and personal credentials, the silver issue ended his congressional career. Cleveland rewarded him with the post of ambassador to Russia, where he served with distinction.[7]

Early in 1896 rumors were afloat that Uriah M. Rose, a distinguished jurist, would step down as national Democratic committeeman because his sound money views offended most Arkansans. A few weeks before the national convention met in Chicago he resigned. Rose never held an elective office, but his legal opinions and counsel in the party won him high esteem across the state and nation. In 1895 Arkansas Senators James H. Berry and

James K. Jones called on Cleveland to appoint him to the United States Supreme Court. Rose joined with labor leader De Emmett Bradshaw, in 1899, to found the Arkansas Bar Association. During his career, he served as president of both the state organization and the American Bar Association. Theodore Roosevelt, in 1906, appointed him to represent the United States at the Hague International Peace Congress in 1907. Congressman Thomas C. McRae replace Rose on the National Committee during the crisis period of 1896. McRae was a silver man but moderate enough to promise to vote for the Chicago nominee whatever his currency position might be. With McRae's accession, the party set aside an able leader. Rose's son, George B. Rose, a Little Rock attorney, also lost sympathy with the regular party organization and became state chairman for the sound money Democrats.[8]

During the summer and fall of 1895, two leading silverites visited the state to advance the cause of bimetallism. William Jennings Bryan quickly became a popular idol in Arkansas. In the spring of 1895, a Fort Smith physician informed him that in Arkansas's border city enthusiasm for the Great Commoner was growing. He invited Bryan to visit the state in August and even ventured to suggest that Fort Smith might provide a more hospitable environment for his political future than Republican Nebraska.[9] Bryan visited the state and his efforts there helped prepare the way for his nomination as a presidential candidate. Governor James P. Clarke and former Governor William Fishback met Bryan when he arrived in Fort Smith aboard the southbound Cannon Ball. Clarke made a silver speech at a morning rally, and after a barbecue lunch William Jennings Bryan addressed a large crowd for three hours. The newspapers did not record the speech, but the Fort Smith *Weekly Elevator* reported, "It was a strong effort and received closer attention than any speech made in this section for years past." After his Fort Smith speech, Bryan spent the evening addressing a Van Buren rally before leaving the state. During his stay, he praised Arkansas Congressman John S. Little for his loyal stand on the currency problem. "The friends of silver," he said, "rely on him for valuable work in the coming congress."[10] Shortly after Bryan's August trip, Congressman W. L. Terry announced his support for free silver.[11]

In December 1895 another silver leader, William Hope Harvey, visited the faithful in Little Rock. *The Helena Weekly World* suspected Col. James N. Smithee and Charles Collins of working closely with Harvey. Before long, two of these three men became citizens of Arkansas. Smithee, formerly an Arkansas editor, had flirted with Populism during his Colorado years, and in 1896 returned to his home state to assume the editorship of *The Arkansas Gazette.* Charles Collins was an early advocate of the Bryan nomination for president and became a favorite whipping boy of *The Helena Weekly World.* After two unsuccessful Bryan campaigns in which he led fund raising drives, Harvey moved to Rogers in northwest Arkansas in 1900. The *World's* most hated triumvirate—Smithee, Collins, and Harvey—now resided in the state.[12]

The Helena Weekly World polled the opinion of the Arkansas Democratic press in March of 1896 and discovered to its chagrin that approximately 80 percent of the newspapers favored the free coinage of silver at a ratio of sixteen to one. The newspaper sent out 163 inquiries and of the 108 answering, 87 indicated loyalty to silver. Among the leading goldbug papers were *The Helena Weekly World, The Pine Bluff Press-Eagle,* and *The Arkansas Democrat* (Little Rock). James Mitchell, of the latter newspaper, held the position of postmaster of Little Rock and gave only nominal support to the Democratic nominees in the fall election.[13]

The greatest victory in the journalistic realm for the silver men came with their capture of *The Arkansas Gazette.* In mid-May, W. B. Worthen, president of the *Gazette,* resigned his connection with the paper. Worthen was a Little Rock banker and a Cleveland man. The day after Worthen left, the newspaper drastically altered its tone. With Worthen out, the *Gazette* could now speak of national banks of issue as "leeches upon the body politic." In January, Worthen had warned the state not to listen "to the shrieks of calamity howlers" who would force a "national issue" in a state election; now *The Conway Light* complained that "a Populist editor on a Democratic paper beats the devil." James N. Smithee secured a controlling interest in the newspaper in May 1896 and served as president and editor. Smithee was no stranger to Arkansas journalism. He had worked for the *Gazette* in 1876 and a few years later for *The Arkansas Democrat.* In 1886 he received an appointment from Cleveland as land agent in New Mexico Territory but soon moved on to Denver. When he returned to Arkansas to steer the *Gazette,* gold men claimed he had

become a Colorado Populist at heart.[14] How he acquired sufficient funds to take possession of the newspaper is unclear. *The
Weekly Elevator* repeated a Little Rock rumor when it reported
that New York attorney John R. Dos Passos, who had fought the
Fishback repudiation amendment "and who spent several days in
Little Rock last week, is concerned in the deal."[15] Dos Passos was
a leading corporation lawyer, had participated in the reorganiza-
tion of several leading railroads, and served as attorney for the
sugar trust.[16]

During the latter half of 1895, the two factions established organizations in Arkansas and prepared to battle for control of the
party. But the silver men already held the upper hand in the
Democratic state central committee. As the primary elections
drew near, most candidates expressed support for silver.[17] Attorney General E. B. Kinsworthy represented those few who remained loyal to Cleveland and still regained their offices. All of
Arkansas's congressmen succumbed to the silver virus, although
Hugh Dinsmore and Thomas McRae affirmed their willingness
to vote for a goldbug presidential nominee in the hope that currency reform might be achieved later.[18]

Some of those who took their place in the silver parade did so
with little enthusiasm. A southern Arkansas politician from the
town of Camden recalled in later years his reluctant capitulation
to the "silver shiboleth" [*sic*]. R. Minor Wallace had established a
law practice in Texarkana by 1896. He had voted faithfully for
the Democratic nominee through the years and considered himself a "uniform party" man. He had hoped to see Cleveland's tariff reform become the campaign issue rather than silver. Despite
his misgivings, he went on the stump for the ticket in 1896.
Thomas McRae heard a sample of Wallace's impressive oratory at
Camden, Arkansas, and wired Arkansas's Senator James K. Jones,
chairman of the National Democratic Committee. At Jones's request, Wallace undertook a series of speeches for Bryan in 1896.
A few years later, when Arkansas gained a seventh seat in Congress, the new place went to Wallace. He became a firm Bryan
supporter and gained a reputation as a prohibition orator.[19]

Not all of Bryan's Arkansas allies shared wholeheartedly in the
Commoner's philosophy. According to Raymond O. Arsenault,
the Bryanists in Arkansas were divided into two groups. The
moderate or conservative Bryanists were planters, businessmen,

and other urban dwellers. The radical Bryanists were drawn from among the "small farmers, timber workers, and village merchants. . ." The town versus country or agrarian versus New South cultural clash which had been apparent in earlier decades manifested itself within Bryanism. The moderate Bryanists, who were, in Laurence Goodwyn's phrase, the "shadow movement of Populism," did not espouse radical reform. Some moderate Bryanists had no interest in reform at all. These men identified more with Northern economic interests than with agrarianism. According to Raymond Arsenault, Jeff Davis's rise to power can be explained by the fact that he recognized the vulnerability of the moderate Bryanist leadership of the Arkansas Democratic Party. Men like James P. Clarke, Daniel Webster Jones, James K. Jones, and James H. Berry had more in common with the old Bourbon Democracy than with the movement that emerged with Jeff Davis.[20]

The contest for the 1896 Democratic gubernatorial nomination afforded an outlet for party tensions over the silver issue. In January 1896 when the old-line Democrats met together for their Jackson Day Banquet at Little Rock's Capitol Hotel, it became clear that the silver issue would dominate the campaign in Arkansas. Many former presidents of the Old Hickory Club were in attendance, men like Joseph W. House, whom Cleveland had appointed as a United States district attorney, and James Mitchell, editor of *The Arkansas Democrat* and postmaster of the city. The speakers of the day called for party unity whether nominees stood for silver or gold.[21] Whether primary loyalty belonged to the silver cause or to the national party became the theme of the gubernatorial primary campaign.

Many candidates for the governor's office sent up trial balloons during January and February and quickly withdrew. The first serious contender to enter, James H. Harrod, formally announced his candidacy in a letter to the voters. Harrod had identified himself with the faithful at the Old Hickory Club, and he now asserted his allegiance to the party as his foremost conviction. Since the age of twenty-one, he informed his readers, he had voted a straight party ticket in every election. But he also asserted his devotion to bimetallism and called for a return to the coinage of silver "as it was before demonitization." His espousal of the railroad commission also ranked Harrod with those demanding change. His stance in favor of a low tariff, encouragement of immigration, and support for the common school represented the usual allegiances expressed by almost every Democratic candidate in every Arkansas election of the era. Late in January he affirmed his support for the 16 to 1 ratio and the adoption of silver by the United States independently of the rest of the world.[22]

The second major contestant for the nomination, A. H. Sevier, announced his intentions in February. *The Helena Weekly World* warned the descendant of a family which had dominated Arkansas in the ante-bellum period that unless he came out "for sixteentooneorbust, regardless of the world, and fall down and worship Marse Charley Collins, Marse Dan Jones and Marse Judge McCain, his name will stand as a synonymn for damp soil."[23] In 1894 Sevier had presented a foredoomed resolution to the state Democratic convention endorsing the administration of Grover Cleveland, and in 1896 he remained loyal to the president.[24]

In his campaign, Sevier proposed to give the state "a business administration." He thought the Chicago convention should have a silver plank but should leave the ratio to congressional determination. He opposed creation of a railroad commission primarily on constitutional grounds. The state constitution prohibited the general assembly from creating any permanent offices other than those provided for within the basic law. Sevier objected to the commission's power to subpoena witnesses like a court, and he estimated the loss to the state in operating expense at fifty thousand dollars annually. Setting maximum rates by statute seemed less complicated and more economical than creating a new government agency. These views failed to gain much support for Sevier. The first primary election came in the state's second most populous county, Sebastian, on February 15. Sevier polled only 572 votes to Harrod's 1,738. During March and April he lost in each primary. By May he surrendered to the inevitable and left the race.[25]

At the end of January, Harrod had been the only announced candidate, but the fortunes of Daniel Webster Jones were on the rise. Jones grew up in Hempstead County, just six miles from the home of his boyhood friend, Senator James K. Jones. Both men came from the Southern planter class. Senator Jones studied law for a time under Daniel Jones. A contemporary described Daniel Jones's manner as democratic despite genteel origins.[26] At times,

Jones directed his appeal along class lines. Speaking to a group of representatives of the state's Bryan-Sewall clubs, he proclaimed a state of war between "the toiling masses of mankind" and the "insidious . . . money changers" who were "corrupting men in high places."[27]

On January 29, *The Helena Weekly World* reported that Daniel Jones might be a candidate for governor. The *World* thought he would be acceptable to the silver people, but wondered if they could overlook his career as a railroad attorney. Jones had lobbied for the Iron Mountain Railroad to block passage of Joseph T. Robinson's abortive railroad commission bill in the 1895 legislature. Now he favored both free silver and a railroad commission. Jones commended himself as a preferable candidate to the disturbed party because he represented the older, respected leadership class while identifying himself with the more militant silver men. His candidacy would be another move toward undercutting Populist strength and maintaining Democratic supremacy in Arkansas.

Through his aggressive leadership in the Democratic Bimetallic League of Little Rock, Daniel Jones brought his claims to leadership into view. He stood adamantly against all attempts to mollify the gold men. In late January, at a meeting of the league, Judge W. S. McCain proposed appointing a committee to look into the views of candidates on the currency question. The suggestion evoked a counterproposal to give a "fair consideration" to those gold men who sought "minor offices." Jones denounced the latter proposition. Justices of the peace and sheriffs were those most likely to arouse the populace, and the silver forces needed a strong base of support, he warned. "We come to make war," exclaimed Jones.[28]

A preamble and resolution that Jones presented to the league reveals his root-and-branch policy. The statement condemned Grover Cleveland and his followers as betrayers of the Democratic Party and called for a decision in the state primaries on the currency issue. The preamble made the usual arguments in defense of silver, but a more dramatic statement followed in the resolution:

> Resolved, that we will support no candidate for nomination to office from President down to Constable, and that we will vote for no delegate to a convention, or committeeman of our party, unless

he be a pronounced advocate of the free and unlimited coinage of silver at the ratio of 16 to 1, without regard to the action of any other nation on earth.[29]

This position became the major issue of the Harrod-Jones contest.

At the February 3 meeting of the Bimetallic League, Jones introduced a second resolution to clarify the first. The resolution scored those newspapers which had announced that Jones and the league "had expressed an unwillingness to accept the result of the Democratic primaries." The resolution accused the newspapers of misrepresentation of the facts. Actually, Jones explained, the resolution meant silver Democrats would support only silver men in the primaries in Pulaski County, but in the fall election, they would vote for the nominees whatever their views. Jones refused to compromise with moderates who flinched at attacks on fellow Democrats. "'The man who is not with us on this question,' said Jones, 'is not a Democrat, I don't care what he calls himself.'"[30]

On the evening of February 20, the two major candidates debated at the state house in Little Rock before a large audience in Representatives Hall. Harrod attacked Jones for his silence and noncommittal attitude on local issues. He defended regulation of the railroads by a commission as necessary and just. Jones accused Harrod of being a latecomer to the railroad commission forces—an argument that could have been applied to Jones as well. He saw "no burning state issue" in the primary fight. The attempt to center attention on local issues represented a dodge to avoid the currency issue. The free silver question towered over all other issues of the campaign. Then Jones reminded Harrod of a statement the latter made before the Old Hickory Club. If the Democrats "nominated the devil and Rothschild wrote the platform he would support the action." Harrod freely admitted before the assembled crowd that he had made the statement. By contrast, Jones assured the people of the capital city of his determination not to give support to a goldbug presidential nominee. Throughout the campaign, Jones used Harrod's remark with devastating effect.[31]

The Weekly Elevator (Fort Smith) praised Harrod's speech but condemned Jones's "hair-triggered mouth." The Helena Weekly World said the speech by Jones classed him as a "blatant demagogue." The World excoriated him for abandoning state issues.

"What has the Governor of Arkansas to do with the settlement of the free coinage of silver?" queried the newspaper. Later the *World* called Jones a "shameless and hypocritical traitor" who would bolt the party. His election would signal "the death knell of the Democratic Party in Arkansas."[32]

In mid-April Sevier, who soon left the race, met with Jones and Harrod in a debate in Pine Bluff, seat of Jefferson County, in the eastern lowlands. The local goldbug paper claimed that Sevier, with his promise of a "business administration," had the best reception of the candidates. Jones made his usual reference to Harrod's remark, "I draw the line on Rothschild and the devil, and Cleveland too." The Populists also had something to say about Harrod's statement. *Morgan's Buzz-Saw,* the voice of Winfield Scott Morgan, ran a satirical series entitled "Letter from the Devil." Commenting on Harrod's willingness to support Satan himself the Devil wrote, "Say, I like a man like that J. H. Harrod that is running for governor of Arkansas. He's a man after my own heart."[33]

Although Jones came into the race a month later than most candidates, he swept by his opponents quickly. His name was not on the ballot in the first primary, in Sebastian County. During the first week in April, Jones won in four county primaries (Chicot, Conway, Scott, and Polk) while Harrod won only in Craighead County. By the middle of May, the *Gazette* estimated his delegate total for the state convention to be 228 to Harrod's 90. Despite reform efforts, Arkansas had not yet adopted a uniform primary system, and the county elections came on various days from February through June. On June 10, twenty-five counties held primaries. The Jones bandwagon captured twenty-four of the twenty-five primaries held that day and clinched the nomination for the silver leader.[34]

The victory of Dan Jones in the primaries indicated the strength of the silver sentiment in Arkansas. Some of the counties also included a referendum question on silver in the primary election. Even in the two most urban counties, silver rolled up a favorable vote. In Pulaski County, the voters supported silver by 3,059 to 439, and they supported silver in Sebastian County by 1,361 to 94. Rural Independence County gave silver an impressive 1,174 votes with only 15 opposed. Plainly, the voters of Arkansas believed in bimetallism, and even a candidate for state office had to face the issue.[35] Not only in Arkansas but across the South and

West, Grover Cleveland and his followers were rapidly losing control of the Democratic Party.

The race for United States senator also served as an outlet for tensions within the party. Since both candidates for the office had previously announced their firm allegiance to silver, they now tried to convince the voters that their own zeal for silver surpassed their opponent's commitment. Senator James K. Jones surprised no one in his decision to seek reelection to the seat he had occupied since 1885.

The bald, large-headed senator stood over six feet tall. He dressed in ante-bellum fashion, wearing a "suit of black broadcloth, with long wide skirts to the coat" and displaying "a wealth of immaculate shirt front." Jones's father, a wealthy Mississippi planter, brought his son to southern Arkansas before the Civil War and after the conflict gave him a "fine black land plantation." For a time in the 1870s, James K. Jones entered into a law partnership with Daniel W. Jones, a boyhood friend.[36] Willis J. Abbot recalled him as a "magnificent survival of the old school of Southern statesmen." The "admirably proportioned" senator was "handsome of face, with a noble brow, a beard just whitening and blue eyes." He could be "bluff and decisive" or gentle. His "placid, even stolid temperament" deceived many into thinking that he took his responsibilities lightly.[37] Texas Senator Horace Chilton remembered him as a man who was "large, tall, and rural in cast." His hair was "yellowish gray" and he wore a "moustache, with a goatee which gave him an air of impressiveness and force." He was not by nature a "frowning or gloomy" individual, "but he devoted little time to the social interchange of the cloak room because he had always some task of management to work out." Like Senator Arthur Pue Gorman, Jones had the ability to go "to the individual men composing the Senate, to go to one today, to another tomorrow, to another the day after, and so continually trying to find a common ground upon which all could meet." Chilton thought Jones had "deeper convictions than Gorman" but was sufficiently practical in his approach to politics to content himself with securing his ends little by little.[38]

Senator Jones ranged himself on the side of silver early in Grover Cleveland's second term. When the president called for repeal of the Sherman Silver Purchase Act in 1893, Jones cast his vote in the Senate Finance Committee against repeal. But Jones failed to defeat the repeal bill in committee. Debate raged on the floor of the Senate until Arthur Pue Gorman presented a compromise plan to bring silver and gold Democrats together. Thirty-seven of the forty-four Democrats in the Senate signed Gorman's statement, and Jones, according to the *Gazette,* was the last of the thirty-seven to put his signature on the compromise plan.[39] When Grover Cleveland rejected the agreement and called for unconditional repeal, Senator Jones "declared he would never again be a party to a compromise on the silver question."[40]

The part Jones played in smoothing the path of the Wilson-Gorman Tariff Bill through the Senate set the stage for one of the issues in the 1896 campaign. His position as reconciler of divergent interests became a basis for later charges that he had deserted basic Democratic tariff doctrines. But his role in the revision of the tariff also marked him as a national leader, one who might later help unite a party rent by divisions.

The Democrats in the 1890s suffered from a lack of organization and cohesiveness at the national level. All American parties have been coalitions of diverse interests, but the Democratic Party, as a truly national party, has exhibited greater divisiveness and localism than the Republican Party. The currency issue, the tariff debate, and the seething discontent resulting from depression opened wider the rifts in Cleveland's party.[41] No single ideology secured the approval of Democrats across the nation. Leaders of the party based their strength upon state and regional support, or they claimed the loyalty of one faction. No individual arose to weld the diverse interests into a forceful and powerful unity. Cleveland's unbending dedication to the sound money views of the conservative wing of his party—and his obstinate and uncompromising behavior—alienated many in his own party and prevented him from assuming the role of party leader.

As an experienced politician and party man, Jones might have helped cement the party. His reputation as the man who engineered efforts to compromise Democratic differences raised hopes that the Arkansan might give direction to the rudderless party. But his own steadfast commitment to the silver forces rather than to the principle of party unity also produced fears of further disintegration and disaffection. Journalist Willis J. Abbot pondered the reasons for the choice of Jones as national chairman. He came not from "doubtful territory" but from a safe Democratic state, had no reputation "for political astuteness and for skill in the more devious processes of scientific politics as Senator Hill," and lacked personal wealth or connections with the rich. He was chosen because a revolutionary-minded convention wanted a leader of the same mood. "Now James K. Jones is as outspoken and as frank as the most radical of the Democrats who gathered at Chicago." Because he was known as a "long time silver man" he was chosen "to lead a campaign in which the cry is 'No compromise!'"[42] The choice of Jones could not cure the division in the Democratic Party. Although more capable in the art of compromise than Cleveland, Jones also gave allegiance to one particular wing of his party, and his dedication to the silver camp further contributed to the polarization of the party of Jackson. His chief claim to the role of conciliator derived from his handling of the Wilson-Gorman Bill in the Senate.

The tariff confusion afforded abundant opportunity for a master of compromise to demonstrate his talents. Because of Alabama's opposition to placing coal and iron ore on the free list and Louisiana's determination to keep sugar off the free list, the tariff bill made little headway in the Senate during the winter of 1893–94. Finally, the Democratic caucus appointed a subcommittee of three senators to reconcile the conflicting interests and produce a compromise measure. Jones, a recognized authority on the tariff, served on the smaller committee and joined in the decision to place light duties on coal, iron ore, and sugar. Newspaperman Arthur Wallace Dunn believed Jones's "knowledge of what was in the" Wilson-Gorman Tariff Bill "was superior to that of any other man in the Senate."[43] The industrious Arkansan asserted his own leadership in securing agreement. He talked to individual senators, made a tally of their objections, determined where concessions had to be made, and then presented the results of his research to Secretary of the Treasury Carlisle and to Grover Cleveland. In the end, the Democratic caucus accepted the 408 amendments proposed by Jones. Only one senator of the forty present at the caucus cast a vote against his compromise plan.[44]

James K. Jones and his colleague on the finance committee, Senator George Vest of Missouri, were dedicated to low tariff principles, but found themselves in the uncomfortable position of arranging for amendments to transform the original low tariff bill into a protective measure. In the process, Jones abandoned ad valorem duties, a favorite Democratic tariff concept, and gave support to specific rates for individual items. Although few raw materials stayed on the free list, lumber and wool did remain untaxed. Arkansas timber interests resented the senator's role in passing a high tariff measure while leaving a major Arkansas product unprotected. During the 1896 campaign, Harmon L. Remmel, the Republican gubernatorial candidate, reminded voters that the Republican Party had placed a duty of one dollar per one thousand feet on lumber but that Jones had placed the industry in competition with Canadian lumber. Jones's action was not in harmony with either his state's industrial interests or its generally low tariff sentiment.[45]

Moving onto forbidden ground with Jones, fellow Arkansas Senator James Berry also risked the disapproval of his constituents. Arthur Wallace Dunn believed the old "one-legged Confederate veteran" was "more of a free trader than any man in the Senate." Senator Calvin S. Brice of Ohio, a protectionist, found Berry's support for the Jones amendments very amusing. According to Dunn, Brice spoke to Berry in the following way:

> 'Berry, I see you have just voted for protection again. What will your Arkansas constituents say about that? Voting for protection! Allied with the plutocrats and robber barons! Tied up with the money devil! Berry, I'm afraid those Arkansas people will say you have been corrupted.'[46]

But it was Jones who had to face the home folks in the upcoming 1896 primary election. In that contest, he preferred to emphasize his silver position rather than his tariff record.

Rumors were afloat during the winter of 1895–96 that Governor James P. Clarke might not seek the traditional second two-year term accorded Arkansas chief executives. Clarke ended speculation by announcing, on January 6, his intention to seek the place of Senator Jones in the primary elections. The governor declared himself in favor of "the immediate free and unlimited coinage of silver at a ratio of 16 to 1, without waiting for the consent or cooperation of any other government." He condemned the issuance of interest bearing bonds as a means of retiring greenbacks "or any similar device or makeshift."[47] This statement was an attempt to cast himself in the role of loyal silverite in contrast to the supposedly moderate Jones, who had spent much of the previous year seeking "makeshift" compromises with those desiring bond issues to bolster up the treasury.

Clarke's entry in a race against the formidable James K. Jones seemed rash to most political observers. But by 1896 Arkansans expected the unusual from the volcanic Clarke. Contemporaries often commented on his unusual temper and independent spirit. On one occasion in April, 1895, Governor Clarke displayed his famous temper in a dramatic manner. He went to Gleason's Hotel in Little Rock to search out a political rival, W. R. Jones, a legislator and publisher of the Yellville *Mountain Echo*. After some heated exchanges, Clarke spit in Representative Jones's face and then reached for his pistol. Only timely intervention of friends prevented further violence.[48] On another occasion, Clarke stunned his auditors when invited to address the Arkansas River development conference. He told the assembled enthusiasts that they might as well gather their luggage and go home—he would be glad to see the river "dry up so a road could be built in its bed." He frankly told them that a river with "caving banks and sand bars" gave no hope of navigational promise.[49]

Clarke had little popular appeal among the common people of the state. He disliked handshaking and mingling with ordinary people.[50] Yet this eastern Arkansas Democrat later aligned himself with the spokesman for the rednecks, Jeff Davis. Clarke's home town, Helena, lay in the heart of the Delta country, and his home county, Phillips, held the dubious distinction of being one of the state's most frequent scenes of voting irregularities.

Although Clarke's oratory at times had a populist ring, he was at heart more of an aristocrat than a champion of the people. "I have become satisfied," he warned the general assembly in his final speech as governor, "that there exists a wholesale and systematic plan to oppress and outrage the poorer classes of the people for the sake of the costs involved in a conviction." He saw a conspiracy of lawyers and justices of the peace to extract money from the ignorant poor. He demanded that justices of the peace cease from inflicting "barbarous punishment." But in the same address, he insisted on a cautious approach to the problem of relief for drought-stricken counties in southern Arkansas. The state will not allow starvation, he promised, but "where want and wretchedness are to be dealt with, we are much disposed to be governed by a maudlin spirit of sympathy." Such sympathy, he feared, "unguarded by a sober judgment," might lead the legislature "to establish precedents that in time will prove highly demoralizing."[51]

Few Arkansans expected Clarke to succeed at the primaries. *The Little Rock Times* predicted that if Clarke ever entered the

Senate, "diamonds as big as saucers will rain from heaven."[52] According to *The Arkadelphia Southern Standard*, fifty-two newspapers endorsed Jones and only twelve favored Clarke.[53] Clarke's only hope lay in convincing the voters that the prestigious Jones had only a mild loyalty to silver and had surrendered to those interests seeking a protective tariff. His tactics suggested the kinds of local pressures forcing Democratic leaders like James K. Jones to adopt extreme positions. Regional and local demands helped rend the weakened Democratic Party.

The Helena Weekly World, Clarke's hometown newspaper, did yeoman service for the governor. Although the editor was a convinced goldbug, he bent every effort to warn the state of the insincerity of Senator Jones's silver position. The *World* reminded readers that during 1895, Jones had introduced a bill to issue low interest bonds and retire greenbacks. But when Arkansas's other senator, James Berry, returned from mending political fences at home, he informed Jones about the increasing clamor for silver. Suddenly Jones took on a more rabid silver position, and "he bobbed up" at the Memphis Silver Convention to mingle with Marion Butler and Benjamin Tillman.[54]

William Hope "Coin" Harvey had also questioned the orthodoxy of Senator Jones because the latter had a hand in the Senate Finance Committee's bond bill measures. As a part of one such bond issue act, he attempted to shepherd through the Senate an "unrestricted coinage bill." In March 1895, the young "Coin" warned his auditors that the Jones's bill was "another makeshift." "Take no promises," he warned, "and rely on no politician who claims recent conversion to the cause of the people." But by early 1896, Harvey's quarterly declared Jones's views sound. According to *The Helena Weekly World,* the senator acceded to a more inflationary view during the summer of 1895. Winfield Scott Morgan, prominent middle-of-the-road Populist, was also unimpressed by Jones's maneuverings. He characterized Jones as one of those "political bunco-steerers" who deceived the common people with "a gold basis confidence game."[55]

During January 1896, Jones labored for a free coinage measure in the Senate. He wished to crown his efforts, just before the primary election, with a victory for silver. The House of Representatives had sent a bond issue bill to the Senate which fulfilled, at least partially, the expectations of President Cleveland. It provided for the issue of bonds to finance the redemption of greenbacks but did not, as Cleveland wished, specify redemption in gold coin only. Senator Jones, a member of the Senate Finance Committee, submitted to the Senate an amendment to strike out all of the provisions in the House version after the enacting clause. He wished to substitute to open the mints to free coinage of silver, to issue fifty million dollars in silver certificates based on seigniorage in the treasury to offset the gold reserve deficiency, and to redeem greenbacks with either silver or gold coin at the option of the Treasury Department.[56]

In a two-hour address, Jones presented the merits of his plan. He denounced bond issues as an "unmitigated evil." He justified his own past record on silver as realistic and loyal. Specifically, Jones took pains to explain the bond measure he had introduced just one year earlier. The president had given plain notice that he intended to issue bonds whether Congress authorized a new issue or not. Although he personally "was opposed to the issue of bonds," he knew a free coinage bill without provision for bonds could not pass. Accepting the realities of the situation, Jones presented his plan to issue bonds at a lower interest rate, at 3 to 5 percent rather than 5 percent. The same plan included provisions for unlimited coinage of silver and substitution of silver certificates for the greenbacks. If the Senate had passed the bill, Jones now believed, "there would have been no more bonds, and we certainly would have had the unlimited coinage of silver." The silver provisions would have quickly obviated the need for bonds.[57]

Silver stalwarts preferred a stronger statement on silver and prohibition of bond issues. Senator William M. Stewart of Nevada said the bill had no importance. Those who framed it knew it could not pass, and to him it seemed a "mere dress parade" for those wishing to "make a silver record without hurting anybody." The radical silverites preferred Marion Butler's amendment permanently outlawing bond issues, but in the vote on Jones's proposal, they joined the moderates to pass the measure by a forty-three to thirty-four vote.[58]

Jones had led the "dress parade." His bill could never pass in the Republican dominated House of Representatives; but Jones could return to Arkansas with fresh political ammunition. On February 1, he managed to bring his measure to a vote. "I chance to know," remarked one senator, "that it is a matter of importance to him to leave here at least on Saturday afternoon." As soon as the Senate had cast its vote, James K. Jones took a train for Arkansas to face James P. Clarke in a joint campaign in Sebastian County.[59]

Although alignments and factions in Arkansas politics have often ignored sectional or geographical differences in the state, a section usually supported its own local candidates for statewide and congressional offices. Clarke might count on some support from his own Delta section, as indicated by the loyalty of the *World*, which heartily disliked his silver views. Southern Arkansas would stand behind her own son from Hempstead County, James K. Jones. Northern and northwestern Arkansas would decide the election, and if he were to have any chance of securing support from the Arkansas legislators, Clarke had to win the early primaries in that region.

The Weekly Elevator (Fort Smith) welcomed the governor and senator to the fray. The journal hailed the "meteoric" rise of Clarke from Phillips County representative in the statehouse to the executive office. "He is now and always has been for the free unlimited coinage of silver." But the *Elevator* reflected the sentiment of much of the state when it reprimanded Clarke for presuming to pit himself against a senator who had demonstrated national leadership abilities.[60]

At the little town of Mansfield, south of Fort Smith, the two candidates met in debate on February 5. Clarke attacked Jones's part in the bond issue bill and asserted that Jones was not a genuine silver man. Clarke insisted that a real silver man did not want the difference in value between gold and silver placed in the treasury. By Jones's plan, "the silver is guaged [*sic*] by a gold standard." A devout silver man would insist a gold dollar equals a silver dollar and would fight for the 16 to 1 ratio. Senator Jones replied that he could not see why the mine owners should receive more than their silver was worth. If they were reasonable they would grant the seigniorage to the government.[61]

Clarke, in his Mansfield speech, vigorously assailed the senator's tariff record. Jones had aided passage of the Wilson-Gorman Bill which flouted the will of the Democracy as expressed in the national platform. The duties on sugar, which Jones had supported, cost the people of Arkansas a million dollars. Although the bill endorsed the principle of protection, it did not provide protection for Arkansas's lumber industry. Jones had compromised with Eastern senators at the expense of Arkansas consumers without getting any compensating advantages for his own state. Replying to the attack, the senator insisted he had supported sugar duties in order to break the back of the sugar trust. The duties lowered the trust's profits and placed them in the treasury. He reminded Clarke that the tariff bill had lowered the tax on textiles and thus aided the common man who purchased clothing.[62]

While campaigning in the northwest, Clarke continued his assault on Jones's tariff and currency record. In a joint debate at Hartford, in Sebastian County, he compared the Wilson Bill to the McKinley Tariff. At least under the Republican bill there was no tax on sugar. Instead of enlisting support on the tariff issue, Clarke now found himself ensnared by the charge of Republicanism. After he campaigned in nearby Yell County, the local Republican newspaper reported Clarke had "declared the McKinley Tariff law to be the better of the two; excoriated Senator Jones for his non-action in regard to our lumber industry, in fact made a first-class Republican speech." The *Elevator* scolded Clarke for using "Republican ammunition" to fight Jones.[63]

Harmon L. Remmel, a Little Rock businessman and perennial Republican candidate for governor, came to Clarke's defense. During his quest for the governor's chair in 1894, Remmel had denounced Jones's part in placing lumber on the free list. Now, soon to be a candidate for governor again, Remmel spoke with approval of "this righteous position taken by Governor Clarke," which demonstrated patriotism "in forwarding the industrial interests of the south." A nice compliment, but such support was a major liability in Arkansas.[64]

In a speech at Dardanelle, in Yell County, old "Cotton Top" Clarke attacked on another line. He described Jones's vote against the Hatch Act as "larceny and robbery." Jones defended his action; he did not believe in regulating those who gambled in futures. They were criminals and the law must make their activities a crime.[65]

Clarke portrayed himself as a "straight-foward Democrat," a man who wanted reform, and his opponent as a "compromiser," but he was unable to elicit much support. For a time his campaign overshadowed the governor's race, but the contest came to an abrupt end. On February 15, Sebastian County gave Jones 1,502 votes to Clarke's 1,148. The vote on the silver referendum (1,361 for silver to 94 against) showed no resemblance to the division on candidates. Apparently Clarke made little headway in convincing the voters of his own greater dedication to the cause. In the Yell, Pope, and Johnson county primaries on March 14, Clarke lost again. Without a county supporting him in four attempts, he suddenly announced his decision "not to prosecute further the contest for the United States Senatorship."[66]

Many Arkansans approved of Jones's record on silver. Perhaps they agreed with the advice offered by an out-of-state newspaper. "If the Democrats of Arkansas, confessedly so nearly a unit for free coinage that every candidate is a professed advocate of silver restoration . . ." do not return Jones, it will be a major error since many Americans consider him a spokesman for currency reform. The nation would herald the replacement of Jones, "even for another pledged to silver restoration, as a severe blow to the cause of silver."[67]

The primary contest demonstrated the concern over the silver issue in Arkansas and the interest in national rather than specifically local issues in 1896. Although the more radical candidate on silver secured the victory in the gubernatorial race, the issue was not as clear in the senatorial contest. Probably Jones's prestige, and the habit of returning an incumbent, which has been especially strong in Arkansas, secured the victory for Jones. The manner in which the senatorial candidates fought the contest indicated the firm commitment of Arkansas to silver.

During the primary campaigns, the two factions in Arkansas continued to struggle for control of the party machinery. William M. Fishback, a Sebastian County citizen and governor in the early 1890s, made public his disgust with Grover Cleveland. In four and a half large columns on the front page of *The Weekly Elevator,* he published his vehement attack on the president. He regretted now his canvass of Indiana and New York for the presidential ticket in 1892, the same year in which he won the governor's chair. He accused Cleveland of ignoring the interests of the Southern and Western states. "The conspiracy," he warned, "which seems to have been formed here and in Europe to destroy by legislation and otherwise from three-sevenths to one-half of the metallic money of the world is the most gigantic crime of this or any other age."[68] The frequency of such statements in Arkansas and elsewhere clearly indicated that Cleveland and his Bourbon Democrats were losing control of the Democratic Party. Early in Cleveland's second term, William C. Whitney, a wealthy

New York financier and a devoted Cleveland man, urged the president to consider the doctrines of international bimetallism. Moderate Democrats hoped the New Yorker might be instrumental in bringing Cleveland to a more realistic position, but all such dreams quickly faded.[69] Cleveland remained firm and encouraged his followers to do likewise.

In Arkansas the Cleveland men made a hopeless but determined stand. During May, they attempted to secure greater influence over the Pulaski County Central Committee by forming a "committee at large." According to opponents of the plan, the select committee was to be a goldbug group which would seek to dominate the party machinery. The Democratic Bimetallic League unanimously condemned the plan. One league member, C. H. Whittemore, Democratic candidate for Pulaski County treasurer, insisted silver men were exaggerating the strength of gold men in the county. Only three of the twenty members of the County Central Committee were, in his opinion, goldbug Democrats. But if any county offered refuge for gold Democrats, it was Pulaski County. The area sent George Naylor, one of the most zealous apostles for sound money, to the Arkansas House of Representatives.[70]

The state Democratic convention met on June 17 and declared itself totally committed to silver in a number of planks on the currency question. The convention favored the 16 to 1 ratio and the use of "both silver and gold as money of final redemption." The platform opposed the federal government's relegating the power "to furnish a circulating medium to any private corporation." The party also advocated the income tax and a tariff for revenue only. In state affairs, the platform called for establishment of a railroad commission and submission of an amendment to the voters to grant to the legislature the power to create the commission. Such an amendment would remove doubts about the constitutionality of establishing new state offices. "Railroads are public highways," declared the platform, "and the interest of the people demand a constant supervision of their management." Although national issues predominated during the campaign, the winter of 1896–97 witnessed an increased interest in the railroad commission question.[71]

Because of a new method of apportionment, the 1896 state convention had more delegates than ever before. Yet, the 748 men who came to Little Rock had less to do than in the past. The primaries had accomplished much of the work of nominating candidates, and it was only necessary to hold a one-day session. The temporary chairman, Thomas Taylor of Jefferson County, opened the convention with a fervent silver address and shortly later the permanent chairman, John B. Jones of Little Rock, lashed out at the Cleveland administration in a lengthy barrage.[72]

Among the important decisions facing the convention was the choice of a presidential favorite. William Jennings Bryan did not receive major attention at the convention. By June, a majority had determined upon the popular Richard Parks Bland of Missouri. But a few Bryan supporters of influence angled for his nomination early in 1896. Bryan's leading supporter was that target of the *Helena World*'s most colorful vituperation, Charles Collins. In February, Collins sent Bryan a copy of an article in the *Little Rock Tribune* supporting the Nebraskan's candidacy. He hoped Arkansas would lead off for Bryan early in the first roll call of the states. He believed Dan Jones would win in the primaries and a Jones victory would "point unerringly to you as our leader."[73] Bryan's southern tour of 1895 and his contacts with silver Democrats of the South laid the groundwork for his movement toward the presidential nomination. Although Bryan was not considered the leading candidate, his reputation in Arkansas and elsewhere made him available when the proper opportunity came.

Five counties held presidential preference primaries in 1896 and four, Montgomery, Garland, Hot Spring, and Jackson counties, supported Richard Bland. Only Saline County favored the anti-Cleveland, pro-farmer leader, Horace Boies of Iowa. In an interview in Washington, D.C., Senator James Berry called for selection of a silver candidate but refused to declare a specific choice. Senator Jones, according to Bryan, had been a firm supporter of Bland. Some of those who came to the state convention hoped to secure a delegation instructed for James K. Jones. But the senator gave no overt encouragement to these efforts.[74]

The platform committee proposed that the Arkansas delegation go uninstructed to the national convention, but did bind the delegates to support only a 16 to 1 silver candidate. Although both Arkansas senators pressed vigorously for an uninstructed delegation, the delegates gave enthusiastic support to a substitute resolution in support of Bland. The committee resolution lost to the substitute from the floor of the convention by a vote of 421 to

327, and a delegation with instructions for Bland headed for Chicago in July.[75]

After Bryan delivered his cross of gold speech to the Chicago convention, many of the Arkansas delegation, including the chairman, wished to cast their votes for Bryan, but the majority insisted that Arkansas remain firmly with Bland as instructed. On the fifth and final roll call, Arkansas and California cast all their votes for Bryan early in the balloting. Arkansas had made her move somewhat late to fulfill Charles Collins's hope that Arkansas would set the pace. Yet, in the final stretch, Arkansas helped secure the victory for the Great Commoner.[76]

James K. Jones and William Jennings Bryan developed a close association during 1895 and 1896 that led to Jones's selection as chairman of the Democratic National Committee. The two men first met when Bryan came to the House of Representatives in March, 1891. After Jones met Bryan, he remarked to a friend, "Did you notice that young man's jaw?"[77] Four years later, in June 1895, Jones and Bryan worked closely together while participating in the Memphis silver convention. The Tennessee gathering placed Jones in the chairmanship of a committee of five to promote a silver plank and a silver candidate for 1896.[78]

At the Chicago Democratic National Convention, both men sought the chairmanship of the Committee on Resolutions but because of Jones's advanced age and his leadership at Memphis, Bryan deferred to him. Bryan had little chance of achieving the position since his Nebraska delegation was not seated until after the committee completed most of its work. It was James K. Jones who selected Bryan to deliver the address on the silver plank and thus gave him the opportunity to demonstrate his abilities as a campaign orator. Jones told Bryan later that he chose the Great Commoner for the speech because he was the only prominent Democrat who had not appeared before the convention. The action of Jones also led directly to Bryan's choosing him to command the Democratic forces, a position Jones held during the 1896 and 1900 campaigns. Bryan turned to Jones because "the Senator had been the head of the organization through whose efforts we had won the Convention."[79]

In James K. Jones, Bryan found a leader with whom old-line Democrats could identify. Jones had little sympathy for third-party movements. Although he became a spokesman for fusion with the Populists, Southern Democrats could rely on his party regularity. His innate conservatism stood in contrast to Bryan's progressive tendencies. During the 1900 campaign, Jones admitted his views on the platform might "be getting too conservative," but he feared extremists might inject their views in the platform. "We must I think keep clear of 'isms,'" he wrote to a colleague, "the claims for election of judges by the people and for a term of years and all such things should not even be brought up for consideration—municipal ownership should I believe be left to state platforms."[80] James K. Jones, a Bourbon Democrat, had moved far enough leftward to satisfy Arkansas agrarians. His political sagacity brought a primary victory and then national leadership. One of Jones's major concerns after the Democratic National Convention was to woo Populist voters. He sought to influence the agrarians at the national level and also gave some attention to the movement in his own state.

In the 1896 election, the Populist Party put up a local slate of candidates in only a few counties. They had experimented with fusion with Republicans at the county level in earlier elections, but in 1896 the number of these arrangements reached their apogee. Washington, Sebastian, and St. Francis counties had not tried fusion since the days of the Union Labor Party. Now they joined hands with Republicans. Franklin, Hempstead, White, and Johnson also tried fusion. In some counties, the debate over fusion brought racism to the fore. "The Fusion ticket is another attempt to foist negro domination on this county," fumed a St. Francis County editor.[81] In Miller County, the Populists were nearly evenly divided for and against supporting the Republicans. After a bitter struggle, the county became one of the few to avoid cooperation.[82] But Polk County also followed the example of Miller County and ran a "straight-out" Populist slate which took every local office except one. Drew County offered an example of Republican and Populist cooperation without fusion. The Republican County Convention chose to support the Populist nominee for the general assembly because of a Populist endorsement of a fair election law.[83]

During the campaign of 1896, the Democratic Party of Arkansas coaxed the Populists to return to the party of Jackson. The Drew County Democratic Central Committee passed a resolution cautioning Democrats "to deal gently with our good friends of the Populist persuasion whose intentions, we feel sure are good, and many of whom we trust will return to the folds of Democracy." The committee called on the faithful to welcome those who returned. Later *The Drew County Advance* reported Populists were voting in the Democratic primary for local offices and interpreted the trend as an indication the agrarians were returning to the party.[84]

Some of the Populist leaders of Arkansas favored cooperation with the Democrats in 1896. In Ouachita County, Henry Jones, a "dashing leader of the Greenbacks," who became a Union Labor Party member and then a Populist, told a *Gazette* reporter early in January that Populist strength was on the decline and the best hope for the agrarians lay in joining forces with the Democrats.[85]

Middle-of-the-road sentiment dominated the Populist organization in Arkansas as it did in Texas and some other Southern states. When the state convention met on July 15 in Little Rock, the *Gazette* reported "a very pretty fight on in the Populist ranks." The temporary chairman, J. M. Pittman of Nevada County, made a middle-of-the-road address. The fusionists pressed hard but unsuccessfully for a commitment of delegates to Bryan before the Populist national convention met, just one week later. S. P. Van Patten of Garland County, a pro-Bryan delegate, announced his conversion to socialism and the necessity for revolution but warned that Populists must realize the nation was not prepared for drastic change. The present situation suggested, he believed, an alliance with Democrats. One of the leading Populists of Arkansas and a national labor leader, James R. Sovereign, gave strong support at the convention to the Bryan movement. But the convention voted 178½ to 21½ for an uninstructed delegation.[86]

According to one delegate, J. W. Dollison, the twenty-five man Arkansas delegation to the St. Louis convention stood three to one for a "straight-out Populist ticket" for president. But he believed most of the delegates would support Bryan if he would endorse the Omaha platform. Arkansas Democrats expected J. R. Sovereign to lead the delegation into the Bryan fold, but they were furious to learn that Sovereign had delivered a seconding speech at St. Louis for the nomination of Thomas Watson for vice president. The Arkansas delegation followed Sovereign's lead and cast all of its votes for Watson and for Bryan in the ballots for vice president and president.[87]

Although members of the Populist and Democratic Party spoke at times of cooperation, no widespread movement for fusion developed until after the Democrats and Populists had held their national nominating conventions. After Bryan had won the nomination of both parties, James K. Jones, the new chairman of the Democratic National Committee, pressured his native state to cooperate with the fusion movement.

One observer of the St. Louis convention, Arthur Wallace Dunn, listed Jones as one of the chief wire-pullers at the Populist gathering. The senator made his way to St. Louis several days before the Populist convention convened and met frequently with fusion-minded Populists. His activities behind the scenes gave many the impression that he played something more than the role of a passive onlooker. William L. Wilson, Cleveland's postmaster general, wrote in his diary of the "mortification" that the chairman of the Democratic National Committee should be at work in the Populist convention to secure a nomination for Bryan. During the hours preceding the nomination of Watson, Jones had been in touch with the Populist leader William V. Allen, of Nebraska, warning that he, Jones, had a wire from Bryan insisting he would not accept a Populist nomination for president unless the Populists also nominated the Democratic vice-presidential candidate, Arthur Sewall. The Maine banker, financier, and railroader was hardly in the vanguard of the fight against monopoly and privilege. Allen, desiring the Bryan nomination, but realizing how far his party could compromise itself, refused to follow the dictates of the Jones-Bryan forces. On July 25, the day the convention nominated Watson, the St. Louis newspapers reported Bryan's request not to be nominated without Sewall. General James B. Weaver, in his speech nominating Bryan, made reference to the newspaper accounts. But Senator William V. Allen did not publicly reveal the existence of the Bryan wire in Jones's possession. Apparently the convention leadership hoped Bryan would accept the nomination once it was a *fait accompli*. Jones and Allen did not conspire to keep the convention ignorant of Bryan's attitude.[88]

Although Jones engineered fusion at St. Louis, he had little love or respect for Populists and especially for the Southern variety. Western Populists compromised the principles of the Omaha platform in exchange for emphasis on the silver panacea with less anguish than the agrarians of the South; consequently, Jones found the westerners more tolerable. The New York *World* reported Jones's comments about the Southern delegates to the St. Louis

Convention. They were, in Jones's view, "not a creditable class." They were not sincere in their alliance and would bend every effort "to harass the Democracy and create confusion, and in the end they will do just as they are doing now in Alabama, fuse with the Republicans and vote for McKinley." Jones expected the Southern Populists to "go with the negroes, where they belong."[89] Such statements did little to endear the senator to the Populists or to further the success of the Bryan campaign.

Chairman Jones returned several times to Arkansas during the campaign and used his influence to press upon the Arkansas Democratic committee the importance of fusion. Marion Butler, a North Carolina Populist, had put pressure on Jones to secure the fusion of Southern Democrats with Populists. Some Arkansas Democrats embarrassed Jones by their reluctance to agree to fusion on the presidential ticket. *The Arkansas Democrat, The Pine Bluff Press-Eagle,* and *The Helena Weekly World* led the attack on fusion. The latter newspaper condemned Jones for his dictation to the state central committee, and when fusion had been effected it told voters to strike out the names of the Populist electors from the ballot. *The Arkansas Gazette* chided the reluctant Democrats. "We want the Populists to come back home," said the editor, "we want good feeling between them and their old time associates." The *Gazette* regretted the choice of Watson instead of Sewall but argued that Democrats should accept the situation and reorganize the ballot to allow some Populist electors to participate.[90]

After the Populists completed their conventions, *Morgan's Buzz-Saw* maintained a continual barrage of criticism against fusion. Winfield Scott Morgan's middle-of-the-road paper vilified Chairman Jones for his refusal to support Watson instead of Sewall. Morgan could not understand why Populists should always be the ones to rise above interests. He opposed "making the silver issue paramount" and thought it would lead only to "fusion and confusion." To Morgan, middle-of-the-roadism meant "straight ahead and no monkeying with the disreputable politicians of either party."[91]

During September and early October, Marion Butler exerted pressure on James K. Jones to secure a fusion ticket in Arkansas. Butler led the way by securing an agreement in his own state, North Carolina, to name five Populists, five Democrats, and one silver Republican as electors. The arrangement would give Watson five electoral votes. Butler believed the Democratic national chairman's own state should set a similar example. William Jennings Bryan also asked Arkansas Democrats to help set the pace.[92]

Efforts by Chairman Jones to prod the Democrats of Arkansas to give the Populists a place on the electoral slate failed to bring significant movement by October 1. Thomas Fletcher, chairman of the Populist State Central Committee, announced he had never received "any proposition . . . from any authorized source for a fusion of the electoral ticket." The *Gazette* also reported inaction in both Populist and Democratic camps. But by October 8, the *Gazette* spoke of "a disposition" on the part of many rank-and-file Democrats "to make room on the Democratic electoral ticket for J. R. Sovereign." The paper also announced that a Democratic State Central Committee meeting on October 10 would consider fusion. James K. Jones, said the *Gazette,* desired the unification of silver forces, not to win Arkansas for Bryan, but "for the moral effect" on other states. Arkansas, in Jones's mind, must set an example of fusion.

As a result of their October meeting, the Democrats hammered out a plan accepted by the Populists. Subcommittees of the two central committees met together to work out details of the agreement. The arrangement gave little advantage to the Populist Party. The agrarians presented the Democrats with a list of eight nominees for elector from which the Democratic subcommittee chose three. The Democrats retained possession of five of the eight electors. The Democratic Central Committee approved the arrangement by a seventeen to two vote while the Populist Central Committee gave it a unanimous endorsement despite the presence of middle-of-the-roaders on the committee. One of those approved by the Democrats as an acceptable Populist elector was James Sovereign; and gallantly stepping aside to make room for him on the electoral ticket was future "Popocrat" Jeff Davis. In the fall election, Arkansas's Populist electors gave Thomas Watson three of his twenty-seven electoral votes. Arkansas's example failed to achieve its desired effect in the South. Louisiana leaders had earlier agreed to accept fusion. Butler hoped Mississippi might follow the same pattern, but she did not. Only Arkansas, Louisiana, and North Carolina gave electoral votes to Thomas Watson. In Georgia negotiations ended in failure when the Georgia Democratic State Central Committee refused Populist demands that all thirteen electors on the proposed fusion ticket vote for Watson. Both Populists and Democrats at the grass-roots level balked at fusion.[93]

Arkansas Democrats continued to hold out against fusion. *The Helena Weekly World* advised readers to vote the Democratic ticket but suggested scratching out the names of the three Populist electors. The *World* roundly condemned the Democratic State Central Committee for the fusion deal and even chided fellow goldbug newspapers on their decision to remain close-mouthed on the issue. The Republicans mocked the new position of the Democrats. The Isaac C. Parker Republican League Club of Fort Smith issued a circular ridiculing the attempt to bring in the millennium "by the lying down together, in obstensible harmony and peace, of the DEMOCRATIC JACKASS and the POPULISTIC BILLY GOAT." In a circular addressed to the voters of Sebastian County, the local Democratic committee extended "a hearty Democratic handshake" to those who would vote for Bryan, "no matter what their past party affiliations may have been."[94]

After the excitement of the primary elections, the fall campaign held less interest for Arkansans. The Republicans had virtually no chance of winning any state office, but they did place candidates in the field. Harmon L. Remmel, the Republican nominee for governor, launched an attack on both James K. Jones and Dan W. Jones during the August campaign. Remmel berated the senator for his failure to secure tariff protection for Arkansas lumber against Canadian competitors. The Republicans also made their usual attacks on the election laws. Dan Jones responded to both Populist and Republican demands when he promised to ask the general assembly for a revision of the election law.[95]

In the state election, Dan Jones polled 91,114 votes to 35,836 for the Republican candidate and 13,990 for the Populist. With a majority of over 40,000 votes, the Democrats emerged as the clear victors.[96] Arkansas had committed itself in the primary elections to the silver panacea. In this one cause, the discontented farmer, oppressed by depression, found a rallying cry. He wanted a railroad commission and an end to monopoly too, but this one issue became a symbol of his demands and hopes. Arkansas demanded change, and its voice joined the chorus of those who ousted Cleveland and the sound money leadership.

William Jennings Bryan captured the hearts of the Arkansas people and his followers gained control of the Democratic Party.

His movement to center stage in the Democracy encouraged the development of traits already evident in Arkansas's political culture. The Nebraskan championed simple and moralistic solutions to the complex problems of an industrial age. He approached political causes with an emotional and evangelistic fervor. Arkansans appreciated a man of his stripe and within two years, they elected an attorney general who manifested these characteristics. Jeff Davis was much more than a carbon copy of Bryan. He had a greater flair for the dramatic and the cataclysmic, but he preached many of the same doctrines and exhibited the same penchant for moralistic solutions and panaceas.

The 1896 election contributed further to the tensions and divisions within the Arkansas Democratic Party. Daniel Jones won the governorship in 1896 because of his bold attacks upon the party's right wing. In 1899 Jeff Davis's slashing campaign for the governorship further divided the ranks and created a bitterness hardly paralleled in the state's history. Arkansans now chose Democratic leaders whose main talents lay in their ability to unveil the conspiracies and corruption of government and business leaders. Those men who excelled at denunciation and abusive rhetoric captured the popular imagination. Such leaders could hardly salve the wounds of the national party. James K. Jones, the loyal silverite, lost his Senate seat in 1902, partly because of his modest conciliatory advances toward the sound money men in the Democratic Party. After the 1896 election, the national Democratic Party again resumed its role as the opposition party, but its constituency could not agree on a positive alternative to Republican rule.

The election of 1896 had not created the tensions that divided the party. The process of disruption began with Cleveland's handling of patronage, his intransigence toward even meager silver legislation, and his tactless assaults on the representatives of the party from the South and West. A long depression and the bungling of an administration which failed to find any positive program of action to combat economic suffering had alienated Democrats. The events of 1896 afforded an outlet for accumulating tensions and led the national party further toward disunity and chaos. While the party foundations shook because of tensions within, an independent party threatened its supremacy in the South. In Arkansas, the Populist threat caused the party to veer farther to the left.

3

The Triumph of the Populist Spirit in the Democratic Party

During the 1890s, the People's Party threatened the dominance of the Democratic Party in the Southern states. Although presidential candidate General James B. Weaver did not carry a single Southern state in 1892, he did win a significant minority of votes in some of the states. Two years later, the Populists polled a large vote in Alabama, North Carolina, and Georgia. In the latter state, the agrarians won nearly 45 percent of the ballots cast. In North Carolina, in the same election year, the Populists attracted many Democratic voters to their fold. By fusing with North Carolina Republicans, the agrarian coalition won a majority in the state legislature and elected four Populist and three Republican congressmen.[1] Voting statistics alone do not reveal the extent of the agrarian threat to the one-party system. The protest movement had sufficient power to force Democratic capitulation to some demands of farmers. The Southern Democracy also began making room in its own ranks for such "Popocratic" leaders as Pitchfork Ben Tillman of South Carolina and James Hogg of Texas. The power of the rebel farmers did more than poll votes for independent parties; it also changed the character of the Democratic Party in the South.

Arkansas Democrats responded to the Populist tidal wave in the same manner as other Southerners. Alarmed by the threat to the party of white supremacy, they made concessions to Populist doctrine and granted places of influence in the party to men like Jeff Davis. The Populist revolt never attained the heights in Arkansas that it reached in North Carolina or Alabama. Because the dominant party in Arkansas successfully absorbed much of the Populist spirit, it weathered the agrarian storm with a minimum of loss. The Democrats also profited from early attention to election "reform" in favor of the majority party. With new electoral machinery and a talent for vote manipulation, the Democrats of Arkansas could blunt the farmer's attack.

Geographic and economic characteristics also offer some explanation for the failure of Populism to assume a larger role in the political life of the state. Arkansans frequently boast of the diversity of their resources and industries. Although cotton has been an important crop in the state, it has not overshadowed the rice, lumber, fruit, and cattle industries. One county, Benton, produced more apples before the First World War than any other single county in the United States. Populism in other southern states flourished mostly in the cotton producing areas where small farmers protested the control of large landowners. This class division was not so prominent in the western two-thirds of Arkansas where few large farms existed.[2]

A charting of Populist strength shows two distinct centers of agrarianism on either side of the Arkansas River. One cluster of Populist counties lay in the Ouachita Mountain region in the western section of the state and to the south of the Arkansas River. The second cluster lay in the north central section along the dividing line between mountain and prairie counties.[3]

Often the generalization is made that Populist discontent centered in the hilly areas. This is somewhat misleading. The northern Populist area centered in the area where hills and lowlands meet. Some of the Populist counties were at the very edge of the gently rolling approaches to the Ozarks. Of the seventeen counties voting at least 30 percent Populist in one of the gubernatorial elections of the 1890s, only four lie within the area classified by the Census Bureau as the Ozark region.[4] The four Ozark counties voting 30 percent Populist included Van Buren, Cleburne, Stone, and Washington, although the latter county reached this percentage only in 1892. Washington County on the western border of the state was not a part of the Populist cluster in the north central part of Arkansas as were the other three counties. Outside the Ozark region but bordering on it were three more counties in the 30 percent category, Faulkner, White, and Independence. The heart of the Arkansas Ozarks leaned more toward

POPULIST PERCENTAGE OF TOTAL
GUBERNATORIAL VOTE IN
THE 1892 ELECTION

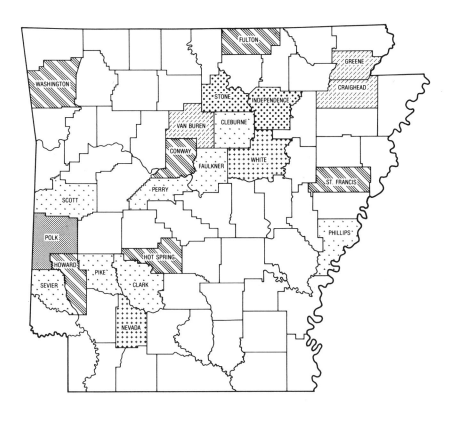

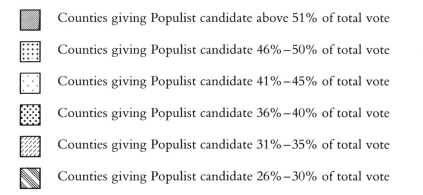

Counties giving Populist candidate above 51% of total vote

Counties giving Populist candidate 46%–50% of total vote

Counties giving Populist candidate 41%–45% of total vote

Counties giving Populist candidate 36%–40% of total vote

Counties giving Populist candidate 31%–35% of total vote

Counties giving Populist candidate 26%–30% of total vote

POPULIST PERCENTAGE OF TOTAL
GUBERNATORIAL VOTE IN
THE 1894 ELECTION

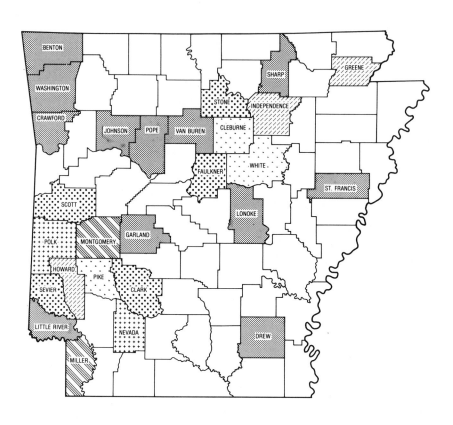

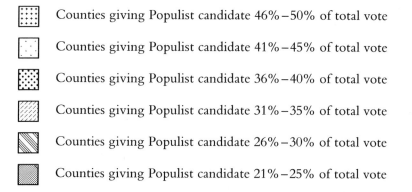

Counties giving Populist candidate 46%–50% of total vote

Counties giving Populist candidate 41%–45% of total vote

Counties giving Populist candidate 36%–40% of total vote

Counties giving Populist candidate 31%–35% of total vote

Counties giving Populist candidate 26%–30% of total vote

Counties giving Populist candidate 21%–25% of total vote

POPULIST PERCENTAGE OF TOTAL
GUBERNATORIAL VOTE IN
THE 1896 ELECTION

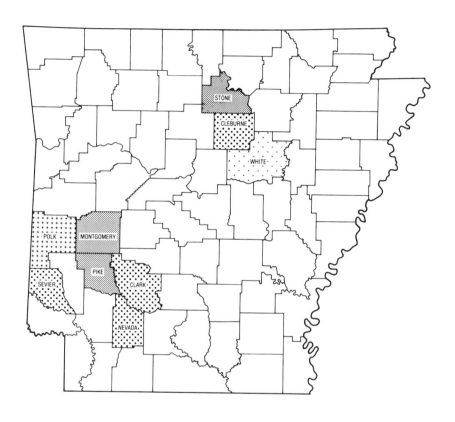

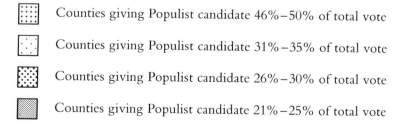

Counties giving Populist candidate 46%–50% of total vote

Counties giving Populist candidate 31%–35% of total vote

Counties giving Populist candidate 26%–30% of total vote

Counties giving Populist candidate 21%–25% of total vote

Republicanism than Populism. Newton and Searcy Counties remained G.O.P. islands in a Democratic sea.

The second Populist center lay in the Ouachita Mountain area of western Arkansas. Polk County, the most loyal Populist county in the state, is situated in the heart of the Ouachita Mountains. This county gave 53 percent of its vote to the Populist gubernatorial candidate in 1892, 47 percent in 1894, and 48 percent in 1896. Six other counties in the Ouachita area cast 30 percent of their votes for the Populist gubernatorial candidate in one or more of the elections of the 1890s. At least two of these, Nevada and Clark, are at the far edge of the hilly region and have elevations ranging from only one hundred to five hundred feet. Sevier, Pike, and Perry counties are somewhat closer to the mountainous area, but Scott and Polk were the only Populist counties in the heartland of the mountains.

The Populist Party gained least support in the Delta region of eastern Arkansas. The party also made a weak showing in the counties bordering the Arkansas River valley. Many of the larger towns of Arkansas, such as Fort Smith, Russellville, Little Rock, and Pine Bluff, were situated in this valley. The townspeople and the wealthier farmers of the river valley did not usually vote with the Populists. The party gained only two strongholds in the valley. The borders of Faulkner and Perry counties met at the river and together formed a Populist bridge between the two major areas of Populism in the state. Along with the Delta and the river valley, one other area displayed a reluctance to accept the third party. Several of the Ozark Mountain counties, such as Boone and Marion, polled extremely low Populist votes.

Apparently Populism won most support in Arkansas among the rural folk who operated farms in the areas where hills and plains met. The remote mountaineer who scratched his living from a rocky hillside and the large landowner of the lowlands did not vote Populist in large numbers. As in Texas and Louisiana, Populism in Arkansas found most of its adherents in poor farming areas.[5]

But economic and geographical considerations alone cannot explain the distribution of Populist strength. The popularity of local politicians brought into play the force of personality. In Phillips County, on the Mississippi River, the Populist party polled 44 percent of the 1892 gubernatorial vote. In 1894 the party won only 0.02 percent of this county's vote. The sudden collapse of Populism can be explained in several ways. Phillips County had managed during the 1890s to eliminate the Negro as a force in county politics. Also the county had a reputation for expertise in ballot manipulation. Apparently those blacks who had supported the Populists in 1892 were counted out in 1894. Another contributing factor in the turnabout was the successful gubernatorial candidacy of one of Phillips County's own Democrats, James P. Clarke. His local popularity and his influence in the county helped to attract voters. Disfranchisement of blacks, electoral fraud, and the popularity of local personalities help to account for the varied pattern of support for Populism in some accounts.

In some states, Populism flourished among those of evangelical faith with very few Populists coming from the ritualist or liturgical communions. Since almost all Arkansans were evangelicals, no religious distinction is apparent between loyal Democrats and the Populist rebels. In the 1895 and 1897 general assemblies, of the seventeen different Populists serving, there were seven Methodists, five Christians, three Baptists, and one "Independent." This does not distinguish them from the Democratic or Republican membership of the general assembly.[6]

Almost all of the Populist leaders of Arkansas listed their profession as farming. A very few were teachers, editors, and physicians. Some of the leaders, like Dr. J. A. Meek of Craighead County, were well-to-do. Winfield Scott Morgan, Arkansas's leading middle-of-the-road Populist, used his newspaper to boost immigration to the state. Morgan's paper advertised itself as "The King of Fun. Wit, Humor, Irony, Sarcasm, Parody, Satire, Ridicule." In its sheets, Morgan boasted of his town's (Hardy, Arkansas) location on the Kansas City, Springfield and Memphis Railroad. The town, with its population of six hundred and located in Sharp County in north Arkansas just 130 miles from Memphis, looked for new settlers. Occasionally he announced his land offerings to potential Arkansans. In one issue he offered twenty-five hundred acres for sale.[7] During the 1896 campaign, James R. Sovereign, a leading Arkansas Populist, in a letter to Marion Butler of North Carolina, complained of the extreme poverty of the Arkansas party. In his reply Butler indicated that Populists across the nation suffered from scarcity of funds.[8] In

Arkansas, as elsewhere, the rank-and-file Populist came principally from poor farming areas, but some of those who led the movement were men of wealth.

The Populist Party in Arkansas had as its reason for being the securing of justice to those farmers of the low-lying hills and rolling prairie land. The movement provided a political vehicle for expression of discontent within the established order in the South. This vehicle took the form of a third-party movement, and, because of the antagonism of the Democrats to any rising political threat, the movement immediately assumed a defensive position. Because of its precarious existence, the Populist Party in Arkansas turned its attention to electoral reform more than any other issue. Without change in the manner of conducting elections, agrarian dissent could not hope to achieve reform. To be an Arkansas Populist meant to champion the cause of electoral change.

The state platform of 1896 condemned the Arkansas election law and called upon the Democrats to allow Populist election commissioners to serve wherever the agrarians were second to the Democrats in voting power. The platform also called for the consolidation of state and national elections. In Arkansas, the state election preceded the national elections by nearly two months. Democrats, conjuring up recollections of the Force Bill, feared consolidation might mean more federal control of elections. "We declare it to be our unalterable purpose," stated the Populist platform, "to wage unrelenting warfare upon this arch-iniquity of freedom and human rights until every free American citizen shall have the right to vote according to the dictates of his own conscience, and can have his vote counted precisely as he cast it." Democratic candidate Dan Jones courted the dissidents by promises to press for fair election laws. The gubernatorial candidate had given his support to the 1891 election law when it passed the legislature, but he now believed experience had demonstrated a need for some modification, and he gave his assurance to the Populists that changes would be made.[9]

The Republican candidate for governor pressed the same issue in a joint debate with Dan Jones in Faulkner County. Harmon L. Remmel reminded Jones that twenty-three thousand poor whites were unable to read or write in Arkansas and could not prepare a proper ballot. If a "political emblem" appeared at the top of the ballot—a rooster for the Democrats and an eagle for the Republicans—the illiterate voter could mark his ballot without the aid of another person. Refusal to modify the system, Remmel feared, would simply enable Democrats to "perpetuate themselves in power, if they wished to be dishonest."[10]

Thomas Fletcher, chairman of the Populist State Central Committee, did not share the optimism of those agrarians who praised Jones for his stand. In a campaign speech in August, Fletcher said:

> This question of personal liberty is of more importance, just now, than any question of finance or tariff; to be a 'freeman' is of more importance than having 'free silver.' The Democratic party is wholly responsible for the present vicious, barbarous, un-American, undemocratic election laws, and some of the leaders, even though they profess to favor honest elections, are largely responsible for its present condition. They opposed any and every amendment looking to any improvement or modification.

Fletcher also affirmed his belief in the sincerity of Dan Jones's promises, but he could not believe the Democratic Party would stand behind Jones in the general assembly. Most Democrats, he noted, were satisfied with the existing election law. Reform, he warned, "will not and cannot be had by electing the Democratic ticket." Fletcher's doubts were well founded. In 1898 the *Gazette* chided those Populists who still condemned the existing system. "Do they want reforms in the state election laws?" asked the *Gazette*. "Let them get in the Democratic boat and there do battle for what they believe is right."[11]

The 1896 platform indicated some of the other basic emphases of Arkansas Populists. The agrarians asserted their determination to stand by the Omaha platform. On the state level they called for "a state board of arbitration to adjust all differences between corporations and employes [*sic*]." The party condemned the granting of state lands to the "levee corporations." Levee Boards in eastern Arkansas had acquired thousands of acres of public land in order to finance the construction of dikes. While these organizations aided in the drainage of land, their operations swallowed up much of the available land area in the Delta region. Populists also believed the state should provide, without charge, a uniform "series of text books" for the common schools.[12]

The depressed condition of the economy constituted another major Populist concern. Philip D. McCulloch, Jr., of Marianna, a Democratic congressional candidate, speaking in Greene County, a center of Populist agitation, recognized the force of the depression issue. "The people," he affirmed, "are not listening to campaign speeches this year because they are entertaining or amusing. They listen because the great issue involved touches their interest. They can't understand why cotton has fallen from 10 to 5 cents." "Stacks of goods," he said, "lay unsold on merchant's shelves." The candidate saw a solution in the free coinage of silver and praised the Populists for their endorsement of Bryan. He welcomed those Populists joining with Democrats to end monometalism and alleviate the depression.[13]

The election year of 1896 was a year of drought in the hills of Arkansas, Texas, and Louisiana.[14] During the hot Arkansas summer, livestock ponds dried, cotton wilted on the stalk, and both early and late corn crops failed to mature properly. In central Arkansas, timber began drying out. Only in the northeastern section of the state had rains been adequate. A long, dry summer added to depression woes and helped fuel the discontent of the farmer class.[15]

The decline in the proportion of yeoman farmers to tenant farmers gives some indication of the extent of distress in Arkansas. Farm tenancy increased at a rapid rate in the state during the 1890s. Although tenancy in Arkansas was common, a few states exceeded Arkansas in the percentage of farmers who did not own land. Mississippi's sharecroppers and tenants composed 62.4 percent of the total farm population in 1900, while Arkansas's percentage was 45.4. But during the twenty-year period from 1880 to 1900, landless farmers increased in Arkansas by 14.5 percent. Only three southern states exceeded this rate of increase. Almost all of the Arkansas increase came in the decade of the 1890s.[16]

Beset by depression, threatened with the specter of tenancy, the distressed farmer, who lost faith in the ability of the Democratic Party to respond to his needs, turned to the third-party movement. But his forces seemed always too small to capture the fortress of political power, and Democratic control of election machinery discouraged his efforts. One course of action offered some promise.

Fusion had always seemed to offer the agrarians some hope for their party's quest for victory in the elections. Ironically, the best hope of success also contained within itself the danger of suicide by assimilation into another party. In Arkansas, as elsewhere in the South, the farmer's parties usually looked to the Republican Party for support since it stood as another opposition voice to the entrenched Democrats. Many Southern Populists vehemently opposed the nomination of Bryan by their party at St. Louis. To the Southern agrarian, fusion with Democrats meant joining hands with the enemy, with those who had frustrated their quest for power by using fraud and intimidation, with those who represented the established interest they hoped to dethrone.

It had been through fusion with Republicans that the Union Labor Party narrowed the gap between themselves and the Democrats in 1888. Although fusion seemed a powerful weapon in 1888, the agrarians failed to make successful use of it in Arkansas in later elections. The Populists almost always rejected fusion with the Republicans on statewide offices. Some county organizations were able to agree on local fusion tickets, but state cooperation proved unattainable. In 1894, Arkansas Populists, like those in North Carolina, Alabama, Georgia, Louisiana, Virginia, and Texas did enter into some type of arrangement with the Republican Party. While in North Carolina, the Populists were able to agree with the Republicans on a single slate including candidates from both parties, most states cooperated in a less organized manner. In Arkansas, Populists and Republicans agreed to run a single slate for most statewide offices. Republicans ran unopposed by any Populist for some offices while Populists received the same advantage in others. But middle-of-the-road Populists refused to support the plan to nominate a Republican for governor. Since the Populists and Republicans failed to agree on a single candidate at the highest level, fusion proved to be ineffective, and the two opposition parties ran their own gubernatorial candidates. Both Populists and Republicans polled approximately twenty-five thousand votes each for governor, splitting the opposition forces down the middle.[17]

The fusion effort of 1896 became another stage in the downward movement of the Populist Party. With the decline of the organization, whose very existence seemed to endanger Democratic fortunes, the one-party system could now achieve greater mastery over Arkansas politics. In the 1896 election, A. W. Files, the Populist candidate for governor, carried only Polk County and received less than 10 percent of all votes cast in the gubernatorial election. The Populists slightly enlarged their small delegation to the general assembly. Clark, Cleburne, Independence, Lawrence, Montgomery, Nevada, Polk, Scott, and White counties sent a total of eleven Populist representatives to the statehouse in Little Rock for the 1897 session. But it was the last time the Populist Party made any kind of showing in the legislative elections. In 1898 not one Populist won election to the general assembly. In 1900 and again in 1904, the voters sent one Populist to the statehouse.[18]

The number of counties voting 30 percent or more Populist in gubernatorial elections declined from seventeen in 1892 to twelve in 1894. But in 1896 only three, Polk, Clark, and White, remained in this category, with Nevada trailing close behind at 29 percent. By 1898 no county maintained this level of Populist strength.[19] The 1898 election sounded the death knell of the Populist Party. The Populists were unable to carry a single county in the gubernatorial election. In Polk County, a bulwark of Populism, the Democrats experienced a rebirth of power. White County voted Democratic "all along the line" for the first time in fourteen years. Counties once disputed hotly by Democrats and agrarians now fell into Democratic hands.[20]

John M. Wheeler, a student of Arkansas Populism, has asserted that while many Populist voters did return to the Democratic Party in 1896, as the Democrats claimed, the actual situation was more complex. "Another dominant trend," he suggests, "was for third party voters to simply 'sit out' the election." Former Populists stayed at home because they were simply disgusted or were unable to decide how to cast their vote. A smaller number of voters turned to the Republican Party. This was a natural response to the passing of their own movement, since for over a decade they had experienced cooperation with the Republicans.[21] Another historian, Raymond Arsenault, has stressed the effect of disfranchisement on the former Populist voter. Despite the fact that Arkansas Democrats billed disfranchisement as a cure for the Black voting situation, they also knew that it would weaken the Republican and Populist parties. Arsenault has illustrated the effect of disfranchisement on whites. He found that voter participation between 1890 and 1898 fell over 30 percent in the twenty-five counties having a white population of 94 percent or more. Even admitting that other factors accounted for part of the decline, it seems clear that the poll tax had effectively disfranchised a large number of poor whites who had once voted Republican or Populist.[22]

Despite the fact that many former Populists had been disfranchised and had joined the Republican Party or abandoned the political system altogether, at least some former Populist voters must have returned to the Democratic Party. It is clear that a few of the better known agrarian politicians made their peace with the one-party system. But many of the leaders of the movement in Arkansas refused to give up on their party no matter how moribund. In 1904 A. W. Files was still chairman of a Populist state central committee. And as late as 1907, Reuben B. CarlLee, a Populist from England, Arkansas, who had served in the Arkansas House from 1883 to 1886, wrote to Tom Watson asking if he thought the faithful should "hold up the skeleton of the People's party or align themselves with the democratic party or try the Independance [sic] League."[23]

Most of the Populist leaders left little trace of their later political activities. Many of them had reached their fifties or sixties in the 1890s and were not active after 1900. A large number of those in the leadership probably lost interest in political activity, joined leftist parties, or aligned with the Republicans.[24] Winfield S. Morgan in 1899 rebuked those socialists who exulted over the death of Populism. He conceded a few Populists had joined the socialists but not so many as the socialists seemed to believe. Populism, Morgan believed, embodied as much socialism as the American people could absorb for many years. Despite Morgan's statement, it is clear that the socialists in the southwestern United States did recruit many of the more militant former Populists. During the 1890s, many former Union Labor Party leaders from Sebastian and Pulaski counties turned to the Socialist Party. Finally, Morgan himself, during the years 1911 to 1918, became a regular contributor to the *National Rip-Saw,* a St. Louis socialist magazine that claimed Eugene V. Debs as one of its editors. But surrender of the party did not come easily. Even as late as June, 1906, *The Arkansas Gazette* reported that Cleburne County, though it stood alone, had a slate of Populist candidates.[25]

The Democratic press in Arkansas heralded the news of any Populist leader returning to the fold. Partisan bias may have led many to believe that the Populists had realized their sin and repented in abject humility. The blare of trumpets for the few prodigals should not lead one to the conclusion that the malcontents returned in droves.

In 1897 the Arkansas press welcomed Homer Prince, "boss" of the Populists, back to the Democracy. Prince served as a member of the Populist Central Committee representing White County.

He had been prominent in agrarian movements for many years. *The Helena Weekly World,* not an admirer of Homer Prince, published a statement of Prince's thoughts on his conversion. "If the principles now advocated by the reorganized Democracy do, in all essentials, coincide with those of the Populists, then we fail to see wherein anything is to be gained by fighting each other instead of the common enemy." Having acknowledged the absorption of the Populist spirit by the dominant party, Prince announced his determination to "do all our fighting on the Democratic side where there is some hope of reaping the reward we have sought for so many years, and that reward is relief for the masses." By 1899 the *World* noted that Homer Prince, "once a tearful Populite," had gained some sense since he had married a Helena woman.[26]

Dr. J. A. Meek of northeast Arkansas, a physician, lawyer, and minister, also made a dramatic return to the Democracy. He had served Poinsett and then Craighead counties in the state legislature on many occasions and as early as 1866. Beginning his career as a Democrat, he became a Greenbacker, Granger, Populist, and then a Democrat again. In 1894 he ran on the Populist ticket as a candidate for attorney general. In February, 1898, Meek sent a letter to the chairman of the Populist Central Committee announcing his reconversion. Chairman Thomas Fletcher replied in an open letter to the *Gazette.* Fletcher reminded Meek of how he discovered him in earlier years as "a bright and sparkling gem of Populism" and had "selected you as my star of promise." Meek campaigned unsuccessfully in the primary election of 1898 for a place in the general assembly but failed to unseat the incumbent in Craighead County. The physician believed the Chicago platform needed some amendment in the Populist direction but advised fellow agrarians to submerge their differences with Democrats until after the election. Meek discovered that restoration to power in the party was not readily granted to the rebels.[27] Another agrarian leader, Dr. C. M. Norwood, a former Union Labor Party candidate for governor, ran in the Democratic primary in 1906. Norwood lost his bid for the Democratic nomination to the Arkansas Senate.[28]

In order to determine the extent to which former Populists returned to power in the Democratic Party after 1900, a search for Populist leaders has been made among the members of the general assembly for the sessions from 1901 to 1920. Newspaper lists

of members of Populist central committees and delegates to national conventions and other similar positions yielded a working
group of 110 names. Of the 110 leading Populists of the 1890s,
only 7 ever gained entry to the Arkansas General Assembly after
1900 for even a single term. None of the 110 ever held a seat in
congress or won a statewide elective office in Arkansas during
the first two decades of the twentieth century. The leaders of the
Populist crusade were not even a minor force in the Democratic
Party in the new century. The agrarians were in no position to
give direction to the progressive movement in Arkansas. Populism in Arkansas did give impetus to a rising demand for change
within the Democracy at the close of the 1890s. But the change
came through Democratic absorption of the Populist spirit and
through accommodation to some of the agrarian demands, not
through a movement of Populists into positions of Democratic
power.[29]

One of the seven Populists who served in the legislature after
1900, Robert Wesley Chrisp of Searcy, won election on the Democratic Ticket to the assembly in 1902 as a representative of that
bastion of Populism, White County. He had served as a Populist
representative to the assembly in 1895 and 1897. In 1896 Chrisp
tried his hand at uniting the reform forces in the Democratic
Party and Populist Party behind one ticket for White County but
did not succeed. In 1898 he made a bid for the state senate as a
Democratic candidate but lost in the primary election. After his
victory as a Democrat in the 1902 election, he made an unsuccessful race for the state senate in 1906.[30]

David E. Barker, one of Arkansas Populism's best known lu-
minaries, won election to the state house of representatives in
1905, 1907, and 1911. He had been the Populist candidate for
governor in 1894 when the party still retained its vitality. In his
quest for the Democratic nomination in the 1908 Drew County
primary, Barker asked the aid of Congressman Joseph T. Robinson. He believed Robinson might be supporting his opponent.
Barker lost the 1908 race but did come back in 1910.[31]

Edgar R. Arnold, a delegate to the St. Louis convention in
1896, ran successfully as a Clark County Democratic candidate
for state representative in 1904 and for the state senate in 1906.
Willie B. W. Heartsill, who ran as a Populist candidate for Congress in 1892, served Sebastian County in the general assemblies
of 1907, 1909, and 1913. Henry B. Walker, a farmer from Logan

County, served in the assembly as a Populist in 1895 and as a Democrat in 1907. Samuel Emory Sweet, a delegate to the St. Louis Convention in 1896, sat in the 1909 assembly for St. Francis County. Another prominent Populist, J. O. A. Bush of Prescott, who failed in his race for Congress in 1892, won election in 1896 to the general assembly. The Nevada County editor returned to the statehouse for a four-year senate term beginning in 1915. The experiences of these seven men indicate that a few agrarians did recover some political influence within the Democratic Party. But they were not sufficiently influential to give direction to the party in the twentieth century.

One Arkansas Populist, James R. Sovereign, achieved power at the highest level in the national Democratic Party. His influence in the Populist Party and Democratic Party rested primarily on his position as a national labor leader. Sovereign, aided by Daniel De Leon and members of the Socialist Labor Party, forced the removal of Terence V. Powderly as Grand Master Workman of the Knights of Labor. Sovereign shepherded the organization during its declining days. Under his direction, the Knights of Labor became increasingly an unskilled and rural workers' union and moved in the direction of political cooperation with agrarian movements. In 1896 Sovereign served as a member of the Populist national executive committee. He went to Chicago after the Populist convention to direct a "Bryan–Free Silver Campaign Labor Bureau" and elicited some labor support for the cause. During the campaign he worked assiduously for a coalition of silver forces behind Bryan. His fusionist zeal provoked barbed comments from *Morgan's Buzz-Saw*. The Sharp County paper called him "the greatest political fakir in this country just now," and a "Jumping Jack for the Democratic Party."[32] Morgan and other middle-of-the-roaders attacked Sovereign for his efforts on behalf of Democratic candidates in other states. Sovereign had made a speech in Memphis on behalf of E. W. Carmack's candidacy for Congress when he knew that a Populist candidate also sought the office. His flirtations caused the Populist state convention in 1898 to terminate his position as national committeeman for Arkansas.[33] The majority of Arkansas Populists by 1896 were middle-of-the-roaders and did not approve of Sovereign's fusionist ideas.[34]

The 1896 election began a pattern of cooperation between Sovereign and William Jennings Bryan. In the spring of 1897 the

Grand Master Workman requested Bryan's aid in securing the moral support of all silver forces for the struggling labor organization. Sovereign had lost one hundred local union organizations within a three-month period. He believed gold men and their money were at work to destroy the organization. Sovereign was not content to hitch the Knights of Labor to the silver star. He also presided over the creation of a new secret order to advance the free silver cause. Assuming the office of grand chief of the National Order of Mohawks, Sovereign established his headquarters at Sulphur Springs in the Ozarks. Sovereign hoped to induce free silver men in the Republican, Democratic, and Populist parties to accept secret membership. The Grand Chief hoped also "to make it agreeable for a certain school of reformers to work with the silver forces who would otherwise go into the Social Democracy and might aggregate sufficient forces in doubtful centers to endanger the chances of the silver ticket in 1900." [35]

During the years from 1898 to 1900, Sovereign corresponded with Bryan and spent some of his time lining up support in the Western states. During May and June of 1898, he campaigned in Oregon for the silver forces and then returned to Arkansas. In the next year he moved briefly to Idaho where he became editor of a local newspaper, took an interest in the state's labor turmoil, and promised Bryan to tour the East before the 1900 campaign. During 1900 he was again at his Arkansas home offering to organize laboring men of the West behind Bryan. [36]

It was not necessary for Populists to convert to the Democracy in order to effect change in the dominant party's ideology. The few agrarians who returned did influence the party leftward, but the response to agrarian pressure began before the return of the insurgents. When Arkansas's legislature met in 1897, the pressure for railroad and antitrust legislation broke through the dam of conservative resistance. The absorption of the Populist spirit had begun earlier, but as the legislatures of the late 1890s proceeded, the agrarian tendencies within the Democratic Party became more pronounced.

The checkered career of the Bush Bill exemplified the accommodation of Democrats to agrarian demands. The proposal, introduced by Populist Representative J. O. A. Bush, provided for the construction and ownerships of railroads by the state. To the Populist Party, the measure was at least a small move in the direction of government ownership and control of the railroads, one of the ideals of the Omaha platform. Although the bill bore the name of a Populist, it elicited the support of some gold Democrats. J. M. Moore, a prominent conservative Democrat, joined with other gold men to boost the state railroad concept at a Board of Trade rally. The business leadership of Little Rock gave the scheme its blessing during December of 1896 before the convening of the January session of the legislature. Col. John G. Fletcher, president of the German National Bank in the capital city, saw in the measure an opportunity to bring a new railroad line to Little Rock.[37] The curious coincidence of Populist theory with the business community's interest in the development of new transportation facilities created an unusual coalition of forces behind the state railroad plan.

In his inaugural address, Governor Dan W. Jones called upon the state legislature to follow the example of several other Southern states by utilizing convict labor to construct a state railroad. The new executive envisioned a north-south route and an east-west route with trunk lines reaching into all parts of the state. The state railroad could be leased to a private corporation which would actually operate the line. Jones suggested that the legislature create a board composed of state officers to form a corporate body "capable of sueing [sic] and being sued." The board could borrow money and float bond issues, but in no case would the state be liable for the board's debt.[38] The latter proposal was an attempt to silence critics who remembered Reconstruction bond issues and repudiation. Strong opposition to bond issues of any kind pervaded the state. Jeff Davis later used the bond issue to arouse the latent suspicions of the hill people against the state railroad plan. The Bush Bill of 1897 incorporated the basic concepts suggested in Jones's inaugural speech.

When the Bush Bill came to its final test in the general assembly, only one Populist member voted in the negative, and the bill had the support of every Populist who voted for James R. Sovereign for United States senator. The bill passed the house by a vote of fifty to thirty-six and the senate by a twenty to ten vote during an extraordinary session of the general assembly. Among those voting for the measure was Senator R. W. Worthen, representative of the Little Rock area, who had bitterly opposed all efforts to establish a railroad commission. "Why, what would we do," queried Worthen in the senate, "without the Iron Mountain Railroad, the Oil Trust or the Standard Oil Co.? We must stop pandering to the Populist Party—why, it made me, 'a gold Democrat,' vote for three Populists, but I took my medicine, and wrote on the back of the ticket 'd—— the platform.'" To secure a new railroad, goldbug Worthen joined hands with the hated Populites.[39]

As a Populist measure the state railroad scheme represented an attack upon Jay Gould's Iron Mountain Railroad and its monopolistic grip on the state's transportation system. Some conservatives agreed with the *World's* fulminations against the "Populite baby" being nursed by a Democratic governor. When Jones set out during the summer and fall of 1897 to gather financial support for his plan, the voice of the "Swamp Democracy," *The Helena Weekly World,* mocked his "iridescent dream." The governor secured pledges from five Little Rock financiers to assume the responsibility for the sale of bonds at $10,500 per mile of track and at 6 percent interest. The plan hinged upon prior commitment by Little Rock to make a $75,000 contribution and upon similar contributions of other communities on the line. The *World* correctly predicted the failure of the scheme. Although Arkansas never built a state railroad, the issue provided a fertile field for political rhetoric.[40]

The Arkansas Gazette during the late 1890s vigorously championed the building of a railroad into the undeveloped zinc fields of northern Arkansas. The Bush Bill could have been the means of building such a line. Arkansas's secretary of state, Alex C. Hull, speaking at the Arkansas Real Estate Conference in 1899, deplored the absence of railroads in the marble, lead, zinc, and timber areas of the Ozarks. But Jeff Davis took up the issue in his bid for the gubernatorial nomination and in his zeal helped lay to rest the ambition of Populist and capitalist. He told a Conway crowd that even Reconstruction governor "Powell Clayton in his palmiest days never conceived a more iniquitous measure." Davis was not a member of the House of Representatives in 1899 when that body revoked the measure by a narrow margin, but he claimed to have had "a hand in the fray." The aspiring candidate predicted that if Governor Jones should have his way and the Bush Bill were reinstated, the board would issue bonds without any restriction on amount before ten miles of track had been built. Not only would limitations on bond issues be ignored, but the board of state officers would involve the state in a massive debt. Despite statutory prohibition of any state assumption of liability for the board's bonds, Davis foresaw action in the courts to force the public to make good on any defaulting by the board. Furthermore, he believed those sponsoring the bill intended to make the state liable. The bill also opened the door for possible fraud and profiteering by the state officials serving on the board.[41]

According to Davis, a certain merchant approached him, during a train ride between Little Rock and Arkadelphia, with an offer of money in exchange for an end to his opposition to the Bush Bill. The irate businessman denied any offer of a bribe and it is quite possible that Davis elaborated on the truth.[42] Jeff Davis possessed a capacity for distorting an incident to squeeze from it the maximum political benefit. Tales of unscrupulous dealing in high places found a ready hearing among the suspicious and credulous hill folk. What began as a Popocratic measure supported by some business interests became for Davis one of the earliest targets in his continuous battle against chicanery and corruption.

While some Democrats gave approval to the Bush Bill, many of those who resented the Populist nature of the measure gave support instead to an alternative. The Smith Bill, according to one Populist representative, was the darling of the Cleveland Democrats and those opposed to the Chicago platform. J. O. A. Bush, in a half-hour speech, denounced the measure as an attempt not to aid the people "but to advance the interest of a heartless, soulless corporation." The Smith Bill granted up to one thousand acres of delinquent tax land for each mile of track laid by the Springfield, Little Rock, and Gulf Railroad. Although by far the largest share of stock in the company belonged to a Chicago financier, former Governor James P. Clarke held one share and sat on the board of directors. The ex-governor appeared before the senate Railroad Committee in an evening session and called for postponement of consideration of the bill until other advocates of the measure had been heard. The Little Rock Board of Trade also gave its blessing to the Smith Bill. The Populists lost their battle to defeat the measure, and in June of 1897 the state chartered the new railroad.[43]

Another evidence of Populist influence upon the Democratic Party appeared in the very first proposal made by the new governor to the 1897 assembly. Dan Jones spoke at length to the legislators on the need for a more fair election law. But his statements won little support from staunch Democrats, and his address came at the conclusion of a farewell speech in which retiring Governor Clarke insisted on maintenance of the status quo. Jones called for amendment of the constitution to remove the provision for numbering of ballots since the practice made it quite simple to determine how an individual cast his ballot. Jones recognized that a man with a family looking to him for support could not easily ignore the intimidation of an employer, and laws which prohibited such coercion could not be enforced. A secret ballot was the only remedy to improper influence over voting.

The new governor's speech parroted many of the arguments of the Populist dissenters concerning the election system. Jones favored granting to the largest minority party in a county at least one representative on every election board, "including judges and clerks of election." For illiterate voters, the governor proposed two judges of opposite parties aid in preparing the ballot. "A political party which cannot maintain its supremacy except by unjust or unfair laws," Jones warned, cannot "retain the confidence . . . of the people."[44]

Governor Clarke insisted that the State Board of Election Commissioners had, without exception, named one minority member to each County Election Board in the 1896 election. Contrary to minority party charges, the retiring governor asserted that the state board had granted to each county's minority party the member of their choice. In each case the minority party "constituting the most numerous opposition" received the appointment. He strongly opposed granting to the minority representative on the county board an unrestricted right to name one of the judges of election for each precinct. The primary purpose of the 1891 election law, he reminded the legislators, "was to free a certain large class of persons having legally the right of suffrage from the control and coercion of another class."[45]

Clarke feared the appointment of election judges by partisans of a minority party would bring unscrupulous judges to power who would exploit illiterate voters. With Delta blacks and Republican whites in mind, he issued the following warning to the assembled legislators:

> To allow the opposition county commissioner to name without question such person as would suit his partisans, would often result in the selection of a person whose chief recommendation for the service was his ability to take advantage of his appointment to compel the illiterates, who are supposed to be the vassals of his party, to

vote according to directions, and to put him in position to report the names of any one who proved refractory.

Although the former governor could not approve of an unrestricted right to choose minority judges, he did make a slight concession to the minority parties. He suggested that the minority member on county boards nominate three persons for each precinct from which the board could select one opposition judge of election.[46]

During the campaign of 1898, eastern Arkansas raised its voice against Jones's proposal of consolidation of federal and state elections. *The Helena Weekly World* feared a revival of Negro voting and a return to Republican supremacy in the Delta region. In his reelection campaign, Jones announced that he had not changed his views on consolidation but in deference to the "Swamp Democracy" would not recommend consolidation to the general assembly.[47] Although the legislature made some changes during the next two decades, Governor Brough found it necessary in 1917 to call for the same reforms Dan Jones proposed in his 1897 inaugural address. Laws prohibiting coercion and intimidation of voters were not always enforced. But legislation alone could not have eased the difficulties of minority parties. Only a more determined enforcement of laws at the state and local level could have relieved the situation.

Although the state railroad plan and the electoral reform debate did not lead to substantial achievement, they demonstrated a tendency in the Democratic Party to seek at least a partial accommodation with the agrarian protest movement. Two Populist concepts that never did win general acceptance by the Democrats were the subtreasury scheme and nationalization of the railroads. But some other Populist ideas did get a hearing. In their 1894 state platform, Democrats accepted a plank proposing a graduated income tax, and in 1896 their convention advocated the abolition of the national banking system.[48] The general assembly of 1897 initiated a decade of agrarian tendencies within the Democratic Party. During the 1899 session, the Railroad Commission became a reality, and in 1903 the assembly gave broader powers to the regulatory agency. In 1897 the only Populist senator in the Arkansas assembly, Thomas Hayes, pressed for a law to prevent the creation of monopolistic combinations within Arkansas, and a mild bill passed both houses.[49] In 1899 a slightly more effective antitrust law, the Rector Act, received the governor's signature.

Although Jeff Davis in his early political career was no friend of the Populist Party, he did identify with the yeoman farmers of Arkansas and adopted a rhetoric that would appeal to the most downtrodden. The middle-class redneck leader espoused some of the popular agrarian causes. He pressed the antitrust issue with dogged determination. In his three administrations (1901–07), the state legislature demonstrated a new interest in the regulation of corporations. Not every Democrat shared the new spirit, and the party entered a tempestuous period. The personality of Jeff Davis had about as much to do with the incubation of the storms sweeping the party as the new issues themselves. The Davis rhetoric did not in the long run lead to the weakening of the business interests in Arkansas. The progressivism of Donaghey and Brough's time would be more professionally and business-oriented than Davis's brand of reform. But whatever the long-term result of his crusade, Davis had sensed the drift of the times and was able to capitalize on the issues in a manner that won an almost fanatical devotion from the people. Dan Jones had led the way with his more dignified manner of wooing those of agrarian sentiment. But Davis, a more masterful politician, took a page from Jones's book and then pictured the author as a moss-backed conservative. Davis, more than any other Democrat in Arkansas, capitalized on the discontent that led to the third-party movements.

4

One-Gallus Democracy

The assault on the one-party system by the agrarians did not
achieve its aim: the creation of an opposition organization powerful enough to challenge conservative control of the state. But in
Arkansas, as in many other areas of the South, Populism bore
fruit by its bifurcation of the Democratic Party. Conservative and
liberal factions emerged within the party at the turn of the century. On the one hand were the Bryanite, silver, anti-monopoly
forces who gained most support from the western two-thirds of
Arkansas, while on the other hand were the black-belt conservatives, the Swamp Democrats, who had scarcely been able to
choke down the Chicago platform of 1896. The factionalization
of the party initiated a more democratic era in Southern politics.
With the development of the primary system at the turn of the
century, the white voter had an opportunity to express a genuine
choice at the voting place. Personalities frequently overshadowed
issues, yet the division in the party represented something more
than controversy over a new breed of politicians. The rise to political importance of the hill people and the initiation of the primary system gave to Mississippi, James K. Vardaman, to South
Carolina, Coleman L. Blease. In Arkansas, likewise, Jeff Davis
rode to power on the discontent of the rural voter.[1]

The era of Jeff Davis initiated a period of colorful elections and
lively campaigning in Arkansas. Despite the showmanship and
hoopla of the campaigns, the factions within the Democratic
Party raised significant issues and gave white voters an opportunity to express their will at the primary elections. Although

politicians of the era sometimes manufactured issues as the need arose, they often wrestled with the questions of most interest to the average voting man of their own day. If in retrospect some of the debates seem to be sham battles fought on the periphery of what seem now to be the major problems of that age, it may be because of our inability to perceive with empathy the concerns of the voter of 1900.

Some of Davis's efforts may have been misguided and negativistic, yet he continually championed one cause. He believed in the rural people of Arkansas who constituted the bulk of the population. He fought passionately to give them control of their own political system. This became his major issue—to dispossess those who abused power and to restore government to the hands of the people. His altruism was not undiluted by selfish ambition, and to some extent he may have exploited the masses for his own gain. But as complex as his own motivations may have been, he sincerely dedicated himself, at least by his own lights, to the task of bringing the forgotten people to political power.

According to Jeff Davis, a politician needed an issue to be successful. He believed Bryan gained fame because of his successful use of the silver issue. Bryan became one of Davis's models, and the Arkansas leader maintained an affection for the Great Commoner throughout his life. Although Bryan may have been an inspiration to Davis, the Arkansan developed a political style of his own. Davis once told his secretary, Charles Jacobson, that people supported issues rather than men. In many of his campaigns, Davis campaigned on themes he believed to be important. But he frequently threw his support to candidates who had not especially been identified with his causes. He supported John Little for governor in 1906, not because of any past associations or because of any burning question of the day, but rather because of Davis's own personal hatred of the opposing candidate. Some of the serious problems of Arkansas did not enlist the support or interest of politicians. Josiah Shinn, prominent educator, complained in an open letter to the *Gazette* in 1900 of lack of interest in the state's public schools. "Is there no candidate for governor who will take up the cause of the common people?" he queried. To the correspondent, the "burning public question for Arkansas" at that time was the necessity of increasing the school term to "not less than six months with power to increase this to eight." Rural areas had four-month terms while cities had terms from six to ten months. The politicians, he believed, talked too much of imperialism and trusts and too little of the need to increase education tax levies. The towns, he believed, should subsidize the rural areas by paying a larger share of the cost of education.[2]

The coming of tempestuous Jeff Davis on the scene initiated a political revolution in Arkansas.[3] To many contemporaries it seemed as if the redneck leader had singlehandedly accomplished change in the political traditions of the state. But disruption of the Bourbon Democracy had preceded Davis's political ascent. Looking back upon those years, Governor George Donaghey (1909–13) wrote of the overthrow of the aristocratic dynasty by the democratic forces of Jeff Davis. In Donaghey's view, the aristocrats dominated state politics before 1900. No one dared seek office without the consent of the inner clique which held a stranglehold on the state's government. Voters who thought they had some voice in the affairs of state really only chose between leaders within the approved circle. Nearly every newspaper in Arkansas supported the system and crushed all those who ventured an attack upon the establishment.[4]

Before Davis began his campaign for the governorship, during 1899–1900, politicians relied upon a visit to the county seat to win support. A candidate met with the politicians and leading merchants at the courthouse to enlist their aid. He might leave a gift with the local editor to secure an endorsement by the newspaper. Moving on to the next county, he followed a similar pattern, but he spent little time appealing to the masses. Until the primary began to replace the convention system at the turn of the century, it seemed unnecessary to spend time campaigning among the people. Davis established a new style of campaigning in Arkansas. He knew the leading politicians in each county usually opposed him, so he pitched his appeal to the common people of the rural areas. Davis found time to visit the hamlet, the crossroads, and the solitary farmer on the hillside. He could launch a fiery tirade before a village gathering, or he could swap homey tales over the fence with a dirt farmer. He was the first Arkansas politician to make extensive use of printed speeches, sending out one hundred twenty-five thousand in the 1900 campaign alone.[5]

Davis's long-time personal secretary believed the redneck leader brought a political revolution to Arkansas. He destroyed the old order by sending the older and long respected leadership into political limbo. He brought new men to Arkansas's congressional delegation, into the courts, and into state and local offices. He championed the primary system and made his appeal directly to the masses, bypassing those in established positions of authority. Thriving on controversy and emotional issues, he divided the party into factions that reached down into the county and city levels.[6]

The new firebrand in Arkansas rode the trains into the hills and bayous, to the prairie land and the Delta. Where the trains didn't go, he sometimes rode a mule. According to one newspaper, Davis branded his mule with the letters C.S.A. to encourage the myth that his animal had been an old Confederate army mule. Not the least of his advantages was the name, Jefferson Davis. The aspiring politician capitalized on his respected and illustrious name, much to the disgust of those Confederate veterans who opposed him. Davis himself, unlike most Arkansas politicians preceding him, had not fought in the Civil War. But the fact that he had been an infant during that glorious struggle did not deter him from decking himself in the heroic trappings of the war. He invariably wore a plain suit of Confederate gray, refusing even on the most elegant occasions to don formal attire.

The Chicago *Inter-Ocean* described Davis as a man of the Joseph W. "Bailey brand." He had a "portly build" and a "baby-like countenance, sparkling with good nature and geniality." Bailey not only had the same roundish, smooth features, but also gained a reputation for distinctive dress, often wearing the garb common to politicians half a century before his time. Davis's boyish features, according to his secretary, remained with him into his later years.[7]

Davis's father had been county judge in Little River County in southwest Arkansas. Judge Lewis W. Davis had also been a Baptist preacher, and his son maintained a connection, though sometimes a stormy one, with this denomination. Young Davis studied law briefly at the Arkansas Industrial University in Fayetteville, and then, following in the same path as Joe Bailey, he moved on to Vanderbilt and Cumberland University at Lebanon, Tennessee. With a modest amount of training, he entered his father's law practice, located by that time at Russellville in Pope County. During his days at Russellville, Davis developed a close friendship with Jeremiah Wallace, his father's law partner.[8] Wallace, twelve years older than Davis, helped shape the younger man's political philosophy. Like Wallace, he came to see politics as a battle against the malignant forces of evil. Perhaps Davis's Baptist upbringing also accounts for his moralistic approach to politics.

Davis began his public life as prosecuting attorney for the fifth judicial district (Pope, Yell, Conway, and Johnson counties) in 1890 and served for several years. He attended the Democratic State Convention in 1894 and took part in the debate on the silver plank. Davis gave vigorous support to the 16 to 1 ratio and opposed attempts to allow financiers to fix the value of silver at a ratio acceptable to themselves. His views prevailed, and Davis continued his defense of the silver plank. In the 1896 election, he made an unsuccessful attempt to unseat the congressman in the fourth district, W. L. Terry. Since Terry had also announced his support for free silver, the campaign did not hinge upon this issue. Davis withdrew early in the campaign when he foresaw defeat. His own county met in convention on February 1, and the Democratic delegates supported Davis's candidacy by a forty-two to twenty-two vote. Believing the margin of support in his own county too small, Davis announced to those assembled at Russellville his decision to withdraw before the meeting of the congressional district convention. Returning to his Russellville law practice, he did not seek office again until the 1898 election.[9]

The development of the primary system for nominating candidates enabled Jeff Davis to secure a place of power in the Democratic Party. Some counties had used primaries for choosing local candidates before the 1890s. The general assembly of 1895 legalized primaries without making them mandatory or requiring a uniform date for elections. By the time of the 1896 election, the primary had begun to supplant the convention system as a means of selecting statewide officers. During the next few years, counties exercised the freedom to use either a convention or primary, and they sometimes resisted efforts by the Democratic Central Committee to enforce a uniform day for the holding of their primary elections or conventions.

During the campaign and state convention of 1898, the primary system excited much controversy in Arkansas. In February the Democratic State Central Committee accepted former Governor Clarke's proposal to establish a uniform day for holding either primaries or conventions. The Clarke plan passed by a slim twelve to ten vote, but many counties ignored the committee's call for a uniform day. *The Helena Weekly World* joined with the

Gazette in supporting May 7, 1898, as the uniform and proper day for primaries.[10]

Similar conflicts over the primary system occurred in many other states. The Mississippi experience paralleled that of Arkansas in many respects. During the 1890s, Mississippians opposing the dictatorial county committees sought to use the primary to wrest power from their hands. The "ring" politicians might control the county convention, but their domination of primaries seemed less certain. The desire to reduce the power of established politicians also motivated the struggle for the uniform day. A system of staggered primaries had made it possible for county bosses to trade off state or district offices with the leaders of other counties. But opposition to boss rule was not the sole motivation for supporting the uniform primary. Allies of the same statewide candidate might favor primaries in some counties while opposing their use in others. They favored primaries in counties where the politicians opposed their favorite, and they opposed primaries where they could rely on strong backing from local leaders.[11]

In South Carolina, Mississippi, and other Southern states, the primary became a vehicle for limiting the power of the "rotten boroughs," where Delta chieftains controlled the votes of the black population. In some states, a geographical shift of power occurred. The Delta country lost voting power in relation to the sections where whites were in the majority. The primary encouraged white democracy by granting to each white man an equal vote, and it became the means for the hill farmer's rise to political power. For the Democratic Party, the primary was a means of adjusting to agrarian demands. It gave a voice to the dissidents and encouraged them to work within the party. It also offered a means for disfranchising blacks who had threatened to cooperate with third-party movements, undergirded white supremacy, and ensured the continued domination of the Democratic Party in the South.[12] These forces, at work in Mississippi, South Carolina, and other Southern states, were also moving Arkansas toward adopting a primary system.

Because of the new primary system, the Arkansas Democratic State Convention of 1898 was the briefest held up to that time. The primary election decided the nominations and left little of significance for the convention to do. The Democrats took only one day to affirm the election results and to debate proposed changes in the primary system. A minority resolution from the platform committee eliminated county conventions as a means of choosing statewide nominees and made a uniform day for primaries mandatory. A Conway man told the delegates the convention system had perpetuated courthouse rings. He believed the uniform primary would end their domination. But many delegates feared changes might somehow encourage Negro voting. The chairman of the state central committee assured the hesitant that a law to forbid Republican blacks from crossing over in the primary would eliminate this danger. Others disliked the "centralizing" tendencies of the minority resolution. Whatever the reason, the convention defeated the proposal and adopted in its place the majority resolution. The latter provided for either conventions or primaries, as the "respective central committees" of the counties might choose. The resolution also allowed the county central committees to choose and instruct "delegates to the state convention as they may deem best; and, further, that candidates for state offices shall be nominated by a majority of the delegated state convention." The decision left the county politician's control of his bailiwick unchecked. The advocates of a more uniform system received a slight rebuff, but they were more successful during the first administration of Jeff Davis (1901–03).[13]

In 1902 the state central committee finally succeeded in forcing all Democrats to observe the uniform day. On March 29, the *Gazette* announced: "For the first time in the history of Democratic politics in Arkansas primary elections to determine all the nominations for elective offices will be held on the same day—today." In all seventy-five counties, voters expressed preferences for candidates from justice of the peace to governor and senator. Other Southern states were in the process of expanding the use of the primary. In 1902 Mississippi became the first state to require political parties to hold a primary. The Mississippi law provided for a runoff primary when no candidate received a majority vote. In 1905 the Texas legislature amended the Terrell election law to compel counties to participate in the uniform primary. The Texas law reinforced the one-party system by requiring minority parties to take on the financial burden of administering primaries.[14] In 1895, 1909, 1911, and 1916, the Arkansas General Assembly enacted legislation which made party primaries legal elections but did not provide for runoff primaries. Arkansas law did not require all parties to make use of the primary but bound them to the uniform day and all other legal provisions, if they chose to hold primaries. The statutes provided detailed regulations to insure against fraud and intimidation.[15]

Because Jeff Davis depended upon the support of the masses to retain power, he became a firm proponent of the primary. In the Democratic state conventions, he stood with those seeking to strengthen and extend the use of primaries. Like his South Carolinian counterpart, "Pitchfork" Ben Tillman, Davis contributed more to the development of the primary in his state than any other individual. During the 1904 convention which he dominated, Davis extracted from the delegates a resolution declaring the winner of the 1906 Democratic primary the official candidate for United States senator. The delegates ruled that the 1906 convention accept as the nominee the candidate polling a majority of all votes cast in the state as a whole. The resolution also committed all Democrats in the general assembly, regardless of the outcome in their own district, to vote for the candidate obtaining a statewide majority. Knowing many politicians would gladly bury him, Davis tried to secure his political future by espousing a binding primary system. His success in the 1904 convention smoothed the way for his primary victory and election to the Senate in 1906. Davis's use of the primary to mitigate the influence of party bosses resembled the strategy of Robert La Follette. The Wisconsin Progressive launched his direct primary crusade after losing a bid for the 1896 Republican gubernatorial election. Because of popular backing, La Follette's personal ambitions could be achieved by adopting a nominating process that appealed to the public rather than established politicians. For both Davis and La Follette, self-interest and the people's interests seemed to coincide.[16]

Because of the presence of a large black population in southeastern Arkansas, white Democrats feared an open primary system. In the 1896 election, 40,289 blacks and 160,816 whites paid poll taxes and were eligible to vote according to the *Gazette*.[17] Responding to the fear of black voting in the primaries, the convention of 1898 passed a resolution recommending "a strict observance of the party lines in the holding of county primaries and convention." The resolution gave judges of the primary elections responsibility for determining whether an individual applicant was a "known Democrat in county, state and national politics." By 1902, many county central committees had ruled that only white Democrats could vote in primaries. In its *Digest of Rules* adopted by the 1912 convention, the party stated explicitly, "The Democratic party of Arkansas shall consist of all eligible and legally qualified white electors who have paid a poll tax." In Arkansas the white primary and the poll tax effectively eliminated the Negro vote.[18] The 1912 state Democratic convention refused to endorse the grandfather clause, and the voters rejected the device in a referendum in the fall of that year. During the two decades beginning in 1890, all Southern states disfranchised the Negro by means of the poll tax, grandfather clause, white primary, and other devices.[19]

The primary system became Jeff Davis's vehicle for attaining power, but the popular basis for his strength consisted of the small farmer, mechanic, country schoolteacher, and all those of the rural areas who looked with suspicion on the financiers, businessmen, urban dwellers, and Little Rock politicians. At the same time, Davis also relied on a "shadow movement" that included planters who had moved to town, some merchants, and other members of the middle class who identified more with Davis's Southern anti-colonial rhetoric than with specific economic reforms. Many Southerners looked upon their economy as a colonial one, dominated and exploited by Northern and Eastern businessmen and by those Southern commercial leaders who were in league with them. Davis had not been the first Arkansas Democrat to utilize Jeffersonian agrarian rhetoric. Shortly after the new year began in 1897, Governor Dan W. Jones drafted a letter "on the Industrial Progress of the State." In a lengthy statement, he expressed his views on the question of bringing Northern capital and corporate development to Arkansas. Arkansans, he thought, should not seek to establish large cities or big corporations. The future of Arkansas and of all the South still lay in agriculture. "Great cities and powerful money combinations," were, in his opinion, "the worst and last expressions of a character of progress not to be desired." He condemned the large Northern corporations for failing to pass on to the workers their reasonable share of the wealth.[20]

Despite his rhetoric aimed at the discontented, Jeff Davis never did develop a clear definition of economic classes. He was no Marxist. Davis once described socialism as "durn foolishness gone to seed."[21] Raymond Arsenault admits that Davis "relied heavily on class rhetoric" but sees Davis's statements on class as "purposely ambiguous." Davis avoided attacks on the white planter class and failed to clearly pitch his appeal to tenant farmers. More than half of Arkansas's Democratic voters were farmers who owned their own land, and Arsenault believes it was to these yeomen, whether prosperous or down on their luck, that Davis directed his rhetoric. He could not have won an election by enlisting only the very poor. For this reason, he avoided making specific class distinctions in the hope that both well-off and poorer farmers would stand with him against the town and the North.[22]

But if Davis failed to announce in academic terms his definition of class divisions, he certainly did in his speeches pit the common man against wealth and privilege. "He labors to divide the people against themselves," charged the *Gazette,* "in order that he may become the champion of the bigger class." Setting himself up as a "tribune of the people," he portrayed the inhabitants of Little Rock as "an aristocracy of purse-proud plutocrats who menace the interests of the plebeians."[23] When a legislative committee in the general assembly heard testimony on an antitrust bill, Davis scolded them for calling in businessmen but not farmers:

> They sent for the high-collared crowd—that crowd that wear collars so high they can't see the sun except at high noon, looking over the top of their collars. They sent for that crowd that when they shake hands with you, they only give you the tip of two fingers.[24]

After Davis's death, *The New York Times* recalled that he "adopted the 'pitchfork' style of oratory and posed as the friend of the people." Senator Chauncey M. Depew of New York believed Davis's "ideal state would have been made of small landowners and an occasional lawyer. He himself was a lawyer."[25]

While he solicited the sympathies of the farming community, Davis also deliberately courted the antagonism of established authorities. He spoke of Richard Brugman, the editor of the *Gazette,* as "the meanest, most contemptible little Republican in Arkansas, who just a few years ago was the president of a 'nigger' club in Little Rock." He defied convention by refusing to pay the *Gazette* for a political announcement of his gubernatorial candidacy. One of the *Gazette* editors so detested Davis that he allowed his commission as a notary public to expire rather than seek an extension while Davis remained in office. To the governor, most of those who ran Arkansas's newspapers were "squirrel-headed editors."[26]

Davis was no Populist. He had opposed the third-party movement, and his political allies in the emerging "Davis faction" would not be former Populists but faithful Democrats. Yet Davis's rhetoric, style, and expressed views often resembled those of Populist leaders, and eventually he did win strong support among the voters in former Populist counties. By 1905 Davis was ready to admit a certain sympathy with the views and spirit of the agrarian party. He praised their courageous opposition to Cleveland's goldbug policies and rejoiced that they were now back in the Democratic Party, "voting the Democratic ticket as bravely and loyally as any man that ever cast an honest ballot." In 1905 Bryan merely reiterated doctrines "the Populists advocated twenty years ago; that is public ownership of public franchises." Davis now affirmed his agreement with the old Populist doctrine that, "if this Government does not soon own public franchises, if it does not soon own public carriers, that the public carriers will soon own this Government."[27]

While it is demonstrably clear that Davis courted the Populists in his 1906 senate race and won by large margins in former Populist areas, it is not so easy to track this kind of Populist support in the 1900 election. Records of county primary election returns for some areas are not available. Also, the 1900 vote was so lopsided for Davis that it would be questionable whether quantitative studies of the differences would be significant. In addition, the fact that many counties cast their ballots after the election of Davis was a foregone conclusion adds to the confusion. Raymond Arsenault's analysis of selected precinct returns led him to the conclusion that in the 1900 election, it is impossible to assert with confidence that former Populists were a significant factor in Davis's rise to power. The evidence from county to county is too inconsistent to support the view that significant numbers of Populists turned to Davis in 1900. What is clear is that Davis did well in rural areas and that his strongest opposition came from urban precincts.[28] Yet, even Arsenault's analysis of precinct returns shows Davis receiving a very large vote from Populist precincts in the 1902 and 1904 primary elections. Davis received 66.1 percent of all primary votes in 1902, but Populist precincts cast 78.1 percent of their votes for Davis. In 1904 he received 57.8 percent

COUNTIES INCREASING DEMOCRATIC
STRENGTH IN 1900

*Populist counties, i.e., counties casting 30% or more of total votes cast in 1892 for Populist gubernatorial candidate (figures indicate percentage of increase of Democratic vote for 1900 gubernatorial election over county's total in 1896 or 1898, whichever is higher).

of all votes cast for governor, but Populist precincts cast 75.2 percent of their votes for Davis.[29]

It appears that at least a significant minority of Populist voters may have returned to the Democratic Party in 1900. Polk County's swing to Jeff Davis suggests this interpretation. Polk County had a higher Populist vote than any other Arkansas county during every biennial election beginning with 1892. In 1900 the bastion of Populism increased its Democratic gubernatorial vote by 64 percent. No other county changed its voting pattern so drastically. Stone County, a part of the north central Populist region, ranked second to Polk County with a 38 percent increase. Only one other area experienced more than a 25 percent rise. Searcy County, in the heart of the Ozarks, had very few Populist voters. It gave the Populist nominee a mere seven percent vote in 1892 and only one percent in 1896. Yet in 1900, the county increased its Democratic vote by 35 percent. Searcy, like Newton County, was a stronghold of Republicanism in the Ozark region. The drift toward Davis by Republicans in Searcy County did not set a pattern for Republicans in other areas of the state.[30]

Davis's success as a politician did not depend solely on courting the independents. He also mastered the demagogic tactics that became a trademark of many Southern politicians. Davis's appeal to class and racial prejudice, his use of epithets against enemies, his crusade against the newspapers, his theatrical tactics, distinctive garb, and identification with rural people by his use of the "plain folks" device all contributed to help him conform to the demagogue stereotype. If his enthusiasm for antitrust crusades and "running Red-River" through the political dens of Little Rock did not always achieve substantial reforms, he at least brought a greater measure of democracy and interest into the state's elections. This in itself was a worthwhile achievement, but the accomplishments came at the expense of a lowered political tone and a continuation of racial oppression.[31]

His ability to entertain and warm the hearts of the country folk partly accounted for Davis's popularity. He adopted a campaign style similar to that of the Taylors of Tennessee. During the 1886 campaign in Tennessee, Robert Love Taylor and his brother, Alfred A. Taylor, ran on opposing tickets for the governorship. Both men were adept at recounting humorous tales that evoked tears and laughter. Democrat "Bob" Taylor, who served as governor during the 1880s and 1890s, played his fiddle before campaign crowds. Although he came from a prominent Tennessee family, he won the enmity of most city newspapers while capturing the hearts of the "wool hat boys." Davis followed a similar pattern but was more bombastic and aggressive than Robert Taylor, who made moderation and harmony a theme of his campaigns.[32] Davis did not come from a prominent family like the Taylors, but he certainly did not come from the lowest economic strata of society. For all his down-home rhetoric, he was very much a middle-class lawyer, and while he tried to recruit hill folk, he always had a realistic recognition of his need for winning votes and allies from the professional and middle class.

Davis excelled in the employment of epithets and vituperation. Cal Ledbetter has described him as thriving on "confrontation and combat." Davis, by this interpretation, had a "deep-seated emotional need" that could only be satisfied "by pushing people and handling events so that excitement was always present. . . ." Politics became an arena for "continuous warfare." His continual need for crises and crusades to whet his appetite for aggression helps to explain why Davis would seek out political confrontation even when it might not seem to be necessary or even politically desirable.[33] During a trip to Arkansas, Huey Long heard Davis speak and fell under the spell of the hillbilly orator. Long admired the way old Jeff flayed "the potbellied, pussle-gutted" aristocrats. He also heard Davis address the rural people as "rednecks" and "hillbillies." But the Arkansan used the expressions as terms of endearment, and country folk accepted them as such. They thought of Jeff Davis as one of their own kind. Huey Long discovered that Louisianans reacted in the same manner, and he inherited the techniques used by Davis and some of the other Southern demagogues. Because the term "demagogue" when used of men like Davis, Long, Blease, and Tillman can convey a negative connotation which may at times be inaccurate or unfair, it is important to note, in the case of Davis, that the term is not used in a patronizing sense. Nor does the term imply that Davis was a deceitful or duplicitous person. As Arsenault prefers to express it, Davis was one of the "legitimate folk heroes" of the South.[34]

The redneck leader frequently exploited racial feelings to attract white voters to his ranks. During a campaign for governor, in the fall of 1903, Davis accused his opponent of the heinous crime of appointing black men to office. Judge Carroll Wood selected a Negro to serve as one of three jury commissioners charged with the duty of selecting juries for the judicial district. "Did you ever hear of such a thing in Arkansas before?" wailed an indignant Davis. If Wood gave such "recognition" to blacks when a judge, what might he do as governor? He reminded his listeners of an often repeated pledge "that no man could be appointed to office under my administration unless he was a white man, a Democrat, and a Jeff Davis man."[35]

In 1902, he gained national attention by pardoning Andrew Thompson, a black, on condition that he settle in Massachusetts where there were so many Negro sympathizers. Thomas Wentworth Higginson of Massachusetts, famed leader of a black Civil War regiment, waved off Davis's action as empty "bravado." Not long afterward, when an attorney sought a pardon for his client, Davis replied, "If you will show me a ticket to Boston for this negro I will immediately issue his pardon." By such grandstand actions he sought to silence Northern critics of Southern racism.[36]

Like many other Southern whites, Davis denounced the extension of voting to the blacks during reconstruction days:

> The most cruel blow that was ever struck a helpless and defenceless people was the action of the general government in placing in the hands of an ignorant, illiterate and irresponsible race of people, the ballot of a free man, giving them the same rights and privileges under the general government as were exercised by their former masters.

Enfranchisement was despicable, he believed, but even in his own time the black voter was an "ever present eating, cankerous sore." The Negro should never be given the vote because he "is not susceptible of higher education, he is not susceptible of higher moral culture."[37]

On September 1, 1904, in a speech at Pine Bluff, Davis scathingly denounced attempts to force the South to enfranchise blacks. The Republican national platform called for a reduction of Southern congressional representation proportional to the number of blacks disfranchised. This was an attempt to implement provisions in the Fourteenth Amendment. To a courthouse crowd, Davis cried:

> I refer to the race question, to nigger equality, to social equality, attempted to be forced upon the people of the South by Mr. Roosevelt. I stand for the Caucasian race in the government, I stand for a

white man's government, and I say that nigger domination will never prevail in this beautiful southland of ours, as long as shotguns and rifles are around loose and we are able to pull the triggers.[38]

Davis also believed in segregating school taxes so that whites need not pay the cost of educating blacks. White property taxes should go only toward the education of whites. Davis's views on Negro education echoed the pronouncement of Mississippian James K. Vardaman, who believed the idea of educating Negroes was nearly "criminal folly."[39] Before the 1904 general election campaign, Davis had not favored school tax segregation. But during the course of the campaign against Harry Myers, the Republican candidate for governor, Jeff Davis had adopted a more racist tone than he had used in earlier campaigns. He denounced the very concept of black education by taking up a slogan once used by James K. Vardaman, "Every time you educate a 'nigger' you spoil a good field hand."[40] The segregation of taxes would have destroyed the black educational system since blacks could not have provided sufficient revenue to maintain even minimal standards of education. Despite this, Davis in January, 1905, asked the state legislature to enact such a measure. Davis's speech to the legislature reveals a new depth for racial demagoguery. He assailed the Negro race as "degenerate and improvident" and as "not susceptible of higher education." The Negro in his view was a "servant made so by God Almighty, bred and born as such," and any effort to educate him would be futile. "Attempted education," he asserted, "proves harmful rather than beneficial, so I have come to the point where I, for one, am willing to step out and say, 'From this day forward let the negroes in Arkansas educate themselves.'"[41]

Republican leader John E. Bush led a counterattack by blacks to defeat tax segregation. Bush was a former slave who became the receiver of United States Public Lands in 1898. He argued that blacks paid taxes to support public facilities that were off-limits for them. Fortunately *The Arkansas Gazette* joined with the Arkansas Teachers Association in speaking forcefully against the proposal. J. C. Burgess of Pope County introduced a tax segregation bill in the Arkansas House of Representatives in January, 1905, but it was defeated by a fifty-six to twenty-nine vote. The Burgess bill was not the first attempt to segregate taxes, and it was not to be the last. Apparently most politicians viewed segregation of taxes as an extreme measure, and Arkansas never did adopt the scheme.[42]

Not all Southern leaders appreciated Davis's racial rhetoric. While attending the Dallas State Fair, he launched a tirade against Theodore Roosevelt's Negro policy. Rising before a crowd of five thousand, Gov. James Hogg took some pains to renounce the ill-tempered speech. "The Governor of Arkansas is a good fellow, but I don't want him or any other man to build up race prejudice in Texas."[43]

Davis's racism was reprehensible, but it was not much more virulent than the strain that affected many white Southerners.[44] In Arkansas after 1891, although every politician was expected to endorse white supremacy, it was not necessary to make racism the major campaign theme. There was no need for Davis to launch an all-out anti-black crusade of the Benjamin Tillman or James K. Vardaman variety.[45] He was asserting the accepted white supremacist doctrines of the Democratic Party in the South. He would have agreed with a Georgia newspaper's warning to agrarian rebels in 1890 that "White Supremacy is the very foundation of our civilization," and voters should not "forsake the party and principles of their fathers."[46] When Hoke Smith campaigned for governor in 1905, he proposed that Georgia adopt an amendment to its constitution to "insure a continuation of white supremacy."[47] In the early 1900s James K. Vardaman declared that "the matter of white supremacy or black domination in the South is at fever heat." Vardaman's racism was more pronounced than Davis's brand. The Mississippian frequently made race a major theme of his campaigns.[48] In a speech accepting his party's nomination for governor, Democrat John S. Little summed up the philosophy of the Arkansas Democratic Party:

> The white man in the South while protecting the negro in his property rights and peaceful pursuits will control the destinies of this state and of this country and the sooner this fact is acknowledged by all men the better it will be for us all. The Democratic party of Arkansas and of the South is, irrevokably [sic], committed to the doctrine of the white man's control in a white man's country, a position from which it will not recede and from which it cannot be driven.[49]

The more erudite and respected often couched the same views in more elegant language. A university town minister, Reverend

Nathaniel Ragland, speaking of the founder of the First Christian Church of Fayetteville, praised him as a "rare specimen of the Anglo-Saxon race in whose veins flows the best blood of the world." Robert Neill, a Batesville attorney, wrote to William Jennings Bryan, in 1901, to warn him not to discuss the visit of Booker T. Washington to the White House. The incident had damaged Theodore Roosevelt in the South, and any attempt to evaluate the situation in Bryan's newspaper, *The Commoner,* could only anger Southerners. The attorney believed "the incident" would only "encourage and stimulate a large number of his race to be more pressing and importunate for social equality, and social recognition."[50]

In almost the same breath, Davis could move from appeals to the basest instincts of man to stirring the heart with stories of tender emotion. He was a "Master of Humanics," as the *Gazette* described his ability to portray the human, the pathetic, the touching scenes of life. During his bid for the United States Senate in 1906, Davis used this device against the incumbent. Senator James Berry had cast a vote against the Hatch Act, a bill to regulate the sale of futures by taxation. Berry wanted, as he put it, a complete prohibition of the practice, not a licensing or taxing of it. Davis launched his attack on Berry, in one speech, by portraying speculators as monsters of greed who cynically sold the labor of the poor and wretched. After taking his hearers in a flight of imagination to the sordid scene at the New York Cotton Exchange, he returned them to the cotton fields of Arkansas. He had traveled once along the White River and had seen "little children, girls and boys, thinly clad on a cold, frosty morning, children just as dear to their parents as yours or mine are to us, picking the cotton, pulling it from the bolls, their little hands almost frozen." The speculators on Wall Street were "gambling in the flesh and blood and bone of the children of the South."[51] Suddenly, respectable old James Berry seemed like a villain who had locked arms with cruel Eastern financiers to oppress little children.

If Davis's use of touching stories was an artful device, it is also true that he had a large heart. He was a man of deep emotions, who could also parade them for effect. As governor he gained a reputation for granting pardons when confronted by a tearful mother or a lonely wife with babies. When critics complained of his generosity, he told them to keep broken-hearted relatives from coming to his door because he could not resist a mother's plea. Davis's inability to resist the supplications of the unfortunate was reminiscent of the reputation of Tennessee Governor Robert Love Taylor. The Tennesseean frequently moved his audiences with tales of pardons granted to the wretched and poor. Though other governors may have pardoned even more convicts than Davis and Taylor, few excelled them in exploiting the image of a merciful and compassionate executive. Pardons may have gained some votes, but Davis's use of the power went beyond political expediency. When Charles Jacobson, his private secretary, grieved for an imprisoned cousin, Davis made an emotional appeal to Theodore Roosevelt. The cousin, a young Jew, was sentenced to five years in a federal penitentiary for embezzling twenty-five dollars from the post office. In his letter Davis called his aide, Jacobson, "the gentlest, kindest friend I ever had." To the president, Davis suggested, in a second appeal, "all you need is more heart, more tenderness of spirit, to make you a great good man." [52] Roosevelt did not grant the pardon.

Davis made the suffering of convicts in Arkansas prisons a continual object of concern and battle. William N. Hill, veteran prisoner, who later revealed many of his experiences in a book, *Story of the Arkansas Penitentiary,* had many kind words for the warm-hearted governor. The ex-convict told of the lashing of a black man who was too sick to report for work. Although he was almost delirious with fever, the guards, after beating him, chained him to a post where he sat in the sun without water for one whole day. He saw prisoners working on the railroad who had such ragged shoes that their feet froze in the snow. When Davis, and later Governor George W. Donaghey, declared war on the prison system, they earned the bitter hatred of prison officials. [53]

Armed with the support of discontented farmers, capitalizing on the new primary system, and using the art of the demagogue, Jeff Davis captured control of the state government. The agrarians who had tried in vain to seize the reins of government could now abandon their third-party hopes and support the new idol of the masses. A whole new breed of politicians came to power and with them a new issue-consciousness. As Arkansas entered the new century, its Democratic Party divided into Davis and anti-Davis factions. New issues and new personalities offered the voters a significant choice at the polls or at the least an exciting spectacle.

5

Issues of the Davis Era, 1897–1900

"They say I am a demagogue," Jeff Davis told a throng of voters at Conway. "Every time a man comes out and stands for the interests of the people he is denounced, either as a crank or a demagogue." The defense had some truth in it. Then and later, critics of popular Southern leaders have discounted their claims of concern for the common people and accused them of trumping up phony issues to gain power. But if some of Davis's crusades seemed more iconoclastic than constructive, they did involve issues and questions that the rural masses perceived as involving their interests. If his manners were rude and his antics suggestive of a buffoon more than a statesman, Davis used these techniques to achieve changes in government policy. The state moved further toward the concept of government regulation of corporations and toward more humane treatment of convicts. The "demagogues" of the South, despite their limitations and bigotry, served a useful purpose. Although they did not drastically affect the power of the established economic interests in the South over the long term, they did weaken the older political leadership and provided a psychological outlet for the passions of those who were frustrated by the dominance of the city folk.[1]

In much of his rhetoric, Davis pitted the farmer and worker against the city folk who consumed the fruit of their labors. The governor spent too little time in his Little Rock office to be an effective administrator, but he did traverse, almost continuously, the isolated areas of the state to arouse the masses. He believed his appeals informed the people of issues vital to their own welfare. In a Conway speech, in 1899, he accused the wealth-consuming class of exploiting the wealth-producing class. Lawyers, judges, governors, legislators have come too often from the wealth-consuming classes and they have made the laws to protect their own interests. "I want to tell you," he cried, "that it is woe to the robbers who have gathered in the fields that they have not sown, who have stolen the jewels from labor and built upon them a throne." The Haymarket riot had not surprised him. A worker could not "be a patriot on an empty stomach." The only solution lay, he believed, in transferring the law-making power to those who produced wealth.[2]

The people trusted Davis, and they indicated their interest in the causes he espoused by standing with him in primary after primary. Some of his themes struck a responsive chord and drew the hill people to his side. In Arkansas as in many other states, the farmers' grievances against the railroad made regulation of these corporations a major concern. Davis did not initiate the struggle to subject all corporations to the police power of the state, but he soon became the dynamic leader of this movement. The management of the penitentiary had frequently yielded politicians a convenient battleground, and Davis relentlessly led new assaults over this old field. He also developed new issues. When Dan Jones and the majority of the general assembly laid plans for construction of a new state capitol building, Davis used every legal device and obstructionist tactic available to block their efforts. He labeled the scheme a "steal" and pictured those responsible for the project as either incompetent or corrupt.

The debate over railroad regulation engaged the attention of Arkansans long before Davis appeared on the scene. During the administration of Governor James Berry, in 1883, the state began demanding payment of property tax by the railroads. In that year, the legislature established a railroad commission composed of the governor, state auditor, and secretary of state. The commission had no power to set rates or regulate the conduct of the railroads, but it did have authority to assess railroad corporations which had artfully dodged payment of property taxes. The Iron Mountain Railroad went to the state supreme court, and ultimately the United States Supreme Court, in its unsuccessful attempt to prevent the railroad commission from assessing its property. In the mid-1880s, Daniel V. Jones, as attorney general, hauled the railroads into state and federal courts to collect unpaid taxes for the period from 1874 to 1883. Eventually, through a compromise plan, the Iron Mountain Railroad paid the state two hundred and fifty thousand dollars as full compensation for the years it escaped taxation.[3]

In 1895, Joseph T. Robinson led the movement in the general assembly to secure a regulatory commission. At twenty-two, he was the youngest member of the house of representatives, but he made a distinct impression during his one term by his authorship of the commission bill. The bill provided for regulation of freight and passenger rates by a commission and for prohibition of rebates. Surprisingly, in light of his later career, Dan Jones appeared before a house committee as a railroad attorney speaking in opposition to the Robinson Bill. By a lopsided vote, the house of representatives crushed the commission bill.[4]

Popular support for the commission concept gradually produced a change of Democratic doctrine. The 1896 Democratic state platform affirmed that "railroads are public highways and the interest of the public demand [*sic*] a constant supervision of their management." The platform called upon the legislature to set up a commission and to submit a constitutional amendment to the people to remove any possible limitations on the assembly's power to create such an agency. The state constitution prohibited the establishment of any new, permanent, statewide office. Critics of the bill had seized upon this constitutional restriction and interpreted it to include commissions. The platform statement coincided with the views of Governor Dan Jones. In his 1897 inaugural address, he reminded the assembly of the constitutional mandate (Section 10, Article 17) given to them "to correct abuses and prevent unjust discriminations and excessive charges" by railroads. Legislation had been ineffective in the past, and now "the people demand *adequate* legislation." Jones recommended creation of a temporary commission until the people approved a constitutional amendment. The railroads, he believed, should pay the full cost of the commission's operations. Except for their "extortionate charges and unjust discrimination" such a commission would be unnecessary. "Their own unlawful conduct renders the creations of such a commission absolutely necessary for the protection of the people," and they justly should bear its expense.[5]

The Arkansas Gazette, in early 1897, gave its encouragement to the movement to establish a commission. The party had committed itself to correct railroad abuses, and the legislators had a solemn duty to their constituents to pass the bill. The newspaper believed the measure, as proposed by Governor Dan Jones, could pass court tests.[6]

Although a number of similar commission bills came to the railroad committees of the house and senate, the major proposal came from Senator Middleton J. Manning of Monroe County. Through most of the session, he battled furiously in the Senate Railroad Committee while other members placed obstacles in his path. Finally, in early February, Manning polled the committee demanding they state clearly whether they wanted a commission. One by one, he questioned committee members. Senator F. M. McGehee asserted definite support with no qualifications. Senator A. G. Gray was for a commission but not the one proposed. Senator William F. Grace of Jefferson County replied, "Yes," but "with proper restrictions." Senator R. W. Worthen and Senator B. D. Williams from Pulaski County spoke in opposition to the commission. Williams couched his answer in vague terms but did assert that railroads should not be subject to the absolute power of three men. Worthen, who less than a week earlier had favored a commission, now definitely opposed the idea since it would disturb business. When Manning moved to report the bill, only McGehee voted with him. Angrily, Manning "jammed his hat down on his head" and walked out of the committee.[7]

While the pro-railroad forces maintained control of the senate, the house of representatives was far more responsive to the mood of the people. The house passed its version eighty-one to three with one of the two Republican members voting against the commission. The youthful Festus O. Butt, who later donned penitentiary prison stripes after his conviction in the "boodle cases," was among the two Democrats opposing the bill. But the lower house's enthusiasm was to no avail. *The Drew County Advance* lamented in early March the evident determination of the senate to kill the measure.[8] The session ended with no progress toward creation of a commission.

Governor Dan Jones made a second attempt to secure the commission bill when he called the general assembly into an extraordinary session on April 26. The special session was also a necessity since the legislature had not appropriated the funds required for the operation of the state government. Again the house took action, and it designated the commission bill as House Bill #1, thus giving the bill priority above all other issues to be discussed.[9]

A dramatic battle took place during early May in the senate. The railroad commission caucus, which had been meeting frequently ever since the beginning of the regular session, thought it now had a chance to secure passage of the latest version of the commission bill. The caucus members determined that the senate stood divided over the new bill at sixteen in favor to sixteen opposed. When one of the major opponents, Senator David L. King, from the Twenty-first District (Columbia, Lafayette, and Miller counties), made a trip to Memphis, the caucus members attempted to steamroll the measure through the senate. The opposition delayed the vote by lengthy speech making until late in the afternoon. When the final vote came, one of the supposedly loyal caucus members, R. D. McMullin of Yell County, stunned the senate by answering the roll call with a no vote. The turncoat senator had signed a statement of support which appeared in the *Gazette,* and he had pledged himself along with others at a caucus meeting earlier on the day of the final vote to stand firm. Angry caucus members demanded an explanation, but the senator refused to state his reasons for deserting the commission, except to say the afternoon speeches had impressed him.[10]

The *Gazette* thought the platform was now "meaningless" and called upon the people to view the record of the senate with care to see "those who have betrayed the party and the state." Governor Jones expressed amazement at the desertion of the party's platform. By June, *The Pine Bluff Weekly Press-Eagle* called upon the house to accept defeat and terminate its fight for the commission bill so that the special session could adjourn.[11]

Some of the conservatives of Arkansas, when threatened with the uncertainties of direct regulation of corporations by statute, saw a glimmer of righteousness in the commission idea. Senator J. A. C. Blackburn, representing Benton and Madison counties, had not been "over anxious" for a commission because he believed in "letting every man do as he pleases with his own," but with the right kind of law and respectable commissioners, a commission might be beneficial to the railroads. "I think," he said, "with a commission of intelligent men, the railroads would feel secure and would know just what they could depend upon." He did not see how the railroads could tolerate the "present prejudice" against them and the continual "agitation by every would-be politician." *The Helena Weekly World* expressed a similar view. The *World* condemned attempts in the legislature to enact a provision limiting passenger rates to two cents per mile. Undoubtedly the railroads would soon beg for a commission rather than suffer the vagaries of regulation by statute.[12]

Despite the acquiescence of some conservatives, the railroads hardly received the commission concept with unrestrained enthusiasm. Little Rock merchants and manufacturers welcomed the prospect of an end to discrimination against their city in favor of Memphis and St. Louis, but railroad men did not share their views. According to the *Gazette,* it was not the businessmen of Little Rock, but the railroad attorneys and lobbyists who gnashed their teeth at a commission bill.[13]

During the time of the debates in the assembly over the commission question, a prominent railroad entrepreneur spoke at the Arkansas Commercial Convention in Little Rock on the reasons for Arkansas's failure to develop as rapidly as other states. He did not mention the commission bill but made several indirect comments on the subject. The speaker was Samuel Fordyce of Hot Springs, who held a position of influence in the Democratic Party during Cleveland's hegemony. He blamed Arkansas's backwardness upon repudiation of bonds, the flooded condition of eastern Arkansas lands, and the diversion of potential immigrants and railroads to other areas because of the obstruction created by the Indian Territory on the western border.

Fordyce also warned the state of other and more recent evils on the political scene. The political climate seemed inhospitable for potential Northern investors who might otherwise furnish capital for development. A hostile mood toward corporations pervaded the state. He did not believe the general assembly had accorded the railroads a fair hearing before considering legislation affecting their interests. Since politicians were not expert on railroad affairs, he suggested they seek out the counsel of the railroads and make their approaches for advice with a more friendly spirit. He wished, if possible, to offer the "olive branch" to the people of Arkansas and to draw the state and the corporations together. *The Pine Bluff Weekly Press-Eagle* summed up the speech as a call for "more business and less politics" and gave its encouragement to a more generous state policy toward railroads and corporations.[14] Fordyce's statements do not offer any hint of railroad encouragement of the commission idea. The Fordyce speech followed a line of reasoning commonly used by railroad advocates to oppose regulation. In Alabama, the Mobile *Register* made the "timid capital theory" its chief argument. The newspaper attacked the elective commission concept on the grounds that increased distrust and court fights between government and business could only disturb the state's economy and hinder prosperity.[15]

During the few years of James N. Smithee's editorship, *The Arkansas Gazette* ranged itself squarely with those who favored railroad regulation. When the general assembly of 1897, after lengthy maneuvering, finally buried the commission bill, the *Gazette* printed daily on its editorial page the names of those state senators who had voted against the bill. In bold type the editor listed their names under the headline "BETRAYERS OF THEIR PARTY." The *Gazette* also singled out the Iron Mountain Railroad as a special object of scorn. A typical editorial castigated the Gould system for swallowing the Little Rock and Fort Smith Railroad. Its next victim, the Memphis and Little Rock, lay "limp and lank and powerless in the sapping, poisonous grasp of this unholy and unclean monster." The *Gazette* saw the Gould system as an "octopus" which strangled any new potential competitor.[16]

Politicians and newspapers frequently charged railroad lobbyists with exerting extreme pressure on the legislators in Little Rock to prevent passage of unfavorable legislation. *The Helena Weekly World* claimed the lobby had paid legislators in 1897 to prevent passage of the "inquitous" commission bill. It was common knowledge, said the *World,* that Thomas L. Cox was the real boss of the state legislature. Whenever a bill restricting the railroads came before the legislature, Cox would appear on the floor of the senate and "beckon his satellites" to go with him to his Capital Hotel room. In 1908, before a Pulaski County Grand Jury, Thomas L. Cox admitted to having had a part in bribing legislators to secure favorable railroad legislation. Because the statute of limitations in felony cases exempted citizens from prosecution after three years, Cox was free to reveal what he knew about improper influence of the legislature. The "boodle cases" beginning in 1905 resulted in the conviction of a number of Arkansas legislators for accepting bribes. The payments brought pro-business votes on pure food and drug legislation, railroad measures, and capital construction acts.[17]

Although some businessmen and some conservatives accepted the concept of orderly regulation by a moderate and responsible commission, the railroads of Arkansas did not originate the movement for regulation and fought its progress during the 1890s and early 1900s. If at times the railroads surrendered to the inevitable, it was with the hope that they might influence the restrictive legislation to make it more palatable. The farmers of Arkansas were in a militant and angry mood, and the regulatory movement owed more to their Populist spirit than to initiatives from the business community.

In Texas, Georgia, and some other states, the reaction to the regulatory movement was comparable to the reaction in Arkansas. The railroads of Texas bitterly opposed James Hogg's railroad commission bill of 1891. When the legislature met in Austin to consider the measure, a horde of lobbyists descended on the capital where they feasted and entertained the legislators in hopes of turning a few votes. Only a few railroad men in Texas accepted the commission idea. Backing for the measure came from the farmer's alliances, agricultural shippers, merchants, bankers, and lumbermen. The railroad regulation movement reached high tide in the nation about 1907. In that year Hoke Smith tried to instill new vigor into the ancient Georgia railroad commission, created in 1879. Although almost every state in the Union had a railroad commission by 1907, the railroad lobby exerted strong pressure against Smith's aggressive measure. The Georgia statute increased the rate-setting powers of the commission, extended its control to include utilities and all types of transportation facilities, and gave it broad supervisory control over corporation securities. In Wisconsin the railroads neither maintained an obstructionist stance nor initiated the regulation crusade. By 1905 the railroads of Wisconsin accepted the inevitability of some type of legislation, and rather than continue a hopeless foot-dragging strategy, they turned their energies toward securing a moderate law. Also the large shippers and manufacturers, who had been the chief opponents of the commission and who had profited from the complex rate system of the railroads, finally adjusted to the regulation concept since they saw some hope of shaping the commission to protect their interests. The Wisconsin state legislature accommodated the various interest groups and passed a moderate commission measure.[18] The railroad regulatory movement of the 1890s and early 1900s reached its peak in Arkansas during 1898 and 1899.

In the primary election campaign of 1898, candidates for the Arkansas state legislature sang out a chorus of support for the railroad commission. Even Pulaski County, the most urban area in the state, turned out of the senate one of the members of the railroad committee, B. D. Williams, who helped embalm the commission bill. During the primary campaign the wayward senator endeavored to explain his heresy and to assure the voters of his conversion. John F. McNemer, one of his opponents, wondered aloud why Williams had not voted for the railroad commission in the 1897 legislature since he was just as aware then of popular demand for the measure. Five candidates seeking the same Pulaski County senate seat debated at the Sam Jones Tabernacle in Little Rock, and each one swore allegiance to the commission. The campaign did not spark much enthusiasm or excitement. More interest focused on the brewing conflict with Spain than on state politics. But the voters displayed some interest in railroad regulation and the platform repeated the party's commitment to create a "commission to supervise and regulate" railroads.[19]

Jeff Davis entered the 1898 primary race for nomination as attorney general. He faced four opponents including the highly respected Prof. F. M. Goar, dean of the University of Arkansas Law School. His other opponents were J. B. "Buck" Baker of Izard County, John T. Hicks of Searcy, and E. P. Watson of Bentonville. All of the candidates for attorney general had agreed to a "joint speaking" at the scenic Ozark town of Eureka Springs in April. The weather was damp and rainy on the scheduled day, and only Jeff Davis put in an appearance. Having suffered a stroke just before the campaign began, he remained seated during his speech. His attacks on the respected law professor were somewhat restrained in comparison to later tirades. He chided his opponent for requesting an endorsement from an out-of-state man, Governor Stone of Mississippi. Davis recalled that the governor had "followed Mr. Cleveland off on the money and got the wax beat out of him." If Davis were to seek help outside Arkansas, he "would go to the plains of the Platte."[20]

In this first major campaign speech of his career, Davis raised three major issues, and all three bordered on the railroad question. He condemned the Arkansas debt settlement with the United States, the Smith Railroad Act, and the Bush railroad measure. "First," announced Davis in reference to the debt settlement, "I am bitterly opposed to the attempted steal of 273,000 acres of land by the Iron Mountain Railroad." The question of Arkansas's debt to the federal government had a long and complex history. Arkansas began accumulating debts to the United States during its first year of statehood. The two governments made claims and counterclaims against each other. The issue became more complicated in 1850 when the United States Congress passed the "swamp land act" granting to the state all the unsurveyed overflowed lands within its boundaries. In 1853, Congress granted to the Cairo Fulton Railroad and other lines a total of 273,000 acres of swamp lands previously confirmed to the state of Arkansas. This vast grant passed into the hands of the Iron Mountain Railroad, i.e., the Missouri Pacific system of Jay Gould.

During the 1890s, representatives of Arkansas negotiated with the Interior and Treasury Department to secure a settlement of conflicting debt claims. Both governments claimed a right to collect on obligations of the other. Governor James Clarke arrived at a settlement with the Cleveland administration, but the deal required acceptance by the Congress and the Arkansas General Assembly. The state of Arkansas probably would have accepted the compromise except for the sudden addition of an amendment by the House of Representatives' Committee on Public Lands. The so-called "Meiklejohn Amendment" required the state to surrender all claims to lands granted by the United States to the predecessors of the Iron Mountain Railroad. Arkansas had consistently refused to acknowledge that she had lost title to the land. G. A. A. Deane appeared before the committee on behalf of the railroad and successfully lobbied through it the amendment granting its claim to two hundred seventy-three thousand acres. Deane argued that two-thirds of the land had already gone into the hands of settlers. The committee conceded the railroad claim and the amendment passed both houses of Congress.

In the view of Arkansas Governor Dan W. Jones, Congress had bowed to railroad pressure. Although the Arkansas congressional delegation had previously opposed any such move, they suddenly added their approval to the amendment, and the Arkansas General Assembly followed their lead by passing a resolution to approve the compromise. Governor Dan Jones fired off a laboriously detailed veto message charging undue railroad pressure. But the general assembly promptly passed the resolution over the governor's veto.[21]

The settlement presented a ready-made issue for Jeff Davis's 1898 campaign. Although he usually found Dan Jones somewhat closer to the conservative camp than himself, Davis praised the governor for his abortive attempt to kill the compromise. Davis told his audience at Eureka Springs that the railroads were literally stealing lands from the state. The Arkansas Supreme Court, he recalled, had upheld the state's claim that the lands had never been legally transferred to railroad ownership. The railroads should compensate the settlers, who bought their lands in good faith.[22]

The second major issue in the Eureka Springs address involved a railroad land grant. The general assembly of 1897 enacted the Smith Bill to grant tax delinquent lands for construction of a new railroad. Davis did not believe the proponents of the act were sincerely interested in creating a line to compete with the Iron Mountain. He saw a more sinister motive behind the proposal. "I charge that it was conceived in sin and brought forth in iniquity for no other purpose than to defeat a railroad commission bill." Apparently, Davis saw the scheme as an artful ploy to divert those concerned about monopolistic practices away from regulatory measures. The expectation of new competing lines might temper the enthusiasm for a commission.[23]

Finally, Davis raised the specter of the 1897 Bush Bill, a Populist measure authorizing the building of state-owned railroads to compete against monopolistic lines. He was "unalterably opposed because it is Populism boiled down, placing the building and ownership of railroads in the hands of the state." The Board of State Officers created by the act would be open to the temptation to deal dishonestly. He feared a reversion to Claytonism (a reference to Powell Clayton, Reconstruction governor) and the evil of placing the yoke of excessive bond debts on future generations. Davis did not discuss some of the positive aspects of the plan. Outgoing Governor James P. Clarke had told the general assembly in 1897 that a state railroad between Little Rock and the coal-mining region of Fort Smith could be a means for supplying coal to Little Rock at a fair price. He believed the lack of a cheap coal supply kept industry from entering the state. A railroad commission and a state-owned railroad could force the Iron Mountain to charge a fair rate. Davis himself referred to the common complaint of independent coal mine operators that the Gould system often refused to supply them with cars. Governor Clarke thought that the state railroad concept offered a solution to the problem of finding some method of securing capital for building new roads. The constitution prohibited the state from making loans to railroads, but it did not forbid the building of a railroad by the state itself. These advantages of a state railroad system did not engage Davis's attention during his 1898 campaign.[24]

Davis also explained his views on the commission concept in his Eureka Springs speech. He advocated the creation of a commission, but he wanted the voters to ponder some additional possibilities. Although the commission should be granted broad authority, the legislature need not abdicate its power to regulate railroads directly by statute. The legislature by law could revoke charters, require companies to provide cars, establish rates, and regulate wages and hours of railroad workers. It was true, he admitted, such laws might face a judicial test in the courts, but the same prospect faced any commission decision. He had complete confidence in the fairness of the courts. "The judiciary of the state of Arkansas is as true as in any state in this Union." This accolade for the courts stands in stark contrast to Davis's later attitude toward the judiciary after they had spiked his antitrust crusade. Davis did not insist upon regulation by statute but considered it a matter for further thought. But he clearly ranged himself on the side of those who struggled to bring about some kind of effective regulation.[25]

An early primary in Lincoln County upheld the popular view that Professor Goar was far ahead of the other four candidates for attorney general. But death suddenly removed him from the competition, and Jeff Davis quickly took the lead in the four-cornered race. Davis did not secure a majority of popular votes in the primary election, but he won a plurality almost twice as large as the next highest contender, J. B. Baker. He gained 220 delegates in the county primaries and 9 more at the convention. Arriving in Little Rock before any of the other candidates, he began bargaining for the nomination. One week before the state convention met, he had already set up headquarters at the Capital Hotel and was seeking out uninstructed delegates. His labors bore fruit when he won the nomination on the first ballot without a single vote to spare.[26] Davis was not yet the leading voice in the war on railroads and corporations. In 1898 he rode the crest of a wave of protest. It would not be long until he would place himself at the forefront of the anti-corporation drive in Arkansas.

Although the general assembly had not been able to agree on a commission in 1897, it had voted to submit the question to the people in the 1898 general election. By a vote of 63,703 to 16,940, the voters ratified a constitutional amendment to empower the general assembly to create "offices and commissions" to regulate railroads. When the legislature convened in January 1899, Governor Dan Jones again demanded passage of a commission law. Regulation by statute had been inadequate, he told the legislature, but a commission could effectively enforce the law. The assembly of 1899 accepted its mandate from the voters and enacted a statute to create an elective commission.[27]

The commission faced serious criticisms and initial difficulties in its attempt to regulate the railroads. Even some Populists were unimpressed. Winfield Scott Morgan in his Populist paper announced, "Arkansas now has a Railroad Commission; now let us see how it 'controls' the railroads. About the only thing it will control is its salary." Morgan believed government ownership alone could bring railroads under control. Controversy also surrounded the choice of commissioners. The members of the first commission were appointed to serve until the general election of 1900 when commissioners would be elected. *The Helena Weekly World* admitted the three men chosen by Governor Jones were lawyers of some ability but was indignant at the choice of Charles Collins, an ardent silver man, as secretary of the commission. Collins, according to the *World,* was continually carrying volumes of statistics about and kept pestering people with his ideas.[28] Jeremiah Wallace, whom Jeff Davis fervently admired, received an appointment and served several two-year terms.

Many states had already experimented with railroad commissions. Some of them served only as advisory bodies. The Massachusetts commission heard grievances, held investigations, and made suggestions to the corporations. But other commissions possessed a larger measure of regulatory power and actually established rates. Some of the latter could only set a specific rate after conducting an investigation. But in Arkansas, as in some other states, the commission could produce a whole schedule of rates. Those states which established commissions during the 1870s and 1880s usually conferred on them an advisory function.

But the commissions formed after 1890 usually had more authority. The Southern states generally created strong railroad commissions. The Southwestern states did not establish commissions until after 1890 when the stronger agencies were in vogue. Texas had not created a commission after the Civil War because of the need to entice new railroads into the undeveloped state. As in Texas, the frontier environment of Arkansas discouraged the creation of a regulatory commission until the 1890s.[29]

A regulatory commission did not automatically achieve greater success than a purely advisory one. The most important factor determining whether a commission operated effectively was the ability and expertness of its commissioners. Arkansas's commissioners lacked the requisite knowledge and experience to establish realistic rates. Many Arkansans complained that the First Railroad Commission actually raised railroad rates. In its first report, a work of 459 pages written mainly by Jeremiah "Jerry" Wallace, the commission endeavored to defend itself against these charges. The commissioners admitted to having "naively adopted" the published rates of the railroads and having set out to enforce these rates. Previously, cut rates to favorite shippers had been common, and it was always possible to bargain for lower rates. When the commission enforced the published rates with no exceptions, the cost to shippers increased. Eventually, the commissioners argued, their experience enabled them to establish lower rates.[30]

The Arkansas Railroad Commission manifested a certain amount of zeal without knowledge in its attempt to vigorously prosecute the railroads. The commission made an ill-advised attempt to regulate interstate commerce by attacking the Kansas City Southern Railroad. On a shipment of chairs from Fort Smith, Arkansas, to Grannis, Arkansas (Polk County), the railroad charged a rate above the maximum prescribed by the commission. Much of the Kansas City Southern track lay in Indian Territory across the border from Arkansas. The line ran for nearly 29 miles through Benton and Washington counties in Arkansas and then through Indian Territory for 128 miles until reentering Arkansas just south of Fort Smith. The railroad line accepted freight and passengers at five junctions in Indian Territory. A branch line ran from Fort Smith for sixteen miles to a junction at Spiro, Indian Territory. Although most of the line lay outside state boundaries, the commission prescribed rates for shipments originating and terminating in Arkansas on a through bill-of-lading.[31]

When the commission ordered the Kansas City Southern to lower its rates, the railroad secured from United States Circuit Judge Jacob Trieber a temporary restraining order. Although Indian Territory had no legislative powers, Trieber believed these powers had been reserved by Congress to itself and could not be exercised by the state of Arkansas. Trieber went beyond the immediate question of interstate as opposed to intrastate commerce. "No state," he declared, "has the power to authorize a Commission to fix rates arbitrarily with no power in the courts to stay the hands of the Commission if it chooses to establish rates that are unequal and unreasonable." In the fall of 1900, Judge Trieber made his temporary injunction permanent.[32]

The Arkansas Railroad Commission appealed to the United States Supreme Court to reverse the action of the circuit court. The chairman, in a written opinion, explained the position of the commission. He did not believe the entrance of goods into a territory outside Arkansas for a part of their journey classified them as goods in interstate commerce. He gave some indication of the weakness of his case by declaring, "We are aware that the Interstate Commerce Commission has held a similar transaction to be interstate commerce, which holding seems to have been acquiesced in by the Texas Railroad Commission." The commission based its appeal to the Supreme Court on an earlier case in which the court had upheld Pennsylvania's right to tax railroad receipts on a line which operated partly in a different state. Chief Justice Fuller of the Supreme Court dismissed the argument. The earlier case involved a line entering another state solely to avoid the kind of engineering problem created by a lake or mountain.[33] In the early twentieth century, the commission pursued an aggressive policy but had only moderate success despite the encouragement and support of Jeff Davis.

During his two years as attorney general from 1899 to 1901, Davis cultivated new issues to bring color and spark to the political scene. Two major concerns engaged his attention during this period, the capitol construction program and the antitrust movement. His fiery activism on these two fronts alienated Governor Dan Jones. Compared to the new tribune of the people, the governor's moderation marked him as an aristocrat, a member of the old Civil War veteran, conservative leadership. Despite Jones's movement toward railroad regulation and trust legislation, Davis stirred more dust and attracted more attention as the nemesis of the soulless corporations.

According to Governor Dan Jones, the people of Arkansas demanded an antitrust law. The rural people were "rabid" in their opposition to the corporations and could speak knowledgeably about monopolies. "They are in for war and nothing but war on the evil will satisfy them." [34] In March 1899, the general assembly passed the Rector Anti-Trust Act, almost a copy of a bill that had been enacted in Missouri. L. B. Leigh, an insurance company agent, complained bitterly of the general assembly's vindictive mood. When businessmen approached the legislature with petitions against the measure, "they were received and treated by the lower house in a manner, which to put it mildly, was not in keeping with the decorous behavior which should characterize the proceedings of a deliberative body." For sixteen years, fire insurance companies had established uniform rates through a state fire underwriters board. Only the politicians, he believed, would consider such a board a trust. [35]

If the legislature's enthusiasm embittered the corporation executives, the implementation of the Rector Act by Attorney General Davis caused them to gnash their teeth. In April, Davis filed more than one hundred test suits against the fire insurance companies operating in the state. The battle became so intense that many of the companies discontinued business in Arkansas, at least temporarily. In the major test case, *Arkansas V. Aetna Fire Insurance Company and the Lancashire Fire Insurance Company,* the defendants argued that the Rector Act "only made a conspiracy to defraud where the combination" to fix a price is entered into within the boundaries of Arkansas. Jeff Davis and his assistant in the case, Charles Jacobson, believed the act applied to corporations fixing prices no matter where they may have entered into such an agreement. Section one of the act declared, "Any corporation organized under the laws of this, or any other state, or country, and transacting business in this State, who shall enter into any pool, trust, to regulate or fix the price of any article shall be deemed and adjudged guilty of a conspiracy to defraud." The attorney general admitted that the Lancashire Fire Company was an English corporation and that the Aetna Company was a New York based firm, but he believed a conspiracy anywhere would cancel their privilege to operate in Arkansas. He asked, in accordance with the penalty provided by the Rector Act, that the "defendant's corporate existence be declared forfeited."[36]

During April of 1899, before the legislature adjourned and before the supreme court made its decision, approximately one thousand men met at Glenwood Park in Little Rock to demand modification of the antitrust act to relieve fire insurance companies from its restrictions. Many of those present denounced the excesses of the legislature. When Jeff Davis made some remarks before the crowd, he was, according to his version, "hissed, hooted, and howled down."[37] Shortly after this incident, the Arkansas Supreme Court ruled against the extraterritorial interpretation of Jeff Davis, and the fire insurance companies returned to normal operations.

Governor Dan Jones considered the attorney general's actions demagogic and extremist. According to Jones, Davis believed that "if an insurance company, operating regularly in Arkansas was a party to a rate agreement in Hong Kong, it was violating Arkansas law." Arkansas's most distinguished jurist, Uriah M. Rose, whose goldbug views had cost him his place as National Committeeman, declared the Davis interpretation clearly wrong. The statutes of a state could not extend beyond its own territory. *The Arkansas Gazette* also began an anti–Davis barrage that continued during the next decade. The newspaper made an essential point: the Arkansas Court had ruled that a conspiracy outside the state was prohibited by the act if the agreement was to fix rates in Arkansas specifically. Davis, if he had been sincere, would now begin amassing evidence proving the existence of such an agreement. Instead, he had dropped the cases and castigated the court.[38] Davis's critics thought he was more interested in the next gubernatorial election than in actually securing a favorable verdict in the courts.

Davis's vigorous prosecution of insurance companies followed a pattern set by a famous Texas attorney general, James Hogg. In the late 1880s, Hogg began a drive against out-of-state wildcat insurance concerns which attempted to dodge Texas laws concerning minimum security capital requirements. As in Arkansas, many companies took flight rather than comply with state regulations. In 1907, when one of Hogg's associates sponsored a law requiring three-fourths of a company's insurance premiums to be invested within Texas, a second exodus occurred. The Texas and

Arkansas crusades preceded the more famous insurance company investigations of Louis D. Brandeis and Charles Evans Hughes in the Northeast. In the early 1900s, Charles Evans Hughes gained fame through his investigation of New York's Equitable Life Assurance Company. A committee of the state legislature initiated the probe into the company's practices and the moves of J. P. Morgan to gain control of the firm. As the number of insurance companies rapidly increased, many states enacted a variety of regulatory laws. The movement for a federal insurance act to bring stability and uniformity to the regulations placed on insurance companies did not achieve its goal during Theodore Roosevelt's and Woodrow Wilson's era.[39]

The decision of the Arkansas Supreme Court against his extraterritorial interpretation gave Davis a valuable issue for his 1900 campaign. In every county square and hamlet he ridiculed the black-robed justices. Although formal candidacies were not announced until 1900, Davis began making political speeches during July 1899. In an address in Sharp County on Independence Day, he launched his attack on the court. "We have an anti-trust law, that would have knocked every trust cold, had the Arkansas Supreme Court not killed it." He preferred to use the ballot box against the courts rather than take hasty action, but he believed if ever we fought another civil war, it would be over "judge-made" law. In his denunciation of the state's supreme court he added an attack on the highest court of the nation for its decision against the income tax provision of the Wilson–Gorman tariff. It was another case of a court legislating.[40]

In a Conway speech, he recalled how the judges had refused to allow him to present his argument in shirt sleeves. "If you will permit me," he told the honest plebeians of Conway, "I will unbutton my collar. I won't take off my coat: it has been judicially determined by the Supreme Court of Arkansas that I couldn't take off my coat." George W. Murphy, successful candidate for attorney general in 1900, joined Davis in condemning the court. The justices had "construed" the Rector Act "into a blank." Murphy's Davis attachment was short-lived; he later became one of the leaders of the anti-Davis faction. Later they made peace again, and Murphy went on to become the Arkansas Progressive Party's candidate for governor in 1912.[41]

Davis broadened his assault to include prosecutions of the express, tobacco, and cotton seed oil trusts. He even began action against a Little Rock "ice trust" which he accused of conspiring to keep the city's ice prices at a high level. After his victory in the 1900 primaries, he directed the drafting of the platform at the state convention, a platform which praised the legislature for enacting the Rector Anti-Trust Bill. One of the planks made Davis's view the official doctrine of the Democratic Party:

> While we are in favor of the passage of such laws by congress as will effectually destroy the trusts and place such restrictions around the corporations as may be necessary to protect the public welfare, yet we maintain that corporations are creatures of the law, and have no rights except those rights granted by the people. We further maintain that a sovereign state has the right and power to exclude any foreign corporation from doing business in the state. We demand the enactment of such laws by our legislature as shall prohibit corporations which belong to pools, trusts or combinations in restraint of trade no matter where organized, from doing business in the state of Arkansas, and that it shall exclude them from its borders.

During his career as governor and United States senator, Davis continued to make the antitrust issue a dominant theme.[42]

The gubernatorial aspirant displayed a more negativistic spirit in his drive to defeat the capitol construction project. The old statehouse was a charming and dignified structure, but it had deteriorated, and the government had outgrown the cramped quarters. Senator John D. Kimball of Hot Springs, who drafted the 1899 Capitol Bill, called the building an "ancient rookery." The legislature in 1895 soundly defeated a construction bill, but in 1898 Governor Dan Jones proposed building a new statehouse on the penitentiary grounds. The legislature responded with an initial appropriation of fifty thousand dollars to begin construction.[43]

The attorney general began an unrelenting campaign to obstruct the project. In May 1899, he filed *Quo Warranto* proceedings against the newly appointed capitol commissioners, questioning their authority to implement the Kimball Capitol Construction Act. On June 5, he tried to secure an injunction from the Pulaski Chancery Court to restrain the commission from beginning construction. A few days later, he initiated a suit to prevent the state auditor from issuing warrants in payment for work done on the building. But the Arkansas Supreme Court upheld the right of the auditor to issue warrants and declared the Capitol Act constitutional. Davis had argued that all appropriations not specifically designated for normal operation of the government must, according to the constitution, receive a two-thirds majority vote in the assembly. Since the Capitol Act had not passed by this margin, he denounced the auditor for issuing warrants. Again the courts had impeded the frenzied efforts of the attorney general.[44]

In his Fourth of July speech, Davis declared the "million-dollar state house . . . will cost three million dollars and prove to be the most infamous steal ever perpetrated against the people of Arkansas." *The Arkansas Gazette* defended the integrity of the capitol commissioners and denied even a hint of corruption. Davis assured a Conway audience that he had not intended to impugn the honest character of the commissioners, especially their own local citizen George W. Donaghey. But he had less kind words for one commissioner, Charles Gordon Newman, who also edited the *Pine Bluff Commercial*. The goldbug editor had characterized Davis as a "buffoon" and a "mountebank." If the editor was not personally dishonest, he was, in Davis's view, "an old broken-down aristocrat."[45]

At the state Democratic convention, the Davis forces blocked inclusion of a capitol construction plank in the platform. Senator James Berry thought the proposal had little chance to secure approval because of the strong pro-Davis sentiment, and he interceded in the dispute to persuade the sponsors of the plank to withdraw it.[46]

After the laying of the cornerstone in November 1900, the state discontinued construction for two years. Charles Jacobson, Davis's secretary, believed that political considerations alone motivated the attack on the capitol construction plan; he did not think the crusade delayed the project by a single day. Jacobson was emotionally involved in the question and could not have made an impartial judgment. The statehouse dispute was undeniably a political football, but later events indicated that Davis's fears were something more than empty rhetoric. Inferior construction, bribery of legislators, and unforeseen ballooning of costs dogged the project during the first decade of the twentieth century. Davis's hostility toward the building project was not insignificant; he contributed to the snail's pace construction.[47]

In his first inaugural speech, Davis explained to the legislature his views on the capitol project. He had never opposed the building of a new capitol *per se*. He had objected to the use of the penitentiary site, the management of the project, and the methods of construction. He proposed dispensing with the capitol commission appointed by Governor Jones and creating a new board of state officers. The state officials could employ a suitable manager to direct the construction effort. The board would be authorized to secure competitive bids as a safeguard to close "all avenues for extravagant expenditures." Governor Jones, in his farewell speech to the same body, had called upon legislators to retain the existing commission. The legislature refused to place the building project in the hands of the state officers. Failing to secure a major revamping of the board, Davis replaced the commissioners with men of his own choosing. In 1901 and later, Davis seemed especially concerned about placing the enterprise under his own supervision.[48]

Other states experienced the difficulty of combining politics and construction programs. Attorney General James Hogg of Texas created a stir when he refused to accept the completed statehouse because of a leaking roof. Texas's building project also suffered serious delays as the governor, the Capitol Board, the legislature, and others squabbled over whether to construct the building with limestone blocks or Texas granite. Arkansas also delayed construction during Governor Donaghey's administration while politicians battled over the use of native as against out-of-state granite.[49]

While Davis developed the issues, he also began one of the most colorful campaigns in Arkansas history. In June 1898 the *Gazette* had speculated on possible candidates for governor two years hence. The editor listed nine men, some of whom made the race; Davis was not among them. But a few months after he had entered the office of attorney general, he announced his intentions. In letters to the members of the 1899 legislature, he said he "had not intended to enter the contest until the scurrilous attacks upon me by the subsidized press of this city forced me to take the defensive, not only for myself, but as they term it, the late lamented legislature." The *Gazette* denied any crusade against the would-be martyr, chided Davis for presuming the assembly needed him to defend it, and advised the hillbilly leader to accept the verdict of the court on the state capitol and antitrust disputes. Most politicians, according to George Donaghey, did not take Davis's candidacy seriously at first.[50]

In the small town of Hardy, in north central Arkansas, the attorney general opened his campaign with an assault on the courts, the corporations, and the old-line politicians. He told the local citizens he had not intended to seek office again, a phrase he used in many campaigns, "but I am in this fight for the people, and I shall not desert them." Davis made frequent speeches during the summer and fall, sometimes joining his opponents in debate. He "has been going up and down the state," said the *Gazette*, "like a political roaring lion seeking whom he might devour." In northwest Arkansas he "sawed the atmosphere with his coarse talk and clown-like antics." At the Ozark courthouse in September, he openly attacked the governor, threatening to "skin him alive" if he did not accept a challenge for a joint debate. Dan Jones was too busy, the *Gazette* replied, to answer the "Quixotic challenge of the attorney general." Never before had Arkansas politicians gone to the hustings with such energy a year before the actual election. Jeff Davis enjoyed campaigning and for him it became an almost continuous pursuit.[51]

Davis courted opposition in order to secure the limelight. He referred to "Old man Mitchell," the editor of *The Arkansas Democrat*, as "a disgruntled old gold-bug crank," and accused the newspaper of "bulldozing" him. He began a vendetta against Senator James Edward Wood, editor of the *Lee County Courier*, who had voted for the antitrust act but had later denounced the measure at the businessmen's rally in Little rock. The two opponents clouded the air with epithets. Senator Wood was "a dirty, filthy little squib." And Davis in his Confederate gray, said Wood, looked like a "Jackass parading" in a lion's skin. In a statement to the *Gazette*, the senator promised to "completely unmask this demagogue." He eventually decided to become a candidate for governor in order to more effectively answer Davis and to meet him in joint debate.[52]

Although it had been customary for politicians to conduct their own campaigns without injecting themselves into other races, Davis defied this tradition throughout his career. He frequently entered other contests lest his own campaign become too tame. By May 1899 politicians knew Governor Dan Jones would be the chief contender against incumbent United States Senator James Berry. Since Davis had increasingly alienated himself from Governor Jones, it seemed natural for him to align with James Berry. In June, he wrote a letter to Berry offering to give the senator his backing in the campaign. Several months later the attorney general, in an address at Dardanelle, claimed that Berry had publicly endorsed him for governor. The assertion brought immediate denial from Berry. No Berry-Davis coalition developed, but the attorney general continued his one-sided struggle for Berry as against Jones.[53] In later years he conducted extensive campaigns for those associated with him.

Apparently, no major issue drew Davis toward Berry. Davis was not averse to making alliances on non-ideological grounds. But the 1900 senatorial contest was the first in which James Berry met an opponent who differed with him on a significant issue.[54] Whether the voters were fully aware of the difference or not, the candidates offered them a choice on the issue of imperialism. On January 29, 1900, Dan Jones wrote an address to the people formally announcing his candidacy for the Senate. The message, written for newspaper publication, set forth Jones's expansionist views and distinctly set him apart from Senator Berry. Dan Jones favored retention of Puerto Rico and the Philippines but with a large degree of self-government. He argued that the insular domains should have a territorial government somewhat like that of New Mexico at the time. The Philippines were the key to the Asian market, he believed, and that vast market could absorb a large part of the Southern cotton crop. "Shall we admit," he asked, "our incapacity to carry out Christian civilization beyond the eastern bounds of the Pacific Ocean?" Like many expansionists of his time, he saw God's hand leading America to her imperial destiny. Nearly a month earlier, he had delivered a similar address to the Arkansas Bar Association, and a leading Democrat replied with "an ardent anti-expansion speech."[55]

Governor Jones was out of step with most Arkansas Democrats on this issue. Both Arkansas senators stood firmly against acquisition of the Philippines. In January 1899, James K. Jones told William Jennings Bryan of his determination to oppose annexation of the Philippines "under any circumstances." Senator Jones believed enough Democrats shared his views to either force an amendment or defeat the Treaty of Paris. Since the Republicans were quite anxious to secure a treaty without delaying until a later session, he thought they would accept an amendment. According to the amendment, Spain would, as in the case of Cuba, relinquish her sovereignty to the Philippines. This would avoid an outright cession of territory. But Bryan argued that the most efficient way to secure Philippine independence was to first accept the treaty as President McKinley sent it to the Senate; then the

Democrats could go to battle on the issue of imperialism. James K. Jones rebuked his colleague: "The feeling is growing more and more intense on this question; and to be perfectly frank with you, I regret exceedingly that you have taken so prominent and pronounced a stand in favor of ratification."[56]

One week later, Senator Jones wrote: "And how any man can vote for a ratification of the treaty, with almost certain knowledge that the intention is to keep them as permanently a part of the United States is beyond my comprehension." For Jones, it was a "matter of conscience" to vote nay on the treaty. In still a third letter, he protested any attempt to simply pass a resolution rather than amend the treaty. Spain could not resume the struggle, and the United States was unwilling to fight. Certainly, the treaty could be amended. Many other Democrats echoed Jones's view. The Arkansas Democratic platform of 1900, which Jeff Davis scrutinized and sanctioned at the convention, opposed annexation by force, demanded self-government for the Philippines, and denounced "the carpetbag government foisted on the people of Porto Rico and Cuba."[57]

On many other issues, the two candidates for the Senate were in agreement. Both gave enthusiastic support to the popular election of United States senators. After Berry had defeated Daniel Jones in seven of the first eight county primaries, the governor retired from the race.[58] Arkansans usually returned an incumbent, and most voters probably chose the old one-legged veteran without giving serious thought to the question of imperialism.

The primary election campaigns at the turn of the century brought significant issues before the voters. At times, as in the case of the 1900 senatorial contest, the choice between candidates involved a significant difference. Frequently personalities engaged more attention than the issues, but even the antics of Davis helped focus the attention of hill people on governmental matters of concern to them. If at times the real differences between Davis and his opponents seemed small, he at least captured a place in the public imagination as the chief opponent of corporate and political privilege. He became the symbol of revolt against the established economic and political authorities. With tremendous moral fervor and energy he voiced the demand of the common people for economic change and regulation. His crude manners and self-serving theatrics should not obscure the fact that he gave the regulatory movement a new urgency. His untiring zeal helped mobilize those favoring legislation to restrict the activities of railroads and insurance companies.

Contemporaries seriously indicted Jeff Davis's political style. Critics sometimes admitted he had championed significant causes, but they thought his reformist zeal manifested itself more in the realm of rhetorical skill than constructive achievement. He helped spike the state railroad scheme by his attacks on the Bush Bill in the 1898 and 1900 campaigns. While Governor Dan Jones encouraged the legislature to iron out the defects in the Bush Act, Davis assailed the scheme in his drive for the governorship. Arkansas never built a state railroad.[59] *The Forrest City Times* put it succinctly, "He talks well, and he promises much, but he never brings anything to a head." The governor "tears down, but he never builds up." The newspaper cited the capitol construction project as an example of Davis's negativism. To obstruct the building scheme the governor "employed every frivolous technicality" imaginable. His "malign influence" prevented the capitol commission from making headway with building plans.[60]

Davis achieved more than the entertainment of the masses by his carnival-like performances. His crusades led to concrete achievements. He helped further the drive to force railroads to pay a higher share of taxation, and he had a part in placing franchise taxes on corporations. His vehement attacks on the fellow-servant rule led to legislation prohibiting employers from escaping liability for injuries suffered because of negligence of fellow workers. His efforts to humanize the conditions of convicts led to some mitigation of the barbaric condition of Arkansas prison life. Davis did not have a flair for administration—he preferred to stir the dust. He spent many hours campaigning in the hills. If he had been an effective executive, he might have accomplished more, but he did make substantial contributions. He also helped set the stage for the reform crusades of later governors.[61] The hillbilly leader effectively exploited the issues of his day to wrest control of the state from the conservatives. Davis always considered the controversies in relation to his quest for power. He was both a demagogue bent on achieving high office and a zealot dedicated to improving the lot of his one-gallus friends. To accomplish his goals he chose the role of obstructionist. Iconoclasm was the path to political ascendancy. A capitol site bestrewn with moss-covered building blocks and infested with willows and weeds might lead to power more quickly than the splendor of a stately granite structure. Davis did not build a capitol, but he did establish a powerful political structure that dominated the state during his governorship and continued as a force in Arkansas politics even after his death.

6

The Davis Organization, 1900–1906

The American system of government has not always nourished a strong two-party system. In the days of James Monroe, no opposition party gained a place of power on the national scene. One-party systems have been more common on the state level and have not been confined to the South. Historically, the two-party system has not been the *sine qua non* of a democratic system. Factions have usually appeared whenever a single party has gained dominance within a libertarian society. Whenever these factions have attained a recognizable distinctiveness and a degree of permanence, they have given the voters an alternative or choice of a kind, but they have not been an equivalent for the two-party system. The divisions within the Democratic Party have been transient and fluid. Historic traditions and long-lived organizations have not helped to fix their identity in the minds of voters. Yet, if an alternative choice is an essential element of democracy, the Southern one-party system has sometimes exhibited a democratic spirit.[1]

In Arkansas, factions have been temporary and marked as often by personality differences as by ideological cleavages. But during the early years of the twentieth century, Arkansas voters witnessed the rending of their party into two warring camps. Many ambiguities and fluctuations occurred to obscure the identity of the two factions. Politicians aligned themselves now with one camp and now with another. Some individuals defied classification. But every voter of even slight intelligence knew that in Arkansas there were Davis Democrats and anti-Davis Democrats.

Jeff Davis constructed a powerful political organization and captured control of the party machinery and many of the offices of the state government. The editor of *The Jonesboro Tribune* called him "a self-appointed dictator" whose influence reached down even to the selection of "constable and road overseer in many instances." According to the *Gazette,* Davis had a "satrap" in every province of the state. The newspaper estimated that "two-thirds of the sheriffs in Arkansas are component parts of the governor's machine." Since the county sheriff was the "king bee" of his "shire," the governor exerted strong influence at the county level. Davis's secretary, Charles Jacobson, called his boss "the supreme political dictator of his state."[2]

Opposed by the traditional leaders of the state government, city newspapers, Delta chieftains, and most other respected elements of society, the redneck leader routed all opposition and triumphantly captured the seats of power. The counties held their primary elections on various days throughout the late winter and early spring of 1900. Success in the early primaries rose to a crescendo of victory as Davis won in every county except Pulaski. His stunning achievement compelled many reluctant Democrats to come to his side, at least temporarily. *The Arkansas Democrat,* a goldbug paper and belligerently anti-Davis, acknowledged Davis's claim to power after the 1900 primary. The *Democrat* admitted Davis had been right in his charges that most of the newspapers and politicians of Arkansas opposed his election. And the paper confessed its own opposition. But seventy-four counties had supported Davis and the *Democrat* conceded the necessity of supporting the governor-elect in the general elections. One of his backers, Judge Emon O. Mahoney of Union County, said that Davis had "made more ex-politicians, broken more precedents set by them, had stronger opposition and won out by larger majorities than any other man that ever entered the political arena of Arkansas."[3] But if his towering political strength brought some men to his side, it also alienated others and encouraged the division of the party into Davis and anti-Davis factions.

In the primary election of 1900, Davis asked the voters to elect only his supporters to state offices. As a result he secured an attorney general (George M. Murphy), secretary of state (J. W. Crockett), auditor (T. C. Monroe), and commissioner of mines, manufacturing and agriculture (Frank Hill), who were all personally loyal to him. Davis quickly alienated the officers he had befriended, but he began his term with a group of allies. Since the state officers served on a number of state boards, such as the Penitentiary Board, he could extend his control over the various institutions and activities of the state administration.[4]

Davis absorbed some of the remnants of the Populist Party's dwindling support. *The Arkansas Commonweal,* a Populist sheet, reported that the Independence County Populists had planned to support Jeff Davis in the 1900 election but had instead dissolved their organization. *The Arkansas Democrat* saw little future for the Populists in the state, because one of their most vigorous leaders, Thomas Fletcher, had recently died. Although Davis specifically disassociated himself from the Populist Party, it is possible that his rhetoric appealed to some of those who had looked to men like Fletcher to lead them. It has been questioned whether former Populists came over to the Davis side in significant numbers in the 1900 election. Raymond Arsenault, for example, asserts that many of them voted for the Arkansas Republican Party in 1900. The Republican vote in 1900 increased by 5 percent over the 1896 turnout. Because agrarians had at times cooperated with the Republicans in the past, it would have been natural for them to turn to that party as their own declined. Nevertheless, Davis pitched his appeal to the discontented, and if Populist voters did not come to him in large numbers in 1900, he did attract more of them to his ranks in later elections.[5]

The hillbilly leader dubbed his organization the "Old Guard" and cast it in the role of defender of the common people. "And if I can call the Old Guard around me," he once said, "we will whip this old political Bourbon ring in Little Rock." The Old Guard demonstrated its strength as early as the 1900 State Democratic Convention. Before the platform committee presented its work to the convention, it submitted its draft to Davis for approval. But Davis had not yet won the unreserved loyalty of all those who had moved in his direction. That there was still some uncertainty about the wisdom of an all-out commitment to the new leader is seen by the defeat of Davis's choice for chairman of the state central committee. Davis had tried to install his trusted comrade, Jeremiah V. Bourland of Franklin County. But the convention rejected Davis's choice and reelected Carroll Armstrong of Conway County.[6]

Before the general assembly convened on January 14, 1901, the "Old Guard" made a determined effort to elect a presiding officer of their own choosing for the lower house. In the past, politicians had made their choice months before the actual assembling in Little Rock, but in 1901 and 1903, the election of a Speaker became a protracted struggle. By January 7, seven candidates for Speaker had established headquarters at the Capital Hotel. The *Gazette* predicted a hot fight for the speakership. After Davis threw his support to Thomas H. Humphreys, a Fayetteville attorney, several contestants agreed to give up the struggle before the first ballot. The "Old Guard" rallied behind their nominee and captured the office by a vote of sixty-six for Humphreys to thirty divided between two opponents, George W. Williams of Pulaski County and H. T. Bradford of Lonoke.[7]

In his acceptance speech, Speaker Humphreys indicated his personal and ideological loyalty to Davis. "Trusts, the arch-enemy of nations, states and people, have stalked through our state," he warned. "This arch-fiend took a tilt in the political arena with our governor-elect and the governor left the monster on the field of battle on his hip." Humphreys also declared his agreement with Davis's interpretation of the Rector Act, "a thief in one place will be a thief in another."[8]

Thomas Humphreys continued to support Davis's policies during his tenure. He led a fight in the house of representatives to enact Davis's view on convict leasing into law. The governor sought to invalidate and terminate a ten-year contract granting the labor of three hundred convicts to the Arkansas Brick and Manufacturing Company. As attorney general, and thereby a member of the Penitentiary Board, Davis had signed the contract himself during the Dan Jones administration, but he later repented of his action. Humphreys introduced a bill into the house of representatives to terminate all leasing contracts at the end of the governor's term in which they were initiated. The bill declared all contracts made under the Dan Jones administration void as of January 1901. Critics of Davis charged repudiation. One of the members of the firmly anti-Davis Pulaski County delegation expressed keen disappointment that the Speaker of the House had sponsored such a measure. When a second Pulaski County delegate reminded Humphreys of Davis's own signature on the contract, the presiding officer rose to defend his ally. The governor had admitted to signing the document "hastily" and had come to regret the action and desired cancellation. Although opposition to the bill was strong, it became law, and Governor

Jeff Davis canceled the contract with the Arkansas Brick and Manufacturing Company. Despite this victory, Davis did not have things his own way. In the 1901 legislature, he had insufficient factional support to achieve some of his major goals. Davis failed to consistently unify his followers behind his program. The men who served in the legislature did not come from the poorer economic classes. They came from the same socioeconomic groups that had served in earlier legislatures. The governor's two most ardent supporters in the senate were David King and William F. Kirby. Despite men like King and Kirby, the legislature rejected Davis's bid for a fellow-servant law, a reform school, and an antitrust law. One reason for the failures of the Davis faction was the tendency in the legislature to associate factionalism with bossism. Leading the opposition to the governor were the representatives from urban Pulaski County.[9]

The planters of the Delta region in eastern Arkansas had also vigorously opposed Davis, and the new governor set out to remove them from political power. At his request, the general assembly of 1901 reorganized the various drainage and levee boards of the Delta so that Davis could replace the board members with men of his own choosing. The governor's machine now included elements from the once hostile east.

In the 1902 primary elections, Davis continued his drive for Delta support by endorsing James P. Clarke's attempt to unseat Senator James K. Jones. The contest exhibited a spirit of rivalry between the two sections of the state. James K. Jones came from a southwestern county, Hempstead, and was considered the south Arkansas candidate. Clarke's home was Helena in Phillips County. Because of Clarke's influence in eastern Arkansas, the alliance helped extend the Davis organization's control in the Delta region.[10] The inhabitants of the western two-thirds of Arkansas always looked upon the eastern area as the home of boss rule and machine politics. An alignment of the hill Democracy with the swamp Democracy made little ideological or economic sense, but from the standpoint of political power it was an intelligent move. There were several reasons why Davis chose to fall into line with old "Cotton Top" Clarke. Davis had a certain amount of respect for and perhaps even fear of Clarke. The Delta man's abrasive and volatile personality seemed to fascinate Davis. Clarke, in the *Gazette's* words, had "a tongue like a scythe blade that can cut and carve." He had once spit in the face of an opponent. He was fiercely independent and unpredictable, almost an opposite of his later Senate colleague Joseph T. Robinson, who became a notoriously loyal administration Democrat under Woodrow Wilson and Franklin D. Roosevelt. Davis could appreciate a man of Clarke's temperament. Not the least incentive for the alliance with Clarke was the latter's usefulness to Davis in encompassing the defeat of one of the great idols of the Arkansas Democracy, James K. Jones. But the main lure for the Old Guard was the opportunity to extend its power into an area where it had been politically weak. Despite the advantages of the alliance, many of the Davis men accepted the Clarke contingent into the fold with great reluctance.[11]

In attacking James K. Jones, the governor took on a senator who had earned national prominence as Bryan's campaign manager. But Jones was vulnerable on several points. He had led the national party in two defeats, suffered a serious illness, was the target of criticism from dissident Democrats across the country as well as some who were restive under his leadership in Arkansas. Jones also had a "large interest" in the round-bale cotton ginning patent. Those who operated or ventured capital in the square-bale gins had denounced the scheme as a monopoly.[12] William Jennings Bryan stood faithfully with his political lieutenant, but his kind words could not stave off defeat at the hands of Davis men and Delta colleagues.

Arkansas silver Democrats had been unhappy with James K. Jones since the mid-1890s. Despite his tack on the silver question, he appeared to many to be an old-line or regular Democrat and not a zealot for progressive reform. Charles S. Collins wrote a lengthy letter to Bryan explaining in plain terms the opposition of the more ardent silver men to Jones's leadership. Collins regretted that, in the years before 1896, Bryan had mistakenly assumed Jones to be "the representative and leader of the Arkansas Contingent" in the bimetallic movement. The silver men had chafed at the prospect of working for Jones in his senatorial contest against James P. Clarke. But to have defeated Jones in the primary would have hurt the national ticket since Jones had won acclaim as a national leader of silver Democrats. For this reason, "We turned all our forces for Jones, made a great campaign and beat Clarke." When Jones won the chairmanship of the national committee, "many of us were bitterly disappointed." The silver men in Arkansas were just at the point of convincing the Populists and other "outside parties that our wing of the Democracy" was sincere and trustworthy. Then the Jones appointment "acted as a wet blanket especially in Arkansas." The silver men knew Jones to be a "typical Democratic politician which is only another form of declaring that he has always been a constitutional compromiser, always careful to be technically correct in his postulates" but always more interested in office than in convictions.[13]

Although Jones had built a national reputation as a silver Democrat and had led the movement by silver men to capture the party machinery, he soon earned the distrust of the more ardent silver men across the country. A prominent Boston Democrat, George Fred Williams, complained to Bryan in 1897, "The Senator suggests that gold Democrats should now be treated with some degree of leniency, meaning thereby not to make any sacrifice to get them in but to receive them kindly if they recognize the inevitable and come in." The writer feared the goldbugs would return to places of power in the party. He did not believe it was time "to flirt with the gold deserters of last year." One year later the same correspondent informed Bryan that Jones was seriously considering a 22 to 1 ratio, but the Bostonian believed a compromise better than a monometallic standard.[14]

Senator Jones thought of himself as an organizer and unifier of bimetallists. For several weeks he met with Populists, Democrats, and silver Republicans in Washington during February 1898. Marion Butler, Charles Towne, and James K. Jones agreed to issue a call for solidarity to their own constituencies. In a report to Bryan concerning their messages, the chairman explained, "These all appeal to bimetallists to unite, and I hope will do good." Jones defended his conciliatory gestures toward gold men. His policy toward those who wished to return, he informed Bryan, was to inform them "that we would be very glad to have all Democrats squarely back in the fold; that the party will not deviate one hair's breadth from the line already marked out for us, and that it will be necessary either to come in without conditions, or, in my opinion, join the Republicans." But he did not believe in turning out men like Arthur P. Gorman. Those who were not totally committed to the "straight gold party" might work with the silver Democrats and eventually return to the fold.[15]

Although Bryan generally defended the chairman against all his critics, the two men occasionally had serious differences of opinion. James K. Jones joined with other prominent Democrats on July 1, 1900, to importune the Great Commoner to leave the 16 to 1 ratio statement out of the 1900 platform. Most Democrats preferred a simple affirmation of the 1896 silver plank. The next day Bryan wrote to Jones of his regret that "our conclusions are not the same." "I would prefer to see a fight, even if the advocates of simple re-affirmation won, rather than have the plank which you suggest adopted." Jones feared Bryan might identify himself with too many advanced or progressive causes. He did not want discussion of election of judges, municipal ownership, or civil service reform in the campaign. He did favor laying more stress on strengthening the power of the Interstate Commerce Commission to prevent discriminatory freight rates.[16]

William Jennings Bryan's second defeat encouraged the Arkansas enemies of James P. Clarke. In November 1900, Charles Collins wrote a lengthy letter to Bryan castigating the men at national headquarters who behaved as if the ardent silver men were "guilty of some indefinable offense or folly in advocating 16 to 1." Jones, who recently had suffered a heart attack, lost the political confidence of fellow Democrats as well as his good health. His opponents in Arkansas hoped to bring him down in the next election.[17]

After the November election, James K. Jones returned to Arkansas for a week of rest and discovered that James P. Clarke had declared himself a candidate for his Senate seat. "I hope," Jones wrote Bryan, "to be able to at least make it interesting for him before we get through with it. I don't know on what ground he proposes to set me aside, unless it is because he would like to have the place." *The Arkansas Gazette,* looking back upon the senatorial contest agreed with Jones in viewing it as a battle between personalities. "There was no issue at stake. It was a battle between men—each one a life-long Democrat and in good standing with his party."[18]

In the fall of 1901, Jeff Davis began his campaign for a second term, but he also quickly moved into the senatorial race. At the same time, he called upon the voters to elect Davis men to the state legislature. Not until January 1, 1902, did the anti-Davis faction rally behind a serious contender. They put forward the tall, aristocratic, E. W. Rector, son of a Civil War governor of Arkansas. As the author of the Rector Act, when he was Speaker of the House in 1899, he had gained attention and popularity. When Rector announced his intention to remain uninvolved in the Senate contest, Davis replied in the press, "I do not intend to keep my hands off the senatorial race." *The Arkansas Gazette* commented after Jones's defeat, "Heretofore it has been the custom for a candidate to look only to his own affair and let others do the same." But Davis made speeches and sent letters and telegrams to friends encouraging them to vote for Clarke. According to Jeff Davis, the Jones forces had spent some time searching for a candidate who could defeat him. They had tried "first one gentleman and then another" and kept setting dates for announcing their intentions. Finally, they chose Rector for the task.[19]

The Davis crusade to topple James K. Jones was primarily a tactic to win power in Arkansas. Many of the charges levied against Jones were of a personal and trivial nature. Some of Davis's accusations were probably embellished by his fertile imagination. He excelled at painting his enemies as villains and conscienceless aristocrats. Yet, like Charles Collins, Davis probably sincerely thought Jones was an old-line compromising Democrat who could posture for the times but lacked a basic determination to achieve popular reform. Davis preferred men who could "run Red River" through the halls of government and wash out the corrupt interests. Clarke, on the other hand, had taken a strong silver position early and had made potent antitrust declarations. Although he, like Jones, was an old-line Democrat and something of an aristocrat, Davis liked his volatile nature and approved his antitrust convictions.

In a January 1902 address, Jeff Davis began a bombastic assault on Chairman Jones. He accused the distinguished Democrat of taking thirty-five hundred dollars placed by the court in his hands as guardian of a female ward, and using it to pay off his own debts. Davis reached back to 1868 to dredge up an old case of brawling between Jones and his plantation superintendent in which the senator had scarred his opponent for life. Jones owed a sum of money to his plantation helper but escaped paying because he declared bankruptcy after the Civil War. "I have not brought these things forward" just to dig into a man's past, said Davis. These tales will help the voters judge "the sincerity of the acts of Senator Jones."[20]

The charge which did Jones most damage, in the view of

Charles Collins, was that he owned stock in a trust. Jones had purchased an interest in the American Cotton Round Bale Company. Because of its patent, the company had the exclusive right to manufacture machines which could compress cotton into round bales. The investors hoped farmers would convert to their equipment. Jones claimed Davis confused a patent with a trust. The governor replied by asking why the corporation had filed its incorporation papers in New Jersey, the mother of trusts. In New Jersey it cost forty-one hundred dollars to file but in Arkansas only twenty-five dollars. The reason, Davis said, was the company's desire not to subject itself to the Arkansas law requiring corporations to open their books to state inspection. Davis also condemned Jones for using his influence to "pump morphine" into a recent antitrust measure in the general assembly. "He is nominally in sympathy with the Democratic Party in its warfare on trusts," admitted Davis, "and yet we find him engaged in a trust." [21] Recalling the 1902 primary, Senator Horace Chilton believed Jones's dabbling in business and his possession of a modest Washington home had become "a fulcrum for the demagogue." Actually the senator's "business lines did not run parallel to any subject of Congressional regulation and his home was a cheap looking brick house in an unfashionable part of the city." [22]

Jeff Davis tried to lure Rector into the Jones-Clarke conflict, but his gubernatorial opponent refused to indicate any preference between Clarke and Jones. "I am not in the senatorial race," declared Rector, "it is Governor Davis's scalp I am after." In March, Davis discontinued joint debates with Rector and began meeting Senator Jones on the stump. Leaving Judge Bourland to stand in for him at the Rector debates, the governor went after bigger game. At Forrest City on March 15, Senator Jones wondered aloud why Davis had come to debate instead of Clarke. [23]

Contributing to the difficulties of Senator Jones was the opposition of Thomas C. McRae, who was just completing eighteen years of service in the Congress. McRae was not seeking reelection in 1902, but he did enter the fray to help defeat Jones. [24] *The Arkansas Gazette,* in March, published a letter from McRae to Wood Rainwater, a Morrilton merchant, advising that Jones not be reelected because of "blunders and mismanagement" in the Senate. Somewhat unfairly, McRae accused the senator of not asserting sufficient leadership in the Senate to defeat the treaty with Spain. McRae also condemned Jones's weak stand on the trusts.

The senator had introduced a mild antitrust bill but had not supported full publicity for corporation affairs. McRae thought an antitrust bill should prohibit trusts from using the mails and should place trust-made articles on the free list. On March 22, one week before the primary election, a *Gazette* reporter interviewed McRae in Washington, D.C. The congressman said he had warned the public of the trusts for twenty years and would not give up the fight now at the age of fifty. He did not believe the American Cotton Company deserved its own senator in Washington. McRae's interview revealed a further dividing of the party during the contest. The congressman condemned ex-Governor Fishback who had taken a position for Jones and had lashed out at Jeff Davis. McRae warned the public to vote only for those legislators committed to Clarke.[25]

Governor Davis's assault upon Jones rocked the foundations of the Democratic Party in Arkansas and helped crystallize further the two factions. Ex-Governor James P. Eagle, formerly a close friend and a fellow worshipper with Davis at the Second Baptist Church in Little Rock, broke with Davis because of the latter's campaign against Jones. In March 1902, Eagle told a reporter, "I think Jones should be returned to the senate of the United States." He said he had been a supporter of Davis, "but he cannot reasonably expect those who are admirers and strong supporters of Jones to continue to support him, waging, as he is, an unjust war upon Senator Jones." On one occasion at Lonoke, Eagle made a speech on Jones's behalf. Davis especially resented Eagle's campaigning for Jones while holding an appointment by Davis to the Capitol Commission. The governor asserted the right to control and dictate to those who were part of what he conceived to be his organization.[26]

In the late March primary, James P. Clarke defeated Jones in forty-three of the seventy-five county primaries. A downcast Jones returned to Washington and penned a letter to Bryan. He characterized the campaign as "in many respects the most unpleasant I was ever in." He believed unlimited sums of money had been used to accomplish his defeat, although he did not know the source of the money used against him. Then he gave a more likely explanation of his loss, "The present governor has a singular hold on the more ignorant classes of the community, and he is able to carry them wherever he chooses."[27]

On March 30, 1902, one day after the primary election, Jeff

Davis sent an abrupt message to James Eagle. The whole letter consisted of two sentences, "Come to my office at once. I send my carriage for you." When Davis learned that Eagle had not been at home, he sent another letter calling for the capitol commissioner's resignation. Eagle later asserted that he had not worked to defeat Governor Davis but had simply spoken out for James K. Jones. He demanded an explanation for his dismissal. Davis explained that political tensions would prevent them from working "harmoniously" together.[28]

Because of his assault upon James P. Eagle, Jeff Davis alienated many Baptist leaders in Arkansas and endangered his standing among the Baptists of the state. The governor had maintained a life-long association with this powerful Arkansas institution and had recently assumed the office of vice president of the Arkansas Baptist Association. But ex-Governor Eagle had become an ordained Baptist minister in 1869 and was now nearing completion of twenty-one years of service as president of the state association. Five weeks after the primary election, Eagle became president of his denomination, the Southern Baptist Convention, and twice won reelection to the post. Governor Davis had moved onto treacherous ice by dismissing Eagle.[29]

On April 7, Davis wrote to President Eagle, "I love the Baptist cause and the Baptist church . . . but feeling that those high in the authority in the denomination" had not denied vile slanders against him, he tendered his resignation as vice president. James Eagle sought further vindication by spearheading a movement to oust Jeff Davis from membership in the Second Baptist Church of Little Rock. "I am ready for trial," Davis wrote in early May. The church discipline committee summed up Davis's sins under seven headings, seven being the biblical number of perfection or completeness. Six of them charged Davis with specific instances of public drunkenness. Once at Hot Springs he lost money in a gambling establishment while drunk. On another occasion, he had been drinking and "treating some Negroes" near Benton County. None of the incidents mentioned Davis's dismissal of Eagle, but the last perhaps alluded to it: the governor had violated the church covenant and had been "grossly sinning against the purposes and principles of its organization."[30]

On May 28, one hundred members attended a business meeting at the Second Baptist Church and, with only five dissenting votes, accepted the proposal to "withdraw fellowship" from the wayward governor. The chief executive took the occasion to go fishing in Chicot County, about as far away from Little Rock as one could go without leaving the state. A number of politicians spoke in favor of the dismissal, including the man who would oppose Davis in the next gubernatorial contest, Supreme Court Judge Carroll D. Wood.[31]

Less than two weeks later, before the delegates at the state Democratic convention, Davis replied to the charges leveled against him. The dismissal "almost moves me to tears," he said, but he was thankful for his old home church at Russellville which had accepted his membership. He spoke of the Eagle men as "canting hypocrites" and of the incident as the "last thrust of the dying men of the late senatorial campaign." Since some people had come to believe the charges leveled against him, he must go before the people for vindication. He had faced a packed jury, he thought, but now, four years in advance of the election, he was announcing his intention to seek nomination to the Senate seat of James Berry in 1906. Davis had already begun using the excommunication to his advantage during his 1903–04 campaign for governor. Speaking of the incident at Little Rock, he said, "A lot of high combed roosters down there, Judge Wood among the members, turned me out of the church for political purposes without a trial."[32]

The effects of the Eagle dismissal reverberated during the session of the legislature in 1903. The Senate Committee on Public Buildings and Grounds conducted hearings into the legality of Davis's retirement of Eagle. One member of the committee declared it was "high time to call a halt on 'his majesty's' arbitrary actions." James P. Eagle appeared before the committee and averred he had been dismissed for making a speech at Lonoke in behalf of Senator James K. Jones. Governor Davis refused to come before the hostile committee. Although they failed to force reinstatement of Eagle, the majority of the committee agreed to the declaration that the dismissal was "arbitrary, irregular, unwarranted by facts and without authority of law, and that Hon. J. P. Eagle is still in law and in fact a member of the board of capitol commissioners." A minority held the governor's actions were within the authority granted by the Capitol Act of 1901.[33] The Eagle episode served to clarify the lines between Davis and anti-Davis factions.

Another conflict arose from the ashes of the senatorial contest and further divided the Democrats. Senator James K. Jones balked at conceding the finality of the decision at the primaries. Although he had signed an agreement with James P. Clarke to accept the primary verdict, he persisted in demanding at least the votes of those legislators whose districts had supported him. Jeff Davis warned the voters in a public letter that certain people intended to "wrench from the Democrats" the victory gained at the polls. In January 1903, before the legislative balloting for senator, the Jones men held a strategy caucus. Representative John H. Keel of Jackson County warned that to choose James K. Jones would nullify the primary system. The primary, he said, "is a Democratic institution, made for Democrats and operated by Democrats." Senator Creed Caldwell of Jefferson County declared that Rector's withdrawal from the 1902 race, after Davis had won the primaries and before the convention met, had established a precedent which should not be broken. Senator Hal L. Norwood of Polk County believed the Democrats were so divided that the primary decision must be accepted in order to maintain a solid front against the Republicans. At some future time, the Republican Party might hold the balance of power in the legislature and make the decision which Democratic faction to support. Despite these warnings, the Jones men determined that the senator should at least receive the votes of legislators whose districts supported him. When the roll call took place, the legislators generally accepted the verdict of their own localities and James P. Clarke won by a vote of seventy-seven to fifty.[34]

Another episode arising out of the Jones-Clarke contest indicated Davis's willingness to make a clean break between his own followers and the opposing faction. Jeptha H. Evans, a leading Democrat who had thrown his lot in with Davis in 1900, remained hostile or at best unenthusiastic about the crusade against James K. Jones. After the defeat of Jones, Evans wrote a friendly letter to Davis lauding the governor for his part in securing Clarke's victory. Davis shot off an angry reply to the Booneville politician and charged him with "dissimulation." The success of Clarke had come with no aid from Evans. "I made you chairman of the last state convention," he reminded Evans, "hoping thereby to placate you, but I find that I failed." Friends reported seeing Evans wearing a Jones button. But even worse was Evans's opposition to Jeremiah G. Wallace's candidacy for supreme court judge. Then speaking of the dividing of the ranks, he said, "You know when the Lord went through the vineyard he cut off the branches that were unfruitful, the barren, and I am doing that now." Evans charged that Davis backed various candidates in order to bring a "new crowd" into control of the party and he asserted his determination not to be in "political servitude" to Davis.[35]

In his gubernatorial campaign of 1902, Davis set out to identify his faction with the common people. His opponent was well suited to the aristocratic label Davis intended to place on him. E. W. Rector, in the words of the *Gazette,* was "a gentleman in every meaning of the term." He authored the antitrust bill which Davis had championed so vigorously as attorney general. Rector believed the redneck leader was now riding "into office on my thunder." Davis gave short shrift to Rector's antitrust achievement and spotlighted his genteel origins. All across Arkansas, he repeated a tale about Rector rebuking a schoolmaster for failing his son. The aristocrat had denounced him for giving his son no more consideration than that given "to the children of common woodhaulers." Rector complained of some elaboration upon the story. He had not used the phrase "woodhaulers," but he admitted the essentials of the incident, including the slur upon the laboring classes. Nothing could extract the distinguished candidate from his predicament. He might speak of his early life "cutting and hauling wood and rails, building rail fences, driving oxen," and of being "always the champion of the right of the poorer classes," but to no avail. At one point, Rector suggested that Davis had become something of an aristocrat. The governor had purchased an electric fan for his executive office, Rector noted, instead of using a palm branch as common people did.[36]

Davis raised many of his favorite issues—the Capitol, antitrust legislation, and penitentiary reform—but often the campaign sank to the ridiculous. Rector accused Davis of anointing his body with Wizard Oil to disguise his drunkenness. According to some contemporaries, Davis had, on at least one occasion, scarcely managed to steady himself on a chair before he entered a debate. Such rumors did not endear him to evangelicals and prohibitionists. But he assured any who doubted his orthodoxy, "I'm a hardshell Baptist, . . . and I believe in foot washing, saving your sweet potatoes and paying your honest debts." The masses enjoyed the spectacle, and, on one occasion, at the Capital Theatre in Little Rock, the crowd became so enthusiastic and boisterous that the two debaters could not always be heard. By March the *Hazen Oracle* found "the outpour of hot language . . . monotonous." In the primary elections Rector won only five counties: Sebastian, Miller, Garland, Arkansas, and Lee.[37]

The temperance movement was gaining strength in Arkansas by 1902, but not sufficiently to deny Jeff Davis the election. Arkansas had thirty dry counties in 1900, and within ten years the number increased to sixty-three (out of seventy-five counties in the state). Rector allied himself with the prohibitionists but was unable to sufficiently mobilize the anti-liquor vote. But the Arkansas Anti-Saloon League, founded in 1899, would be a more potent force in future Arkansas elections. Another significant factor in the 1902 election was Davis's improved showing in "very isolated" farming districts. The Populist areas were coming more clearly into the Davis camp by 1902.[38]

The divisiveness of the 1902 campaign helped draw the battle lines for a major confrontation of factions during the 1903 general assembly. The Davis men fought the capitol construction plan as devised by the legislature, struggled to enact their leader's antitrust views into law, condemned the purchase of the Cummins Prison Farm by the Penitentiary Board, and moved to head off a drive to impeach the governor.

Davis maneuvered to secure control of the 1903 legislature as soon as it convened. In line with his strategy to win support in eastern Arkansas, he threw his support behind John Ike Moore of Helena for Speaker of the house. Representative Edwin J. Kerwin of Jefferson County condemned "the efforts of Governor Davis to dictate the speakership." There were, he believed, "many influences that should have been kept out of this contest." The contest was not simply a struggle between factions but was also a sectional fight. Eastern and southern Arkansas had their own candidates, while the rest of the state divided their support. Davis's choice prevailed by a vote of seventy-four to twenty-six. The heavy support given to Moore was not an indication of Davis's strength in the legislature. On other key issues, the redneck leader had a smaller group of supporters.[39]

One of the major issues of 1903 involved the perennial problems of the Arkansas penitentiary. Like Robert Love Taylor of Tennessee and James K. Vardaman of Mississippi, Davis led a crusade to correct the unsanitary and dehumanizing conditions of the prisons and to abolish convict leasing. Following Mississippi's lead, Arkansas formally and legally abolished convict leasing during the early 1890s, but, like Mississippi, Arkansas failed to terminate contract leases until the early twentieth century. When men like James K. Vardaman and Jeff Davis championed the abolition of leasing, they adopted a cause that had been dear to the hearts of agrarians. The Populists of the South had vigorously denounced leasing. The fight against the practice antagonized lowland planters who profited from the use of convict labor on their Delta plantations, and both Vardaman and Davis met strong resistance to their efforts to end the evil. Vardaman secured legislation which brought the practice to an end. He also reorganized Mississippi's penitentiary board to increase the power of the superintendent. Davis failed both in his attempt to abolish leasing and to reorganize the penitentiary organization. His efforts had some value in keeping the reform movement before the public so that a later administration could achieve the desired reforms. The more immediate results of Davis's effort was the bitter enmity of those politicians whom he referred to as the "penitentiary ring."[40]

No issue more clearly separated Davis men from their opponents than the penitentiary investigation of 1903. Jeff Davis carried on a running battle with the other members of the Penitentiary Board that erupted into a major investigation in the house of representatives. The anti-Davis men planned the probe as a prelude to an impeachment of the governor. After a special session of the general assembly in 1897 had authorized establishing a prison farm, the state officers began seeking a suitable farm where the state might employ its convicts. A state-owned farm would, they hoped, provide the prisoners with a means to supply their own living and end the acknowledged evil of convict leasing. Mississippi had successfully removed many of its prisoners from private farms to a state-owned plantation. In 1901 Davis vetoed a measure to authorize a joint legislative committee to receive bids on a farm. One year later, the Penitentiary Board, to the governor's chagrin, contracted for purchase of the Cummins farm. Governor Davis, in protest, discontinued meeting with the board which included himself, the attorney general, the secretary of state, the commissioner of agriculture, and the auditor serving as chairman. He accused the board of acting hastily, without proper examination of the farm. The land was swampy, covered with Johnson grass, and could not support the convicts. Because of these charges, anti-Davis men set out to vindicate the board in a legislative investigation and to prepare counter charges that might lead toward impeachment of the governor.[41]

Attorney General George Murphy, a member of the board and a hot-tempered Irishman, led the movement to impeach Davis. Xenophon O. Pindall, who became a staunch anti-Davis leader, supported a plan to call the governor and attorney general before the 1903 legislature for an open airing of differences. Pindall thought the debate would end in triumph for the attorney general, but the house of representatives, wishing to avoid an embarrassing scene, rejected the proposal. In mid-February, George Muphy hired the Capital Theatre in Little Rock and put on his own extravaganza. Admission was by ticket only and early on the day of the festivities, the box office reported all tickets sold. The meeting, attended by many legislators, was "anti-Davis through and through." George Murphy shared the platform with Secretary of State John Crockett, Auditor T. C. Monroe and twenty other supporters. The fiery Irishman lashed into the governor's record amidst a volley of cheers from the Little Rock audience. The governor had made "libelous charges and insinuations" against state officials. "If they are true they ought to be impeached." If the governor spoke falsely, "justice and right cry out for his own impeachment."[42]

In a two-hour speech, the attorney general outlined the history of the penitentiary dispute. When Davis held the office of attorney general, the board considered twelve different farms for possible purchase, but Davis pressed hard for purchase of the Beakley place. The farm had impressed the attorney general during a visit there to inspect the use of leased convict labor. Davis himself, Murphy reminded his auditors, had admitted the whole Beakley farm was submerged during certain periods of the year; yet, he resented the board's rejection of his recommendation. Later he became interested in the farm of a well-known Republican leader, Louis Altheimer. As governor, he induced the board at one of its meetings to accept a resolution restricting consideration to the Beakley and Altheimer places only. But in September 1902, at a meeting which Davis did not attend, the board rescinded the earlier resolution. In defiance of the governor, the board then purchased the Cummins farm. Davis's determination to dictate to the board and his failure to overawe them, according to Murphy, led to the recent insinuations and denunciations. Finally, Murphy praised the "glorious one-legged old soldier," James Berry, and predicted the veteran senator would trounce Davis in the 1906 senatorial contest.[43]

While the house prepared to investigate the allegations of Davis and the rebuttals of Murphy, the senate also formed separate ranks over the penitentiary issue. Senator Benjamin McFerrin introduced a bill, bearing his name, which would have placed the administration of the penitentiary under the Board of Charities. George Murphy had noted in his Capital Theatre speech that Davis controlled the charities board and now desired to control penitentiary appointments. Senator James E. Wood, an old arch-enemy of Davis from eastern Arkansas, led the attack on the bill in a lengthy speech. He recognized it as an attempt to secure dictatorial control. Joining with Wood, George Sengel of Sebastian County declared the McFerrin Bill imperialistic and undemocratic. Senator Oliver N. Killough from eastern Arkansas, who was president of the St. Francis Levee Board, which Davis was making a part of his machine, straddled the issue. The senator was one of those from the Delta who, having been wooed by the governor, now began to waver. He stated his desire to remain amicable with both parties in the dispute. He was Davis's friend, but he admitted to a small row with the chief. Davis had attacked him "for harpooning his anti-trust bill, but it had not reached the stage of 'pistols and coffee for two.'"[44]

Another Davis man of some importance in the senate was Hal L. Norwood. He condemned Murphy's hiring of a hall for a crusade against the governor as "unprecedented." For one month he had listened quietly in the senate as the members had "nagged at, piked at" Governor Davis. Senator Norwood later won election, in 1908, to the office of attorney general and served two terms.[45]

In the house of representatives, Edward M. Merriman of Pulaski County proposed that the Ways and Means Committee, which he chaired, be authorized to investigate charges made by Davis and by the board members against one another. Actually the committee had already launched its probe unofficially, but it now sought authorization for a formal inquiry. Merriman's anti-Davis stance also became apparent when he authored and engineered through the general assembly a new capitol building program. The proposal for an inquiry won easy approval and hearings began on February 18 and lasted until March 23. The meetings were held in the evening in the supreme court chambers.[46]

George Murphy appeared before the Ways and Means Committee and defended the purchase of the Cummins farm. William W. Whitley of Polk County, the one zealous Davis man harbored by the committee, questioned Murphy about the condition of the farm. The attorney general asserted Johnson grass covered only nine hundred of the ten thousand acres and he had seen "fine cotton growing right up to the edge of the Johnson grass." He accused the governor of pressuring Auditor T. C. Monroe to join with him in forcing purchase of the Altheimer farm. Davis had threatened to support a candidate in opposition to Monroe in the next election if the latter did not follow Davis's lead on the farm purchase issue. Murphy also resented Davis's attempt "to force his will right square upon us, right or wrong, and without consideration, and regardless of their feelings if they refused to agree or side with him."[47]

After hearing almost endless testimony, charges, and countercharges, the committee finally drafted four different reports to the house of representatives. The first report, also called the majority report, was signed by Merriman and other anti-Davis committeemen. It failed to secure approval by the house in a very tight contest, forty-three ayes to forty-four noes. This first vote, more than those that followed on other reports, gave an indication of the division between Davis and anti-Davis forces in the lower house. The report defended Penitentiary Superintendent Reese Hogins for supplying convicts to the Arkansas Brick and Manufacturing Company in accordance with the contract which Davis had declared void. The superintendent had not acted on his own initiative but in line with a decision of the Arkansas Supreme Court upholding the Dickinson Convict Leasing contract. The real reason for Davis's tirade against Hogins was the latter's refusal to place Davis's incompetent brother-in-law in a place of high responsibility in the prison administration. Some years later Davis's secretary, Charles Jacobson, published a letter from Jeff Davis to Reese Hogins which evidenced the governor's bitterness at the superintendent's refusal to hire Davis's relative.[48]

According to the majority report, Davis presented Altheimer's asking price to the board as eighty-seven thousand five hundred dollars when he knew Altheimer had lowered the price of his farm to seventy-five thousand dollars. The testimony of the Penitentiary Board members confirmed that Davis had given them notice of the higher price while Louis Altheimer testified he had given Davis the lower figure. The report, without really saying it, insinuated that Davis somehow intended to pocket the difference. The charge was serious but was not cast in plain terms and could not have been proved. The report also denied charges that the Cummins farm had been the scene of brutal incidents. According to Davis, one James Rector, a convict, had died as a result of a beating administered at the penitentiary. The majority of the committee agreed that Rector's "emaciated condition resulted from non-assimilation of food." They accepted the penitentiary physician's testimony as sufficient evidence for the cause of Rector's death.[49]

The majority report also presented analyses of several trivial charges made by the state officers against Davis. Supposedly, the governor had received free coal from a company which had also been granted the privilege of supplying coal for the charities board; he had taken a free ride on a special railroad car with friends on a hunting trip; he accepted payment of thirty-five dollars from his contingency fund as well as a fee from the University of Arkansas to pay for travelling expenses to make an address at Fayetteville.[50]

After the Davis men had scuttled the majority report, the lower house turned to consideration of report number three. Those who signed the third report declared the Penitentiary Board free of any "corruption" and found no evidence to indicate "culpability, misconduct or criminality" on the part of Davis. In one sense, the report offered a compromise, but it did not provide the anti-Davis forces with an indictment of the governor as a basis for impeachment. Xenophon Pindall spoke for the disappointed anti-Davis men when he intoned against a "whitewash." The majority of the committee in the first report, he observed, had found Davis "guilty of misconduct in office." In another close vote, forty to forty-four, the lower house rejected the third report.

Report number two, on the other hand, received the support of the legislators by a sixty-six to twenty vote. The second, or minority, report seemed a more acceptable compromise because it declined to offer any judgment on the charges. Like the third report, it made no allegations, but in contrast to report number three, it did not absolve any party from blame. The two committee members who signed it believed the task of the Ways and Means Committee consisted only of receiving testimony and presenting the accumulated evidence to the house of representatives so that the whole body could interpret the evidence for itself. The report, in effect, sidestepped the controversy. Having broken a few lances without a decision, the members found the minority report a convenient way to end the spectacle.[51]

William Whitley, Davis's disciple, signed the third report which avoided making serious charges, but he also prepared a fourth report signed only by himself. He wished to express certain objections to accusations and statements made during the investigation. Whitley could not see how it was possible to examine "judiciously" the ten thousand acre Cummins farm in ten or twelve hours; he could not accept the suggestion that purchase of a one-hundred-and-forty-thousand-dollar property, after a one-day examination, could be characterized as "prudence and caution." He condemned the bestiality of the penitentiary system. Brutality had been common before the Rector incident and had continued unchecked afterward. The prisoner overseers served unpalatable food and whipped inmates "on the naked back." Whitley also presented a defense of the peccadilloes charged against Davis. But his report never came to a vote, partly because the lower house had voted favorably on the minority report before Whitley could call for consideration of his views. One of the anti-Davis legislators accused Whitley of being a Populist who had donned Democratic garb. The Davis man denied Populistic origins but admitted to having led the movement in Lonoke County against Grover Cleveland. During the battles in the Ways and Means Committee, the anti-Davis men had labeled Whitley "the governor's attorney."[52]

Many of the same legislators who supported Davis in the penitentiary struggle also stood by him in the 1903 antitrust debate. During his three terms as governor, Davis fought for passage of an antitrust act to outlaw the operation of corporations in Arkansas that had entered into price-fixing arrangements outside the state's boundaries. Davis's secretary copied, almost verbatim, the Missouri antitrust law, and Senator David L. King sponsored the measure in the state senate. The revision was necessary, Davis said, because the supreme court had "cut the very life and vitals out of the Rector Anti-Trust Law and left its dead and mangled corpse lying prostrate at the very door of the Temple of Justice." In his 1901 message to the assembly, Davis had admonished the legislators to enact a law with his "extra-territorial" interpretation. He also advised that the law compel corporation officers to appear with their books and records at a place designated by the attorney general. It was impractical, he believed, for state officers to travel to a company's home office to secure testimony.[53]

In 1901 and again in 1903, the Senate Judiciary Committee, in response to pressure from the business community, tried to pigeonhole the King Anti-Trust Bill. Sebastian County's conservative Senator George Sengel boasted during the 1903 legislative debate that he had mustered the business forces against the old Rector Act. He campaigned against the antitrust act in the primary, and his opponent had favored the law, yet Sengel won the Fort Smith area voters to his side. "I repeat," he said, "that I am here standing for the commercial interests of our great state." Sengel feared the antitrust law would damage the manufacturing and commercial progress of Fort Smith. Jobs would be lost and credit destroyed. The *Gazette* reported that the large insurance companies of Arkansas had sent letters to their agents urging them to defeat the King Bill. The Little Rock Board of Trade sent a statement to the two Pulaski County senators: "Gentlemen, This business community is considerably exercised on account of the danger threatened their business interests by the proposed law." The board predicted destruction of credit and "a chaotic condition in commercial circles, as it will be impossible to secure insurance." The Commercial Club of Texarkana passed resolutions condemning the King Bill. John Gould Fletcher, president of the German National Bank and recently one of the gubernatorial candidates opposing Davis, told a large gathering of business leaders in Little Rock that the "whole thing was gotten up to make somebody a congressman, or senator, or a governor."[54]

State Senator Hal L. Norwood, who supported Davis in the penitentiary case, also fought on the Davis side in the antitrust debate. To pass King's Bill, he said, would "bring gladness to the cottages and cabins of the poor and lowly," but he sensed a mood of retreat which "would bring gladness to the palaces of the rich." Those who opposed censure of Governor Davis in the penitentiary struggle were usually the same men who had struggled to enact the King Bill.[55]

But the King Bill did not become law during the 1903 general assembly. Although the Senate passed the measure and though an identical bill except for title passed the house of representatives, the two bodies never managed to agree to an absolutely identical bill. The obstructionists succeeded in their attempt to destroy the measure in a maze of parliamentary maneuvering. The house had its Keel Bill and the senate its King Bill, almost precisely the same. During the latter half of April, Senator David L. King tried to unravel the snarl. After an aroused senate had just repassed the Merriman Capitol Act over Davis's veto, King rose to call up consideration of his antitrust measure again. The senate had become accustomed to his efforts and "there were cries of 'I object! I object!' from all parts of the chamber mingled with laughter." The chair ruled Senator King out of order. Over and over again King rose during the next two weeks to call for consideration of the bill, but the senate refused to revive the question.[56]

The capitol construction issue also became a test of loyalty or opposition to the governor. The anti–Davis men investigated the dismissal of Capitol Commissioner Eagle and denounced the action as illegal. They once again passed a capitol measure, the Merriman Bill, to revive the lagging construction program. When the governor vetoed the Merriman Bill, the most devout Davis men held firm, but the 1903 assembly was Davis's most hostile legislature, and the bill easily passed over his veto. The Merriman Bill provided for a new Capitol Commission staffed by members elected by the general assembly. Davis refused to recognize the authority of the new legislative commission, and for half a year the state had two capitol commissions. Finally, the attorney general, George Murphy, won a case in the Arkansas Supreme Court which relieved the governor's commission of its "shadowy existence."[57]

In late 1903, when Davis began his campaign for reelection to a third term as governor, he found the antitrust issue especially useful. The governor told a crowd that his opponent, Judge Carroll D. Wood, had lobbied against the bill. "He was as busy as a cranberry merchant: he kept the path from his room to the Senate chamber as slick as an otter slide going in and out." Davis warned the people not to be deceived into believing the statute could be understood only by trained lawyers like Wood. Even "the humblest, the most uneducated sun-burned son of toil can understand the plain wording of this plain statute."[58]

During the winter of 1903–04, the gubernatorial campaign continued the process of dividing the Democratic Party. The anti-Davis men flocked to the various Carroll D. Wood Clubs in the state. At a January meeting of the Little Rock chapter, Judge F. T. Vaughn, a Wood man, announced to a cheering crowd that he intended to oppose any county candidate who allied with Davis. "I will not support a single man who is for Jeff Davis." One of those present at the meeting was an old Cleveland Democrat, Joseph W. House. The goldbug leader, in a vitriolic speech, derided the governor for bringing more shame to Arkansas than any other hundred men. Senator James Berry joined hands with the Wood people since a Davis defeat would improve Berry's position in the senatorial campaign against Davis in 1906.[59]

In the 1904 primary, Jeff Davis faced one of his stiffest challenges. The Wood campaign was the best organized and financed opposition force that Davis had encountered. The Davis faction no longer could enjoy the distinction of having the only well-organized political force in the state. Davis suffered a dimunition of his factional strength as some of his followers joined the Wood forces. One of the more significant defections was that of Congressman Joseph T. Robinson. During the course of the contest the two factions in the Democratic Party became more sharply distinguishable than ever before. From the highest state offices to the lowliest local contests, every candidate could be identified as either a Davis or Wood man.[60]

Davis won decisively, carrying fifty-eight of the seventy-five counties. He polled 71,502 votes to Wood's 52,216 in the primary election. The election demonstrated a weakening of Davis's strength in eastern Arkansas because of Clarke's decision to remain neutral in the 1904 election. The urban–rural conflict which Davis had fostered bore fruit in the 1904 contest. Little Rock, which had given Davis 52 percent of its vote in 1902, now only gave him 37.3 percent. Raymond Arsenault has found that precincts that had cast at least 40 percent or more of their votes for a Populist governor in either 1892 or 1896 cast 75.2 percent of their votes for Davis in 1904. These Populist precincts had given Davis 78.1 percent of their votes in 1902.[61]

Despite Wood's challenge, the Davis men took control of the convention machinery, secured Davis a place as chief of the delegation to the national convention, forced approval of his primary proposal, and dictated the choice of members for the new state central committee. Joseph W. House led the fight on the floor of the convention to seat an anti-Davis Independence County delegation which had been recommended by the retiring state central committee. House's proposal lost by a 191 to 251 vote. The credentials committee had recommended that the whole convention decide whether to seat the Davis or the anti–Davis Independence County delegation. After House failed to get approval from the convention for seating both Independence County delegations, he denounced the appointment of a credentials committee consisting of fifteen Davis men. A number of leading members of the Old Guard served on the credentials committee. Among them were William Whitley, Jephtha H. Evans, and George Washington Hays who later served as governor. The convention rejected the anti–Davis delegation and seated Davis's Independence County delegates.[62]

Davis pushed through the 1904 convention a primary proposal to insure his election to the Senate two years hence. The resolution declared "That the Democratic nominee for the next United States Senator shall be selected by the popular vote in the same manner that state officers are chosen." The candidate receiving a majority of votes cast in the state "shall by the state convention be declared the Democratic nominee and the same shall be binding on all Democratic members of the legislature." This arrangement eliminated the possibility of a Davis victory at the primary election but a defeat in the convention or legislature. James K. Jones had been reluctant to surrender his claims after the 1902 primary defeat, and in the 1904 gubernatorial election, James Berry took a Carroll D. Wood delegation to the convention from Benton County, even though the county had given a majority of its votes to Davis.[63]

Although Davis won extensive support in the 1904 convention, he did not have his own way at every point. Robert L. Rogers won the nomination for attorney general over Davis's close friend, Judge Bourland. In his acceptance speech, Rogers told the convention he intended to wear only one yoke, that of his party. The convention voting pattern, as indicated by voting on the Independence County question, also showed a strong anti–Davis minority. Support for the two factions was scattered fairly well across the state. But Davis received the least delegate support from the Delta region. Only two of the seven counties bordering the Mississippi River voted with him, and within the St. Francis Levee District (in northeastern Arkansas) there were thirty-six anti-Davis votes to ten for the governor. He also garnered more votes from his home congressional district (the fifth district) than from other areas of the state.[64]

In his 1905 inaugural speech before the legislature, Davis chided those who had "knifed" the King Anti-Trust Bill. "Look about this General Assembly," he suggested, "Ah, Gentlemen, there are strange faces here today." Despite the presence of many anti-Davis men, the 1905 legislature passed the King Bill in short measure. The bill had little real effect because the attorney generals did not attempt to enforce it, and in 1911 the legislature removed some of the controversial sections of the act.[65]

Jeff Davis began his Senate campaign in July 1905, but he soon found a single contest too confining, and he set out to defeat Robert L. Rogers' bid for the governorship. He accused Rogers, who held the office of attorney general during Davis's third term, of insufficient dedication to the antitrust cause. He had not vigorously prosecuted the corporations. The governor turned to popular Congressman "Bass" Little from southern Arkansas to help defeat Rogers. At one point, Little wished to leave the race because of nervous exhaustion and begged to be relieved. But Davis and his lieutenants kept Little's hesitation to themselves and pressed him to continue the race. Samuel Q. Sevier of Union County, one of the candidates for governor in 1906, explained why he gave up the struggle after two months of campaigning. "My defeat was a foregone conclusion from the day" two lesser candidates dropped out, and the "Davis strength combined on Little and the anti-Davis vote was driven to Rogers."[66]

Although others saw the anti-Davis bloc moving toward Rogers, the latter denied ties with any group. He refused to identify himself with Davis or Berry in the senatorial contest, but it was clear that he despised Davis and had the support of those who shared his views. In a speech at Lake City, printed for distribution, he entitled one section, "Running On His Own Hook." "I am advocating no other man for office. Must you," he asked, "follow the dictation of nay one man as to how you shall vote for governor?" He did not care for whom men voted so long as they cast a vote for him. Probably many voters associated John Little with the redneck hero and voted for the two men. The victory of Little over a field of several candidates suggests the importance of the alliance. Yet, some voters refused to align themselves in strict factional groups like their political leaders. One Jeff Davis man in Lonoke County, Joe P. Eagle, expressed surprise that so many in his area supported both Davis and Rogers.[67]

"Bass" Little had replaced Clifton R. Breckinridge of Pine Bluff, a prominent goldbug in the 1894 congressional race, and he became an ardent proponent of silver at the state and national level. The *Gazette* called him the "Great Commoner" because he wore plain clothes and mixed with the average man without affectation. His support for several Davis crusades indicates a certain ideological similarity between himself and the redneck leader. Little favored placing the penitentiary under the control of an independent board appointed by the governor (he did not insist upon appointment by the governor if the legislature desired otherwise). He agreed with Davis in favoring local option rather than statewide prohibition measures, and he had long advocated that fellow-servant legislation be revised to give effective protection to employees. Like Davis, he denounced the legislative bribery and corruption that had come to light during Davis's last term in office, and he called for strong legislation to restrict lobbying. Charles H. Brough, a political science professor at the University of Arkansas who became Arkansas's leading progressive governor (1917–21), threw his support to John Little.[68]

Robert L. Rogers also favored revision of the fellow-servant law and opposed convict leasing, but unlike his opponent, he thought the penitentiary had been managed efficiently and needed no basic change in administration. He had brought suit against the harvester trust and other companies and promised to continue the suit, but he lashed out at the King Anti-Trust Act which Davis pressed upon the legislature. "This illegitimate anti-trust law, evidently illegitimate, because it has so many 'daddies,' has been threshed out so often that it is nearly threshed to death." Rector, Davis, David L. King, and others claimed to be its "daddy," but it was really, he believed "an adopted child, . . . from the state of Missouri."[69]

Although Rogers claimed to be running only in opposition to John Little, he gave much space in his Lake City speech to an attack upon the Davis-Clarke combination. He accused the governor of participating with Clarke in an unholy settlement with the railroads. The railroads operating in Arkansas had joined forces to seek in the courts an order restraining the Railroad Assessing Board from imposing upon them what they considered excessive rates of taxation. Jeff Davis held membership on the board in September 1904, when it hired Senator James P. Clarke to negotiate a settlement with the railroads. In the famous "railroad tax compromise," Clarke agreed to accept from the railroads a payment for the state of $334,794 instead of the original tax claim of $586,567. When he became attorney general, Rogers denounced the surrender of a quarter of a million dollars to the railroads. As a candidate for governor in 1906, he implied that Clarke's thirty-thousand-dollar fee, paid by the railroads, seemed more like a bribe than a legitimate legal payment for services. Clarke had put less than a week of serious effort into the negotiations, Rogers observed. He did not think Clarke would have entered into the compromise with the railroads if they had not agreed to pay him the legal fee of thirty thousand dollars.[70]

In a speech at Bentonville, the county seat of James Berry's home county, Jeff Davis defended his role in the tax compromise. He reminded the voters that railroad assessments had increased during his tenure. The assessment board had not compromised away a promissory note or a bond which would have been a firm claim, but an assessment which had been stymied in the courts by railroad initiative. Because of litigation, none of the taxes were being paid for several years. Davis believed the settlement was "the best piece of financiering that has ever been accomplished for Arkansas in the matter of assessing railroad property." Senator Clarke also made an effort to defend his reputation in a lengthy statement, "To the People of Arkansas," in January 1906.[71]

The contest between Berry and Davis did not reveal major ideological differences. The two men made an early commitment to a greater measure of democracy in the American government. Since the late 1880s, Berry had championed the direct election of senators. Arthur Wallace Dunn remembered him as a senator who always cast his influence on the side of democratic measures. Senator George F. Hoar often told Berry that the primary system and direct election of senators would lower the quality of men chosen to the Senate. But Berry believed the people had the ability to choose men of integrity. It was only after the 1906 primary election that James Berry confessed to Dunn that he had been mistaken in his faith in the people.[72]

In addition to the direct election of senators, James Berry supported a federal income tax and a lower tariff.[73] But his democratic progressivism did not reach to the heights of Bryanism. During 1907 and 1908, Bryan expressed support for government ownership of railroads and the initiative and referendum in a Southern tour. James Berry told the perennial candidate that championing such visionary causes was certain to destroy any chance for electing a Democratic president. He asked the Nebraskan to take up issues that could lead to the White House.[74]

If the contest between Davis and Berry resembled a power struggle more than a clash of philosophies, there were at least some differences in the image the two men presented to the voters. Davis represented a more ebullient and youthful Democracy, while Berry suggested to the voter the image of an older leadership which had lost touch with the people of the hills and villages of Arkansas. To the fellow up the fork of the creek, Davis seemed a more likely man to smash the trusts and drive the interests from the halls of government.[75]

Davis charged Berry with obstructing the right of the people to make their own choice of senator in the primary. The senator, according to the governor, had left the 1904 Hot Springs Convention when the resolution came up to declare the winner of the 1906 senatorial primary the Democratic nominee. Berry denied he had left the hall to squelch a "blanket primary." He had left for home because one of his children had had a serious accident. Berry also labored to explain his vote against the Hatch Act to place a tax on dealing in futures. Like Davis, he opposed gambling on Southern crops, but he did not believe in taxation as a means of regulation. He had favored the George Bill which made it a felony to engage in such speculation.[76]

In early April 1906, as the primary returns filtered into Little Rock, it became apparent that Davis had won another victory. Although his votes were fairly well scattered across the state, some weakness was still apparent in eastern Arkansas. He did not win a single county bordering the Mississippi River. Also, the western tier of counties and those in the southern part of the state did not hold as firmly as in the past for Davis. The governor's strongest bastion lay mainly to the north of Pulaski County, and to some extent on the county's eastern and western borders. This urban county, which supported Berry, lay like an island in a sea of Davis supporters. Davis carried fifty-one of the seventy-five counties. In the popular vote he won by a generous margin of almost fourteen thousand votes. The committee canvassing the vote for the Democratic State Convention gave the total vote as 68,469 to 54,688.[77]

When the result of the primary became clear, Col. J. C. Yancey, a prominent planter, who had led the anti-Davis delegation from Independence County at the 1904 State Democratic Convention, put his property up for sale, and announced plans to leave the state. "The most lawless and vicious elements in the state," he complained with some exaggeration, "are in control of the entire political machinery." It seemed apparent that Davis would now control Governor John Little's administration. *The Record* (Russellville) took notice of Governor Little's appointment of John H. Page as his private secretary. Mr. Page had served as secretary of the Davis-dominated state central committee for several years. He had also been secretary of the Board of Charities which Davis made an essential part of his organization. The appointment, said the *Record,* "would seem to indicate that the present administration will dominate the incoming one."[78]

The victory of Jeff Davis in the senatorial primary and of John "Bass" Little in the gubernatorial contest of 1906 demonstrated the cohesiveness and continuing strength of the Old Guard. After James Berry lost the race for the Senate, he explained the defeat as a result of Davis's coalition with the James P. Clarke forces and John Little's supporters. *The Arkansas Gazette* theorized that Clarke wished to continue the alliance of his eastern Arkansas supporters with the Davis men because if that combination could win in 1906, it might help secure reelection for Clarke in 1908. Senator Clarke also entered the campaign against Berry, in part, because of his own personal antipathy toward the old veteran. The two men kept "on different sides of the street at Washington." In nearly every county of Arkansas, Davis had an organization working for his candidates. For three terms, almost six years, he had been building up his support throughout the state.[79] By 1906 the Davis organization had reached the high-water mark of power.

The Democratic Party of Arkansas in the first years of the twentieth century seethed with unrest, but out of the turmoil emerged two factions which gave the voters a colorful political spectacle and, at times, a choice at the primary elections. If the differences between candidates appear to later observers to be more rhetorical than substantial, they seemed significant to those of an earlier day. The voters sought to turn out the old crowd and bring in a new team dedicated to destruction of the trusts and interests. While Democratic divisions afforded the voters a more democratic choice, Republican divisiveness severely crippled the opposition party. The two factions in the Democratic Party did not offer the potential for a well-organized, permanent, and effective alternative to the two-party system, and the divisions in the Republican Party prevented it from fulfilling its role as challenger to the party in power.

7

The Republican Party in a
One-Party State

The dominance of the Democratic Party in state politics forced Arkansas Republicans to turn their attention chiefly to federal patronage and presidential politics. The Republicans maintained a continuing organization in most counties and ran candidates for statewide offices in many elections at the turn of the century, but their cause seemed nearly hopeless at the state level. Yet the opposition party was hardly a nonentity. Harmon L. Remmel, the number-two man in the state Republican machine wrote to Powell Clayton, the number-one Republican of Arkansas, to express his resentment "of the unjust slur that" the party "is simply organized for the distribution of patronage." He reminded his chief that the party had carried one of the congressional districts in a recent gubernatorial election, almost elected a congressman in one district, and had covered the state during each campaign "with an array of competent speakers."[1] Despite Remmel's optimism, no Republican sat in the executive chair at Little Rock from Reconstruction until the 1960s. Nor have the Republicans, since the 1880s, been able to send more than a handful of legislators to the general assembly.

Harmon L. Remmel typified the Little Rock coterie that gave direction to the Arkansas Republican Party. He served as an agent of the New York Mutual Life Insurance Company and was also a banker. Remmel was president of two Little Rock banks, the Bankers Trust Company and the Mercantile Trust Company. He was a highly respected financier, although one of his most important financial efforts ended in embarrassment. Remmel tried to promote the Arkansas Anthracite Coal Company, which aimed to develop a railroad system and mining operation in the Scranton area (east of Fort Smith), but he overestimated the value of the coal fields acquired by his company. Eventually his coal and railroad effort suffered financial collapse. But Remmel was a man who experienced success more often than failure, especially in politics. He frequently held the chairmanship of the Republican State Central Committee. He ran as his party's candidate for governor in 1894, 1896, and 1900. Like many of the party leaders, Remmel secured some of the most desirable patronage positions for himself. From 1897 to 1902, he held the office of Collector of Internal Revenue, and later he became United States Marshal for eastern Arkansas. A crafty, devious man, he sought continually to ingratiate himself with Powell Clayton and to undermine rivals.[2]

The Republican Party in Arkansas reflected a pattern seen in many states of the deep South. It had the same focus on patronage and the presidential nominating process. The party also divided into lily-white and black-and-tan factions.[3] The divisions further weakened the party's effectiveness as an opposition voice. The blacks began showing signs of an independent spirit within the Republican Party as early as the 1876 state convention. They surprised the imperious Powell Clayton by nominating a Negro, Edward A. Fulton, to be temporary chairman. Clayton had expected smooth sailing for his own nominee, D. P. Upham. Although Clayton's nominee did win, blacks demonstrated that they would not passively accept white domination of the party.[4]

The dissension between blacks and whites in the Arkansas Republican Party was evident again in April 1888, when black representatives again nominated a candidate for temporary chairman of the state convention. They put forward J. A. Simmons of Drew County, but the convention relected Judge Jacob A. Trieber, a white man, to be temporary chairman. Two months later the rift widened when Pulaski County Republicans formed a whites-only organization that later became known as "The Lincoln Club."[5] Despite these "lily-white" episodes, blacks continued to play a role in the party organization. Their loyalty to the Powell Clayton organization helped ensure them a place in the Arkansas Republican Party. Blacks helped Clayton prevent white insurgents from gaining power in the party. For their help, Clayton rewarded them with at least a small share of the patronage. Both Clayton and Remmel identified with the "black and tans." Remmel did not weaken his opposition to the "lily-whites" until they came to dominate the party after 1913.[6]

During the 1890s, the tension between the lily-white and black-and-tan factions increased. In Pulaski County in 1896 racial dissension made it impossible to field a slate of candidates for county offices. Blacks refused to go along with an all-white slate. The lily-whites preferred and got no ticket at all rather than acquiesce to an integrated slate. As disfranchisement progressed, white Republicans concluded that the black man was of no further benefit to the party.[7] Since Republicans were already at a great disadvantage in their competition with the white supremacist Democratic Party, it seemed that non-voting blacks would be an obstacle to future party victories. After 1894 the blacks no longer held any of the higher elective offices in Arkansas. The poll tax had helped to curb black political influence in the Republican Party.[8] Black dissatisfaction reached a peak in 1897 when a white man, W.S. Holt, became secretary of the state central committee. Holt replaced a black, Judge Mifflin W. Gibbs. Blacks had controlled the position before and believed it should have gone to a black again.[9]

In 1899 the Republican organization failed to secure the appointment of a Negro physician to the Pension Board. The disappointment helped fuel the growing discontent of blacks with the Republican leadership. Although Clayton and Remmel supported Dr. G. W. Hayman and secured the approval of the state central committee, they were unable to overcome lily-white opposition and Democratic attacks. Asbury S. Fowler led the lily-white opposition to the appointment of Hayman and gained the backing of many members of the Grand Army of the Republic. Clayton viewed the opposition to Hayman's appointment as an attack on his own regular Republican machine and its black-and-tan allies. President William McKinley favored a bipartisan board, but Remmel tried in vain to find a Democratic physician who would agree to serve on a board with a Negro. Remmel blamed Fowler for the failure of the Hayman appointment. "Fowler," he said, fails to understand the importance of blacks for the Republican Party and "criticizes . . . me for having sustained the darkey."[10]

In 1900 the racial tensions within the party increased. John C. Bush, a black leader, remained with the regular organization and condemned the action of blacks, led by white insurgent H. F.

Auten, in holding a separate black convention for Pulaski County. Speaking to the regular Pulaski County Convention, Bush praised Asbury Fowler for his part in the Hayman incident, called Dr. Hayman a "fool," and chided whites for going "to the mourners bench for a negro." "When the whites are arrayed on one side and the blacks on the other," warned Bush, "then the whites will go to glory and the blacks go to hell." The organization had given John Bush the position of receiver in the Internal Revenue office at Little Rock, after McKinley took office. Because of loyalty to the lily-whites, he held the office until 1913 when Wilson brought the Democrats into control of the patronage. Bush held the highest office of any black in Arkansas and was one of the very few permitted by the Republicans to receive an elevated office.[11]

One of Arkansas's leading Negro Republicans, Scipio A. Jones, although he held the office of secretary of the Republican Pulaski County Central Committee, refused the enticements of the regulars in 1900. He joined H. F. Auten and the blacks on the sidewalk outside the meeting hall of the regular convention. The open-air convention chose delegates to the state convention, but the rebels failed to gain recognition at that gathering.[12] In the 1902 election, the black Republicans of Pulaski County bolted the convention a second time and chose Negro candidates to oppose the lily-whites. The blacks polled only 5 percent of the county's votes.[13]

In 1909 the Clayton organization offered the enticement of federal office to bring Jones back to the fold. Remmel wrote to William Howard Taft that the organization had promised blacks "when the fight was on" two federal jobs in Washington, and he sought one position for Jones. But the Taft administration rejected the pressure to place Jones as register of the District of Columbia Internal Revenue Office. Instead the Republicans gave him a minor census position to last during the 1910 enumeration. Although Remmel made repeated attempts to secure a more suitable position for Jones, who practiced law before the United States Supreme Court, and though Booker T. Washington used his energies in Jones's behalf, the federal patronage system found no room for him. The frequent disappointments probably encouraged his participation in the serious insurgency of 1920, when Arkansas blacks placed an independent ticket in the field.[14] But the federal administration was not alone in denying a place to Jones. In 1907 the Clayton organization rebuffed his quest for the position of assistant district attorney for eastern Arkansas and pressed instead for the selection of Clayton's nephew and namesake, Powell Clayton.[15]

An indication of the growing restiveness of Arkansas blacks in the Republican Party can be seen in the career of Mifflin W. Gibbs. Gibbs was a wealthy and well-educated black leader who had immigrated to the state in 1871 from Oberlin, Ohio. He became a close ally of Clayton and carefully avoided maintaining too close a link with the black and tans. Clayton relied on Gibbs to keep black delegates to the conventions in line. For his loyalty to the regulars, Gibbs enjoyed a variety of elective, patronage, and party positions during the 1870s and up to 1901. From 1887 to 1897, he was secretary of the state central committee, his highest post in the party. In 1897 President McKinley asked Gibbs to serve as consul to Madagascar. The distant post was not Gibbs's first choice. "It was a surprise," he confessed in his autobiography. "Madagascar had not come within my purview. . . ." He remained at the consulate from October 1897 until the summer of 1901. From Madagascar Gibbs watched the growing power of the lily-white faction with deep concern. By 1908 he had decided to abandon the increasingly segregated Republican Party. Other leading blacks followed him out, including Dr. Elias Camp Morris of Helena, who was president of the Negro Baptist Convention. In 1908 the nomination of William Howard Taft, combined with the growth of lily-white power, led blacks in the South to join the cause of William Jennings Bryan. The disaffection stemmed in part from the fact that Taft had served as Roosevelt's secretary of war during the Brownsville affair. Taft had been directly involved with the high-handed and unjust treatment of black troops who were accused of being involved in a riot.[16]

During the early 1900s, the lily-whites became increasingly bold in trying to deny blacks a role in the party. In 1910 in Jefferson County, whites organized a lily-white delegation to the state convention. In so doing they tried to supplant Ferd Havis, a wealthy black who had served as chairman of the county Republican committee for the twenty years preceding 1906. In 1910 Havis shared the leadership of the delegation with a white man, R. C. Thompson. Havis's group won the battle and was seated. Despite Havis's victory, whites continued to press the issue. Because segregation had become firmly established, the lily-whites began to try to use segregated facilities for conventions. In 1914 the Pulaski County lily-whites arranged for their convention to meet at the segregated Hotel Marion in Little Rock. The blacks were automatically shut out of this facility, and they responded by holding a separate county convention.[17]

In the year 1920, the factional conflict reached a new level of volatility. Harmon L. Remmel's nephew, Augustus C. Remmel, used the now familiar tactic of choosing a segregated hotel for the Pulaski County Convention. Hearing that blacks planned to ignore the racial barrier and attend the convention, Remmel switched the meeting place to a second segregated hotel. In protest, the blacks held a separate Pulaski County Convention. When the state convention met on April 28, it accepted the credentials of the lily-white delegation from Pulaski County and refused to seat the black and tans. To protest the move, about fifty blacks walked out of the convention. The black Republicans then held their own state convention at the Mosaic Temple in Little Rock and chose, for the first time in the state's history, a black candidate for governor. J. H. Blount, principal of a black school in Helena, polled 15,627 votes in the 1920 general election, about one-fourth of the total for the white Republican candidate and approximately one-eighth of the Democratic contender's vote. After the 1920 election, racial tension in the party eased somewhat. The exciting events of 1920 should not be taken as an indication that the black-and-tan movement was on the verge of gaining new strength. One student of the black-and-tan movement in the South has suggested that "Black and Tanism in Arkansas died in its beginnings." Arkansas, like Tennessee, had a very weak black-and-tan movement. During the 1920s, blacks won a slightly greater degree of representation in the organization, but the Republican Party in Arkansas continued to be the captive of those of lily-white sentiment.[18]

In addition to the racial division, the Arkansas Republicans were also divided between the "regulars," those in control of patronage like Clayton and Remmel, on the one hand and the "insurgents" on the other hand, who were primarily outsiders seeking power. To some extent the insurgents represented a more youthful element seeking to replace the stalwarts of the Reconstruction era. *The Fayetteville Democrat* described the division as one between "old-line Republicans" and younger men who resented Powell Clayton's "bossism." In 1901, Clayton wrote to party chief Harmon L. Remmel to warn him of attempts at "organizing the young Republicans, a mischievous movement, fraught with much danger." Clayton suggested that Remmel choose "some young men whom you could trust, and who have not been too prominent heretofore, in some back counties" to feign interest in the movement in order to gather intelligence about the dissidents and their plans.[19]

Less destructive for the Republicans in Arkansas was the divisiveness over the sound money issue. Very few Arkansas Republicans ever joined the silver Republican movement. Some of those who did join the silver Republicans later associated themselves with the black-and-tans. One of the Republican insurgents of the 1900s, W. D. Matthews of Stuttgart, delivered a free silver speech before a Little Rock Democratic rally in 1896.[20]

The Republican Party in Arkansas drew its support from Delta blacks, hill country farmers, and urban businessmen. Most prominent in the party's leadership were a small group of Little Rock financiers and businessmen. The manager of the Southern Cotton Oil Company at Little Rock, C. C. Johnson, told a reporter for the Little Rock *Globe-Democrat* that the regular Republican chiefs were the "leading promoters" of Southern business interests. During an insurgent Republican uprising in 1902, the *Globe-Democrat* interviewed a number of supporters of the regular organization. Those speaking in defense of the regulars included the president of a lumber company, two bank cashiers, a railroad official for the Iron Mountain, a "retired capitalist," the secretary of a hardware wholesale company, and a real estate man.[21] Most of those holding positions on the state central committee were also government employees and many of them had offices in the federal building in Little Rock.

A few sound money Democrats flirted with the Republican Party in Arkansas. In 1900 the "General Attorney" for the Iron Mountain Railroad, George E. Dodge, informed William McKinley that a large number of Democrats in Arkansas "are now heartily in harmony with your administration." Another gold man, Oscar L. Miles, complained to Theodore Roosevelt that he had become a Democrat in political isolation because of his pro-Cleveland stance.[22] The Republicans in Arkansas increased their efforts to woo businessmen during Jeff Davis's governorship. Mark Hanna, in 1900, allowed himself a bit of optimism about the prospects of electing a Republican governor in Arkansas. "By reason of the extremely populistic and revolutionary character of the democratic candidate," he predicted, "thousands of leading Democratic business men of Arkansas will support Mr. Remmel's candidacy for Governor." Although his expectations were too sanguine, a few Democrats did vote the Republican ticket during the Davis era to express their contempt for the redneck leader. In 1902 Powell Clayton reported to Theodore Roosevelt that Davis had polled eight-seven hundred votes fewer than the Democratic field and by Clayton's estimate, three thousand Democrats had "rebuked" the governor by casting their votes for an insurgent Republican candidate. The Republicans never had great success in winning dissident Democrats, but they continued their efforts to capitalize on the factionalization of the dominant party. As the 1904 campaign approached, Clayton wrote to Roosevelt of plans to delay the Republican State Convention "to allow the democratic disaffection and apparent disruption to become as fully developed as possible." With some relish he informed the president that "the anti-Davis men are very bitter, and apparently irreconcilable." [23]

Democrats in Arkansas often found it useful to cooperate with Republicans to gain some influence over patronage. During his early years in Congress, Joseph T. Robinson frequently negotiated with Republicans about appointments in his district. As one of his constituents put it, "We Democrats here have our preference as between Republicans who ask appointments." In 1905, Robinson, in a "To Whom it may Concern" letter, denied that he had attempted to control Republican patronage but asserted his right to express a preference. Republicans who had received his support paid their political debts by discreetly aiding him at election time. The Republican postmaster at Pine Bluff, Fred C. Furth, promised to do everything possible to elect Robinson short of casting his own vote for a Democrat. He would deliver "the solid Jew vote," and his inlaws, the Altheimers—especially "the old man Louis"—who were leading Republicans, would give him their aid. "Tough Republican that I am," wrote the postmaster, "I recognize merit at all times, even in a democrat." The two men also worked closely on plans to secure a generous congressional grant for erecting a new federal building in Pine Bluff. [24]

According to Jeff Davis, the level of cooperation between parties had been greater before the decline of Republican strength. The governor accused Senator James K. Jones of establishing co-operative ties with Republicans during the 1880s when fifteen to twenty members of that party served in the state legislature. Davis wondered why Jones had not gone to President McKinley to protest the appointment of Powell Clayton as ambassador to Mexico. "The simple fact is, that until the present election system was inaugurated in Arkansas it was quite to the profit of Senator Jones to stand in with Clayton."[25]

The Republican Party managed to display moderate strength even in one of the nation's strongest one-party states. In the presidential elections between 1892 and 1920, the Republicans mustered an average of 34 percent of all votes cast.[26] In the 1900 election, the Arkansas Republicans rebounded from the 25 percent vote of 1896 to a more substantial 35 percent. The return of better economic conditions affected the outcome in Arkansas as it did in much of the nation. After the election, Senator James K. Jones informed William Jennings Bryan that his majority in Arkansas had dropped "from seventy-two thousand in 1896 to thirty-five thousand in 1900, and in my own county, men who have voted the Democratic ticket all their lives, voted the Republican this time, openly boasted of it, and gave as the reason, that they didn't want any more '5 cent cotton.'"[27] In 1904 and 1920 respectively, Theodore Roosevelt and Warren G. Harding raised the Arkansas Republican vote to approximately 40 percent of all votes cast for president. The Arkansas pattern was not a unique one in the South. The border states and even the old Confederate states retained a surprisingly strong Republican percentage in national elections as late as 1900. In that year Texas gave 31 percent of its vote to the Republicans, Georgia 28 percent, and Alabama equaled Arkansas's 35 percent. In the border states, Republican percentages reached even higher levels. The role of Southern Republicans in national elections did not become insignificant even after 1900.[28]

Roosevelt earned a special place in the hearts of Arkansas Democrats. One of Jeff Davis's closest supporters, Jeremiah V. Bourland, said of him, "the President has his own way of doing things which I like very much." Bourland was "especially pleased" that Roosevelt had appointed gold Democrat Uriah M. Rose to a place on the court of International Arbitration.[29] Governor Davis's relationship with the president was less cordial. He refused to attend a banquet given by the Board of Trade in Little Rock to honor Roosevelt who was making a Southern tour. Davis excused the insult to the president by explaining he could not sit at a banquet table with Powell Clayton, the man who had murdered his aunt. The story of Clayton's homicidal act evidently sprang from Davis's fertile imagination. Although Clayton's militia force had been in Davis's aunt's town when she took ill, her later death had nothing to do with the occupation of the town or with Clayton.[30] Yet, even Davis harbored a certain admiration for Roosevelt. In 1902 he confidently predicted the president's nomination and election in 1904. The governor confided, "I know we cannot defeat you. I feel it in my heart."[31] Davis snubbed William Howard Taft in a similar manner. When Taft had his aide, Archie Butt, prepare a list of guests for a diplomatic reception, he instructed him to "invite all the Senators with the exception of Senator Davis of Arkansas. A man who accepts an invitation from me to dinner, and then refuses to come without sending an excuse, will not get another."[32]

The Republicans dominated only two counties during the 1890s and early 1900s. In Searcy and Newton counties, they controlled local offices and won majorities in presidential elections. In the congressional contests of the era between 1896 and 1920, the Republicans never elected a congressman although a few counties gave them a majority in each congressional election. In 1900, the Republicans received a majority of the congressional vote in only six counties and were very close in five more.[33] During the 1890s and until 1920, they managed to send at least two, but never more than six, members to the state legislature.[34]

The general assembly redrew the congressional districts in 1891 and 1901 to dilute Republican strength as fully as possible. Most of Arkansas's Negroes lived to the southeast of a line drawn diagonally from the northeast to the southwest corner of the state. The tier of counties along the Mississippi contained a heavy concentration of blacks, as did the lower river valleys of the Ouachita, the St. Francis, the Arkansas, the White, and the Red rivers. In 1900, *The Arkansas Democrat* called for an end to the "shoe-string district" which had served to "offset the 'black-belt,' or the river-bottom counties, where a large majority of the voters were negroes." In order to keep blacks a minority in all districts, the newspaper admitted, politicians had included hill counties with the valley counties.[35] The resulting pattern showed districts fanning out in varied directions from the southeast corner of the state.

In 1901, Arkansas's population increase entitled the state to a seventh congressional seat. *The Arkansas Democrat* rejoiced that square districts were now a possibility. The poll tax and the election law of 1891 had removed the fear that blacks and Republicans might regain control. When the committee on redistricting in the Arkansas House of Representatives met, it excluded Willis W. Moore of Newton County, the lone protesting Republican committee member from the chamber. After the assembly had finished its task, *The Arkansas Gazette* reported each district was "safely Democratic." The legislature drew the boundaries so that each one contained about half as many Republicans as Democrats. Based upon the 1900 congressional vote, the new areas would average about twelve thousand Democratic to six thousand Republican voters.[36] While the new districts were slightly more compact than those established in 1891, they still swept into the black belt to neutralize Negro voting power.

The Democrats did not rely on gerrymandering as their basic weapon to control the electoral process. The new first congressional district demonstrated that an area with a large black population could be a Democratic stronghold. Democrats won heavy majorities in congressional elections in this eastern Arkansas area. In 1906, a disputed election in the fourth congressional district dramatized some of the common devices used by Democrats to keep minority party strength at a minimum. The district included the tier of counties along much of Arkansas's western border. Some of the counties of the Ouachita Mountain region, which traversed part of the district, sometimes polled a respectable Republican vote. Scott and Polk counties had sent a Republican to the state senate in 1904. George Tilles, the Republican candidate for the district, appealed to the United States House of Representative's Committee on Elections to unseat Democrat William B. Cravens. According to Tilles, Cravens and his cohorts had entered polling places and did "handle and attempt to count said ballots before the time for closing the polls, as prescribed by law." In 650 cases, he claimed, judges of election had marked ballots for Cravens when illiterate voters had indicated a preference for Tilles.

Arkansas Republicans frequently condemned the provision of the 1891 election law which provided that all voters clear the polling area while judges of election marked the ballot of an illiterate voter. Since Arkansas had a high rate of illiteracy and since Democrats controlled the selection of election officials, there was ample opportunity to manipulate the votes of illiterates. In some counties, according to Tilles, the Democrats "made away with" 250 or more ballots. He thought Democratic officials conducted the election in a "partisan and wholly unjust" manner, but he failed to secure vindication from the congressional committee. The charges were typical of complaints made against the Democratic electoral machinery.[37]

The Arkansas Republican Party, demoralized by Democratic election manipulation and regularly defeated in contests for elective offices, turned its energies toward securing federal appointive offices. Long periods of Republican presidential leadership also encouraged the pursuit of patronage. What the Republicans lacked in electoral strength they compensated for with a powerful political dynasty that controlled Arkansas appointments.

The Republican machine dominated by Powell Clayton and Harmon L. Remmell kept a firm hold on Arkansas's federal patronage. The silver Republican *Stuttgart Free Press,* referring to the 1896 state convention, declared "the fact was too patent to be contradicted that Gen. Powell Clayton was complete master of the convention as absolute a tyrant as the czar is in Russia."[38] By 1902, when insurgency reached a peak in Arkansas, the Republican State Central Committee passed a resolution accusing the rebel Republicans of trying to destroy "the most complete, harmonious and approved political organization in all the southern states." One insurgent, George P. Dent, spoke of the central committee as "a *close* corporation . . . a political office trust."[39]

In 1910, the Department of Justice prepared a summary statement concerning appointments in Arkansas. The Republican Central Committee, a group of about ninety-five men, chose a smaller executive committee that cleared all applications for federal appointments. Candidates appeared before the executive committee and the latter made its recommendations to the whole central committee. Approved candidates were then recommended to Washington.[40] But the statement, which summarized the bare mechanics of the procedure as outlined by Remmel and Clayton, did not reveal the practical workings of the system. Charles D. Greaves, insurgent candidate for governor in 1902, issued a more revealing statement in his campaign pamphlet, *A Few Reasons Why Claytonism Should Be Rebuked.* According to Greaves, those on the central executive committee held all the important federal jobs in the state. Both U.S. marshals, one district attorney, the collector of Internal Revenue at Little Rock, the Little Rock postmaster, and the register and receiver of the land office at Little Rock were all members of the executive committee. For thirty-five years Clayton had dominated the party machinery. After William McKinley appointed Clayton ambassador to Mexico, the Republican boss continued to run the machinery through his henchman, Remmel. In 1900, Clayton feared losing control of the organization and temporarily returned from Mexico City to engineer the choice of central committee members. He and Remmel dictated the membership from a list they had agreed on in advance of the state convention.[41]

A decade later, one of Arkansas's Bull Moosers, J. A. Comer, made similar revelations to the Republican National Committee. The state conventions, he charged, continually nominated the same central committee members that had held office for years. By 1912, Clayton had not resided in Arkansas for sixteen years, but the state central committee sent appointments on to him in Washington, D.C., for his approval before presentation to the administration. J. A. Comer gave the national committee several biographical sketches of office holders who had served on the state central committee from twelve to twenty years and who held the major federal offices in the state.[42]

Powell Clayton assumed leadership of the Republican Party in Arkansas for half a century. *The Arkansas Gazette* once theorized "that without Clayton there would be no Republican Party in Arkansas. It would be another case of Hamlet with the title role of the play expunged." He originally came to Arkansas during the Civil War with a Kansas regiment. After the war's end, the general stayed on to become a carpetbag governor. Contemporaries thought he dressed in an elegant manner for an Arkansan. At Clayton's July 4 inauguration, retiring Governor Isaac Murphy observed with amusement the new chief executive wearing gloves on a hot Arkansas day. A "determined jutting jaw" added to the military bearing of the carpetbag governor. Although in later years, baldness left only a swatch of hair at the sides of his head, he retained a mustache and beard.[43]

In 1896 *The Washington Post* declared that "Powell Clayton is prepared to trade the vote of Arkansas for a cabinet job, Interior Department preferred." Arkansas Republicans also expected Clayton to enter McKinley's cabinet. But Clayton preferred, he told Remmel, to receive the Mexican mission, and in 1897 he left the state for Mexico City. Clayton did not have any great enthusiasm for Theodore Roosevelt before he became president, but the Rough Rider retained Clayton in office. The general was gratified, "as I had no personal claims on President Roosevelt and from the fact that we were generally in different political camps inside of the Republican Party." Clayton did not resign from his post as Arkansas's National Republican Committeeman until January 1913. Remmel expressed regret that his chief did not remain at the post to the end of his life.[44]

The crafty Remmel became one of Powell Clayton's most faithful lieutenants. In 1898, he informed the ambassador he had the collector's office "thoroughly well in hand and have a field force which I can effectually use in an emergency to render service to both you and myself." A few days later, anticipating the death of Cooper (which did not occur), Remmel wrote about plans to secure greater control of the party. If he could "make agreeable arrangements" with the marshal in the western district and the new marshal in the eastern district "we would virtually have matters in our own hands throughout the state and you would know definitely then that you had a lieutenantcy that could positively be relied upon." One year later, Clayton advised Remmel, "If we get our friends in control of the Convention, we can then shape things to suit ourselves."[45]

The insurgent Republicans directed their attacks against Remmel, Clayton, and the executive committee. To some degree, insurgency in Arkansas represented the dissatisfaction of those without federal offices. The Democratic State Central Committee in 1902 viewed the situation in terms of patronage:

> It [the Democratic Party] is opposed to two aggregations, each styling itself the Republican Party. They are both essentially the same and have been aptly distinguished, the one as the 'Pie-Eaters' and the other as the 'Pie Hunters.' So far as we can see, the only essential difference between these rival factions apparently arises out of the fact that the Federal offices are not numerous enough to be so parcelled out as that every member of each faction may enjoy the fees, perquisites and emoluments of at least one office.[46]

Just before McKinley's death, Powell Clayton expressed fear of an alignment between the insurgents and Vice President Roosevelt. "I think," he told Remmel, "we may expect the opposition to rally around the Roosevelt standard." Two months after the assassination, Clayton wrote of his fear that Roosevelt might "at first, be imposed upon by people of the Mathews stripe and he may be fooled by the palaver of Southern democrats."[47] But the new president did not make an all-out attack on Clayton's organization. In line with his strategy elsewhere, he adopted a wait-and-see policy and eventually embraced the regular Republicans in Arkansas.

Theodore Roosevelt's quest for the 1904 presidential nomination motivated and shaped his policy toward Southern Republicans during his first term. Senator Mark Hanna, his foremost rival, had already secured a following among the black-and-tan factions in the South. He appeared to have sufficient Southern support to carry him to victory at the national nominating convention. The Cleveland millionaire also began making accommodations to the rising lily-white faction. In South Carolina, William McKinley and Hanna allied with wayward Democrat John L. McLaurin, who sought to align Gold Democrats with white Republicans in support of the national Republican Party. When President Roosevelt took command of the patronage, he moved cautiously. In the first months of his administration, Southern white conservatives took heart at the appointment of Gold Democrats. In South Carolina, the lily-whites understood that Roosevelt would appoint no Negro to a major office. Then came the stunning news of his appointment of a Negro physician as collector of the Charleston customs office. Mississippians were enraged when he refused to replace the Negro postmistress at Indianola and shut down the office rather than surrender to the demands of militant whites. With racist sentiment on the rise, the president angered lily-whites, blacks, and conservative Democrats in turn. But by 1904, the astute Roosevelt had created a loyal Republican following in the South. He did not use the big stick to destroy the regular Republican organizations, but he did maneuver them into his camp.[48]

During the winter of 1901–02, the Arkansas insurgents made a determined effort to secure the new president's support. A similar upsurge of insurgent factions occurred all across the Southern states.[49] Both Arkansas factions sent their leaders to Washington, D.C., and Powell Clayton kept the telegraph wires between Mexico City, Little Rock, and Washington humming.[50] H. F. Auten, who represented the insurgents, revealed numerous instances of Republican misconduct to Washington officials, and he finally succeeded in his drive to remove several regular Republicans from major offices. Roosevelt's secretary of the treasury, Lyman J. Gage, informed the president of his department's assessment of complaints against Remmel and his followers. He listed charges that had become familiar: Remmel forced Henry Cooper to share his salary with him, Cooper's stroke had incapacitated him so that he was absent from his duties as marshal for weeks at a time, Remmel spent most of his time outside the collector's office doing political work, and the Republican Central Committee had forced Louis Altheimer to share his Pine Bluff postmaster's salary with a black leader who had been passed by for the job.[51]

The accusation against Remmel was especially serious because it had been leveled against a high-level organization man. If the Insurgents could topple him, they might later bring down the whole Clayton machine. During 1902, both Insurgent Republicans and malevolent Democrats recounted frequently the well-worn Cooper-Remmel tale. Remmel had promised to secure for Henry Cooper the United States Marshalship for the eastern district. At first he had opposed the choice of Cooper, but after the candidate agreed to pay five hundred dollars annually from his marshal's salary to Remmel, the latter agreed to support the appointment. Remmel's letters reveal the truth of the charge. In 1898 when Cooper suffered a light paralytic stroke, Remmel wrote to Clayton in Mexico to insist on the right to name Cooper's replacement, and he desired the same relationship with the new appointee, "known only to yourself," that had existed between himself and Cooper. When the scandal surfaced in 1902, Clayton wrote to Remmel to express his disappointment that the "arrangement between you" had become public knowledge. Theodore Roosevelt gave meager encouragement to the Insurgents when he dismissed Remmel from the office of collector of Internal Revenue because of the incident. Despite the president's abandonment of Remmel, Powell Clayton kept his lieutenant in power. In June 1902 the state convention chose the indestructible Remmel to be chairman of the state central committee. Clayton wrote to Theodore Roosevelt to justify his retaining Remmel. The convention, said Clayton, believed the loss of the collector's office sufficient punishment for Remmel's "indiscretion."[52]

The Insurgents did not gain the places lost by the ringleaders of the Republicans, but they did succeed in ejecting a few key figures from office. Despite the Remmel-Cooper revelations, the Roosevelt administration intended to reappoint Henry Cooper as marshal. The appointment had already gone to the Senate Judiciary Committee when intense criticism forced Attorney General Philander C. Knox to withdraw Cooper's name from consideration. The Arkansas Republican Central Committee now turned to the lily-white leader, Col. Asbury Fowler, and the administration secured his confirmation to the marshalship. Captain F. W. Tucker received the appointment of collector. This was no clearcut Insurgent victory since both Fowler and Tucker gave at least nominal allegiance to Clayton. On the other hand, both men were allies of Theodore Roosevelt and potential rebels against Clayton's control. Tucker had been one of Roosevelt's trusted advisors on Arkansas politics. The struggle between the Insurgents and the Regulars took a violent turn when H. F. Auten and Harmon L. Remmel grappled on the floor of the latter's insurance office. Auten seized Remmel by the throat and struck him with a loaded cane. Only the intervention of onlookers prevented a more serious incident. Powell Clayton was in a precarious position in his state party, but he survived with his power intact. After the 1902 election, Roosevelt indicated his final determination to stand by Clayton. The president asked him not to make any decision about resigning his ambassadorship "without writing me well in advance and letting me have time to communicate with you. The result in Arkansas was to my mind absolutely conclusive as showing that the voters were with the regular organization." [53]

Early in 1904, before Mark Hanna's death, Clayton promised to back Roosevelt's quest for the Republican Party's nomination, but he alerted the president to the presence of a "strong Hanna undercurrent." Clayton warned Roosevelt that the agents in Arkansas's federal land offices resented the administration's condemnation of their political activities. The Interior Department had reprimanded Arkansas officials for leaving their offices to meddle in the elections of distant counties. Clayton's letter expressed agreement with Roosevelt that federal office holders should not be delegates to the national convention, but Clayton did not think the administration should forbid them to attend state conventions. Roosevelt replied in a conciliatory tone. "I have not even gone so far as you thought, for I have not felt that all officeholders should be debarred from going to the convention. I have simply made the request that as few as possible shall go." Later Clayton promised to use his influence to see that only dedicated Roosevelt men represented Arkansas at the national convention.[54]

Sometime before January 15, 1904, Roosevelt made some kind of commitment to restore Harmon L. Remmel to a federal office.[55] The president perceived that his greatest hope for Arkansas's delegate support lay in aligning with the regular organization. After the election of 1904, Clayton set his sights for placing Remmel in the office of United States Marshal for eastern Arkansas. Asbury S. Fowler had held the position since Roosevelt's removal of Henry Cooper. As Fowler put it, Clayton was now "making the fight of his life to have Remmel appointed Marshal." Fowler had not been one of Clayton's more dedicated followers in years past. As early as 1897, Clayton had warned Remmel that Fowler intended to create divisions between Remmel and Henry Cooper in order to elevate himself in the party hierarchy. In 1899 Clayton and Remmel complained of Fowler's campaign against the black leaders of the party. By 1906 the Insurgents had welcomed Asbury Fowler to their ranks. Charles Greaves, an Insurgent leader, commended Fowler for not seeking the endorsement of the Republican Central Committee in 1906. Greaves informed Roosevelt that the reappointment of Fowler "would disarm criticism."[56]

As viewed by *The Arkansas Gazette,* Roosevelt's decision to appoint Harmon Remmel as marshal represented a tremendous victory for the regular organization. Asbury Fowler made a vigorous fight to retain the position, and his loss was a stinging defeat for the Insurgents. It had now become clear that Roosevelt would give his full support to the Clayton forces. For Remmel it was a personal victory. The marshal's office was a more important position than that of collector.[57] A few years later, when the William Howard Taft administration searched for records of the formal investigation of the Remmel–Cooper arrangement, nothing could be found. Perhaps Roosevelt had decided not only to reinstate Remmel but also to expunge the investigation from the record.[58] With the return of Remmel to full privileges, the regular organization had weathered the crisis.

A notable example of Powell Clayton's determination to control Arkansas patronage was his frenzied crusade to place Martin

A. Eisele in the office of superintendent of the Hot Springs Reservation. President William McKinley, believing the position to be legally within the civil service, refused for several years to remove the Democratic appointee, William J. Little. Remmel and Clayton battled with gold Democrat Samuel Fordyce over the right to dictate the appointee. Fordyce completed his railroad line between Little Rock and Hot Springs in the late 1890s. He had established his home at Hot Springs, although business interests took him frequently to St. Louis and elsewhere. He meant to have a hand in choosing the appointee and had some support from the secretary of the interior, Ethan Allen Hitchcock. In 1900, after much cajoling, McKinley removed the Democratic superintendent and placed Eisele in the coveted office. Along with the new position a number of lesser government jobs in Hot Springs fell under Republican control and helped strengthen the Republican organization.[59]

In a strong one–party state, the Republican Party had become a patronage machine and a vehicle to deliver delegate votes at national nominating conventions. Harmon L. Remmel and Powell Clayton cared for little else but maintaining their domination of the state organization and keeping appointments within machine control. Their paths led continually to Washington. The Democrats in 1897 entered a long dry spell and only occasionally were they able to influence patronage before 1913. Often they gave their encouragement to the Insurgents, but in Arkansas the dissident Republicans remained an ineffective force. While the Arkansas Republican Party played a significant role in the presidential nominating process, in national elections, and in patronage distribution, they were unable to serve as a viable opposition party at the state level. The only hope for a real choice at the polls rested, not in the general election, but in the Democratic primaries. For much of Arkansas's history, the Republicans remained a voice crying in the wilderness.

8

Decline of the Davis
Faction, 1907–1912

When Jeff Davis left the governor's office in January 1907, his political influence waned but did not suffer complete eclipse. Politicians could not ignore the existence of the Davis faction, although the organization lacked some of its earlier cohesiveness and permanence. New factions arose and declined to further confuse the political scene. After the redneck leader's death in 1913, his organization continued to be an important element on the political scene. Candidates might make a concerted effort to enlist the support of the old Davis forces, or they might try at least to mollify them. But not many years passed before the Davis phenomenon became more of a lingering sentiment than an identifiable faction.

During 1906, when Davis occupied the governor's chair, successfully campaigned for the United States Senate, and placed his organization's support behind the candidate who won the governorship, he seemed to have reached his political zenith. But the course of state politics and his own performance in the United States Senate brought a decline in support. Almost as soon as Governor John Little assumed his office in 1907, Little fell victim to severe emotional stress. With his departure to a mental institution, the president of the senate, in accordance with the 1874 constitution, assumed the office of governor. In May 1907, before the legislature adjourned, the upper house chose Xenophon Pindall to be president pro tempore of the senate. Since the state constitution provided that the president of the senate succeed a deceased or disabled governor, Pindall now claimed the office. The recent incumbent stepped down, and Davis's arch-foe took command of the state's administration.

Jeff Davis sometimes compromised his crusading ideals when politics dictated the necessity for making terms with the enemy. Some contemporaries thought he had a hand in placing Pindall in the governor's chair. Congressman Joseph T. Robinson believed Pindall attained his office "by accident or suspicious combination." He had allied with Davis and then made terms with the railroad lobby. According to one of Robinson's friends, state Senator Alexander Yopp of Hazen, Davis gave his support in exchange for Pindall's promise to veto a local bill.[1] If Davis gave aid to Pindall, it was clandestine and temporary. The two men had not been in the same political camp. Before Pindall had completed a year in office, Davis made a public reference to him as the "mouthpiece" of the penitentiary gang and a member of the crowd that had always opposed "Jeff Davisism."[2] The redneck leader's organization failed to control or influence the Pindall administration.

The "Old Guard" faction made early preparations for the battle to regain control of the governor's mansion. Six months before the 1908 primary election, Davis decided to regain power by placing his faction squarely behind William F. Kirby in opposition to George Donaghey.

If the Davis organization stood for zealous reformism, it had chosen well in backing William F. Kirby. The candidate had gone to the 1897 general assembly as one of the leading contenders for creation of a railroad commission. He joined with J. Marion Futrell of Marion County, a Populist member of the same assembly, in a demand that the commission bill be amended to exclude from the commission any person who had ever received a free railroad pass. In the 1901 Arkansas Senate, Kirby fought for passage of a bill to force the railroads to pay the expenses of the railroad commission. When conservatives moved to postpone consideration, Kirby denounced their obstruction. "I know the bill will not pass," said Kirby. "The disposition of the senate from the first days of its organization has been to crush all legislation tending to regulate the railroads. There is a sentiment here that has been felt by every senator upon this floor." Kirby's efforts failed. In 1903, the general assembly authorized him to compile an authoritative digest of Arkansas statutes. Rumor indicated, though many denied it, that Jeff Davis had dictated the choice of Kirby.[3]

In 1906 when the ill-fated John Little won the campaign for governor, Kirby secured the office of attorney general. During his single term, Kirby took a leading part in litigation designed to enforce Davis's antitrust act. The Arkansas Supreme Court upheld the state in its contention that the Hammond Packing Company had illegally entered into price-fixing arrangements and could be subjected to legal penalties for violation of the law. The company appealed to the United States Surpeme Court. In asking the Supreme Court to advance consideration, Kirby stated the heart of the case. He had sued a commission "to take evidence" from an agent of the Hammond Company, and the company refused to produce its books and papers. He maintained that the company's answers to charges were constitutionally stricken out in the state supreme court, "and judgment rendered against it, as by default," since the company denied access to material evidence. The United States Supreme Court agreed that rejection of the company's testimony in court did not constitute a denial of due process because of the company's refusal to turn over its books.[4] The decision was a major victory for the antitrust forces.

Although the Davis organization had chosen a progressive candidate, the Old Guard could not easily picture itself as the only alternative for reformist Democrats. Kirby's chief opponent, George Donaghey, had also identified himself with the rising progressive sentiment in the South. Davis's decision to oppose Donaghey further weakened his influence in Arkansas. The electorate had become weary with politicians and looked to the business community for a new leader. In his campaign, Donaghey denounced the involvement of the capitol construction project with politics. He offered the state his experience in the construction industry as a suitable qualification for shepherding the building program toward completion. His election indicated a reaction against professional politicians and the checkered career of the famous project. A national periodical, *The World's Work,* commended the state for its choice of Donaghey. The conduct of "some of its political representative" had brought Arkansas "political notoriety." But by the spring primaries of 1908, "the feeling became strong . . . that it was time for a business administration of public affairs rather than for another merely political administration." The journal estimated contractor Donaghey's fortune as "perhaps half a million dollars."[5]

During the primary campaign, William F. Kirby made reckless charges against opposing candidates. He accused one respected educator, who entered the lists against him, of corrupt use of funds granted by the Peabody Foundation. *The Malvern Times Journal* warned Kirby that "he has bit off a great chunk when he undertakes to besmirch the character of John H. Hinemon."[6] In order to bolster his candidate, Jeff Davis left Washington in February 1908 to take an active part in the battle against Donaghey. One indication of Davis's declining fortunes was the surrender of his beloved personal secretary, Charles Jacobson, to the enemy camp. Jacobson broke ties by supporting the anti-Davis candidate for attorney general, Oliver C. Ludwig. He wrote Joseph T. Robinson, who had made a similar break a few years before, "the only politicks [*sic*] I am fooling with now is Ludwig's race and I am certainly going to see that he is elected."[7]

The election was a serious setback for the Davis organization. George Donaghey easily won the spring primary election in the three-cornered contest for governor. He garnered 53,479 votes to Kirby's 40,220. John Hinemon, the educator, trailed both with 35,160 votes. The redneck leader secured for his candidate a little below one-third of all votes cast. Also, in the attorney general's race, the Davis candidate lost by a vote of approximately sixty-four thousand to fifty-eight thousand.[8] The *Arkansas Sentinel* (Fayetteville) saw Kirby's defeat as a rebuke to bossism. "If the people had nominated Mr. Kirby for governor the people would have thereby said they would suffer to be built up in Arkansas a mighty political machine," which would permit Jeff Davis to control "state affairs."[9]

Joseph T. Robinson also viewed the election as evidence of a rebellion against the Davis machine. As chairman of the Donaghey controlled state convention, he told his fellow Democrats the party had given notice, "that no political boss, however crafty or aggressive, can dominate its policies or stifle the voice of its members." He believed boss rule and factionalism were on the wane in Arkansas. Governor X. O. Pindall, who also allied with Donaghey during the campaign and served as temporary chairman, spoke in similar terms: "Democracy, tired of partisanship, sickened at factional strife, deserted the accustomed haunts where availability had in the past seemed to prevail." Pindall saw the election as a repudiation of politicians and orators in favor of a man of the masses.[10]

Jeff Davis, ever a master of sleight of hand, sought to convince the voters his defeat had been a victory. In a public letter to the winning candidate, he spoke of his great pleasure at Donaghey's victory, since the contest was in reality "a choice between two Jeff Davis men—yourself and Kirby. I selected one Jeff Davis man and the people selected the other, which they thought to be a Jeff Davis man."[11] Donaghey replied that he had "never been identified with" either of the factions in the party and had asserted his independence as early as October 1907. He had not been part of the organization, but his denial of any tie with Davis was not fully candid. George Donaghey had given financial aid to Davis in his 1906 campaign for the United States Senate, and Davis had praised "Honest George" for his exposure of corrupt links between the capital construction company (Caldwell & Drake) and legislators.[12]

The 1908 Democratic State Convention, in the *Gazette's* words, brought a "crushing defeat" to the Davis machine. "It was apparent," the newspaper reported, "that the convention was overwhelmingly against Davis and was determined to force him into the background."[13] Early in May, Pindall announced his intention to run as a candidate for delegate-at-large to the national convention. He specifically stated his determination to seek the position to the exclusion of Jeff Davis. It had been customary to choose the two Arkansas senators as members of the "big four" (the four delegates-at-large). Davis had a penchant for smashing precedents, and Pindall now gave notice of his intention to do the same. "Frankly, I state," said Pindall, "that Senator Davis and myself cannot consistently and with reason be members of the same delegation to the Denver convention." The *Gazette* rebuked Pindall for his course, "Haven't we had enough of bitterness and factional fighting for six months past?"[14]

George Donaghey quickly sustained Pindall and agreed to a big four slate of Donaghey, Clarke, Pindall, and the anti-Davis candidate for attorney general, Oliver C. Ludwig. The anti-Davis men later chose to substitute James Harrod for Pindall. Harrod had been a moderate candidate for governor against silverite Dan Jones in 1896, and like Donaghey, he became one of Woodrow Wilson's early supporters. By convention time, the two opposing forces were prepared for a showdown. Some of the western counties adopted an independent stance. They placed in the field a slate of non-officeholding delegates. When one of the Old Guard, Judge Jeptha Evans, placed Senator Jeff Davis in nomination at the convention, both cheers and hisses rent the air. The delegate could not complete his speech amid the hubbub and finally acceded to the cries of "sit down." When the vote was tallied, the Donaghey faction elected its entire slate of four, and Davis trailed in seventh place.[15] The redneck champion had failed in his bid to choose the governor, to control the convention, and to represent the state at the national convention.

Jeff Davis also failed to maintain his position as the preeminent leader of Arkansas progressivism. The champion of the people had to make room for a new scourge of the interests, George Donaghey. The Democratic platform of 1908, Donaghey's own handiwork, demonstrated his progressive stance. It denounced trusts but without any reference to Davis's distinctive views on foreign corporations fixing prices beyond state borders. It called for conservation legislation to protect the state's coal, timber, and mineral reserves from outside exploitation. The platform opposed entering into any new convict leasing. Another plank suggested increasing the power of the railroad commission "to regulate and control transportation of freight and passengers—the equipment and roadbeds of railways, and that necessary relief in such matters may be granted, without the necessity for special legislation." Donaghey also secured a provision favoring submitting to the people a constitutional amendment providing for the initiative and referendum.[16]

One of the Donaghey planks incurred the wrath of many Arkansas bankers. During the annual meeting of their association in 1908, a Little Rock banker, George W. Rogers, reported with chagrin concerning a recent conversation with Donaghey. "He has in mind this idea of guaranteeing deposits. He said he intended to recommend the passage of a banking law to the next legislature." Harmon L. Remmel, the Republican leader, introduced a resolution disapproving the guaranty idea, and his proposal carried. The retiring president of the association, John Q. Wolf, represented a more progressive view, "Letting well enough alone would never have put skates under the life insurance grafters, nor put rebating, stock-jobbing railroad officials on the rack, nor uncovered the packing house filthiness and rottenness." He believed the time had come for a guaranty law.[17] Donaghey allied himself with those favoring William Jennings Bryan for the presidential nomination in 1908, and he suggested Woodrow Wilson as a second choice for the vice presidency. Some years later William F. Kirby spoke of Donaghey as "an original Woodrow Wilson man." [18]

George Washington Donaghey's performance in the campaign and during his two terms in the governor's office between 1909 and 1913 enhanced his reputation as a progressive and weakened Davis's claim to be the leader of the Democratic Party's reformist wing. Before his inauguration, Donaghey took the state superintendent of education and the president of the University of Arkansas on a tour of the University of Wisconsin, the University of Chicago, and other institutions, to determine how he might improve educational facilities in Arkansas. Under his leadership, the state established four agricultural colleges patterned after farming schools Donaghey observed in Wisconsin. [19]

Donaghey also stole Davis's thunder by carrying on a vigorous attack on the railroads. When Donaghey entered the race for governor, the railroads had just won a round in the regulation controversy. They secured an injunction restraining the railroad commission from enforcing its freight rates and a two cent per mile maximum passenger fare. Representatives of the railroads met with George Donaghey after his victory in the 1908 primary. They hoped to influence him to take a stand for compromise on the rate issue, but the governor-elect was adamant. In his 1909 inaugural speech, Governor Donaghey declared war on the railroads. "Now evidently," he told the legislature, "the railroads have selected this state as the weakest point in the territory of their operations, upon whose ground their battle shall be pitched to practically defeat the state's rights." He lamented the success of the five major trunk lines in overruling the railroad commission's attempts to enforce maximum rates. The legislature responded almost immediately with a fifty-thousand-dollar appropriation to press the battle in the courts. Two years later Donaghey reported the failure of the state to force its rates on the railroads. Judge Jacob Trieber, in June 1909, had ordered the commission to negotiate a rate schedule with the railroads. In the course of these talks, the state finally agreed to increase its maximum rates by one-third. Donaghey believed "the state's right to prescribe rates, while theoretically free, is practically gone." The federal courts had obstructed the efforts of Arkansas to control even intrastate rates.[20] But if Donaghey failed in his railroad battles, he did win some of the acclaim that had once gone to Davis as the chief foe of the interests.

No issue had been dearer to the hearts of the Old Guard than the capitol construction project. Donaghey again captured the imagination of the voters by making one of Davis's crusades his own. During his two terms, the governor battled the construction company, the architects, and the legislature on the capitol issue. Eventually, he demolished part of the structure, on the ground that it was unsafe, and rebuilt it to suit his own notions. By the time he left office, the state capitol was almost ready for occupancy.[21]

Donaghey pressed the convict leasing issue with Davis-like ardor and brought abolition close to fulfillment during his administration. Before he left the executive office, Donaghey drew national attention to his cause by pardoning 360 convicts and releasing them from the penitentiary. At the turn of the century, many Southern states moved to abolish the leasing system. Hoke Smith of Georgia had not been a strong advocate of prison reform, but in 1908 he called a special session of the legislature to terminate the practice. In Alabama the movement did not gain impetus until the 1920s. After a bitter struggle, Alabama reform groups prodded the state assembly to end the practice in 1928.[22] Arkansas achieved abolition of leasing a few months after Governor Donaghey left office.

While Governor Donaghey assumed leadership of the rising progressive forces in Arkansas, Jeff Davis fought to maintain his hold over his rural admirers. But his career in the United States Senate failed to add luster to his name or to significantly bolster his political organization. He had created a stir when he delivered a major address shortly after his installation as senator. Robert La Follette had raised eyebrows in early 1906 when he entered upon a Senate career by presuming to occupy the floor in a two-day oration.[23] Davis's address seemed no less presumptuous to the Senate club. In his maiden speech, he presented for consideration his antitrust bill. The measure was essentially the same bill Davis shepherded through the Arkansas legislature, refurbished for the federal government. "The best object lesson to-day for the suppression of the trusts," he told a bemused audience, "would be to see John D. Rockefeller or some fellow just like him with stripes on." He also expressed the hope "that the laboring people would organize all over this land . . . God speed the day when their organization will prove so strong that Senators on this floor will turn to them eager and anxious to know their desires and wishes."[24]

The New York Times reacted to the redneck senator's tirades with amusement or boredom. When the Congress convened in December 1907, the *Times* reported, "Senator Tillman was compelled today to divide attention with Jeff Davis of Arkansas and fiddling 'Bob Taylor' of Tennessee." After his initial speech, the newspaper credited him with "one reform which has long been dear to the hearts of certain Southern Senators." He had "put an end to the abbreviation by Democratic Senators of the name of the former President of the Confederacy, Jefferson Davis." The *Times* rated his address "a disappointment even to his friendliest colleagues. It did consume time, but it was not even a good show." When Davis died, a little over five years later, the *Times* recalled how the Arkansan "told his people that he wished to go to Washington to make the dry bones rattle in the Senate." He was going "to rattle them," the *Times* observed, "by pure lung power." After nine days into the first session he made the attempt, but "it was a failure." The New York paper asserted that Davis "did not again figure prominently in the Senate."[25]

If the "Popocratic" senator shocked and amused the country during his initial days in the Senate, his later behavior caused the nation to take him less seriously than ever. Davis's antitrust bill remained a dead letter during his whole career although he often reintroduced it and chided the Senate for inaction. As he became more embittered, the senator's flamboyant oratory stunned an age accustomed to overblown rhetoric. In 1908, he delivered a lengthy tirade against the interests which had bottled up his antitrust bill in the Judiciary Committee. For the first time during his political career, he spoke from manuscript lest any "intemperate or unguarded language may escape my lips on this occasion." In denouncing the "plutocratic press" and the monopolistic interests he said:

> Go! damnable imps of pelf and greed. I defy your taunts! Tear to fragments my political career, if it comport with your execrable will; stifle and distort my every utterance; not satisfied, if such be your brutal frenzy, lash my poor form into insensibility; then, if it be your further pleasure, gnaw from my stiffening limbs every ves-

tige of quivering flesh; howl in wretched bestiality through my own innocent blood as it drips from your fiendish visages; drag then, if you want what remains, into the filth and vermin of your foul den and burn it upon the altar of Baal, or scatter it before the friendly winds of heaven to your betters, the carrion crows of the field![26]

As Davis spoke, according to *The Arkansas Gazette,* the press gallery emptied. Only a few senators persisted to the end. Davis mispronounced dozens of words which evidently were not part of his normal vocabulary. The *Gazette* reporter wondered if Davis had ever seen the manuscript before since he continually stumbled over words and phrases. *The Arkansas Democrat* thought "the damnable imps of pelf and greed" would "consider the source and look upon it all as a huge joke."[27]

In 1909, Davis made another foredoomed effort to secure approval of his bill to prohibit any "scheme, or plan to speculate or gamble" on agricultural futures. Again he challenged those who would oppose his reform proposals:

> I would not be an alarmist, sir, but I predict here and now that unless conditions change, that unless the Congress of the United States turns a listening ear to the lamentations of an outraged public, that within ten years there may be another Shenandoah Valley, there may be another Gettysburg; the red broom of war may sweep this Government as it has never been swept before, and when that day shall break in all its fury, woe to the crowd working the field of legislation that have laid these grievous burdens upon the backs of the crowd working the field of human endeavor.[28]

One of the damaging episodes in the Senate career of Davis was his involvement in the "sunk lands" controversy in 1910. The dispute came to a head during an investigation by a subcommittee of the United States House of Representative Committee on Public Lands. Davis testified before the committee and did little to enhance his image in the process. At one point he wired his old friend Jeremiah Wallace, "What shall I do?" and the Judge replied, "Keep your mouth shut." Wallace's biographer, his own son, wrote: "Those were unhappy days for Senator Davis, and the worry and irritation incident to them were calculated to increase his natural volatility."[29] Another ally of Davis, who came under fire during the investigation, remarked, "Every time Senator Davis opens his mouth he prejudices the matter. It would be better to pay his expenses to New York and keep him there until it is disposed of." [30]

The subcommittee hearings inquired into the views of parties interested in a bill introduced by Arkansas Representative William Oldfield at Davis's request. The senator drafted a bill "To Quiet and Confirm The Title To Certain So-Called Sunk Lands." He intended to use congressional action to settle a land dispute in the interest of his own clients and friends. The lands in question were in the low-lying country of the northeast. An earthquake, in 1810, had dropped thousands of acres to a lower level and much of the section became swampland. In 1850, the United States Congress granted the lands to the state of Arkansas, but through legal technicalities the ownership of Arkansas was disputed by the federal government. Two secretaries of the interior, one during Grover Cleveland's second term (Hoke Smith) and another during Theodore Roosevelt's administration (Ethan Allen Hitchcock), argued that the federal government did not have a just claim and should not contest Arkansas's ownership. [31]

Meanwhile, the state had granted the lands to the St. Francis Levee Board, which in turn sold them to private individuals. In 1908, the Roosevelt administration, ignoring earlier opinions, insisted the lands were legally United States property. Homesteaders, who anticipated a victory by the national government, moved into the sunk lands area. A major dispute erupted between those speculators who had purchased quitclaim deeds from the levee board and those settlers who had staked a claim. Jeff Davis served as the legal representative of the St. Francis Levee Board. He also had a number of friends in eastern Arkansas among those engaging in speculation. Among these friends was Judge E. A. Rolfe of St. Francis County, who purchased over sixty-thousand acres at $1.50 per acre. [32]

In his conduct and testimony Jeff Davis indicated less concern for the rights of those at the lower rung of the economic ladder than he had in the rhetoric of his campaigns. Many homesteaders deluged the Public Lands Committee and Arkansas congressmen with pleas to respect their claims. One supplicant wrote:

> For my sake, and hundreds of others, do all you can to knock out that bill. I have moved down here on public lands for a home, and it is fine land 90 per cent good farm land, and for that bill to pass we would all lose our homes. The land is nearly settled, and that bill would give it to the levee board and timber corporations. [33]

Congressman Joseph T. Robinson informed his fellow committee members that the homesteaders were "relying on that decision of 1908" to insist on United States ownership. But Davis told the committee to quiet the title to Arkansas and let the litigants fight it out in the courts. "It may be that it would work some hardship on the little fellow, but the great good of the public is what we want." Robinson pressed Davis hard on this point. The Arkansas Supreme Court had rendered a decision unfavorable to the speculators, and now they were "applicants" for the Davis Bill. To seek a settlement through a statute after losing ground in the courts was an unfair maneuver designed "to cut out the little fellows." As Robinson continued to ask embarrassing questions, Davis suddenly announced he had to leave.[34]

Like other Southern demagogues of the age, Davis lost some of the zeal of his earlier "Popocratic" phase once ensconced in the Senate chambers. Senator Chauncey M. Depew, who had little reason to admire Davis, remembered him as "loudly, vociferously, and clamorously a friend of the people. Precisely what he did to benefit the people was never very clear, but if we must take his word for it, he was the only friend the people had." On one occasion Davis castigated Senator Depew for his associations with the monster corporations and railroads. When he had finished his attack, Senator W. M. Crane walked to Davis's seat and warned him that Depew might "be dangerous to him personally" and by "ridicule . . . make him the laughing-stock of the . . . country." Chauncey Depew recalled that Davis "waddled over" to his seat, and said, "'Senator Depew, I hope you did not take seriously what I said. I did not mean anything against you. I won't do it again, but I thought that you would not care, because it won't hurt you, and it does help me out in Arkansas.'" *The Arkansas Gazette* chided the redneck leader for his laugh-provoking rhetoric when the nation needed genuine "tribunes of the often oppressed people!"[35]

The sunk lands dispute created a rift between Senators James P. Clarke and Jeff Davis. The redneck leader had informed Congressman Oldfield that Clarke gave assent to the sunk lands bill. He had also told the subcommittee about Clarke's concurrence with the plan. An angry Senator Clarke appeared at the hearings and condemned Davis for placing him "in a false attitude, and one which I do not want to occupy." Clarke wondered why Davis did not bother to walk across the Senate floor to ascertain his views before speaking for him. "I do censure Senator Davis," announced Clarke, "if I may use such a strong word, for having accepted second-hand the statement as to my views."[36]

During the 1911–12 primary campaign, Congressman Stephen Brundidge, in a bid for Davis's Senate seat, made generous use of the sunk lands episode. In a major address at Morrilton in December 1911, Davis answered Brundidge's attack with a long history of the affair. He told the voters that his connection with the St. Francis Levee Board had been as counsel to help obtain judgment against timber depradators. Because of the uncertain nature of land titles, the Chapman and Dewey Lumber Company had "cut and carried away a great quantity of valuable timber." If the title had remained with the federal government, the St. Francis Levee Board could not recover damages from the company. The timber interests had pressured the government to assert its title. Davis's version cast him again in the role of savior. He had delivered the public from the corrupt influence of greedy corporate interests.[37] Brundidge called on Davis to meet him in debate, but the senator consented to only four joint speaking engagements. Davis had pilloried James Berry, in 1906, for refusing joint debates, complained Brundidge, "but the senator has cold feet now and wants to take it alone."[38]

Congressman Brundidge attacked Davis's attendance record. The senator had been out of Washington for extended periods and had involved himself in campaigns for state office. He had wept when he told workers how he wished to go to Washington to help lift their burden. But he was not present to vote for an employer's liability act. Davis was not paired; he simply did not vote.[39] Charles Jacobson, who had broken with his former boss, came to the side of Brundidge in the struggle. Two other leading Davis men, John H. Page and Judge Jesse C. Hart, also broke ties with the senator.[40]

The senatorial campaign of 1912, like the Kirby-Donaghey contest, was not a struggle between progressives and conservatives. *The Literary Digest* remarked about the unusual faith of the common people in supporting Davis despite his setbacks: "they believed in him so strongly that they renominated him at a recent primary over an opponent who was supposed to represent the progressive element that is helping Arkansas to catch up with the more advanced states." But Davis viewed Brundidge as a Johnny-come-lately. "When I was fighting for the Arkansas antitrust law all over this state," complained Davis, "he was training with the other crowd with his nose turned high in the air." He has joined the ranks of other "high-collared lawyers" who "have tucked their wings and ceased their barking."[41]

Despite setbacks Davis mustered enough strength to defeat Brundidge in the 1912 primary by a sizeable margin. He won approximately seventy-two thousand votes to sixty-two thousand for Brundidge. Davis made his poorest showing in the eastern half of Arkansas where resentment against his sunk lands position as well as the traditional anti-Davis sentiment of the area combined to weaken his support. *The Literary Digest* commented on Davis's knack for holding the loyalty of "rural admirers" despite the amusement of Washington with their hero. "They took his word for it when he went back to Arkansas and told them that the reason he was laughed at in Washington was that Congress was packed with aristocrats who were naturally prejudiced against him."[42]

By the end of 1912, Davis's power had begun to erode. George Donaghey, who belonged in the opposing political camp, had emerged as a progressive leader with credentials as impressive as Davis's. The redneck leader had failed to influence the electorate to send William F. Kirby to the statehouse. While exerting less influence over state policies, Davis failed to play a stellar role in the Senate. Although his control over state affairs diminished during the years after 1908, he and his organization continued to be a major political force, and to some extent, Davis's path-breaking attacks on corporate privilege in Arkansas smoothed the way for Donaghey and later progressive governors.

Davis informed the 1912 state Democratic convention, "I am going to be in politics until I die." Death came swiftly and unexpectedly to the fighting senator. He had been dieting during the winter of 1912–13 and had lost fourteen pounds. His law partner, Frank Pace, thought Davis was in good health, but shortly after midnight on January 3, 1913, he died of a heart attack. *The Arkansas Democrat* surmised that the campaign against Brundidge "probably contributed more than anything else to undermining his robust physique."[43] With his departure the Davis organization lost much of its cohesiveness and power, but it remained a force in Arkansas politics during the next few years.

9

Changing Patterns in
the Democratic Party,
1912–1917

The election campaigns of 1912, the victory of a Democratic presidential candidate, and the death of Jeff Davis triggered dramatic changes in Arkansas's political life. The shifting alliances and the weakening of the Old Guard altered and confused the political scene. Personalities had always been a major focus of politics in Arkansas. A dynamic personality constituted the chief foundation stone of the Davis organization. But when the redneck leader passed from the scene, no single individual rallied permanent support or provoked his enemies to coalesce into a continuing institution. Now a host of individuals sought out temporary allies when and where they could find them.

In Arkansas, as across the nation, the election of Woodrow Wilson meant an end to the long Democratic patronage famine. By birth and training, Wilson was a Southerner, and the old Confederate states looked expectantly for a new influence in the counsels of Washington. But the rivalry of those seeking preference created bitterness and further confusion in Arkansas, and many believed Wilson had bypassed the state as well as his own faithful progressives. A succession of bitter primary elections spiced with Delta vote manipulation added to the political ferment. In 1912, Arkansas elected Joseph T. Robinson governor and Jeff Davis to the Senate. But when Davis died in January 1913, the new governor induced the legislature to send him to fill the vacancy. This turn of events brought a succession of governors to the executive office during 1913. As in 1907 when Governor John Little retired, constitutional technicalities produced another debate about the rightful successor. Two governors held the office after Robinson's departure until the inauguration of George W. Hays, who won a special primary election in July 1913. Somehow persisting through it all was Stephen Brundidge, a former congressman. He lost the 1912 Senate contest to Davis, the Senate race of 1913 to Robinson, and the July 1913 special gubernatorial primary to Hays. In the fall of 1913, William F. Kirby launched a determined crusade to unseat Senator James P. Clarke. Though he failed, Kirby got the place in 1916 when Clarke died. By that time Arkansas politics had weathered its season of rapid change.

During these turbulent years, progressivism became a major theme in Arkansas politics. Most politicians shifted at least part way toward the reform causes that Jeff Davis had earlier espoused. Arkansas came to resemble the Western states in its drive toward a democratic and individualistic form of progressivism. Some of the state's congressmen joined forces with the agrarian or radical Democrats who pressed for government intervention in the economy to aid depressed economic classes. Arkansas moved at least partially toward a more activist philosophy of government responsibility and away from an earlier extreme state's rights emphasis.

This era of political turbulence brought to the fore one of Arkansas's most famous political leaders. Joseph T. Robinson served in the United States Senate during Wilson's two terms and continuously until the days of Franklin D. Roosevelt's court-packing attempt in 1937. He became an unusually loyal administration senator during the two Democratic presidencies. Robinson was not a "radical" progressive, but he did spearhead several Wilsonian reforms and became the chief congressional strategist for New Deal programs in the 1930s. "To him is largely due," said Arkansas Congressman W. L. Terry, "the credit for the smooth functioning of the legislative processes involved in putting in the statutes most of the New Deal policies." Arkansas's United States Senator John Miller remembered him as "an economic and political liberal," a man who never became a "popular idol," but who proudly championed the cause of the poorer classes.[1] He became known nationally as Alfred Smith's vice presidential running mate in 1928. Robinson had reddish hair and a somewhat volatile temperament to match. Newsmen sometimes called him "Scrappy Joe." George Donaghey recalled that

"there was something extraordinarily commanding in his appearance. His large head and well-fleshed body seemed to radiate
power."[2]

Before Robinson had entered his twenties, he made a political
speech denouncing the Populists and their "socialistic" concep-
tions. In 1895, he served in the general assembly and gained fame
in Arkansas for his youthful crusade to establish a railroad commission. After the 1900 census, Arkansas received a seventh congressman, and Joseph T. Robinson won the contest in the newly
created sixth district. He acquired some support because of his
identification with the less populous areas of his district. His
home county, Lonoke, had few towns of any size while his competitor in the 1902 election came from Jefferson County, the location of the district's most populous town, Pine Bluff. Few
issues distinguished the two candidates for Congress except that
Robinson's opponent, Sam Taylor, campaigned primarily in
towns while Robinson traveled to towns and country areas. In
the 1902 contest, Robinson allied with the Jeff Davis organization
to further enhance his standing with rural Democrats.[3]

Congressman Robinson did not maintain a firm alliance with
the Davis forces beyond the 1902 election. He opposed Governor
Davis's bid for a third term in 1904, and in 1908 Robinson backed
George Donaghey for governor rather than William F. Kirby, the
Davis man.[4] A more serious assault upon the Old Guard came
when Robinson announced his intention to challenge Jeff Davis
in the 1912 United States senatorial race. Robinson had debated
whether to pursue the office of governor or senator. During
Donaghey's first term (1909–11) most politicians expected him
to run for governor in 1912. But by 1910 he had made his decision to seek a place in the Senate. During the next year, his prospects of success in the Senate race dimmed. When a tour of the
state revealed insufficient enthusiasm for Robinson's candidacy,
he withdrew from the contest. Since Congressman Stephen
Brundidge was also a serious contender, Robinson feared a three-
cornered fight would only bring victory for the incumbent Senator. Brundidge, a round-faced, large-framed Searcy politician,
never gave up on a political fight. His hatred for what he considered demagoguery, and his own consuming passion for higher
office kept the White County leader in the ring with Davis. But
Robinson turned his interest toward the gubernatorial nomination. When his campaign gained momentum in early 1912, Davis

sought to restore friendly ties with him. Jeff Davis wanted no opposition from Robinson during his difficult campaign for reelection.[5]

Both Robinson and Davis courted the other's aid. In January 1912, one of Robinson's followers, A. H. France of Gillett, spoke with Jeff Davis and reported that Davis "would prefer Yourself (Robinson) to Gov. D (Donaghey) in the coming election. He was pretty well 'stewed' but you know a drunk man speaks the truth sometimes." Another Robinson man, Attorney Earl Hardin of Fort Smith, reported that "Judge Bourland is now very Favorable." Robinson wished to avoid any indication of a breach between himself and the Davis forces. When *The Arkansas Gazette* reported Robinson had criticized Davis in a Booneville speech, Robinson men were quick to ask the newspaper to correct the slip lest votes from the Davis men be lost. The newspaper conceded the attack had been made on Donaghey and not Davis. In mid-March the *Gazette* reported that Davis had begun attacks on Robinson's foe in the campaign, George Donaghey. "Senator Davis," the paper noted, "has taken a more or less active part in the race for governor since the campaign opened, although he announced at the beginning that he would keep hands off."[6]

Three major candidates campaigned for the 1912 gubernatorial nomination. Hal L. Norwood and Joseph T. Robinson sought the office in opposition to the attempt of incumbent George W. Donaghey to return for a third term. Robinson had been allied with Donaghey, but by 1911 their interests had collided. Early in January 1912, Attorney General Norwood announced his decision to withdraw from the race. To Donaghey it was not surprising. "I informed the people of the state a few days ago," he said, "that the gang was going to take one or the other of my opponents out of the running." When Robinson continued to challenge Donaghey to reveal the identity of the mysterious "gang," he eventually pointed to a small clique in the upper house of the legislature which looked to the leadership of Senator Webb Covington. During the campaign Donaghey impugned the integrity of the legislature and tried to tie Robinson to its record, although the latter had been serving as a congressman in Washington. As the governor put it, the campaign narrowed to a fight between "box car Donaghey," who was built like a freight train but delivered the goods, and Congressman Robinson who was a Pullman car, "handsome, persuasive" but unable to carry a large cargo.[7]

The prohibition question had become increasingly important by the time of the 1912 election. The issue further confused the political scene but did not become as disruptive a force in Arkansas as it did in some other Southern states. The Tennessee Democratic Party suffered a severe rift in 1910 as that state elected a governor, Ben Hooper, who was both a Republican and a devout prohibitionist.[8] In Alabama and Texas the liquor question also seriously factionalized the Democratic Party.[9] The preponderance of evangelical churches in Arkansas and their commitment to prohibition brought early victory for the movement. By 1912 only nine of the seventy-five counties were wet. Three years later the legislature passed a statewide prohibition act. Reverend E. R. Steele, pastor of the Asbury Methodist Church in Little Rock, expressed the mood of many Arkansas churchmen when he told an Epworth League rally:

> The children of God have the best right to vote and live in the White House. The men who are opposing us are enemies of God and they have controlled this government too long. They have controlled the ballot box and dictated to the voters. It is about time to change and we claim the right to come on the streets on the authority of Jesus Christ and work for the change.[10]

But the prohibition controversy did not become a dormant issue in Arkansas politics. It reared its head in nearly every election of the early twentieth century. George W. Donaghey affirmed his belief in the need for a statewide prohibition statute. Since he did not think a legislature so dominated by the "Whiskey Interests" would pass such a law, he favored the use of the recently adopted initiative and referendum to accomplish prohibition. Joseph T. Robinson disliked the "submission" concept. He believed local option had sufficiently resolved the issue for each locality. But if the people should through the initiative and referendum demand statewide prohibition he would enforce their will.[11]

Charges and countercharges filled the air, as nearly all candidates for office accused their opponents of being tools of the whiskey interests. While Robinson men sought to tarnish the moral rectitude of Donaghey's campaign, they courted the whiskey forces themselves. Ira D. Oglesby, a prominent Fort Smith leader of Robinson's forces, assured his candidate of the backing of the "liquor crowd" in the area. "As you know," he reminded Robinson, "but few Governors have ever been elected without the support of the whiskey ring, and for their support, the Governor must, either directly or indirectly render them legislative assistance." He suggested that Robinson not grant them any political favors since "they will support you from necessity." There should be legal protection for whiskey dealers but destruction of the "whiskey ring." In another letter he informed Robinson of arrangements "to send two men out to mining camps to control Italian votes. Forced liquor men to do this. They are in a position where they must do as requested."[12]

George Donaghey in his *Autobiography* recalled that he "had been the first Southern governor to boldly and openly fight the liquor interests." But Arkansas's prohibition leaders were more skeptical. George Thornburgh, a Methodist layman and the leading light in the Arkansas Anti-Saloon League, endorsed Donaghey in 1912 as the candidate for prohibition men, but he reminded the public that he had not voted for Donaghey in 1908, since the liquor interests were behind his candidacy then. As in Texas, Arkansas temperance leaders usually represented the more progressive wing of the party. Those espousing prohibition looked upon the movement as another enlightened reform to advance social welfare.[13]

Construction of the statehouse and tax reform were also major issues of the 1912 gubernatorial campaign. Donaghey insisted he needed a third term to put the finishing touches on the capitol project. Robinson denounced the governor's quest for large appropriations to complete the building. Donaghey announced his support for the proposed Turner-Jacobson Bill, a tax reform measure, because he believed it would force the "Sugar Trust" to pay taxes on its fifteen thousand acre holdings in Arkansas. He accused Robinson of wooing the Little Rock Board of Trade and the Cotton Exchange by his opposition to the reform. The "ring" which owned five-hundred-thousand-dollars worth of property and "pays no taxes" favored the old tax system which gathered revenue primarily from the small businessman and the farmer. Jeff Davis entered the controversy on Robinson's side, late in the campaign. He told a group of farmers at Robinson's home town, with questionable accuracy, that the measure would force "double taxation" on them.[14]

The voters handed Donaghey a resounding defeat when they elected Robinson by nearly a two to one majority. Far from removing the capitol project from politics, the tempestuous governor had concentrated on the theme: he had torn down part of the structure and rebuilt it to suit his own notions. Possibly many voters remembered Jeff Davis's frequent references to the project as a million-dollar steal. The large vote revealed a distaste for Donaghey more than a popular movement for Robinson. But by the summer of 1912, Robinson was clearly in control as he dominated the state convention.[15]

When Jeff Davis suffered a fatal heart attack in January 1913, Robinson suddenly altered his plans. Almost as soon as he entered the executive office, he prepared to abandon it for a place in the Senate. Campaigning against him were William F. Kirby, Stephen Brundidge, and Hal Norwood. Robinson's three opponents challenged him to allow the voters to choose Davis's successor in a special primary. But knowing the voters would not approve his swift exit from the governor's chair, Robinson determined to secure election through action in the 1913 general assembly. Since the Seventeenth Amendment which provided for popular election of United States senators had not yet taken effect, the Arkansas legislature still had power to make its own choice. Robinson's enemies attempted to delay the organization of the house and senate and to prevent Robinson men from securing places of leadership. But the new governor had sufficient influence to secure a favorable vote in the legislature. His persistence in seeking the post caused widespread resentment among the voters. A Baptist preacher, Reverend H. L. Winburn, wrote to Charles H. Brough, "There is a wide-spread feeling of resentment toward Robinson for his frank and evident opportunism (to put it euphemistically) and an outspoken hope" he will resign. J. H. Andrews of Marianna told Brough that "Robinson's candidacy" was "very unpopular" and many hoped he would "be 'sat upon,' as he deserves." Professor Brough briefly considered entering the contest to fill the vacant governor's chair, but his correspondents warned him that if he spoke out in defense of Robinson he would lose the support of an outraged public.[16] On January 28, 1913, the legislature voted to send Governor Robinson to Washington to occupy Davis's seat in the Senate.

Joseph T. Robinson's victory in the Senate contest opened the door to political controversy about a successor. In March 1913 the president of the senate, W. K. Oldham, became acting governor, but he had held office only one week when the Arkansas Supreme Court declared the more recently elected president pro tempore of the senate, J. M. Futrell, to be the rightful governor. Earlier the legislature passed a resolution that the people should choose a governor, and the new executive called a special election for July 23, 1913.[17]

George Washington Hays, a county judge for Ouachita County, quickly emerged as the strongest contender for the gubernatorial vacancy. A few weeks after Davis's death he wrote to Charles H. Brough at Fayetteville asking him not to enter the gubernatorial contest. "I would regret very much to have to make the race against such men as your-self," he told the professor. Not until April did Brough finally decide to remove himself from the campaign.[18] But Stephen Brundidge remained a candidate in a struggle that generated much bitterness in the party. Brundidge and Hays campaigned actively from late April until the June 21 primary. The contestants raised few significant issues. Brundidge charged that Hays had made an alliance with senators Joseph T. Robinson and James P. Clarke. He hoped that public resentment against Robinson's exit from the executive office might be turned against Hays. At Conway he told a crowd he had sent a letter to Hal Norwood and Robinson asking them to join in a primary campaign for Davis's Senate seat. Norwood had agreed, but Robinson rejected the offer. Hays's refusal to speak a word of criticism against the actions of Robinson, according to Brundidge, implied an alliance. George Hays replied that Brundidge sought the governor's office only as a stepping stone to the United States Senate.[19]

During the canvass, Brundidge's campaign manager claimed Hays had entered into an arrangement with members of the St. Francis Levee District Board. Eugene Williams, treasurer of the board, had originally offered to back Brundidge, providing Williams remained in control of the board and could "control the naming of the St. Francis Levee Board" members. When the Brundidge organization refused, Williams turned immediately to Hays and received a guarantee of support.[20] Perhaps the Brundidge people embellished the tale for effect, but later developments confirmed the existence of an alliance between Williams and Hays. The latter received an unusually high percentage of votes in some eastern Arkansas counties in 1913, and as governor he sabotaged efforts to reform the levee board by making its membership elective.

As the returns trickled into Little Rock, *The Arkansas Gazette* headline read, "Election Hinges On Vote In Phillips County." Incomplete returns gave Hays 31,975 votes and Brundidge 31,205. Four counties had not reported, but Phillips County would determine the outcome. The next day, tabulations narrowed the gap to 504. Observers expected Brundidge to win heavily in Phillips County since it had been part of the congressional district he had once served. Hays had most of his strength in his own southern section of the state. While Hays maintained a paper-thin margin, Phillips County held back its returns. When the county Democratic Central Committee finally canvassed the returns on June 25, four days after the primary and after the election results of the rest of the state had become clear, they gave Brundidge 1,351 and Hays 1,043. The Hays vote was enough to avert defeat. A shocked and angry Brundidge released a midnight statement on June 25 saying, "Phillips County is in my judicial district and I have always carried the county by a large majority." He remembered defeating Senator Davis in 1912 by nearly a 1,200 majority. Candidate Hays had not even bothered to campaign in the county and was almost unknown in the area. A *Gazette* editorial agreed that the vote for Hays was "remarkable" since Brundidge had many close friends who worked hard for his election in Phillips County, while Hays did not visit the county at any time during the campaign.[21]

The action of the Phillips County Democratic Central Committee clearly violated the rules adopted by the party governing primary elections. The rules called for immediate counting of ballots at the closing of the polls without "delay or waiting, recess or adjournment" and the announcement of results "as soon as known." The central committees were to meet on the first Monday morning after the primary "and there and then publish the vote cast for each candidate." The primary had been held on June 21, a Saturday, and the committee should have published the results on June 23, a Monday. They kept the results from public view until June 25, creating the suspicion that they had waited to determine how many votes Hays needed to insure election.[22] Other counties, especially in the Delta, reported returns tardily and sometimes tinkered with the ballots, but no county equalled Phillips County's notoriety for vote manipulation.

Brundidge furiously contested the primary election, and his crusade created a rift in the Democratic Party. On June 30, the state central committee heard arguments from Brundidge's representative, Hal L. Norwood. The contestants asked for sufficient time for pollbooks from four disputed counties to be brought to Little Rock for committee examination. If no fraud were detected in the four counties, the Brundidge forces would drop all charges. The outcome of the contest became apparent when the committee rejected the request and accepted instead a resolution that evidence be presented in time for a decision on July 3, Wednesday night. Norwood insisted that the adoption of the resolution precluded any chance of preparing a case to prove fraud. He also believed the decision violated an order from the Pulaski Chancery Court ordering a fair and reasonable hearing of the Brundidge contest.[23]

The Chancery Court ruled that its injunction had been ignored and declared the committee's hearing a "travesty." *The Arkansas Gazette* agreed with this assessment and condemned the committee for deciding for Hays without examining any of the disputed pollbooks, tally sheets, or ballots. The Hays men controlled the committee and "simply ran the steam roller over the Brundidge men." On July 11 the Arkansas Supreme Court, in a majority decision written by William F. Kirby, declared the case to be outside the court's jurisdiction. This left the committee free to certify the nomination of George Hays. But the breach did not heal easily. Republican Harmon L. Remmel exulted, "The Democratic Party in the state now stands almost evenly divided into two strong factions as a result of the late primary election." Brundidge continued to make public denunciations of Hays during the general election campaign, but most prominent Democrats and the *Gazette* called for unity. One congressman warned Arkansas Democrats against emulating the "Tennessee vendetta" that turned the state over to Republicans. Despite recriminations and divisions, Hays won the July 23 election with 53,655 votes to 16,842 for the Republican candidate. When he took the inaugural oath in August, he became the fifth governor to hold office in 1913.[24] The election demonstrated the growing tensions within the party and the continuing resentment of the Delta political machines by Democrats in other sections of the state.

Poinsett County figured prominently in another close primary in 1914. William F. Kirby challenged incumbent Senator James P. Clarke. Both men had been associated with Jeff Davis, but Clarke had fallen out of favor in his later years, and in 1914 the remnants of the Davis forces aligned themselves to defeat "old Cotton

Top." Poinsett County announced returns showing 1,296 votes
for Delta chieftain Clarke and 615 votes for Kirby, but when it
became evident that Clarke was losing in the statewide returns by
184 votes, the county officials revised their figures to 1,621 to
450. The *Gazette* refused to accept these figures in their tally, and
eventually the county committee changed the vote once more, to
1,521 for Clarke and 450 for Kirby. This turned the tide for
Clarke, and he scraped through to victory. The state auditor
noted that only 1,537 Poinsett County citizens paid poll taxes for
1913 while the total vote certified by the committee was 1,971.
The Log Cabin Democrat in Conway denounced Clarke's "corrupt
bunch of robbers" who had controlled the election machinery.
"This state," said the newspaper, "has so long endured the domination of Eastern Arkansas political thieves that it has become
rather accustomed to having to overcome padded votes and ballot box stuffing by these crooks." Like Brundidge, William F.
Kirby contested the election before the state central committee
and the state convention but without success. The convention
voted 469 to 163 not to take up the question of Kirby's contest.[25]

The election of 1912 and the return of a Democrat to the White
House contributed to the pattern of change in Arkansas politics.
Wilson had many supporters in the state before the Baltimore
Convention, but most of them were not in places of leadership in
the party. Charles H. Brough, professor of economics and sociology at the University of Arkansas, was among the early Wilson
men. In 1910, the future Arkansas governor wrote to congratu-
late Wilson upon his victory in the New Jersey gubernatorial
race. He reminded Wilson that he had been one of the "old boys"
at Johns Hopkins who had listened to his lectures on "historical
jurisprudence." "Wilson for President in 1912," he assured the
new governor, "will now be the slogan of Southern Democrats—
certainly of those of us who know you."[26] In Virginia two months
after Wilson's September 1910 nomination, anti-organizaton
Democrats formed the nation's first Wilson-for-President clubs.
Politicians who had ranged themselves against the organization
Democrats, led by Senator Thomas S. Martin, now joined with
some of Virginia's leading educators to press for the Wilson nomination. Thomas B. Love and other Texas progressives also reacted to the New Jersey victory by taking up the banner for
Wilson. Across the nation, those who identified themselves with
progressivism fell in line with the Wilson movement.[27]

James H. Harrod became one of the most active and loyal of the Wilson men in Arkansas. He had been the choice of moderates for governor in 1896 when the silverite Dan Jones won the nomination. In 1912 he served as president of the Little Rock Woodrow Wilson Club. Early in January he presented a resolution to the State Democratic Central Committee that the serious contenders for the presidential nomination be placed on the primary ballot and the candidate with the highest vote be "accepted" as the choice of the Arkansas delegation to the national convention. Harrod delivered a long speech eulogizing Wilson, but Senator James P. Clarke spoke in favor of an uncommitted delegation. He wanted no discussion of candidates in the state committee, and he refused to align himself with any potential nominee. Clarke succeeded in forcing Harrod to withdraw his proposal. Other original Wilson men who led the Little Rock club included John W. Crockett, Earl W. Hodges, De Emmett Bradshaw, Carroll D. Wood and June P. Wooten. Crockett had been a Davis man briefly, but like Wood, he became one of the fiercest opponents of the redneck leader. Bradshaw was an attorney and labor leader.[28]

Before the Baltimore convention met, Woodrow Wilson came to Little Rock where James H. Harrod and Earle W. Hodges met him and took him to meet Governor George W. Donaghey. The state executive promised, "We're going to work hard for you down in Arkansas, Governor Wilson." But the governor avoided presidential politics during his own struggle to retain his office. William F. McCombs, Wilson's campaign manager, found prospects in Arkansas very discouraging during his tour of the South. He was born and raised in the state, and his father had been "one of the largest planters and merchants in southeast Arkansas." McCombs had "considerable hopes, or rather profound longing," that he might enlist his native state for the Wilson candidacy. But when he arrived in the state capital, he "found that the Clark forces had stolen a long march on us and that the Speaker could not be withheld from carrying the primaries." McCombs left the state "in chagrin." The weak efforts of Donaghey and his progressives could not pull the state into Wilson's camp. The "businesslike" governor had antagonized many of the state's politicians by his vigorous use of the veto to prune appropriations and his refusal to bargain with members of the legislature. Joseph T. Robinson became the rising star in Arkansas politics, and the young man from the prairie rice fields of east central Arkansas was not a Wilson man.[29]

The Wilson movement in Arkansas failed because of lack of organization and because its leadership was unable to control the party machinery. Before the township mass meetings gathered to select delegates for county conventions, Champ Clark men carried their message to each section of the state. By the time county conventions selected delegates for the state convention, the Clark men had built up a large following. Clark's victory in Arkansas came in part because of the campaign led by Jerry C. South. A well-known Arkansas politician from northeast Arkansas, South held the post of chief clerk of the United States House of Representatives. Loyalty to the Speaker of the House prompted South to leave his Washington office to set up Clark headquarters at Little Rock. To the disgust of Wilson men, he remained several weeks away from the national capital to direct the campaign. The Wilson men organized Wilson Clubs but relied mainly on a few newspaper appeals. One of the chief difficulties for Wilson men was the proximity of Clark's state. "The idea," declared the Woodrow Wilson Club of Little Rock in a newspaper advertisement, "that the Democrats of this state should vote against Woodrow Wilson because Arkansas is a neighbor to Missouri is absolute nonsense."[30]

Joseph T. Robinson's victory in the primary election practically ended Wilson's chances of securing Arkansas. Gubernatorial nominees usually dominated the state convention, and the Robinson organization placed itself behind Champ Clark. At the state convention, Clark's twenty-one-year-old son made an appearance to express appreciation for the loyalty of many Arkansans to his father. The state's leaders also, despite the continuing popularity of Bryan, chose to redeem the party from the Nebraskan's leadership. Senator James P. Clarke used the convention as a platform to denounce William Jennings Bryan because the latter had not genuinely forgiven "good Democrats" who had refused to vote for him in 1896. The convention silenced "old Cotton Top" with cheering and cries of "sit down" and "Bryan, Bryan."[31]

At the Baltimore convention the Arkansas delegates, under Robinson's leadership, deserted Bryan in his bid for temporary chairman. To the chagrin of some of the Wilson delegates, the state voted as a unit against the Great Commoner. Robinson not only sought to place Arkansas's forces squarely behind Champ

Clark but also became one of Clark's floor strategists at the con-vention.[32] Although Robinson did not originally favor the Wilson nomination, he later became one of Wilson's most devoted servants during his Senate career.

Oscar W. Underwood and Judson Harmon had very little strength in Arkansas. Underwood, of Alabama, generally gathered those of conservative temperament in the South into his fold. Both Clark and Wilson appealed to the progressives, and William Jennings Bryan had not given public indication of which one he favored before the convention. Texas became Wilson's most potent champion in the South. Texas politicians like Thomas B. Love, Thomas Watt Gregory, and Albert Sidney Burleson admired the manner in which Wilson triumphed over the New Jersey machine forces of James Smith. They hoped to dismantle Joseph Bailey's forces in the same manner. At the Baltimore convention, Gregory and Love allied the Texas delegation with the Pennsylvanians, and the two states spearheaded the operation that brought victory to Wilson.[33]

While Joseph T. Robinson worked for Wilson's defeat, another native son helped marshal allies to secure his nomination. William F. McCombs, who became chairman of the National Democratic Committee in 1912, came originally from Hamburg, Arkansas, and maintained contacts with his home state after moving to New York City. McCombs had been lame since childhood and habitually leaned on a cane. Contemporaries described him as six feet tall with auburn hair "tinged with gray" which was "brushed back from a high forehead." He had a "clean cut" face which gave him an "intellectual" appearance. As a young man he came into contact with the austere Professor Wilson during student days at Princeton. Like James K. Jones a decade earlier, McCombs lost the confidence of many prominent Democrats. During the campaign effort, he also lost favor with Wilson. Three days before the inauguration, McCombs publicly announced his determination not to accept a Wilson appointment, and when Wilson offered him the French ambassadorship, the Arkansan coolly refused. "They are trying to send me to St. Helena," he commented, "after all I have done." One year later the embittered national chairman expressed an interest in an appointment as ambassador to the revolution-scarred land of Mexico. Edward M. House raised the question of the appointment, but the president thought McCombs could not serve in such a critical position. The secre-

tary of the treasury, William G. McAdoo, vigorously opposed
the continuation of McCombs in power, and before the 1916
national convention met, the Arkansan gave his resignation to
Wilson.[34]

William McCombs failed to secure an influential position in
the dispensing of patronage. A loyal McCombs Democrat, T. J.
Pence, stopped by the White House and penciled a note to Wilson's secretary, Joseph Tumulty, in 1913 saying, "Don't let any
one be appointed Supt. of the Hot Springs Reservation until I see
you. McCombs wants it for his brother." Honoring the request
Wilson wrote to Secretary of the Interior Franklin K. Lane, "I am
anxious to have the brother of Mr. William F. McCombs appointed to this post." But the plans never materialized. As early
as March 1913 the *Louisville Courier-Journal* reported that "Mr.
McCombs who did most to capture the nomination at the Baltimore convention" was already marked for exile or retirement.
The newspaper chided Wilson for allowing William G. McAdoo
instead of McCombs to be the "arbiter of patronage." McAdoo
placed a clipping of the article in his files and wrote in the margin,
"Another specimen of McCombs malevolence and lying. . . . He
is a Republican and never loses a chance to lie about me."[35]

The McAdoo–McCombs feud had come to a head even before
the inauguration of Wilson. In early August 1912, Wilson traveled to the New York campaign headquarters to resolve conflicts
between the two men. Later, McCombs sought a cabinet post as
a reward for shepherding the Wilson forces to the Baltimore victory. He wanted to be secretary of state, attorney general, or secretary of the treasury, and he finally decided to press for the latter
office. He was just as desirous of keeping McAdoo from the post
as he was to have it for himself. The choice of his rival indicated
that McCombs faced a bleak political future. Many of McCombs'
colleagues believed his determination to dominate affairs, his par-
anoid temperament, and his nervous collapse after the convention
contributed to his fall. Joseph Tumulty said, "He was sensitive to
a pathological degree, jealous, suspicious of everybody."[36]

As in other Southern states, many of the original Wilson men
in Arkansas complained of the president's passing them by to
court favor with the established powers in the halls of Congress
and the statehouses. Wilson had originally intended to use patronage to strengthen the progressives, who in the South were
those opposing conservative machine politicians. But, as Albert

Sidney Burleson warned, such a program would alienate congressmen and foredoom any chance of passing reform legislation. One of Arkansas's "progressives," who failed to receive a patronage award, was Oscar H. Winn. He boasted of his record on the side of the reform forces in Arkansas. He once initiated a "four years war against the round bale trust" by building seven square bale gins. Winn successfully introduced a bill into the state legislature "doing away with the assumed risk and the contributory negligence feature of our laws which prevented recovery for injuries sustained on account of negligence of fellow servants." He wrote the bill establishing Arkansas's first tuberculosis sanitarium and fought to require railroads to pay one percent of their gross receipts into the educational system. "I have since a long time before I could vote aligned myself with the progressive, reform element of the democratic party. I have been a persistent and consistent fighter for reform in our party ranks." The disappointed Winn wrote to William Jennings Bryan that he had spent fifteen thousand dollars for the Bryan cause yet had never held a federal post.[37]

But more important to the Wilson men was the appointment of James Harrod as district attorney for eastern Arkansas. As Winn informed Wilson, "Jim Harrod was the original Wilson man of Arkansas."[38] But when Jeremiah Bourland's name went to the United States Senate on June 5, 1913, for confirmation as district attorney for western Arkansas, the name of Harrod did not accompany it as many had expected. *The Arkansas Gazette* surmised that "some hitch" had developed. On June 11 the *Gazette* reported Harrod was still favored, but other names were "being mentioned." The next day Harrod ended the controversy by stepping off a curb into the path of a speeding automobile. His death on a Little Rock street removed him from the scene but left Oscar Winn more embittered than before. "You know and I know," he wrote to Bryan, "that if President Wilson's wishes in the matter had been properly respected Mr. Harrod would have been appointed two months ago." The men who opposed Harrod were the same men who had always attacked Bryan's "progressive policies." Winn recalled how he had joined with Charles Collins to win Pulaski County for Bryan in 1896. Now those who had opposed him in Little Rock were seeking the jobs.[39]

Although Senator Joseph T. Robinson had fought for Champ Clark's nomination and had just entered the Senate, he succeeded in pressing his claims for a share in the patronage distribution. He successfully placed his campaign manager in the position of marshal for the western Arkansas district. In appointing him, Wilson again bypassed one of the early Wilson men who sought the position.[40] But the disaffection extended beyond the original Wilson men. As Congressman Otis Wingo put it, "Arkansas has been practically ignored in the distribution of patronage."[41] Wilson's Arkansas policy closely resembled his handling of patronage in Virginia. During the first year of his administration, the president temporized and tried to achieve compromise between the organizaton forces and progressive elements in the Old Dominion. But Wilson's ultimate decision was to grant the bulk of federal patronage to established politicians who in return endorsed his policies. At the cost of alienating progressive friends, Wilson secured a more accommodating Congress.[42]

By the time Arkansas entered the Wilson era, Jeff Davis had died. But his organization survived and became a significant power in Arkansas politics at least until the end of Wilson's first term. The appointment of Davis's life-long friend and political ally, Jeremiah V. Bourland, as district attorney for western Arkansas in 1913 demonstrated the vitality of the Old Guard after the death of their leader. Davis had appointed Bourland as chancellor of the tenth Arkansas Judicial District. After filling out a term in that office, Bourland won reelection. In 1913, he had over five years remaining in his term, but he decided to seek appointment as United States district attorney. Senator James P. Clarke's relationship with Davis had waned, but he endorsed Bourland for the post. Joseph T. Robinson, who had just entered the governor's office at Davis's death and had quickly moved up to the vacant Senate seat, placed his weight behind a different candidate, Troy Pace of Harrison, Arkansas. According to one observer, Clarke vehemently opposed Troy Pace because the latter had "led a crowd in 'hissing' him" at a state convention.[43]

During the spring of 1913, the contest developed into a prolonged battle between the two senators, with the remnants of Davis's following demanding the appointment of Bourland. "I understand our senators are somewhat divided," wrote Thomas S. Osborne, a hopeful compromise candidate, to Josephus Daniels. United States Senator William Hughes from New Jersey spoke of the "bitter fight" between Clarke and Robinson over the appointment.[44] Loyal Jeff Davis men made their position clear in letters to the senators. "As a member of the Davis 'Old Guard,'" wrote Edwin Hines, one of the faithful, "I want to say that the Davis following wants and expects Judge Bourland to receive this appointment."[45] The Davis men sought the appointment as a tribute to their fallen leader. "You will remember with many a thrill," wrote George A. Henning, one of the Bourland men to Senator Robinson, "the hard battles fought by the old guard during the never to be forgotten days, when our beloved Jeff Davis, reigned supreme."[46]

Many politicians advised the new senator, Joseph T. Robinson, to end his opposition to Bourland and to begin courting the Davis element. "Judge Bourland, as you know," wrote Sam R. Chew, "managed largely the several campaigns of the late Senator Davis, and has inherited largely the popularity of Senator Davis with the masses." The writer believed aid for Bourland would insure Robinson's political future. Jeptha H. Evans, an Old Guard leader, expressed similar views. The relationship of Bourland to Davis, he said, gave the appointment a "peculiar significance."[47] Robinson seemed to believe the appointment "could not unify the Jeff Davis element" in western Arkansas. The impression was a false one, wrote Arkansas State Senator George Washington Wagner of Crawford County. Only an endorsement of Bourland could establish friendly relations with the Davis men in Franklin and Crawford Counties (near Fort Smith). It would be, advised the correspondent, the best preparation for the Senate election six years away.[48]

Otis Wingo, one of Arkansas's most progressive congressmen, told Attorney General James McReynolds that Senator Clarke actually favored another candidate but would probably continue to support the Old Guard choice since "Mr. Bourland is a brother-in-law of Ex-Senator Davis." Wingo also favored Jeremiah Bourland. Finally on May 31, both Clarke and Robinson wrote the attorney general of their agreement, after "protracted and frequent negotiations," to recommend Bourland.[49]

During the next few years, Jeremiah Bourland continued to exhibit the Davis flair for pompous and bombastic rhetoric. He also identified himself with crusades to aid impoverished classes. At a mass meeting, he rallied a Fort Smith audience behind angry laundry strikers. At one point in his speech, Bourland "suddenly tore his collar from his neck, ripped it in two and stamped on it." Those who had any respect for wives and mothers would not send white shirts to a "laundry which does not pay its girls at least $10 a week." The usual five-dollar wage "would not support a common hound dog." He had "no more respect for a scab than . . . for a rattlesnake." He hoped his tombstone would bear the epitaph, "Here is a friend of organized labor."[50]

In 1917, Jeremiah Bourland sought reappointment to the office of district attorney. In his effort to convince the administration to renew his appointment, he wrote an ornate fifteen page letter to Attorney General Thomas Watt Gregory. The letter amused Gregory, and he apparently penciled in annotations in the margins. At one point Bourland began a lengthy verbal barrage with "I do not employ ornate or fanciful verbiage, but, . . ." Thomas Gregory commented, "46 word sentence." The very next sentence ran for two and a half pages and totaled 461 words. Somewhat in the fashion of Davis's later rhetoric, Bourland charged Germany with:

> a wanton prodigality of means and methods which pale exploits of Hun and Vandal, and make *light* and *resplendent* the *darkest pages* of Rome or Anthens [sic]; though Pagan Rome and Pagan Athens, at least in their more degenerate epochs, became more degraded in practical fiendishness, barbarity and licentious excesses than had been conceived by even Lucifer himself or by his imps of Hades, in any age of earthly debasement since THE ARCH FIEND was vaulted, as it is said, from the battlements of Heaven.[51]

Senators William F. Kirby and Joseph T. Robinson refused to endorse Bourland in 1917. Their rejection evidenced a decline in the fortunes of the Davis faction. Bourland seemed an anachronism, an old "Popocrat" who had outlived his era. Representatives of the United Mine Workers claimed that "he is supported almost to a man by organized labor." But union strength in rural Arkansas was a weak force. In Sebastian County, Bourland's home, the county central committee continued to support Bourland. But the Wilson administration displayed no great love for him. Attorney General Gregory, in a memorandum to Woodrow Wilson, argued that the Kirby-Robinson candidate "would be a much superior man to the present District Attorney, whose term has expired and whose services have been very unsatisfactory."[52]

While Bourland asked reappointment in the western district, Jeff Davis's son sought the position of district attorney for eastern Arkansas. William F. Kirby, who had been Davis's choice for governor in 1908, now threw his weight behind the son. Tom J. Terral, later a governor of Arkansas (1925–27), also entered the lists for Wallace Davis. He cited Davis's service as national committeeman and as attorney general of Arkansas. Governor George W. Hays (1913–17) had appointed him to fill out the term of an attorney general who died in office. At an early date, according to Terral, Wallace Davis had advocated Woodrow Wilson's nomination. But Charles Jacobson sent a letter to Thomas Watt Gregory warning him against the appointment. "Wallace Davis's only qualification," wrote Jacobson, "is his questionable political influence due to being the son of the late Jeff Davis." Despite the loyal backing of the Old Guard, the redneck leader's son failed to win the nomination. The Davis men had lost much of their bargaining power in Arkansas politics.[53]

As the memory of Jeff Davis receded, his faction's role in the state's primary elections diminished. New groups arose and declined, but no single powerful organization managed to muster the strength of Davis's machine. No longer could the voter choose between two hostile camps at the primary election. A welter of personalities and transient factions confronted the citizen as he considered his primary vote. But much of the color, the rhetoric, and personal abuse of Davis's era lingered on to enliven the election campaigns of Arkansas. But if the Populist style of a Bourland or Davis seemed anachronistic after 1913, the zeal for progressive reform in Arkansas did not wane.

During Woodrow Wilson's first term, Southern congressmen often played a significant role in advancing and shaping the progressive reforms of the era. Southern progressives did not stand consistently on the side of governmental intervention to achieve social and economic justice. Sometimes those who stood firmly for currency reform and trust regulation demonstrated less fervor for child labor legislation and social reforms. But despite inconsistency and lack of solidarity among the Southern Democratic progressives, many times they rallied behind the movement for reform. At least the Arkansas congressional delegation, more often than not, sided with the "agrarian radicals" or "advanced progressives."[54]

Arkansas congressmen of the Wilson era usually identified themselves with those who wished to use government power to redress the inequities of the economic system. In 1906, Senator James P. Clarke was one of the most vocal agrarian Democrats who fought to grant rate-making powers to the Interstate Commerce Commission. He later voted for a children's bureau within the Labor Department, popular election of senators, the Clayton Anti-injunction Act, workman's compensation for railroad employees, and the farmer's free list.[55] Despite Clarke's progressive stance, he was too much of a maverick to ever be a Wilson man of the Joseph T. Robinson brand. The *Outlook,* after his death, commented, "Senator Clarke was not in high favor with the Administration. This is perhaps because the Administration was not altogether in high favor with Senator Clarke." Arthur Wallace Dunn spoke of him as "a 'White House Democrat' in the Roosevelt days." He "had never been regularly on the Democratic reservation, always exhibiting an independence that was at times disconcerting to his fellow Democrats." He broke with the Democratic leadership by speaking out for ratification of Roosevelt's Panama Canal Treaty. In 1913 Clarke complained to Thomas McRae that the Democrats were too submissive to Wilson. Clarke wanted Congress to adjourn even if it meant delay of currency reform so that he could get home to campaign for the 1914 Senate election. Despite his independence and the fact that he was not the most elderly senator, his fellow Democrats elected him president pro tempore in 1913, and again in 1915. An anti-imperialist, the rebellious senator failed in his attempt to add the Clarke Amendment to the Philippine Bill. The amendment, according to the *Outlook,* "would have almost certainly insured the abandonment of the Philippines . . . within a few years." He boldly defied Wilson's leadership by organizing the opposition to the president's shipping bill, and just before his death in 1916 President Pro Tempore Clarke left his seat in the Senate and refused to place his signature on the Adamson Act.[56] Clarke's radicalism stopped short of approving government intervention to dictate an eight-hour day to railroads. Though most Democrats supported the Adamson Act as a party measure, Clarke never felt strongly bound by such commitments.[57]

George Donaghey recalled Clarke as "a man of remrkable [*sic*] magnetism, who had achieved some reputation for his skill in cussing picturesquely." Vice President Thomas R. Marshall remembered Clarke as "a character," a man who was "different from the large body of mankind." He refused to "see or talk to a reporter, and it was only a new man in Washington who dared to approach him with the idea of obtaining . . . his views." On one occasion a constituent asked him why he had not replied to a letter. Clarke replied, "I have already answered too many fool letters that have been sent to me from Arkansas, and when I am reelected I do not propose to waste any time answering every fool who writes me." The vice president thought Joseph T. Robinson was "far more of the politician than . . . Senator Clarke." He believed Robinson was "a man of brains and capacity."[58]

Clarke's individualistic behavior became an issue during his 1914 Senate race. William F. Kirby supporters spread the message that Clarke was "out of harmony with President Wilson" and was an enemy of Bryan. The senator tried to counteract the charges in a pamphlet, *How Does Senator Clarke Stand at Washington*. The tract included a testimonial from Woodrow Wilson that "Senator Clarke has invariably supported the Administration in a most generous way." William Jennings Bryan contributed a statement that Clarke had not been antagonistic toward him and that he had "at all times supported President Wilson in the fight for Tariff reform and currency legislation." If the statements were not entirely candid, they did demonstrate Clarke's fear that his independent course might hurt him in the primary election.[59]

Woodrow Wilson needed the cooperation of Democrats like Clarke in order to strengthen his political base in the states and to drive his programs through Congress. During the year after the inauguration, Wilson's lieutenants established ties with Democratic state leaders in preparation for the 1914 election. To some extent, Wilson's accommodation with entrenched leaders moderated the agrarian impulse of the South. During the 1914 campaign Wilson sent letters of endorsement to aid allies in state elections. In Arkansas Wilson's backing of Clarke meant rejection of the more radical agrarian William F. Kirby. In Texas the president sought to strengthen the progressives by announcing his support for prohibitionist-progressive gubernatorial candidate Thomas H. Ball. The progressives feared election of the demagogic hero of the tenant farmers, James E. Ferguson, would weaken their influence in the state party. Despite Wilson's plea the state turned to colorful "Farmer Jim." In Wisconsin, Joseph E. Davies, one of Wilson's "liaison" men, a liberal Democrat, helped prepare a slate of progressive Democrats to oppose conservative Democrats for the party's nominations. Many state leaders resented the interference of Wilson in state affairs.[60]

Joseph T. Robinson's career furnishes another example of Arkansas progressivism. In almost every situation the young senator followed the lead of President Wilson. He fought for a lowering of the tariff even to the detriment of the cotton and rice interests of his own state.[61] He supported currency reform and took an active part in shaping the Federal Trade Commission Act. His letters to the administration indicated a determination to secure legislation on "interlocking directorates, holding companies and stock watering."[62] Joseph T. Robinson became a firm advocate of a federal child labor law. Many Southern congressmen wavered on the issue, but Texas and Arkansas remained more loyal to this cause than the eastern textile states.[63] Robinson told Joseph Tumulty that despite the "grave controversy among Democratic Senators," he would exert his influence to secure passage of the Keating-Owen Child Labor Bill. In 1924, Arkansans demonstrated further concern for child labor when the state legislature became the first in the Union to ratify the proposed Child Labor Amendment to the constitution. By December 1, 1925, Arkansas, Arizona, California, and Wisconsin ratified the amendment. Ratification passed by a slim margin in the Arkansas house of representatives, 45 to 41, and in the senate, 15 to 13.[64]

The entrance of William F. Kirby to the United States Senate brought an even stronger progressive voice to Washington. To most Arkansans, Kirby represented the agrarian mood and the democratic tendencies of the state more faithfully than the senator he replaced, James P. Clarke. In his unsuccessful campaign to unseat Clarke in 1914, Kirby revealed his advanced progressive sentiments. Instead of merely taxing cotton futures as Clarke proposed, he believed the practice should be prohibited. He thought the Wilsonian banking and currency reforms were inadequate. The system had been designed for the needs of the commercial interests. Land, the farmer's basic asset, should be accepted as collateral for loans. Kirby called for creation of a "rural banking and credit system" and supported a constitutional amendment to provide for direct election of the president. *The Log Cabin Democrat* of Conway compared the two contestants in 1914: "Inherently and by environment, Senator Clarke is essentially an aristocrat and he views the problems of the nation from the aristocratic standpoint." But Kirby, the editor thought, was a man like Jeff Davis who enjoyed "mingling . . . with the common people."[65] Although Kirby failed to unseat Clarke in 1914, he did win the senatorship in a special election held after Clarke's death in 1916.

Most upsetting to the Wilson administration was Senator Kirby's adamant opposition to American participation in war. During Kirby's campaign in 1913, he had warned that the Monroe Doctrine did "not require that we shall regulate the internal affairs of Mexico to protect any financial interest of any of our citizens." He feared war with Mexico might distract the nation from needed currency reform. He hoped Wilson would avoid war with Mexico, "if it can be done consistent with the honor and dignity of the nation, and I believe that it can be done." [66]

After Germany announced her intention to resume unrestricted submarine warfare, Woodrow Wilson broke off diplomatic relations with the Imperial government. On February 7, 1917, Missouri Senator William J. Stone offered a resolution supporting the president's action. William F. Kirby was one of the five senators voting against the resolution. [67] Publication of the Zimmerman note brought the nation closer to belligerency as the Senate debated the Armed Ship Bill. The measure was in line with Wilson's expressed desire to defend American neutrality rights. When Senator Robert La Follette led attempts to obstruct passage of the bill, Kirby gave him loyal support.

On March 2, the Arkansas senator made a determined speech opposing arming of American merchant and passenger vessels. In a statement which might have been a reference to President Wilson's message to the Congress a few days before, he said, "The time has come when we should tear aside cant and hypocrisy and sham." He did not believe Germany's "Sussex Pledge" constituted an "agreement." Germany had never promised an unconditional disavowal of submarine warfare but had insisted on the right to resume U-boat activity at any time. Kirby ridiculed the administration's suggestion that Germany's actions were "in contravention" of a "solemn promise." It was not Germany's actions that had created the war fever, but the business community was "crying for war . . . in order that their profits may continue safe." The real "reason for engaging in war, is that our commercial interests shall be protected . . . in selling supplies and munitions to belligerents." Wall Street wanted the war, "the same Wall Street that revels yonder in the coining of money and that would revel in the coining of the blood and patriotism of the Nation into dividends." He believed "a hireling sensational press—that ought to be in hell" had "inflamed" popular opinion and that Wall

Street pressures made it impossible for the Senate to deliberate in a calm and rational manner.[68] Kirby's rhetoric reflected an anti-Eastern sentiment that ran deep in the Southern brand of progressivism. Like the Populists of an earlier decade, Kirby detected conspiracy on the part of the eastern colonial overlords. His independent course, like Clarke's record of rebellion, indicated a continuing negativism and a democratic emphasis in the state's reform movement.

The dilatory and obstructive tactics of La Follette, Kirby, and others prevented the Senate from enacting into law Wilson's plan to arm American vessels. The overwhelming majority in the Senate favored the bill. To Wilson, the action of the recalcitrants was "incredible." "A little group of willful men, representing no opinion but their own, have rendered the great Government of the United States helpless and contemptible." On March 5, Charles H. Brough sent a lengthy message to the Arkansas General Assembly which offered congratulations on Wilson's second inauguration and upheld the president's policies. Brough suggested "that some resolution or mark of our confidence in President Wilson be expressed by the Forty-First General Assembly." "War may come," Brough warned, "but if it comes the people who have pledged their faith to this great leader will stand ready to protect American institutions. The crew of the common people will not fail him." The legislature voted unanimously to send Brough's message as an expression of their approval of his administration. The Arkansas Senate also approved a resolution commending Robinson for being "true to the people of Arkansas on the 'Armed Neutrality Resolution.'" *The Arkansas Gazette* called upon Arkansans to "repudiate before the nation, by every means that may be immediately to hand, the action of Senator W. F. Kirby." Although former Governor George W. Donaghey stood with Kirby on the issue and informed Wilson of his position, most Arkansans disagreed with the peacemakers. Kirby's position reflected an anti-war sentiment not infrequently apparent among the farming classes of the South.[69]

Kirby was not a wholehearted pacifist, but he did not believe conditions demanded war in early March. Even when Germany's submarines made attacks upon American vessels, he still believed the resort to force a mistake. In the end, Kirby joined with those casting their votes for war. "But if there was the slightest chance on God's earth," he told the Senate on the evening of the declaration of war, "that my vote against it would defeat it, I would stand here and vote a thousand years if it might be that we do not go to war."[70]

During Kirby's reelection campaign in 1920, his opponent, Thaddeus H. Caraway, made use of Kirby's war record to discredit him. Possibly these attacks contributed to the senator's defeat. The Secretary of War Newton D. Baker wrote a letter of support for Kirby to the editor of the *Batesville Record*. He commended the senator's "zeal and fine discernment" as a member of the military affairs committee. The letter excited Caraway to draft a voluminous reply to Baker in which he recited Kirby's record on the war as well as the senator's demand for attaching reservations to the Versailles Treaty. Caraway believed Secretary Baker's sentiments were antithetical to those of the president and the rest of the cabinet.[71]

After Kirby's defeat, the Democratic members of the Senate importuned the president to secure a place for him on the Tariff Commission. Newton D. Baker lent his aid again. "In the early days," admitted Baker, "Kirby acted badly and joined forces with our adversaries, but from the day we declared war until now he has been as stalwart and constant a defender of the War Department and advocate of its policies in the Military Affairs Committee and in the Senate as we have had." Senator Joseph T. Robinson, though "with a great deal of diffidence, and with some embarrassment" also asked the president's consideration for the wayward Democrat. Robinson said he had "not been politically intimate" with Kirby, and he understood Wilson's reluctance "for reasons you have stated to me." In replying, Wilson went to some pains to express his "genuine affection" for Robinson. "You have been a wonderful friend and have excited my constant admiration as well as my loyal friendship." Yet, Wilson refused the request: "I do not know any man who has more grievously disappointed me." The president's adamant rejection of a Kirby appointment served as another illustration of his vindictiveness toward political opponents. Like his predecessor Clarke, Senator Kirby manifested an unusual degree of independence and pluck. His career symbolized the "agrarian radicalism" and the democratic tendencies of his frontier native state.[72]

Not all Arkansas politicians displayed the untamed nature of a Clarke, Kirby, or a Davis, but many others did importune the Wilson administration to adopt progressive reform measures.

Thomas C. McRae, who had served in Congress until 1903, became one of Arkansas's leading bankers and a firm advocate of currency reform legislation. Shortly after Wilson's inauguration, he wrote the president asking him to press for immediate consideration of the money question in Congress. He believed the tariff the most pressing issue but thought a currency law should not be delayed beyond the end of the year. When Congress considered the question, Senator Joseph T. Robinson sent a copy of pending legislation for McRae's advice. Later, in October, McRae spoke before the American Banker's Association at its annual meeting in Boston. When a committee of the association presented a critical evaluation of Wilson's currency proposals, McRae rose to defend the chief executive. He thought it "unfortunate" that the committee "should insert in its report at this juncture reflections upon the pending Administration Currency Bill by characterizing it as socialistic." He told the Boston audience that government, not banks, should control currency, and he condemned the movement to create a central bank. During his speech there were cries of "No, no" and "time is up." [73]

One of the most aggressive advocates of currency reform in 1913 was Otis Wingo, an Arkansas congressman. Wingo had been in his teens when the Populist tidal wave passed through his home county in southwestern Arkansas. He had barely entered his twenties at the turn of the century when he began a law career at De Queen, Arkansas. Quickly he rose to power in the Democratic Party, and at the 1904 state convention he led the drive in the Platform and Resolutions Committee to specifically include a statement supporting passage of Davis's King Bill. The measure incorporated Jeff Davis's distinctive view that a corporation which fixed prices in areas beyond the state borders could be prohibited from doing business within Arkansas. He also took a hand in the fight at the convention for passage of a Davis-sponsored resolution to choose the 1906 Democratic United States Senatorial candidate by means of a primary election. [74] During the 1907 and 1909 sessions of the Arkansas senate, he drafted the Wingo Corporation Act which placed a tax on corporations for the privilege of doing business in the state, wrote the act to establish a state normal school, proposed a resolution which led to the investigation of fraud in the capitol construction program, and directed a successful senate battle to create four agricultural schools in the state. In 1912 he won the Democratic primary nomination for congressman.[75] Wingo's district included the tier of counties running along the western border from Fort Smith to the Red River, and also much of the Ouachita Mountain area. The hilly section had a strong Populist background and continued to show an independent spirit in the 1900s. The western counties sometimes refused to back any of the factions offering a slate of delegates for the state and national conventions. They preferred to choose only non-officeholders as delegates to the conventions. Wingo represented an independent-minded section.

In 1913 Otis Wingo began a career in the House of Representatives that continued until his death in 1930. One of his colleagues said, at the time of his death, "He loved the common man and was the defender of the poor and oppressed." Many of his friends considered his work as a member of the House Banking and Currency Committee in shaping the Federal Reserve System his chief contribution.[76] Wingo's aggressive crusade for a thorough reform of the banking system marked him as an agrarian radical. *The Arkansas Gazette* ranked Wingo, with Texans Robert L. Henry and Joseph H. Eagle, as a radical who refused to give up any of the Baltimore platform promises on currency reform. The three men insisted on including in any banking legislation the reforms proposed by the Pujo Committee. In July 1913 Wingo proposed an amendment to the Federal Reserve Bill prohibiting interlocking directorates in national banks. The agrarian members of the House Banking and Currency Committee adopted the change and also one sponsored by J. Willard Ragsdale and Robert L. Henry. The Henry proposal included, among other things, a form of "agricultural currency" reminiscent of the Populist subtreasury scheme. Woodrow Wilson exerted strong pressure to prevent the agrarians from delaying the measure, and the committee eventually rejected the amendments.[77]

Otis Wingo told Secretary of the Treasury William G. McAdoo of his determination to secure a banking reform bill. He had to be outside the capital city occasionally because of his son's illness, but he was spending nearly all his time in Washington with the Committee on Banking and Currency, "and I think you will agree with me that it is very necessary to hasten the deliberations of that committee" and complete work on the bill.[78] Despite Wingo's effort to produce a bill acceptable to the agrarian radicals, he compromised some of his aims to secure a moderate reform measure. Like Henry, he wished to incorporate the old

Populist subtreasury concept into the act, but he bowed to pressure from the president to save the agricultural credit proposal for a separate bill.[79]

A few Arkansans still rejected the Democratic and Republican parties as potential vehicles for reform. Some of the more militant former Populists joined with labor dissidents to support Arkansas's Socialist Party. Socialists found some support in the three western border counties of Arkansas. Polk and Scott Counties had been centers of Populist strength. Sebastian County could claim a small amount of industry in Fort Smith but also had an active United Mine Workers organization in the coal regions around the towns of Hartford, Jenny Lind, and Huntington. One of the radicals who came to Arkansas to help establish local socialist organizations in the Hartford valley was a maverick Roman Catholic priest, Father Thomas Hagerty. Hagerty had served at churches in Cleburne, Texas, and Las Vegas, Nevada. After his visit to Arkansas in 1903, Hagerty helped found the I. W. W. (Industrial Workers of the World) in 1905. Another leading socialist in Arkansas was Peter Stewart, a coal miner from Hartford. In 1908 he became president of the U.M.W. District 21, and in April 1910 he led the union in a violent strike lasting through the spring and summer. Some workers' families came close to starvation during the strike. In 1912 the city of Hartford elected Stewart as its mayor. Stewart's part in leading union forces in a violent assault against an open-shop mine at Midland in April 1914 led to the charge that he had incited a riot and also had ignored a federal injunction. He was confined at Leavenworth for several months for his part in the "Prairie Creek Mine War." In the same year that Stewart won the race for mayor, 1912, another Sebastian County miner and U.M.W. member, G. E. Mikel, ran as Socialist candidate for governor. He polled 13,384 votes, approximately 5,000 ahead of his fellow Socialist candidate for president, Eugene V. Debs. Although there were pockets of socialism in some of the western tier of counties, by far most Arkansans chose to remain with the one-party system.[80]

Despite the turmoil of political change in the Democratic Party, the loss of Jeff Davis's Old Guard, the shifting alliances, and the rise of new leaders in state politics, Arkansas pressed for progressive change at the state and national level. Maverick politicians like James P. Clarke and William F. Kirby indicated a strong current of individualism and democracy in the state's frontier brand of progressivism. While Arkansas senators and congressmen often stood with those ranked as "agrarian radicals" at Washington, the leadership at the state level continued the tide of change begun by Jeff Davis and the one-gallus Democrats. Especially during the administration of Charles Brough (1917–21) the state entered a new reform era as Arkansas's "scholar in politics" raised the "Popocratic" crusade to a new level of respectability.

10

The Woodrow Wilson
of Arkansas

In the spring of 1916, Governor-elect Charles H. Brough introduced William Jennings Bryan to a Helena audience as a man who "has given us the conception of moral idealism in politics." In the same speech he called President Woodrow Wilson "a notable example of the constructive scholar in politics."[1] Both descriptions could aptly be applied to Charles H. Brough himself. He shared the evangelical fervor of Bryan, and like his presidential colleague received a Ph.D. degree from Johns Hopkins University. Brough received his degree in 1898. When Bryan ran for president in 1896, Brough was only twenty years old. During the campaign, he told a group of Silver Republicans in Utah that the regular Republican Party was guilty of "robbery of the shylocks [sic] dollar." Brough called on Republicans to free themselves from "the criminality of your platform and the corruption of the niggars [sic] that helped to frame it." He spoke of Bryan as "the Child of the prairie, the Champion of the people."[2] He later moderated his racist sentiments but remained an ally of those Democrats striving for progressive change.

Brough grew up in Mississippi, spent a brief period in Utah, and then continued his education at Johns Hopkins and the University of Mississippi Law School. After a year of teaching at Hillman College in Clinton, Mississippi, he accepted a position in the Department of Economics and Sociology at the University of Arkansas. Brough was also well educated in the field of history. He had studied under Herbert Baxter Adams at Johns Hopkins

University. Adams inculcated in his students an appreciation for the objective and scientific study of history. Brough continued his teaching career at Fayetteville until his foray into politics in 1913 and 1916. A fellow student described him as a man with "deep seated religious convictions" who exerted "a wholesome, moral and religious influence over those with whom he comes in contact."[3] Brough maintained active ties with the largest religious organization in Arkansas, the Southern Baptist Convention. He held the office of deacon at Fayetteville's First Baptist Church and later at Little Rock's Second Baptist Church. As early as 1901, Brough delivered an address before Southern Baptists at their New Orleans Convention. He frequently displayed his talents as a Southern orator, and his papers are filled with requests for speeches from schools, churches, and patriotic groups. "He does not pose as a humorist," wrote an old friend, "yet he carries his audience from the pathetic to the amusing at will."[4] Brough became a popular speaker on the Chautauqua circuit and used this talent to earn a living after he left the governor's office. During the 1920s, he devoted his time to boosting the image of Arkansas in an effort to lure business to the state.[5] Brough had been a popular professor at the University of Arkansas, but he finally abandoned teaching for politics. In his 1913 bid for the governorship he failed, but in 1916 the distinguished professor won the coveted office and held it for two terms (1917–21).

By the time Brough became governor, Arkansas had already experienced two decades of reformist crusading within the Democratic Party. Jeff Davis had long ago, as he said, "run Red River through Little Rock." But in Brough, the progressive phenomenon in Arkansas moved further from its agrarian cast toward an emphasis on respectable, sane, and orderly change. The bombastic and negative iconoclasm of Davisism receded and a more positive emphasis emerged. Brough allied himself with bankers, businessmen, teachers, lawyers, and professional people. He preferred democratic reforms, humanitarian improvement, and mild regulatory effort to the earlier massive assaults upon trusts and railroads. He believed government's role in the economy was not that of a passive onlooker, and to a degree he moved away from the negativism implicit in the Southern state's rights philosophy. If government had some responsibility in ordering the business affairs of society, it had an even greater challenge in conforming its own operations to the standards of business efficiency. Brough sought to reorganize the state government so that its agencies operated in a business-like and orderly manner.

In displacing "mountebanks" and "demagogues" with respected leaders, Arkansas followed a pattern set in other Southern states. Two years before Brough's election, South Carolina ousted the turbulent Cole Blease and his chosen successor in favor of Governor Richard I. Manning who revised the state's taxation system and improved state social and educational services. Manning represented one of the respected families of his state and had been a planter and businessman. Like Brough he elicited the support of middle-class groups. In similar fashion, Alabamans sent Thomas E. Kilby, a prohibitionist and a dedicated progressive, to their statehouse. Having earned his wealth in the steel industry, he won the 1918 election with a promise to serve as a "business governor." Virginia also followed the trend toward "business progressivism." Beginning in 1918 a succession of governors including Henry P. Byrd promised to run the state much as one would operate a business concern.[6]

Many of the respectable leadership of Arkansas welcomed the entrance of Brough into politics. One such leader was Carroll D. Wood, an early leader of the anti-Davis faction and a long-time state supreme court justice (1893–1929). His son, Roy Wood, informed the professor that "Dad . . . never ceased to sweat under the yoke placed on the state by Jeff Davis's policies and politics," but now saw the "dawn of a new era." Brough's election would bring the "dethronement of hypocricy [sic], corrupt political practices, scheming and intrigue." He also gained the aid of Joseph House, formerly a leading Cleveland Democrat and a strong sound money advocate. House became one of Davis's mortal enemies, but Brough chose the old-line Democrat for his campaign manager in the 1916 election. Many politicians feared Brough could not win the rural vote. Loid Rainwater, cashier of the Bank of Morrilton, warned, "you will win provided country people do not think you are 'high collared' and have *too much education*." Dr. F. B. Kirby of Harrison thought he stood well "around the towns" but was "very little known" in the "rural parts." His former students constituted a loyal reservoir of support, but one of them, Clarence J. McLellon, warned him not to "mention the University too strongly," since "the people as a whole over the state are not favorable toward the institution."[7]

Brough relied upon the loyalty of his own Baptist brethren, but he also had the aid of many other religious groups. One of his 1913 circulars asserted, "the church going people of Arkansas are for Dr. C. H. Brough, who is a righteous man, and not ashamed of it." Mary Lee Robinson, a Women's Christian Temperance Union leader, assured the professor that he was "unanimously and enthusiasticaly [*sic*] supported by its various members." Labor also came to his side. A railroad conductor, G. T. Schrader, predicted his speech on behalf of the eight-hour day would win "thousands of votes."[8]

Senator Joseph T. Robinson became one of his leading allies, although his aid was not always active and open. When Robinson left the governor's office in 1913 for the Senate, popular antagonism rendered any public avowal of support a liability. But Brough's letters hint at sympathy for Robinson's actions.[9] During the campaign of 1916, Brough answered the charge that he not only had Robinson's aid but was "expecting to lend him the power of the Governor's office in his next race for the Senate." Brough acknowledged Robinson's backing, but he believed the senator was not "unduly active" in his behalf and that other potential senatorial candidates gave encouragement as well.[10]

In 1915 Brough began his campaign with the following statement:

> Some of the main planks in my platform are: Greater efficiency in the state government, a lowering of the rate of taxation, more equitable assessment of property, better rural schools, working convicts on public roads, *a primary election law that will prevent the St. Francis Levee Board and other ballot box thieves from stealing your votes,* payment in full of Confederate pensions, the everlasting supremacy of the white race, and the auditing of the books of Earle W. Hodges.[11]

Brough conducted a vigorous campaign, having visited "seventy of the seventy-five counties" by the end of 1915. He charged that his opponents relied more exclusively upon "organization" and newspaper attacks.[12]

The Fayetteville educator began his campaign on a high level, stating at length his views on taxation reform, educational institutions, election legislation, and other issues.[13] But the campaign soon followed the familiar rut as the candidates abused and vilified one another, and Brough himself wallowed in the muck. Opponents charged that his father had been a "'carpet-bagger' and fought in a negro regiment," and that Charles Brough was a Mormon and a tax-dodger. Brough denounced one opponent as the "Whiskey" candidate and another as an embezzler of state funds.[14]

Thomas C. McRae, L. C. "Shotgun" Smith, and Earle W. Hodges opposed Brough. McRae left the campaign at an early stage, and Smith gained a reputation as the wet candidate. Because Arkansas had already enacted statewide prohibition, the liquor candidate maintained a low profile and his strength was uncertain. The campaign became primarily a contest between Secretary of State Hodges and the Fayetteville academician.[15] Brough made his campaign against Hodges an assault upon Governor George W. Hays and his administration. In an attack on what he termed "the Hays-Hodges Combine," he denounced Hays for "using the governor's office to promote" the Hodges candidacy. The professor recited at length the record of the Hays years and sought to associate Hodges with the governor's "pernicious activity."

Brough condemned Hays for a record of vacillation. On the prohibition question he had done "his best to run with the 'drys' and drink with the 'wets'." When Hays' first legislature convened, he threw his support behind Senator Monroe Smith of Union County, the wet candidate for president of the senate. He also recommended submission of the prohibition question to the voters, the stance taken by the liquor interests in 1915. But when the senate chose Elmer J. Lundy of Polk County, a dry for president and indicated a strong prohibitionist sentiment, the governor "turned a complete somersault on the whiskey question and recommended statewide prohibition." The 1915 legislature did pass a statewide bill, and Arkansas became a dry state. Similarly Hays gave his aid to the Hot Springs Horse Racing Bill to legalize gambling at the "Valley of Vapors." He signed the bill in the presence of its advocates, and when the witnesses had left he "sent post haste after his private secretary and had him bring the bill back to him." Despite the signature Hays proceeded to veto the measure.[16]

Charles Brough reserved his strongest denunciation for the alliance of Hays and Hodges with the St. Francis Levee Board. The organization became a major force in Arkansas politics, and Brough determined to dismantle east Arkansas's most notorious "machine." The legislature created the board in 1893 to administer levee construction and maintenance in eight counties of northeast Arkansas. The levees were to reclaim two thousand five hundred square miles of flooded lands along the St. Francis River, which runs southward through Arkansas to join the Mississippi at Helena. The governor appointed three members for each of the eight counties to a three-year term on the board. The sheriffs, clerks, and judges of eastern Arkansas counties vied for selection to the board as a means of increasing their influence. By Jeff Davis's time, the board had become a powerful political tool for the governor's use. It often divided into factions seeking control of the machine, and the group aligning itself with a successful gubernatorial candidate gained dominance. Senator James P. Clarke once told a congressional committee that "the levee board is sometimes organized along the lines of the factional political differences in the State." Once elected, a governor molded the organization to serve his own purposes. Each year he could choose one-third of the membership and reconstruct the board more to his liking. According to the board's official history, the levee machine sometimes "decided the results of elections in the entire state."[17]

During the 1909 general assembly, efforts to reform the board by making its membership elective failed.[18] But discontent with the political power of the organization increased. Taxpayers within the district were, in Brough's words, "tired of paying thousands of dollars in taxes every year for levee purposes, to be expended by a political board selected by the governor of the state—they were sick and sore of taxation without representation." The Arkansas Gazette reported, in July 1913, a promise by Hays in a Mississippi County speech, to place businessmen on the levee board and not to veto a bill providing for election of board members.[19] Hays later attended a mass meeting in Crittenden County where landowners demanded an elective board. Governor Hays brought cheers from the protesters when he spoke in favor of an elected board. In the 1915 assembly, a reform bill passed the legislature despite the "strenuous opposition" of levee board members. Then, to the disgust of the reformers, Hays vetoed the bill. "Why was it done?" asked Brough. "Ask the governor and the political machine of his perpetuation . . . that machine that he has placed behind Mr. Hodges in an effort to elect him governor . . . that same machine that has dictated every act of Governor Hays, pertaining to eastern

Arkansas, since the first day he hung up his hat in the governor's office." Minnie U. Rutherford-Fuller, a leader of the Arkansas Federation of Women's Clubs, agreed with Brough's assessment of Hays, "I know of no one," she said, "who has more respect for" the machine.[20]

Many Arkansas politicians feared Brough would be unable to secure election with the levee board opposing him. "There is one great factor against you," warned John Gibson of Hoxie, "and that is the machine politician. A man of your reputation and high ideals will not be attractive to this class." Wrote T. P. Johnson, principal of the Earle public schools, "I am with you but Professor, it takes politics to win and can you manipulate the machine—Now of course you know that there is so much machinery that it will take skillful handling." A Fort Smith court stenographer, Guy E. Williams, thought Brough might fail to get control of the "political machinery in the State, and as you well know that is what it takes to elect. For instance had it not been for a combination of circumstances Gov. Hays would never have defeated Brundidge."[21]

Such fears had foundation. Arkansas politicians knew well the techniques of tinkering with the electoral system. During Joseph T. Robinson's campaign for governor in 1912, a loyal supporter in Fort Smith, Ira D. Oglesby, wrote him a letter marked "Keep this confidential." He inquired whether Robinson had enough influence over Attorney General Hal L. Norwood and Secretary of State Earle Hodges "to have them agree to appoint two men as election commissioners? It might be necessary to have another set of election commissioners appointed and I have arranged with a friend of (Governor) Donaghey to have him appoint such men as we agree on." M. W. Hazel, an eastern Arkansas banker wrote in the same month to inform Robinson that three Poinsett County officeholders had gone to Little Rock to promise the county to Governor Donaghey. He warned Robinson of the difficulty in changing the election outcome since the three men controlled election machinery. Harry Lee Williams, a Jonesboro editor, believed county rings in eastern Arkansas could predetermine the result of any primary election with no difficulty. He told of a local Methodist minister's difficulties when Poinsett County voted 100 percent for license instead of prohibition. The preacher was at some pains to explain to his denominational superiors that how he voted had nothing to do with the returns in his county.[22]

Harry Williams asked Brough to spend at least part of his last two weeks before the 1916 primary in the eastern counties, but the professor had nearly written off that part of the state as Hodges territory. Williams pointed out that Craighead and Mississippi counties alone had more votes than six of the hill counties. After some of Williams' friends met with Joseph House, a man who had great experience in Arkansas politics, the campaign manager consented to a tour of the east.[23] Just before the primary election, Brough began to hope for a victory in the east. "Eastern Arkansas is lining up rapidly for me," he exulted, "and I now believe that I will carry that part of the State, which is, as you know, the enemy's territory."[24]

Surprisingly, he carried the Delta country as well as his own northern section. One Phillips County ally, William J. Humphries, explained the outcome, "We had the Political Machine where it did not dare to manufacture the Returns for there was a strong Sentiment for placing an independent Ticket, in the field, for County officers—and if we had received a 'raw' deal in Primary of 3/29, We would have pressed opposition to the County nominees for the general election." A suffragette, Minnie U. Rutherford-Fuller, characterized the mood, "Democrats everywhere, revolted; Helena, even Helena, leading the 'bolting.'" Mrs. John I. Jones, a Forrest City leader of the Arkansas Federation of Women's Clubs, assured Brough that the machine had not been a genuine friend. "Don't let this 'St. Francis Co. Levy Board,' crowd fool you in any way for I happen to know that they did all in their power against you." She rejoiced that Brough would "really rule Arkansas and not ask the judge of St. Francis Co. and a few others how it should be done."[25] The general assemblies of 1917 and 1919 passed legislation restructuring the board and removing it from the governor's control.[26] Some years later in an article on "The Heroic Spirit of Arkansas," Governor Brough lauded the "personnel of the St. Francis Levee Board" as men of "courage and vision" because of their contribution to flood control.[27]

After his success in the spring primary, Brough quickly asserted his new political leadership. When the 1916 State Democratic Convention met, *The Arkansas Gazette* headline reported, "Dr. Brough is in Complete Control." The convention accepted his proposed reforms as the basis of its platform and installed his campaign manager as the new chairman of the State Central

Committee. The platform called for taxation and budget reform, a new primary election law, a "separate millage tax" to provide for state agricultural institutions thereby removing their appropriations from the political realm, and a constitutional convention.[28]

Under Governor Charles Brough the reform impulse in Arkansas rose to a new plateau. The Brough brand of progressivism emphasized efficiency, intelligent regulation, scientific management, and the introduction of business methods into government operations. During his campaign he promised "a safe, sane, business administration." The statehouse, he assured the voters, would "not be a laboratory for experiment with political theories, but a practical workhouse." On the subject of prison reform he pledged "an honest, efficient, and business-like administration of the system of prison labor in the State." He believed "capital and corporate investments should be treated fairly in all legislation enacted." After his primary victory, Brough spoke to the Arkansas Bankers Association in Little Rock and condemned as demagogues those who spoke of bankers as "blood-suckers" and "money-sharks." Allan Kennedy, an agent of the Pennsylvania Fire Insurance Company at Fort Smith, had recognized the new spirit in Brough's politics. He informed Brough in 1913 that the state needed a change in the "office holding element." For too long, Arkansas politicians had been "deficient in that breadth of view and depth of discernment necessary to bring the tangled affairs of the state into businesslike and harmonious position."[29]

Before Brough entered the governor's office, progressivism's emphasis on efficiency and order had been seen in the administration of George Donaghey. But the same reform spirit had also appeared at the city level in the crusade to replace corrupt and uneconomic administration with the commission form of city government. At the turn of the century, municipal reformers proposed the view that an improvement in morality and honesty would be insufficient to solve the problems of the cities. In New York City, in 1906, a municipal research bureau led the way in calling for the application of scientific business methods of management to city administration. Cities began adopting better systems of accounting, budgeting, and auditing, and better methods for improving personnel efficiency. In 1901, Galveston, Texas, adopted a city-commission form of government modeled on the plan of a corporation board. This new form of government dispensed with the separation of powers and gave all authority to a small number of commissioners. Galveston demonstrated that the new system could bring dramatic improvement in handling of revenue and reducing debt. The commission form usually abandoned ward divisions and provided for non-partisan elections. Many Texas cities adopted the reform as a way of "redistributing the tax burden, simplifying administration, and breaking down the influence of local aldermen. . . ." By 1911, there were 160 cities using the new system. Because Arkansas is primarily a rural state, it is not surprising that it was not among those first experimenting with new forms of city government. Fort Smith elected its first city commission on April 1, 1913.[30]

Fort Smith had many of the same problems that had led other cities toward the new form of government. It experienced serious corruption in its police department, an inadequate fire department, dishonest city fathers, and careless management of financial affairs. George Sengel, president of Sengel Hardware Company, and other local business leaders joined hands to call for the city's bankers, manufacturers, and other elites of the business community to organize and give direction to their city. "A few master business minds," they asserted, "must form the nucleus around which we must operate if we are to get anywhere in city building."[31] Fort Smith supporters of the commission form of government argued that it would save money by eliminating many salaried positions. It would also reduce the number of disturbing delays in business procedures, such as the issuing of building permits. The centralization of decision making, they argued, would reduce the influence of special interests.[32] The city's newspaper editors joined with lawyers, physicians, and other elites in a successful crusade to bring commission government to Fort Smith.

In Little Rock, the drive for the commission form of government failed. The Little Rock Board of Trade brought Arkansas mayors together in December 1910 to discuss the possibility of securing legislation to enable cities to adopt the commission form. During the early months of 1911, *The Arkansas Gazette* led a campaign to pressure the general assembly to approve pending commission legislation. But opponents argued that the lack of a party primary election might bring closet socialists or Republicans into the city commission, and the proposal was defeated.[33] Yet, Little Rock did experience the progressive drive for "business-like" efficiency in city government. The prime mover in the capital city reform movement was Charles E. Taylor, secretary of the Dickinson Big Rock Stone and Construction Company and a director of the Citizen's Building Loan Association. He entered politics for the first time when he ran for the mayor's office in 1910 on a promise to run the city "on a sound financial basis. . . ."[34] In his first campaign, Taylor emphasized his belief that as a businessman rather than a politician he could administer the city's affairs in the same way that he would manage a business enterprise. Taylor served as the progressive mayor of Little Rock from 1911 to 1919. After a serious typhoid epidemic, his administration instituted improvements in the water and sewage system, passed a milk inspection ordinance, and established a new health department. The city's purchase of equipment and new fire stations made Little Rock's fire department one of the most modern in the South.[35] In the realm of conservation of human resources, Taylor appointed a vice commission, created a United Charities organization to assist the destitute, and a Bureau of Public Employment to provide at least temporary jobs for the unemployed.[36]

One of Brough's major goals was reform of the financial administration of the state government. "Arkansas has been reveling in a saturnalia of extravagance," he warned. Brough predicted the state's debt would soon reach the six-hundred-thousand-dollar mark because of the inability of the legislature since 1907 to keep appropriations within the bounds of revenue intake. "I do not propose to pinch, but to prune," he said, and to secure "efficiency guaranteed by a wise co-ordination of governmental functions" which could be achieved by creation of an "Efficiency and Auditing Commission." The new organization would audit departmental accounts and recommend economies.[37]

Brough deplored the unusually high taxation rate in Arkansas. The total rate of twenty-seven mills was the highest of any Southern state. He proposed more realistic assessments than the low 30 percent commonly used in the state. Improper assessment procedures had allowed many persons to escape paying a reasonable share. He believed the farmer and real estate owner paid a fair amount, but "let it be proclaimed in the streets of Gad and Askelon that the tax dodger and owner of intangible personalty in Arkansas is abroad in the land, seeking how much of the State's legitimate revenue he may devour and conceal." He proposed an increase in the franchise tax on corporations, creation of a "special honorary tax commission" to study the revenue system, and adoption of a budget system.[38] Texas experimented with similar revenue reforms during the Brough era.

At the 1918 state Democratic convention, Brough presented a record of financial achievement. State warrants which had sold below par for over a decade were now being "cashed at par." The state had been losing at least one hundred thousand dollars yearly because its warrants were honored at eighty cents to the dollar. Arkansas's securities once rejected by New York savings banks were now being accepted. "Arkansas's credit now ranks with that of any other state in the American Union," he boasted. At Brough's suggestion the legislature had authorized a short-term bond issue of seven hundred and fifty thousand dollars to stabilize the state debt situation. In one year, assessments of personal and real property rose from four hundred and fifty million to five hundred and twenty-four million dollars. The increase in the franchise tax had almost doubled the revenue from that source and "to the credit of the corporations . . . there was very little protest to this increase."[39]

While Brough endorsed many of the ideals of the business community, he also closely associated himself with the humanitarian concerns of the state's social reform and religious organizations. He gave encouragement to the Arkansas Conference of Charities and Correction which concerned itself with such problems as child labor and prison reform.[40] He vigorously pressed the legislative programs of the conference during his two administrations. The organization backed the creation of a state-supported school for delinquent girls and establishment of a state charities commission. Brough secured both from the state legislature although he was unable to secure sufficient financing for the commission to operate effectively.[41] He played a leading role in the activities of the Southern Sociological Congress, which represented a Southern movement for social justice and positive action to correct some of the inequities of societies. The congress was formed to study social and economic problems, but not simply from an academic or theoretical point of view. The emphasis was upon action to improve Southern society. The congress gave attention to such issues as race, prohibition, correctional and charitable institutions, and health problems. The Southern Sociological Congress had been founded formally in the spring of 1912. The same kind of spirit that led to its founding at Nashville also brought forth the Arkansas Conference of Charities in the same year. The local organization displayed the same concern for educating the public about social problems and proposed solutions.[42]

One of the most needed progressive reforms was in the field of education. The weak educational system of Arkansas followed a pattern that was apparent across the South. The Southern educational reform movement which responded to these needs at the turn of the century was in the words of Dewey W. Grantham, "a striking illustration of the way in which social action in the southern states almost automatically assumed a regional character."[43] The educational movement won Northern philanthropic aid, elicited the energetic support of professionals and the middle class, and touched the lives of more individuals than any other progressive crusade effort. The education issue touched upon many other major social concerns, including the role of blacks in American society. Much was expected from educational reform. It was viewed as the wellspring of many diverse social improvements. Southern idealists believed educational reform was at the heart of the South's social, economic, and political problems. The school reformers tended to view educational reform "as a redemptive force in the development of a better South."[44]

The chief problem in Southern education was a lack of revenue. Because of insufficiency of taxable wealth, the Southern states could achieve the quality of Northern education only by levying taxes at a rate five times greater than that of the North. Large Southern families and the existence of segregated school systems helped exacerbate the financial strain.[45] One Arkansas historian has estimated that in 1901 only about 40 percent of the state's children attended public school on any given day, and only 66 percent were enrolled. The state had one teacher for every sixty-seven children of school age. The average length of the school year was a mere eighty-four days.[46]

Charles H. Brough did more to advance educational reform in Arkansas than any governor preceding him. But he was not the first progressive leader to give direction to the cause. Grass-roots support had a significant impact beginning early in the century. In 1905 interested reformers in Little Rock established the first school improvement association. By 1911 there were 255 such local organizations with a combined membership of over ten thousand. These organizations gave financial aid from their own resources and also worked to obtain grants from outside the state.[47] Reformers had a partial victory as early as December 1906 when the voters approved by a wide margin the McFerrin Amendment. This measure increased the constitutional limit on taxes for educational purposes at both the state and district level. These limits were raised from five to seven mills respectively.[48]

Governor George W. Donaghey laid much of the groundwork for Brough's later educational reforms. During his 1908 gubernatorial campaign, Donaghey gave his support to an Arkansas Farmers Union proposal to create four district agricultural high schools. In 1909 the state legislature provided for the establishment of these schools at Jonesboro, Magnolia, Monticello, and Russellville. These institutions later became Arkansas State, Southern State, the University of Arkansas at Monticello, and Arkansas Tech. Other reforms of the Donaghey era included: the state's first compulsory education law in 1909, appointment of an education commission to recommend educational legislation, creation of a state board of education, and a measure to consolidate 152 school districts into 64 larger districts.[49]

The election of Charles H. Brough in 1916 greatly encouraged the education reformers. Brough had supported the Arkansas State Teacher's Association, a group he had once served as president, in its bid for a millage increase for school districts. He drafted a plank for the state Democratic platform calling for increasing the local levy to twelve mills. In the 1916 election, the voters agreed with the reformers and accepted the proposed amendment by more than a two to one vote. Also during Brough's tenure, the state adopted a much more effective compulsory attendance law than the measure that had passed in the Donaghey era. The new law required students to attend a minimum of three-fourths of a semester. Although this reform did increase daily attendance by nearly 50 percent, it did not significantly decrease the numbers of children who did not enroll at all. In line with the reformers' emphasis on efficiency and rationalization, the legislature passed a uniform textbook law. The measure aimed to provide better quality texts at a more affordable price. Other reforms included: placing state educational institutions on a millage basis, accepting aid to vocational education through the federal Smith-Hughes Act, and establishment of a literacy commission.[50]

As in the rest of the South, statistical reports for Arkansas indicate some improvement in the twenty years from 1900 to 1920. In this period educational expenditures per student rose from $1.04 to $4.40. The school year length increased from seventy-seven and a half days on average to one hundred and twenty-six days, although it should be noted that only two Southern states (South Carolina and Alabama) had shorter terms. Illiteracy in Arkansas for persons ten years of age and above dropped significantly. White illiteracy fell from 11.5 to 4.5 percent, while black illiteracy declined from 43 to 21.8 percent.[51] The numbers indicate an improving situation for both blacks and whites.

Unfortunately, the educational reforms were aimed to benefit whites more than blacks. The student-teacher ratio for black classes in 1918 was one teacher for thirty-seven students while for whites the ratio was 1 to 25. Enrollment numbers for black students barely increased during the progressive era in Arkansas. Between 1901 and 1918, enrollment of black children increased only from 61 percent of all those of school age to 62 percent. At the same time white enrollment rose from 68 to 74 percent.[52]

Part of the problem for black educational improvement lay in the attitude of whites. Governor Brough was convinced that the black man needed vocational or industrial training rather than the liberal arts. Like most other Arkansans, he agreed with the Booker T. Washington philosophy of black education, which promoted practical and economic concerns above the political and social needs of blacks. Most white Southerners opposed an education for blacks that might induce them to seek social and political equality.[53]

Brough's views on black education were not new. The history of the Branch Normal School of Pine Bluff illustrates the prevailing early twentieth-century attitude toward black education. The Pine Bluff school was the only public institution providing teacher training for blacks. In 1902 Isaac Fisher, a Tuskegee graduate, became the principal of the school on recommendation of Booker T. Washington. Fisher's appointment pleased whites who hoped he would be able to pursue his avowed goal of emphasizing industrial education. Fisher sincerely dreamed of a school with a dairy and with courses in brick making and shoe making. Although he failed to achieve his specific vision, his attitudes on black education pleased William H. Langford, the white trustee-in-residence at Pine Bluff. But many members of the black community viewed his dream as potentially destructive for the educational program at Pine Bluff. In 1910 the school dropped its Latin, philosophy, and ethics programs and moved firmly away from a liberal arts approach. The state's only publicly supported black college now offered an education that was markedly inferior to that available at the tax supported white colleges.[54]

Much of the initiative for improvements in black education came from within the black community. In 1898 at Pine Bluff, a small group of teachers of black children formed the State Teachers Association of Arkansas. The organization aimed to improve the preparation of teachers and to secure better school facilities for blacks. Little is known of the organization's early years beyond information about its leaders. The first president, Joseph Carter Corbin, served until 1904. Corbin, born of slave parents, was a gifted student of languages and math and received a master's degree from Ohio University. He was elected Arkansas Superintendent of Public Instruction in 1872 and served until 1874. In this position he automatically became the chairman of the board of trustees of Arkansas Industrial University (now the University of Arkansas at Fayetteville). He also founded and became the first principal of Branch Normal College at Pine Bluff in 1875.[55]

As in many Southern and Western states, Arkansas progressivism exhibited a strong emphasis on democratic reforms. Charles H. Brough gave enthusiastic support to both woman suffrage and the initiative and referendum. Not all Arkansas leaders shared his enthusiasm. George Washington Hays once declared woman suffrage to be "a Republican move and not the hand of Almighty God." It would be an "outrage on civilization" because it would remove woman from the home, where she was an influence for purity and love, and place her in a sphere where she would be degraded.[56] During his first term, Governor Brough signed a bill granting women the right to vote in Democratic primary elections. Although all of Arkansas's representatives had voted against a proposed woman suffrage amendment in the lower house of Congress in 1915, they voted unanimously for the same proposal in 1918. The victory of Arkansas suffragists at the state level in 1917 had helped change the views of the state congressional delegation. More than forty thousand women voted in the 1918 primary, and in the same year women served as delegates to the Democratic State Convention and as members of the State Central Committee. In 1919 Brough called a special session of the legislature, and Arkansas became the second Southern state to ratify the Nineteenth Amendment. Texas, Oklahoma, Kentucky, and Tennessee were the only other Southern states that took action to ratify the amendment.[57]

Dewey W. Grantham has expressed the view that "Arkansas progressivism was thoroughly consonant with the broader pattern of political and social reform in the South." Despite the rabid assaults on railroads and insurance companies by the Davis movement, the economic interests remained strong in Arkansas politics. As in the rest of the South, Arkansas business and professional leaders had a preeminent position in the reform movement. Although Grantham admits that agrarian radicalism sometimes continued its influence, as seen in the adoption of the initiative and referendum, he still asserts that Arkansas progressivism was not a radical movement.[58] Like the rest of the South, Arkansas progressives sought "the reconciliation of progress and tradition." They wanted moderate change, but they remained committed to social order and traditional values. There should be active pursuit of progress, but change should be accomplished gradually.[59]

Arkansas progressivism, in Grantham's view, was "limited and mild." The grass-roots democracy of the Davis era with its agrarian radical tinge did not bring a full-scale reform movement to Arkansas. In this portrait the disfranchisement process, the continued influence of economic interests, and the state's essentially conservative leadership preempted a full-scale reform movement.[60] Another perspective on Arkansas is offered by Joe Tolbert Segraves. He asserts that "Arkansas participated fully" in the progressive movement. As evidence he points to James P. Clarke's record as a notable Southern progressive during the early 1900s and his reputation as a "La Follette-style" radical. Joseph T. Robinson's record during his first years in the Senate is another striking example. He voted consistently with the most progressive senators. William F. Kirby, who served only one term in the United States Senate is described as "an agrarian radical who stood at the fore of the progressive movement." But Segraves views the movement in Arkansas as one beset with a lack of unity and organization. Each movement "occurred as series of thrusts, each with its own leadership and emphasis."[61]

While it may be accurate to generally characterize Arkansas progressivism as moderate, it certainly must be recognized that it did have some episodes of dramatic reform. The story of the adoption of "direct democracy" in Arkansas is one such episode. When Arkansas accepted the initiative and referendum concept, it identified the state with a more radical brand of Western progressivism. This reform envisioned a drastic change in the manner of decision making and law making. The legislative power once monopolized by the general assembly would now have to be shared with the electorate. In fact, the state voting population would be the ultimate legislative voice in that it could overrule the legislature. Although Arkansas did not utilize the direct democratic methods to enact radical changes, those who pioneered the movement to establish the initiative and referendum did intend the new tools to be a means for changing the status quo. Agitation for adoption of the initiative and referendum in Arkansas began as early as 1896 when the Populists proposed the measure. The idea won some support from the Democratic Party, but it did not gain much attention until 1908 when George W. Donaghey threw his weight behind the proposal during his successful campaign for the governor's chair. The 1909 general assembly voted overwhelmingly in favor of submitting the proposal to the public in the 1910 election.[62]

The 1910 campaign to win the Arkansas voters over to "direct democracy" provides at least one significant illustration of Southern progressives allying with organized labor. The Arkansas Federation of Labor joined hands with the Arkansas Farmers Union to work for passage of the measure, now known as Amendment 10. William Jennings Bryan came to Arkansas before the September 5 election to campaign for the amendment. The silver-tongued orator made fifty-five speeches across the state. Traveling with him by train to support the cause were Governor Donaghey, George A. Cole, president of the Arkansas Farmer's Union, and E. W. Hogan, president of the Arkansas AFL. The measure passed by a vote of 91,367 to 39,111.[63]

Opposition to Amendment 10 came from *The Arkansas Gazette,* the state bar association, and prominent individuals like Charles Jacobson, Jeff Davis's former secretary and by 1910 a Little Rock attorney.[64]

Ashley Cockrill, president of the Arkansas Bar Association, told the membership at its 1912 meeting that the initiative would destroy constitutional government. He lamented Arkansas's adoption of the "Oregon Plan" in 1910 and added, "While 15 states have adopted in one form or another the initiative referendum or both, only Oregon, Oklahoma, Missouri, Colorado and Arkansas permit the initiative by petitions of amendment to the constitution."[65] Despite the fears of the Arkansas Bar Association that Amendment 10, the initiative and referendum amendment, was a radical measure, many progressives expressed dismay at its ineffectiveness. Judson King, secretary of the National Popular Government League with headquarters in Washington, D.C., came to Arkansas in the fall of 1916 to personally direct a campaign for a more satisfactory amendment which came to be known as Amendment 13.

King had the support of many progressive leaders in the 1916 struggle. Minnie U. Rutherford-Fuller, who took a leading role in the suffragist crusade and held offices frequently in the Arkansas Federation of Women's Clubs, lent her encouragement. Charles Brough telegraphed King, "I favor the passage of Amendment Number Thirteen because it represents the extension of the system of the initiative and referendum. My platform endorsed this principle." David Y. Thomas, professor of political science at the University of Arkansas, worked closely with King and took a leading part in shaping the revised amendment. Thomas Mehaffy, later president of the Arkansas Constitutional Convention of 1918, also aided the cause. The leadership of the Arkansas Federation of Labor played a major role in the campaign. Although the Arkansas Bar Association had opposed Amendment 10, it did not take an official position on Amendment 13. Five of the seven Arkansas congressmen gave aid along with Senator Robinson. In *The Arkansas Gazette* the movement had a major foe, but King's lieutenants counted ninety-six newspapers across the state which endorsed the initiative and referendum amendment.[66]

During the campaign, the temperance forces gave mixed support to Amendment 13. Prohibitionists feared the provision because local popular legislation might lead to city or county nullification of the statewide prohibition law. L. H. Moore, editor of the *Arkansas Baptist Advance,* promised to publish a statement to allay such fears but warned that many letters came to him expressing concern about reinstatement of the saloon. William S. U'Ren of Oregon, a national leader of the direct legislation movement, tried to put the fears to rest in a telegram to King. The amendment, he thought, "is one of the very best that has been offered to the people of any state. It does not grant power to counties, cities or towns to establish saloons contrary to statewide prohibition law." William Jennings Bryan gave similar assurance by wire and expressed regret he could not come to Arkansas to help in the struggle. Judson King lost his patience in dealing with the Arkansas temperance leaders. "It is difficult for me," he wrote to Reverend Charles G. Elliot, a Walnut Ridge pastor, "to understand why so many Arkansas ministers are opposing this upon principle." He asked pardon for his bluntness but explained that "after having fought the whiskey interests for years it is hard to restrain myself when I have now to fight the temperance people." In October, King wrote to Oklahoma Senator Robert L. Owen to secure from him a statement on the prohibition aspect of the problem. "It is going to be hard work to run this lie down and nail it," he wrote, but the rumor that direct legislation would open the door to local gambling or whiskey could be scotched by "your emphatic denial as a constitutional lawyer."[67]

The direct legislation organization of King released a lengthy statement by Senator Owen designed to answer objections and make clear the need for a revision of Arkansas's initiative and referendum. The "enemies of popular government," he said, had devised "a great variety of artful jokers" to nullify the initiative and referendum. The supreme court of Arkansas had invalidated the Amendment 10 provision for local popular legislation because of "obscure" language. The courts had also struck down as invalid all amendments submitted after the first three "at any one election" on the basis of an 1874 law limiting amendments to three per election. Amendment 10 did not include such a limitation, but the supreme court used the law to invalidate an attempt to establish the recall of judges and officials. Amendment 13, Owen promised, would remove the limitation. The supreme court had also interpreted Amendment 10 to mean that a majority of all votes cast at an election must be affirmative to enact an amendment to the constitution. Since many voters did not bother to vote one way or the other on submitted questions, a large number of votes were automatically counted against an amendment. The revised initiative and referendum provided for passage by a majority of only three votes cast on the question. Finally, Owen denied that local direct legislation could open the saloons in counties and cities. In support of his view he cited: "Col.

George Thornburgh, President of the Anti-Saloon League of Arkansas, . . . Judge J. V. Bourland, U.S. District Attorney; David Y. Thomas," and others.[68]

Robert M. La Follette sent a message of encouragement to those working for revision of the direct legislation amendment in Arkansas. "Forward looking men" across the country "rejoiced" when Arkansas adopted Amendment 10, but "they were chagrined when the state supreme court by decisions practically destroyed the effectiveness of this amendment." During his campaign Charles Brough, identified himself with the crusade. He expressed regret that the supreme court had limited amendments to three every two years. "Generally, these three amendments are submitted by the General Assembly, and thus the people are prohibited from submitting any amendments." He believed this practice nullified the intent of the initiative. Brough linked his plea for revision of Amendment 10 to a call for a new constitutional convention. If the revised amendment could not be the means of changing the constitution, perhaps the state could call a convention to overhaul the system. Brough thought "that instead of being a great protector of the rights and liberties of the people, some times the ponderous provisions of the present constitution are the greatest menace to their protection."[69]

Despite the endorsement of the Democratic candidate for governor, the voters at the general election on November 7, 1916, voted against Amendment 13 by a vote of 69,817 to 73,782.[70] Immediately after the defeat, Judson King began organizing his forces for a continuing struggle. He wrote to Congressman Thaddeus Caraway of plans for a meeting at the State Bank Building in Little Rock to reorganize the Initiative and Referendum League of Arkansas and work on a "new direct Legislation Amendment." Later he informed Caraway that electing initiative and referendum delegates to the new constitutional convention, if called by the legislature, might be the best tactic. King worked closely also with Professor David Y. Thomas and Attorney Thomas Mehaffy on a redraft of Amendment 13. The progressives faced a steep road in securing the revision. Although the voters rejected the work of the 1918 constitutional convention and the initiative and referendum provision with it, they ratified the amendment in the 1920 election by a vote of 86,360 to 43,662. Then came another setback. While it had the approval of two-thirds of those casting a vote on the amendment, it did not have the approval of a majority of all those casting a vote in the general election, and the speaker of the house of representatives, C. P. Newton of Pulaski County, declared the measure had lost. In 1925 the Arkansas Supreme Court finally reversed its earlier stance and declared the initiative and referendum amendment operative as well as a woman suffrage amendment, which had won almost as large a vote in the 1920 election.[71] When other states enacted anti-evolution statutes in the 1920s, Arkansas became the only state to use the initiative to outlaw the teaching of evolution in public schools.[72]

While Arkansas may have seemed an advanced progressive state in its experiment with direct democracy, its record on conservation of physical resources suggests the more limited and hesitant character of the state's progressivism. In 1907 and 1908, President Theodore Roosevelt established the Arkansas National Forest in southwestern Arkansas and the Ozark National Forest to the north of the Arkansas River. Although some Arkansans supported forest conservation and welcomed Roosevelt's creation of the two national forests, the state legislature displayed no interest in the concept. Sid B. Redding, a Little Rock Republican leader, and F. W. Tucker, a plantation owner in Lawrence County, are representative of a more pro-conservation sentiment in the state. Both men attended the White House Conference on Conservation in 1908. In 1909 the Arkansas General Assembly asked President Roosevelt to abolish the two national forests in Arkansas.[73]

George Donaghey spoke out in favor of protection of natural resources and appointed an honorary, unofficial conservation commission. He appointed an enthusiastic conservationist, Sid Redding, to be the first secretary of the commission. Governor Brough also gave verbal support to the protection of the forests, but he asked the legislature only for investigative powers for his proposed commission. In the progressive era, Arkansas governors were not prepared to ask for effective government regulation of forestry by a professional body. Not until 1931 would the state legislature approve an official forestry commission, and even that body operated without state funding. But foot dragging at the state level was matched by resistance at the national level. Theodore Roosevelt in 1907 saw his conservation thrust slowed by the Congress's revocation of his authority to create new forest reserves in six Western states. Conservatives at the national level frustrated the efforts of arch-conservationist Gifford Pinchot during the Taft administration. Arkansas's resistance to conservation reform does not seem too surprising when the bitter struggles at the federal level are considered.[74]

David M. Moyers has concluded that Arkansas's conservation movement was well within "the traditional concepts of Progressive thought." It showed the same trend toward "efficiency, rationalization, and bureaucratization." These trends are seen in the movement away from the earlier local conservation legislation that applied only to one or more counties, and toward the creation of a statewide commission to give more professional and unified direction to the state effort.[75]

In the Brough era, Arkansas progressivism entered a more activist stage. Politicians began to accept to a larger degree the principle of government intervention in economic affairs. In the 1914 election the voters approved an initiated Child Labor Act by a vote of 72,313 to 25,300. The measure prohibited the employment of children in some occupations and established a minimum age limit of fourteen for any compensated work. In 1915 the state legislature passed a minimum wage law establishing a Minimum Wage and Maximum Hour Commission with supervision over firms employing three women or more. In 1919 the legislature amended the law to include all women under hour and wage regulations. In Brough's time the commission established a $7.50 weekly minimum wage and a six day, fifty-four hour week for women. Governor Brough defended the intervention of government in a speech before the Arkansas Hotel Men's Association. After citing numerous cases of labor exploitation in the Hot Springs area, he insisted that "some limitation is necessary for protection." He rejected arguments of hotel and restaurant owners that profits would drop. He believed patrons would pay the increased costs. The laws regulating the labor of children and women remained on the books during the 1920s and 1930s. The child labor law resembled that of most other Southern states during the post-war era, although Texas had an age limit of fifteen rather than fourteen. Many Southern states permitted women to work ten hours a day and a sixty-hour week. By the 1930s some of the states outside the South had established a maximum work week for women of forty-eight hours.[76]

In large measure, Brough's motivation for seeking a revised constitution for the state was a desire to increase governmental powers to meet the needs of modern society. He recalled the origins of the constitution of 1874. The redeemers who drafted it had "one ideal . . . nearest their hearts. The restraining hand of the people must be laid upon their servants." They placed severe limitations on the taxation power and denied to counties and cities "the right to contract interest-bearing debts." The adoption of such an ideal led to "a Constitution with many restrictions upon the exercise of governmental power." Now, "our ideas and our interests are growing larger," and the old document could no longer serve the state's needs. In his first inaugural address, Governor Brough, in a reference to the need for eliminating constitutional restrictions, said, "The keynote of the present is expansion, rather than contraction; progress, rather than limitation; confidence in our lawmakers and public servants, rather than suspicion of them."[77]

The people of Arkansas, especially the rural folk, distrusted increased governmental power. Jeff Davis recognized this when he said in his farewell message as governor that "it is well known that the people in every section of this State, except in cities where bonds are proposed, the people are opposed to a new Constitution." He saw attempts at revision as the work of a gang "associated with the trusts and railway lobbyists, aided and abetted by insurance conspirators." Such men wanted "all constitutional limits to taxation removed." Because of the constitution "the fraudulent bondholders of the State are bound in chains. It is against this condition that the money power will take any hazard." In 1918 during the battle to adopt Brough's new constitution, Carroll D. Wood recognized the same arguments surfacing again. The enemies were using the "hideous old bogies of 'Bonds' and 'Taxation'" to frighten the average man.[78] Most of the rural citizens of Arkansas still maintained Davis's negativistic view of the state and had not accepted Brough's conception of the increased role of government.

The constitution of 1918 included one of Brough's pet projects, "a scientific budget modeled after the New York Budget." By the new plan, heads of departments in the government would furnish "estimates and itemized statements of the financial needs" to the executive. He would then submit the budget to the legislature with "a complete plan of the proposed expenditures and estimates of current assets, liabilities, reserves, surplus, deficits in the various departments."[79] The new document also included woman suffrage, quadrennial elections, statewide prohibition, and a stronger initiative and referendum. If Governor Brough could have had a free hand, he would have sponsored a proposal authored by Elihu Root that the state of New York had rejected. The Root plan empowered the governor to appoint three state officers. Brough thought Arkansas's democratic views would not tolerate the change. Although the executive had "not one particle of power over" policies in the departments, Brough would not publicly take the position that elective offices be made appointive.[80]

During the spring of 1918, committees completed work on the revised constitution. The Fifth Constitutional Convention met on July 1 to approve the final draft. After eight weeks of deliberation, the convention submitted its work to the people of the state with the assurance that they had "retained the greater part of the old Constitution." Despite such assurances the voters of Arkansas, in a special December election, decisively rejected the constitution by a vote of 23,820 to 37,184. Distrust of government, a negative view of its role in society, and perhaps indifference contributed to the failure of Brough's greatest project.[81]

In Arkansas, as across the South, World War I brought a spirit of change, increased business activity, better cotton prices, and an upsurge of nationalism. Governor Charles Brough spearheaded the patriotic efforts of the state, speaking frequently at liberty bond drives. More than seventy thousand men from the state served in the military. The patriotic fervor and increased contacts with citizens from other sections of the United States fostered a new nationalistic feeling in the state. The Arkansas Council of Defense took significant steps to safeguard health during the war. The council was among the most active in the nation in its efforts to control communicable diseases and sponsored free venereal disease clinics. Little Rock became a major center for training medical officers for service in military camps across the nation. The "Business Progressivism" of Charles Brough did not dissolve as the post-war era dawned. The upsurge of business prosperity encouraged a continued emphasis on efficiency in government during the 1920s.[82]

While the Arkansas progressives of Brough's era addressed themselves to achieving democratic procedures and efficient business methods for state government, they failed to cope with some of the major social problems of their time. Professor David Y.

Thomas, a student of tax reform, called for breaking up land monopolies in the state. In 1917 he complained that "the landed interests" had blocked all efforts in the legislature "to get a progressive tax measure." Like many other Southern states, Arkansas has been afflicted by absentee landlordism. Southerners resenting their colonial status have often blamed alien landholders. Southern demagogues, like James K. Vardaman, often crusaded against the large property owners. In Arkansas, cotton, rice, timber, coal, and bauxite fields were often owned by men in Memphis or the northeastern section of the United States. Timberland owners were holding vast areas in reserve in hopes of an increased lumber price at a future date. The low taxes on unimproved lands made it financially possible for the owners to withhold land from use for long periods. In one county, three persons or corporations owned 85 percent of all the land. The practices of large landowners, Thomas believed, hurt the small farmer who needed land. The problem was not confined to Arkansas. Owners of cut-over Southern timberland held land congresses in the teens to find ways to sell their land at the highest price. While timber men held back land, potential farm land went undeveloped. Thomas thought the solution lay in forcing owners to sell vacant lands by assessing them at the same rate as improved lands. One of the largest land monopolies in Arkansas consisted of the bauxite mine areas of Saline and Pulaski counties owned almost exclusively by a Pennsylvania Corporation, the Aluminum Corporation of America.[83]

Two years later, Thomas complained in *The Nation* of an increase in tenancy both on the farm and in towns. He believed vacant town lots should not be assessed at one-fourth to one-half their actual value. A higher tax would encourage owners to sell to those who could make use of the land. Tenancy increased in the southwestern states of Arkansas, Louisiana, Oklahoma, Texas, and Mississippi until after 1935. Half of those operating farms in 1910 were using land owned by someone else. Absentee owners held two-thirds of all farm land in the Southwest by the 1930s. The tenancy situation was similar in other parts of the South.[84]

Governor Brough's handling of the race riot at Elaine, Arkansas, illustrates the lack of understanding of the economic and social injustices suffered by blacks in the state. It also demonstrates that serious racial prejudices prevented the governor and the army from viewing the events from a realistic perspective. Benjamin Brawley, a black historian who wrote within two years of the event, called it "one of the two or three most far-reaching instances of racial trouble in the history of the Negro in America. . . ."[85] Brawley charged that in eastern Arkansas, as in some other states, planters sold crops without the sharecropper's participation in the sales arrangement and that the planter then settled with the tenant whenever it suited him to do so. Blacks were often charged a lump sum figure for the year's supplies without any itemized accounting so that the temptation for the planter to overcharge was great. The misery and frustration of blacks who believed the planters were delaying settlements and padding accounts so as to keep them in peonage were a major cause for the Elaine riot.[86]

Because of their concern about receiving a fair settlement, the sharecroppers of Phillips County attempted to create a local union which could be a part of the Farmers and Laborers Household Union of America. The white community seems to have interpreted the organizational movement as one that might threaten violence. The actual precipitating event for the riot was the killing of W. D. Adkins, a Missouri Pacific Railroad agent. Adkins was killed outside a black church near Elaine at a place called Hoop Spur. Charles Pratt, a deputy sheriff who accompanied Adkins, was wounded. It may not be possible to unravel the truth about how this incident occurred. What is clear is that a riot followed with confusion, murder, and fear reigning, and that the governor called for federal troops to help restore order. A few whites and at least twenty blacks died in the melee. Governor Brough hastily assumed that the whole affair could be put at the feet of labor agitators. Union organizer Robert Lee Hill seems to have been sincerely seeking justice for his fellow blacks, but in the environment of Attorney General A. Mitchell Palmer's "Red Scare," Hill was easily seen by Brough as a socialist or community provocateur. Brough praised the "white citizens of Phillips County," who prevented further violence and condemned those "bad negroes who were responsible for the outbreak."[87] Most Arkansans seem not to have been greatly influenced by the hysteria of the Red Scare. Brough was an exception to the rule in Arkansas. He feared the influence of Bolsheviks, pacifists, and the I. W. W. or Wobblies. Despite Brough's intense dislike of unionism and radicalism, it does not appear that for most Arkansans the Elaine race riot had much to do with the Red Scare. Most Arkansans viewed the threat as racial in origin rather than as a labor plot.[88]

While tenancy, land monopoly, and injustice to black citizens continued, the Brough era was a period of progressive reform in Arkansas. Efficiency and democracy became the watchwords of the new reform impulse. The impetus for the movement came more from the urban middle class than from rural Arkansas. Urban Pulaski County voted 1,746 to 1,032 in favor of the revised constitution while the old Populist counties such as Polk and White voted heavily against it.[89] Arkansas progressivism doffed its one-gallus coveralls for the city man's business suit. The iconoclasm and negativism of the "Popocrats" gave way to respectable business-like reform and a more willing acceptance of the government's role in economic affairs.

11

Conclusion

As the twentieth century dawned, the national Democratic Party faced the new era divided, defeated, and uncertain of its prospects. The 1892 election had been a glorious one for Democratic presidential and congressional politics. But the tide of fortune turned as the party failed to unite behind a single program or ideology. An unbending president refused to yield to the demands of agrarians in the West and South. Divided in its counsels and rent with dissension, the party could not provide the dynamic leadership for a rapidly growing nation with new economic and social problems. When the Democrats sorely needed healing, compromise, and unity, party factions were further polarized.[1]

The Arkansas Democratic Party contributed to the sectional tensions by its movement toward agrarian radicalism. The drift began even in the 1870s and 1880s as farmers' protest groups threatened to turn to third parties. In the late 1890s, the election of silverite Dan Jones and more especially of the one-gallus Jeff Davis indicated a veering leftward. The eruption of agrarianism in Arkansas contributed to the overpowering of the gold forces in the national convention and the nomination of William Jennings Bryan. The state party also added to the national party's inability to adopt a single-minded view concerning the national government's role in directing and regulating economic and social affairs.

The attitude of Arkansans toward governmental intervention

was ambivalent. Jeff Davis sometimes spoke in activist terms, yet he often reverted to a more Jeffersonian view. He wanted to use governmental power to redress economic injustices and restore a proper balance. But his methods were often iconoclastic rather than rational. With less finesse than Woodrow Wilson, he spoke of taking apart the trusts and destroying monopolistic giants. Jeff Davis showed more interest in policing government to see that it stayed out of areas it had no business in than in extending its supervision over social and economic affairs. The redneck leader's double-minded view resembled that of many Arkansans who desired government aid for levee construction but bitterly opposed federal interference in elections. Yet the crusade against railroad injustices and monopolistic practices did move Arkansas and the South toward a more activist philosophy of government. By the time Charles Brough came to the statehouse in 1917, progressives viewed the restrictions of the old state constitution as archaic dead weights which curbed the state government from acting to improve the economy and society. They also moved toward a less extreme state's rights position and demanded that the federal government take action to control currency, the banking system, and the liquor traffic. A similar shift of emphasis occurred in other Southern states, most notably in South Carolina and Alabama.[2]

During the Wilson era Arkansas congressmen pressed the administration to shape its banking, currency, and antitrust legislation more to the liking of the radical agrarians. Congressman Otis Wingo and Senators Joseph T. Robinson, James P. Clarke, and later William F. Kirby effectively championed progressive reform. Wingo ranked with such advanced agrarians of the South as Mississippi's James K. Vardaman, Texans Joseph H. Eagle and Robert L. Henry, and South Carolinians J. Willard Ragsdale and Asbury F. Lever. Robinson became an administration Democrat, moderately progressive, and one of the South's strongest advocates of child labor reform. Clarke identified himself with the progressives, but his marked individualism occasionally diverted him. He could not tolerate the Adamson Act. Kirby's agrarian sentiments were more akin to Wingo's, and he embodied the latent anti-war tendencies of many farmers of the South. If the voice of Southern agrarian Democrats was not always a chorus in unison, there were many Arkansans in the Congress who spoke in genuinely reformist tones.[3] Arkansas played a significant role in Wilsonian progressivism, even to the point of electing its own scholar into politics.

In Joseph T. Robinson, the state's progressivism touched both the Wilson and the Franklin D. Roosevelt governments. Robinson, a moderate, helped marshal congressional strength behind New Deal measures. Though in his heart he may have been more loyal to Franklin D. Roosevelt than the New Deal program, he played a major role in its legislative enactment. His career does not prove that the reform impulse of the early 1900s moved without interruption to emerge as the New Deal of the 1930s, but it does suggest that for Arkansas the two movements were not vastly divergent.

During the two decades following the 1896 election, the Democratic Party in Arkansas divided into two antagonistic factions. The 1896 election helped crystallize the growing divergence between conservatives and agrarians in the party. Jeff Davis's entrance into the gubernatorial contest of 1899–1900 further divided the party into a militant reformist and a more moderate faction. To some extent the volatile and abrasive personality of the redneck leader produced the rift, but ideology was not an insignificant cause of factionalism. The factions reached their clearest demarcation during Davis's tenure in the governor's office (1901–07). But identification with Davis did not become the *sine qua non* of progressivism in Arkansas. Davis's demagogic tactics and his insistence on personal dominance offended some of those who were sympathetic with government regulation and progressive reform. After 1913 the drift toward a more fluid and transient factionalism increased. The old alignments counted for less as goldbugs and anti-Davis men came to the side of the business-minded progressives. The Davis Old Guard continued to be a force in Arkansas politics after the leader's death, but the movement became more a sentiment than an organization as the years passed. The Old Guard managed to demand its share of patronage for only a few years beyond the redneck leader's death. Personalities tended to again predominate over issues as the party returned to a pattern of "consensus politics."

The bifurcation of the party in Arkansas, a notoriously strong one-party state, afforded white Democratic voters a choice at the primary elections. Sometimes the two factions raised issues that aroused the interest of Arkansas voters. Jeff Davis and his followers used their movement to wrest political power from the conservatives who had not given submerged groups the hearing they desired. If Davis's rhetoric did not always lead to radical or long-term economic reform, he did at least galvanize the country folk into a political force that demanded a hearing for their views. To some extent the gains of the country people were more symbolic than substantial. This is not to say that the gains were insignificant or of no consequence. The Davis faction's "shadow movement," which included townsmen of some economic means and with a middle-class orientation, provided some of the leadership for the movement as well as needed votes. With such breadth, the Davis faction could not press with a unified vision for the kind of drastic economic reform that would have significantly altered the influence of the wealthier classes on the state's political processes. Despite all the noise, Davis did not destroy the power of economic interests in the state. To this extent, the Davis movement was a symbolic crusade whose chief, but not sole, accomplishment was to provide respect and a psychological or emotional outlet for those who believed themselves to be victims of oppression by either Northern colonial or urban elites.

The rise of the Davis faction brought at least an exciting alternative at election time. Arkansas, a state often characterized by issueless politics, now had at least a measure of democracy. Davis's faction did not immediately gain recognizability and relative unity as early as 1900 and 1901. And although the two factions never did attain sufficient cohesiveness and permanence to achieve the identity and visibility of one of the two major parties, the factions did briefly command sufficient loyalty and recognition to stimulate some exciting election contests. The factions did not become an equivalent for the two-party system. They did not have the longstanding tradition and ideological heritage of the major parties. Yet, like some of the other Southern states, Arkansas at times became the scene of significant elections and democratic processes.[4]

The Arkansas pattern bears some resemblance to that of Mississippi. Like James K. Vardaman and Theodore Bilbo, Jeff Davis directed his rhetoric toward farmers and rural folk, and arrayed them against the city. Also, like Vardaman and Bilbo, he has been labeled a demagogue because of the use of bombastic rhetoric to arouse the disadvantaged. Although Davis also pandered to base prejudices, his racism was not of the more virulent type characteristic of other "demagogues."[5] Pitchfork Ben Tillman of South Carolina, Huey Long of a later era, and James Ferguson of Texas adopted similar tactics. Ferguson, whose reforms were more clearly aimed at helping the lower economic classes, aroused the wrath of respectable Texans when he marshaled the forces of the tenant class to secure change. Like Davis, he was the object of an impeachment crusade, but in Ferguson's case the drive of his enemies culminated in his loss of office.[6]

The reform programs of Governors Jeff Davis, George Donaghey, and Charles H. Brough achieved a measure of success. Davis and Donaghey forced the convict-leasing issue to the forefront. Both men used pardons to dramatize the plight of the prisoners, and Donaghey opened the penitentiary gates to hundreds during his last days in office. His critics characterized the act as irresponsible and hasty, but it prepared the way for ending the leasing evil during the next administration. Davis's assault on the railroads and their lobbyists helped establish the regulatory concept in Arkansas. The state railroad commission pursued an activist policy and helped reduce passenger rates. Sometimes the commission's rates were blocked or delayed by court action, but the commission was not ineffective. The state also began to force the railroads to pay a larger share of taxes. The three governors also established and then raised the franchise taxes on corporations. Davis denounced the fellow-servant rule, and state laws in the early 1900s forbade the use of employee negligence as a defense against company liability for industrial accidents. Perhaps Davis's adventurous attacks on the insurance companies were not wholly beneficial. But his flair for the spectacular created greater awareness of the need for regulation of corporations. Before Brough came into office, the state had a blue-sky law to protect investors from fraudulent stock manipulators, and in the same period, the state legislature enacted laws to regulate the hours of working women and children. Arkansas led the Southern states in its dedication to the regulation of child labor and was the only former Confederate state to ratify the abortive child labor amendment of the 1920s.

But the reform governors did not succeed in moving Arkansas from its place among those states having the poorest social and welfare services for its people. This condition cannot be explained solely by a conservative or extreme rightest sentiment. The rural, undeveloped, unindustrialized, non-urban character of

Arkansas explains its failure to provide better education and more services for the helpless and indigent. The state has simply lacked the wealth to finance such programs. Davis, Donaghey, and Brough helped awaken Arkansans to the need for improving state services. Jeff Davis deplored the barbaric conditions in the state prisons and frequently insisted that convicts deserved to be fed and treated like human beings. Brough called for more adequate facilities to aid the insane, and he questioned the failure to provide a reform school for Negro boys who had been placed with adult criminals. He also led a vigorous "good roads" movement that continued to be a dominant theme in the 1920s under Governor John E. Martineau. Yet, most charitable and welfare programs lacked adequate funding. Too often, Governor Brough could only appoint a commission to study and discuss a particular social need while admitting inability to secure revenue to initiate action. Taxation rates to finance education increased during the era, and after 1920 Governor Thomas C. McRae pressed for further increases. But even with increased assessments, Arkansas could not find the moneys to compete educationally with states outside the South. As late as 1971, Arkansas continued to rank forty-ninth among the states in average per capita personal income. While the national average stood at $4,138, Arkansas personal income reached only $3,036.[7]

The reform leaders of the early twentieth century helped spur a continuing sentiment in the state for pressing on toward solution of social and welfare problems. Many Arkansans have refused to be satisfied with a complacent attitude about the state's inadequate social services. Arkansans have always shared a belief in the great potential of their state. The "boosterism" of the frontier era has never died in the "Land of Opportunity" and Arkansans have always anticipated a future period of spectacular growth and progress.[8]

The opposition party in Arkansas failed to present an effective challenge to Democratic leadership. Although the Republican Party garnered respectable minorities in presidential and congressional elections, they dominated local offices in only a few counties and sent only a handful of representatives to the state legislature. They could not elect governors or state officers. The Republicans could not overcome the chicanery and corruption implicit in a system where the dominant party controlled the election machinery. But the party was hardly a nonentity. The

Republican organization remained strong, active, and possessed of outstanding leadership. Powell Clayton and Harmon Remmel were not loved, but they commanded some respect for their ability to hold the regular organization together while insurgents attacked from within and Democrats set the rules of the political game to their own advantage. The Republicans skillfully manipulated patronage and wielded their presidential nominating powers in order to increase their influence in national affairs and to insure the vitality of the state organization. Despite the abilities and energy of the Republican leadership, the party did not seriously threaten Democratic supremacy, and a healthy two-party system did not exist in Arkansas.

The most serious travesty of democracy in Arkansas, as elsewhere in the South, was the disfranchisement of blacks. The Democratic Party announced publicly its commitment to white supremacy. It remained the bulwark of white domination of governmental, economic, and social institutions. Racial intolerance was nearly as virulent in Arkansas as in the states of the deep South. In its 1914 platform the party defined its racial policy, "While the Democratic party does not permit negroes to participate in its primaries, and receives no aid from them, yet it realizes that they are part of the State, are more or less dependent upon the Democrats for sustenance, and the Democratic party has always been considerate of them."[9]

Although the Democratic Party made little response to the needs of blacks, it adjusted gradually to the angry demands of embittered agrarians. Populism in Arkansas did not achieve the power it had in states like North Carolina and Alabama. Gradual accommodation and shifting of ideology cut the ground from under the third-party movements. The Arkansas experience followed a pattern similar to that in other Southern states. Texas Governor James Hogg conducted a campaign for regulation by a railroad commission and made a concerted effort to woo disaffected agrarians.[10] Arkansas Populists made election reform one of their major doctrines. They found it difficult to cooperate with a party that represented established and dominant authority and which threatened to end their existence. Middle-of-the-road Populism flourished in Arkansas as it did in many Southern states. Fusion of the Democratic and Populist parties in 1896 became a reality primarily because of pressures from the national party organizations. The national Democratic chairman's home state could hardly reject the party strategy, and James K. Jones pressured Arkansas Democrats to welcome Populists into the fold. After the 1896 election, Arkansas Populists, like those in other states, rapidly lost political influence.

Leaders of the People's Party did not return in droves to places of leadership in the Democratic Party. A few agrarians did succeed in making the change, but most of those whose names appeared in the newspapers of the 1890s did not crop up again in the political notices of the 1900s. Many had reached the retirement age, and possibly many became disenchanted with the political system. In Alabama only a few Populist voters came back to the Democracy. Instead, many turned to the Republican Party or ended their political involvement.[11] The pattern in Arkansas is somewhat similar, but there is some evidence that many of the agrarian voters did return to the Democratic Party after the entrance of Jeff Davis into the political arena. The Populist influence upon the Arkansas Democratic Party was less a matter of individuals doffing Populist garb to don the Democratic uniform than it was a process of transfer of ideology and spirit. The Democrats espoused some of the Populist doctrines and demonstrated a similar temperament. Jeff Davis discovered that iconoclasm, "running Red River" through Little Rock, and excoriating newspapers, the monopolies, and special interests sat well with the fellows who lived up the forks of the creek.

Progressivism in the era of George W. Donaghey and Charles H. Brough assumes a more respectable tone. The businessman and the professor elicited support from those town folk who were weary of politicians, machines, and demagoguery. Both men strove for business-like reform administrations. Brough especially became the proponent of efficient, scientific, orderly government operation. He favored intelligent regulation by commissions of experts. He did not foster an all-out assault on the business community, but he did favor some supervision and control. The same emphasis on business efficiency in government appeared in other Southern states. Governors Richard I. Manning of South Carolina, Thomas E. Kilby of Alabama, and Harry F. Byrd of Virginia were among those who introduced "business progressivism" to the South.[12] The progressives of Brough's day retained a measure of the rhetoric and the abusive campaign tactics of the Davis era. The state was still emerging from its frontier environment and Arkansans still enjoyed political debates that resembled a clash of prize-fighting cocks.

Arkansas did not sink into a quagmire of reaction and conservatism at the exodus of Charles H. Brough in 1921. A paradoxical mix of conservatism and liberalism lingered on. The progressive sentiment surfaced occasionally, as in 1924, when Arkansas became the first state to ratify a proposed child labor constitutional amendment. Governor Thomas C. McRae pressed for increased revenues to improve the state's lagging educational system. But there were signs of fading idealism also. In 1918, the voters rejected the proposed new state constitution, and in 1920 McRae campaigned on a platform denouncing Brough's penchant for scientific commissions. He fulfilled a promise to discontinue the operation of Brough's Corporation Commission and restore instead the old Railroad Commission. Tenancy, which had never received sufficient attention, became a spreading cancer. In 1920, tenants operated 51.3 percent of all farms in Arkansas, and by 1930 tenancy rose to 63 percent.[13] During the same period, Arkansas became one of the strongest Ku Klux Klan centers in the nation. Despite some evidence of repression and extreme conservatism, a heritage of democratic individualism continued to characterize the state in the decades after 1900. Political analysts still consider Arkansas an enigma. The state has been too isolated and rural to be genuinely liberal in its politics but too close to the frontier and an individualistic heritage to be stereotyped in a conservative mold.

Appendix: Voter Participation in Arkansas

	Total Votes Cast in Gubernatorial Election*	Total Votes Cast in Presidential Election*
1888	183,452	155,941
1890	204,360	
1892	156,186	148,019
1894	126,986	
1896	140,940	149,405
1898	111,218	
1900	132,979	127,866
1902	119,741	
1904	149,780	116,421
1906	151,848	
1908	162,574	151,990
1910	150,578	
1912	169,649	124,029
1913**	83,306	
1914	125,524	
1916	175,734	168,310
1918	72,984***	
1920	200,113	181,466

Biennial Reports of the Secretary of State are source for figures given.
** Special election in July 1913.
*** The Republican Party did not place a gubernatorial candidate in
   the field in 1918.

Bibliographical Essay

Many Arkansas politicians did not preserve their correspondence. Consequently, reconstructing the political history of the period from 1896 to 1920 is a difficult task. Newspapers must be used to secure an understanding of many events not discussed in letters and memoirs. Despite deficiencies and gaps, the state has sufficient source materials to reward the researcher.

Manuscripts

By far the most valuable and extensive collection of manuscript sources for the study of Arkansas is located in the Special Collections division of the University of Arkansas Library at Fayetteville. The library's holdings have been or are in the process of being carefully indexed. The most helpful single source for a study of Democratic politics is the Charles H. Brough Papers. Brough either did not write or did not preserve many letters relating to politics before 1913. The collection is extensive and helpful for election campaign periods but thins out somewhat during Brough's administrations (1917–21). The professor's correspondence reveals much about his anti-machine views, his reform programs, campaign efforts, and his personal affairs before and after 1913. Campaign pamphlets and numerous speeches are also instructive.

The Harmon L. Remmel Papers, also at Fayetteville, constitute the second most valuable collection for the period. Remmel was a prominent Republican in the state organization and his letters primarily relate to the inner workings of his own party with occasional references to the Democratic powers. The collection provides information on the late 1890s and continues beyond the confines of this study. The papers are one of the few extensive collections covering the period before 1913. Powell Clayton, the state party boss who served as ambassador to Mexico under William McKinley and Theodore Roosevelt, kept in touch with Remmel on party matters. Remmel corresponded most often with Arkansas politicians, although he sometimes communicated with Theodore Roosevelt, William Howard Taft, and other national leaders. The letters reveal a crafty, cunning Remmel, who constantly labored to increase his influence over the Republican organization. They also supply a record of the operation of an opposition party in a one-party state.

The University of Arkansas also holds a number of smaller collections which are of value. The Thomas Chipman McRae Papers include five boxes covering the period from 1889–1919. There are several large gaps in the collection, 1902–03, 1905–09, and 1913–14. Many of the letters deal with McRae's land manipulations while a member of the house of representatives Committee on Public Lands. They also indicate his interest in "progressive" currency and banking reform. The George Washington Donaghey Papers contain only 356 items including some letters, speeches, and clippings. The papers must be supplemented by Donaghey's own published writings. The George Washington Hays Papers are in a similar state. Hays kept a few letters on the prohibition debate mainly to disprove the charge of his own ambivalence on the issue. The papers cover the period of his administration, 1913–17, but omit much more than they reveal. The Hal Lee Norwood Scrapbooks are very disappointing. The attorney general preserved a few clippings on his own career, very few letters, and some nearly illegible personal accounts. The David Yancey Thomas Papers contain the letters and writings of a University of Arkansas political scientist during the Brough administration. They are especially useful for a study of the initiative and referendum movement, state tax reform, and the Elaine race riot of 1919.

Other items of significance at Fayetteville include the George A. Thornburgh Scrapbooks covering the years 1875–1923. Thornburgh was a member of the legislature but retired from office as young man and dedicated the remainder of his life to the prohibition cause. His six volumes contain clippings, speeches, pamphlets, and a few letters relating mainly to his temperance efforts. A much smaller collection, the Uriah Milton Rose Papers, contain only a few letters relating to the career of one of Arkansas's most distinguished attorneys. Unfortunately the political activities of a leading Cleveland Democrat are not even alluded to. There is brief reference to his appointment by Theodore Roosevelt to the Hague Peace Tribunal. The Nathaniel Madison Ragland Papers contain letters, sermons, and church minutes. Ragland was pastor of the First Christian Church of Fayetteville, and his papers reveal something of the views of religious leaders of the time. Of only limited value are the Thomas Andrew Futrall Papers which contain the letters and speeches of an Arkansas educator.

The most distressing gap in the source materials is the absence of any substantial collection of Jeff Davis letters. The redneck leader's correspondence can only be obtained by gleaning a few letters from widely scattered collections. But the University of Arkansas is the starting point for a study of Davis. A very small collection, "Political Material Concerning Jeff Davis," has a few political pamphlets. One of the most valuable of these pamphlets, *That Correspondence,* contains letters between Jephtha H. Evans and Davis concerning their political squabbles. The Jeff Davis Papers are a small collection of microfilmed documents including only a few letters, several speeches, clippings, and a brief on one of Davis's antitrust cases while he was attorney general. The John Hebert Page Papers contain a few items preserved by Davis's campaign manager. A notebook records names of Davis supporters in the state. The James Berry Papers contain the letters of Davis's 1906 rival for the United States Senate. The Joseph Taylor Robinson Papers, also at the University of Arkansas at Fayetteville, provide information about one of the state's most famous politicians. Unfortunately most Arkansas politicians did not leave collections of papers for public use.

The Arkansas History Commission at Little Rock has preserved a large number of newspaper sources for the period. Also available there are the R. Minor Wallace Papers. Wallace served in the house of representatives and was an outstanding orator and temperance leader. His papers contain essays and examples of his oratory but almost nothing of political or social significance. The

Governor Charles H. Brough Scrapbooks are housed at the commission. The thirty-four volumes consist primarily of newspaper clippings and material of a personal nature. At Austin, in the University of Texas Archives, the Horace Chilton Diaries contain impressions of Senator James K. Jones.

The Manuscript Division of the Library of Congress holds many collections which have never been exploited for the study of Arkansas politics. The William Jennings Bryan Papers have many letters to and from James K. Jones and many which make reference to the national chairman. Some of these mention Arkansas politics. Most valuable are the letters from Charles Collins to Bryan about the decline of support for Jones in Arkansas and the reasons for his defeat. There is also some correspondence between William Hope Harvey and the Great Commoner. Arkansas Populist and labor leader James R. Sovereign also wrote to Bryan often. The Grover Cleveland Papers provide a few letters of James K. Jones and James Berry. There are some Jeff Davis letters and a large number of Harmon L. Remmel and Powell Clayton letters in the Theodore Roosevelt Papers. The William Howard Taft Papers, like the Roosevelt Papers, contain correspondence with a number of Republican politicians in Arkansas.

The Woodrow Wilson Papers, also at the Library of Congress Manuscripts Division, contain much that is valuable for the reconstruction of Arkansas political history. Arkansas correspondents include many leading Democrats of the state. Much can be learned about Arkansas progressivism from the letters from men like Oscar Winn of Arkansas and Senator Joseph T. Robinson. Wilson's Papers shed much light on the patronage struggles that began in the party with the accession of a Democratic president. The Newton D. Baker Papers provide information concerning Senator William F. Kirby's anti-war record. There is less material in the William G. McAdoo Papers, the Albert Sidney Burleson Papers, and the Josephus Daniels Papers.

The Judson King Papers, at the Library of Congress, report the activities of a prominent direct legislation advocate. During the Wilson era, King took a special interest in passage of a more effective Initiative and Referendum Amendment in Arkansas. His letters reveal something of the nature of the progressive movement in the state. The League of Women Voters Papers contains only a small amount of information on Arkansas's ratification of the Child Labor Amendment to the federal Constitution. The

Cass Gilbert Papers have material on the architect of the Arkansas state capitol but reveal very little about the project in Arkansas.

Many of the materials at the National Archives in Washington, D.C., are a virtually untapped source for the study of Arkansas. The letters in the archives supply information available nowhere else. The Department of Justice, Record Group 60, has appointment papers for the federal judges, marshals, and district attorneys. The Department of the Interior, Record Group 48, contains appointment papers for the General Land Offices in Arkansas. The Land Office records are not available beyond 1907 at the present time. The appointment papers for the superintendant of the Hot Springs Reservation are also available in the Interior Department records. The Department of the Treasury, Record Group 56, has appointment papers for the office of collector of internal revenue at Little Rock. The National Archives hold the papers relating to the contested congressional election between George Tilles and William B. Cravens, for the 60th Congress, Committee on Elections Number Three. Also useful are the transcripts and letters relating to United States Supreme Court cases.

Newspapers

The Arkansas Gazette is easily the most important newspaper source for this study. The *Gazette* published far more extensive accounts of the political events of the day than any other newspaper in the state. It is an indispensable source. Most other newspapers in the state often relied on the *Gazette* for their own information. The *Gazette* supplied the most detailed accounts of debates and activities of the general assembly. No other paper approached the *Gazette* for completeness of detail. Often the *Gazette* has been pictured as a neutral, objective Democratic organ which did not enter into factional disputes. This is only partially true. The *Gazette* turned from Grover Cleveland and its sound money stance toward the silverites in 1896. Within a few years it became one of the many anti-Davis papers.

Also at Little Rock, but less important, is *The Arkansas Democrat,* a sound-money conservative paper. An ill-tempered but colorful conservative "swamp democracy" organ was *The Helena Weekly World. The Pine Bluff Weekly Press-Eagle* maintained a position similar to the *World*. *Morgan's Buzz-Saw* and *The Kicker* are two Populist newspapers still extant. They seldom made reference to state politics, preferring to focus their rather ludicrous satire on national politics. Both were edited by middle-of-the-roader Winfield Scott Morgan. The *Arkansas Sentinel* (Fayetteville) covers primarily Farmer's Union activities and sometimes covered the woman suffrage crusade since the editor, a woman, was active in both movements. Other newspapers frequently consulted were: *The Log Cabin Democrat* (Conway), *The Weekly Elevator* (Fort Smith), *The Mena Weekly Star*, the *Southern Standard* (Arkadelphia), *The Advance* (Monticello), *The Drew County Advance* (Monticello), and the *Fayetteville Democrat*. Also of use was a supplement to *The Forrest City Times* of September 11, 1903, entitled *Governor Jeff Davis: A Review of His Official Career. Some Reasons Why He Should Not Be Renominated*, located in the Library of the University of Texas at Austin. All other newspapers are available on microfilm at the University of Arkansas at Fayetteville and the Arkansas History Commission at Little Rock. *The New York Times* occasionally reported on Arkansas subjects.

Public Documents

The inaugural addresses and other speeches of the governors to the general assemblies are printed in pamphlet form and filed under "Messages to the General Assembly" in the Special Collections of the University of Arkansas Library at Fayetteville. Some of the speeches are found bound with *Arkansas Public Documents*. The *Biennial Report of the Secretary of State* is useful especially for election records. The reports occasionally included material on the members of the general assembly. The *Annual Report of the Railroad Commission* provides valuable material on the state's regulatory movement. A number of investigative committee reports and commission reports contain information about controversial political matters. The Davis faction bitterly opposed the construction of a new State Capitol building. The Capitol Commission reports were issued frequently. The *Report of the Joint Committee on the State Capitol, 1907* and reports of the Secretary of the Treasury for 1902, 1907, and 1908 deal with the Capitol construction issue. *In the Matter of the Adjustment of the Claim of Caldwell and Drake against the State of Arkansas, Abstract of the Record and Testimony* contains over six hundred pages of testimony relating to the building of the State Capitol. For the attempt to impeach Jeff Davis the *Report & testimony of the Ways & Means Committee in its investigation of the differences between the chief executive and the remaining members of the Penitentiary Board* (Little Rock, 1903) is helpful.

Also available at Fayetteville are the *Journal of the Senate of Arkansas,* the *Journal of the House of Representatives of Arkansas,* and *Arkansas Reports.* Kelly Bryant's *Historical Report of the Secretary of State* (Little Rock, 1968), has lists of state legislators and other officials, and a copy of the state constitution. The reports of the Tax Commission, the attorney general, the Penitentiary Board, the Commission of Mines, Manufacturing and Agriculture, and other state offices are bound in a single biennial volume of *Arkansas Public Documents,* available at Fayetteville.

The Library of Congress has a copy of *Address To The People of the State of Arkansas* (Little Rock, n.d.), which is a statement by the delegates to the 1918 constitutional convention, and a copy of *The First Biennial Report of the Board of Control for State Charitable Institutions of Arkansas, 1915–16* (Little Rock, n.d.) and *Third Biennial Report of the Board of Control of Arkansas: 1919–1921* (Little Rock, 1921). At the same location, the *Sixteenth Census of the United States Population* (Washington, D.C., 1942) and *Fourteenth Census of the United States: 1920, Bulletin,* Department of Commerce, Bureau of the Census give population data for the state. For the "sunk lands" controversy a valuable source at the Library of Congress is *Hearings Before The Committee On The Public Lands of the House of Representatives,* Hearings on February 15 to March 2, 1910 on H. R. 19637 (Washington, 1910). The *Congressional Record* provided speeches of Arkansas congressmen. For a survey of the state's mineral and agricultural development in the early 1900s, a helpful source is *Arkansas and Her Resources: The Official Book of the Arkansas Commission, Panama-Pacific International Exposition* (Little Rock, 1915). Two memorial volumes provide some biographical material: *Memorial Services Held in the House of Representatives and Senate of the United States, Together with Remarks presented in Eulogy of Joseph Taylor Robinson,* 75th Congress, Third Session, (Washington, 1938); *Memorial Services*

Held in the House of Representatives of the United States, Together With Remarks Presented in Eulogy of Otis T. Wingo, 71st Congress, Third Session, (Washington, 1931).

Memoirs, Autobiographies, and Contemporary Accounts

Several firsthand accounts help set the scene for the events at the turn of the century. Powell Clayton's *The Aftermath of the Civil War, In Arkansas* (New York, 1915) is a description of the carpetbag governor's own experiences in the Reconstruction era with a few references to later events. William N. Hill, a former convict, wrote about his prison experiences in *Story of the Arkansas Penitentiary* (n.p., c. 1915). Fred W. Allsopp includes a few comments about politics in his reminiscences about Arkansas journalism in *Twenty Years in a Newspaper Office* (Little Rock, 1907). He later made a few minor changes and entitled the revised work *Little Adventures in Newspaperdom* (Little Rock, 1922).

The Memoirs of William Jennings Bryan (Chicago, 1925), written by Bryan but revised and completed by his wife Mary Baird Bryan, tell about James K. Jones's associations with the Great Commoner at the Chicago convention. Other sources of value are: Festus P. Summers, editor, *The Cabinet Diary of William L. Wilson, 1896–1897* (Chapel Hill, 1957); Arthur Wallace Dunn, *From Harrison to Harding: A Personal Narrative Covering a Third of a Century, 1888–1921* (New York, 1922); David S. Barry, *Forty Years in Washington* (Boston, 1924); Archie Butt, *The Intimate Letters of Archie Butt, Military Aide* (Garden City, 1930); Willis J. Abbot, *Watching The World Go By* (Boston, 1933). William Hope Harvey, *Coin's Financial School Up to Date* (Chicago, 1895) has some information on James K. Jones. Three accounts are especially helpful in supplying information about the Wilson era and William F. McCombs. McCombs' own account *Making Woodrow Wilson President* (New York, 1921) was edited by Louis Jay Lang. McCombs died before he had completed his reminiscences, and Lang supplied much of the information in the latter part of the book. Maurice F. Lyons, *William F. McCombs, The President Maker* (Cincinnati, 1922) is not as defensive of Wilson's campaign manager. The Lang account reflects the bitterness of McCombs toward Woodrow Wilson, William McAdoo, and others because they had refused him a cabinet position as a reward for his work in securing the nomination for Wilson. Joseph P. Tumulty in *Woodrow Wilson As I Know Him* (Garden City, 1921) has a chapter on McCombs which provides insights into his and Wilson's profound dislike for McCombs. There is a brief statement of the vice president's impressions of Senator James P. Clarke in Thomas Marshall's *Recollections of Thomas R. Marshall* (Indianapolis, 1925).

An essential work for the study of Jeff Davis's career is his personal secretary's account of his life. Charles Jacobson's *The Life Story of Jeff Davis, The Stormy Petrel of Arkansas Politics* (Little Rock, 1925) conveniently summarizes the political activities of the redneck leader. L. S. Dunaway, *Jeff Davis, Governor and United States Senator, His Life and Speeches* (Little Rock, 1913) is really not a biography but a useful collection of speeches. The same author wrote *What a Preacher Saw Through a Key-Hole* (Little Rock, 1925) which is brief but has some information on the Davis period. Jerry Wallace, *An Arkansas Judge: Being a Sketch of the Life and Public Service of Judge J. G. Wallace, 1850–1927* (Springfield, Illinois, 1928) is a biography of Davis's fatherly friend. It has some discussion of Wallace's service as a member of the Arkansas Railroad Commission and relates a few tales about Davis. There is some comment on Davis's Senate record in Chauncey M. Depew, *My Memories of Eighty Years* (New York, 1924). Two pamphlets bearing on Davis's career are: *The Railroad Tax Compromise and Senator Clarke's $30,000 Fee, Statement by Senator Clarke and the Late Senator Davis* (n.p., n.d.), and *Speech of Robert L. Rogers, Candidate For Governor, Delivered at Lake City, Oct. 16, 1905* (n.p., n.d.). The first pamphlet mainly contains material from the 1906 campaign and is a reprint of information in *The Arkansas Gazette*, January 21, 1906. There is a brief supplemental statement by Clarke written for the 1914 campaign against William F. Kirby. The Rogers anti-Davis speech and Wallace's biography are located in the Library of Congress.

George W. Donaghey has written three books. His *Building A State Capitol* (Little Rock, 1937) is a defense of his demolition of part of the structure and rebuilding according to his own plans. It is of much greater import than his *Homespun Philosophy of George W. Donaghey* (Little Rock, n.d.). The *Autobiography of George W. Donaghey, Governor of Arkansas, 1909–1913* (Benton, Arkansas, 1939) contains a few impressions of Arkansas politicians and some account of Donaghey's early move to Woodrow

Wilson's camp. The book also tells of Donaghey's growing disenchantment with Wilson. Two other autobiographies that sometimes touch on political topics are: Tom W. Campbell, *Arkansas Lawyer: Reminiscences of a Lifetime* (Little Rock, 1952) and a labor leader's account, *My Story: The Autobiography of De Emmett Bradshaw* (Omaha, 1941). Mifflin Wistar Gibbs provides information on the role of blacks in the Arkansas Republican Party in *Shadow and Light: An Autobiography* (New York, 1968 reprint of 1902 edition). Winfield Scott Morgan's *History of the Wheel and Alliance and The Impending Revolution* (New York, 1968) offers insights into Morgan's perspective.

Some of the useful printed documents of the time include: a Bar Association of Arkansas pamphlet entitled *The proposed new constitution: modern proposals for increasing the efficiency of the various departments of government. Papers read before the meeting of the Bar Association of Arkansas held May 31st and June 1st, 1917 at Hot Springs, Arkansas* (n.p., n.d.); *Proceedings of the Arkansas Bankers Association, 1908* (Little Rock, 1908); *Digest of Rules, as Amended and Adopted by the Democratic State Central Committee, July 30, 1912* (Little Rock, n.d.); *Rules of the Democratic Party in Arkansas, Adopted March 4, 1918* (n.p., n.d.). The latter two pamphlets contain copies of election laws as well as party rules.

Secondary Works

Two biographies of limited value are James R. Grant, *The Life of Thomas C. McRae* (n.p., 1932) and Farrar Newberry, *James K. Jones, The Plumed Knight of Arkansas* (n.p., 1913). McRae's biography is very sketchy. The Jones book has more detail but is too enamored of its subject. The following biographies are especially helpful: Allan Nevins, *Grover Cleveland: A Study in Courage* (New York, 1932); the less admiring work of Horace Samuel Merrill, *Bourbon Leader: Grover Cleveland and the Democratic Party* (Boston, 1957); John R. Lambert, *Arthur Pue Gorman* (Baton Rouge, 1953); Paolo Coletta, *William Jennings Bryan,* Volume I, *Political Evangelist, 1860–1908* (Lincoln, 1964); Louis W. Koenig, *Bryan: A Political Biography of William Jennings Bryan* (New York, 1971); Robert Cotner, *James Stephen Hogg, A Biography* (Austin, 1959); Francis Butler Simkins, *Pitchfork Ben Tillman, South Carolinian* (Ann Arbor, 1967); Dewey W. Grantham, Jr., *Hoke Smith and the Politics of the New South* (Ann Arbor, 1967); Sam Hanna Acheson, *Joe Bailey, The Last Democrat* (New York, 1932); C. Vann Woodward, *Tom Watson, Agrarian Rebel* (New York, 1963); Rupert Norval Richardson, *Colonel Edward M. House: The Texas Years, 1858–1912* (Abilene, 1964); T. Harry Williams, *Huey Long* (New York, 1969); William F. Holmes, *The White Chief, James Kimble Vardaman* (Baton Rouge, 1970); Daniel Merritt Robison, *Bob Taylor and the Agrarian Revolt in Tennessee* (Chapel Hill, 1935). An important recent biographical study of Davis that is well researched is Raymond Arsenault's *The Wild Ass of the Ozarks: Jeff Davis and the Social Bases of Southern Politics* (Philadelphia, 1984). For biographical sketches of Arkansas leaders, see Timothy P. Donovan and Willard B. Gatewood, Jr., editors, *The Governors of Arkansas* (Fayetteville, 1981).

The most useful general history of the state is David Y. Thomas's four volume work, *Arkansas and Its People: A History, 1541–1930* (New York, 1930). Unfortunately Thomas did not cover the early twentieth century in the same detail as the earlier period. The last two volumes of biographical sketches pass by many important figures of Thomas's own time. Another chronicle-type history is Dallas T. Herndon (editor), *Centennial History of Arkansas* (Chicago, 1922), in three volumes. A disappointingly thin but useful survey which provides lists of legislators and records some of the achievements of each legislature is Dallas T. Herndon, *Outline of Executive and Legislative History of Arkansas* (n.p., 1922). A colorful account without documentation is John Gould Fletcher's *Arkansas* (Chapel Hill, 1947, reprinted 1989 by The University of Arkansas Press). Other valuable accounts include: Arkansas Writer's Project, *Arkansas: A Guide to the State* (New York, 1941); Lonnie J. White, *Politics on the Southwestern Frontier: Arkansas Territory, 1819–1836* (Memphis, 1964); Fred W. Allsopp, *History of the Arkansas Press For A Hundred Years and More* (Little Rock, 1922); J. S. Rogers, *History of Arkansas Baptists* (Little Rock, 1948); *History of the Organization and Operations of the Board of Directors St. Francis Levee District of Arkansas, 1893–1945* (West Memphis, Arkansas, n.p., n.d.); Winfield Scott Morgan, *History of the Wheel and Alliance, and The Impending Revolution* (New York, 1968); Robert W. Harrison, *Alluvial Empire* (Little Rock, 1961).

Books especially useful for a survey of Southern political history include: C. Vann Woodward, *Origins of the New South,*

1877–1913 (Baton Rouge, 1966); George Brown Tindall, *The Emergence of the New South, 1913–1945* (Baton Rouge, 1967); V. O. Key, *Southern Politics in State and Nation* (New York, 1949); Dewey W. Grantham, Jr., *The Democratic South* (New York, 1965) and Grantham's more recent survey, *Southern Progressivism: The Reconciliation of Progress and Tradition* (Knoxville, 1983) and his *The Regional Imagination: The South and Recent American History* (Nashville, 1979); see also, J. Morgan Kousser, *Southern Politics: Suffrage Restriction and the Establishment of the One-Party South, 1880–1910* (New Haven, 1974); Jack Temple Kirby, *Darkness at the Dawning: Race and Reform in the Progressive South* (Philadelphia, 1972). The views expressed in this study often parallel those of the Tindall and Grantham works. J. Rogers Hollingsworth, *The Whirligig of Politics: The Democracy of Cleveland and Bryan* (Chicago, 1969) and R. Hal Williams' chapter in H. Wayne Morgan (editor), *The Gilded Age* (Syracuse, 1970) analyzes the ills of the national Democratic Party.

For the national political scene the following are very useful: Stanley L. Jones, *The Presidential Election of 1896* (Madison, 1964); Willard B. Gatewood, *Theodore Roosevelt and the Art of Compromise* (Baton Rouge, 1970); George E. Mowry, *The Era of Theodore Roosevelt and the Birth of Modern America, 1900–1912* (New York, 1962); Arthur S. Link's books, *Woodrow Wilson And The Progressive Era, 1910–1917* (New York, 1954); Volume 1, *Wilson, The Road to the White House* (Princeton, 1947); Volume 2, *Wilson, The New Freedom* (Princeton, 1956); Volume 3, *Wilson, The Struggle for Neutrality, 1914–1915* (Princeton, 1960); Volume 4, *Wilson, Confusions and Crises, 1915–1916* (Princeton, 1964); Volume 5, *Wilson Campaigns for Progressivism and Peace, 1916–1917* (Princeton, 1965).

For black history see Thomas E. Patterson, *History of the Arkansas Teachers Association* (Washington, D.C., 1981); Benjamin Brawley, *A Social History of the American Negro* (New York, 1921; reprinted 1970 by Macmillan Co.); B. Boren McCool, *Union, Reaction and Riot: A Biography of a Rural Race Riot* (Memphis, 1970); Hanes Walton, Jr., *Black Republicans: The Politics of the Black and Tans* (Metuchen, N.J., 1975).

On agrarianism, industry, and labor the following are informative: Robert C. McMath, Jr., *Populist Vanguard: A History of the Southern Farmer's Alliance* (Chapel Hill, 1975); Lawrence Goodwyn, *Democratic Promise: The Populist Movement in America*

(New York, 1976); James R. Green, *Grass-Roots Socialism: Radical Movements in the Southwest, 1895–1943* (Baton Rouge, 1978); Norman Pollack, *The Populist Mind* (Indianapolis, 1967); Robert Durden, *The Climax of Populism; The Election of 1896* (Louisville, 1965); Theodore Saloutos, *Farmer Movements in the South, 1865–1933* (Lincoln, n.d.); Fred A. Shannon, *The Farmer's Last Frontier* (New York, 1968); Charles A. Madison, *American Labor Leaders; Personalities and Forces in the Labor Movement* (New York, 1962); Philip Taft, *Organized Labor in American History* (New York, 1964); Edward Chase Kirkland, *Industry Comes of Age: Business, Labor, and Public Policy, 1860–1897* (Chicago, 1967); National Consumer's League, *Labor Laws of Twelve Southern States* (New York, 1934); United States Bureau of the Census, *Statistical Abstract of the United States: 1971* (Washington, D.C., 1971) includes information on Arkansas's recent economic position. Interpretations of the progressive impulse are found in: Samuel P. Hays, *The Response to Industrialism, 1885–1914* (Chicago, 1957); Robert H. Wiebe, *The Search for Order, 1877–1920* (New York, 1967); Gabriel Kolko, *The Triumph of Conservatism: A Reinterpretation of American History, 1900–1916* (Chicago, 1967); Ernest S. Griffith, *A History of American City Government: The Progressive Years and Their Aftermath, 1900–1920* (New York, 1974); Lewis L. Gould, ed., *The Progressive Era* (Syracuse, 1974). For an understanding of the spirit of early America during an age of growth, Daniel J. Boorstin, *The Americans: The National Experience* (New York, 1967) is helpful.

A number of state studies provide points of comparison with the Arkansas experience. Geoffrey Blodgett, *The Gentle Reformers: Massachusetts Politics, 1900–1912* (Cambridge, 1964) argues that Massachusetts had already experienced a long history of humanitarian and social concern. Because the state had already adopted moderate reforms it did not become a hotbed of insurgency at the turn of the century. Stanley P. Caine, *The Myth of a Progressive Reform: Railroad Regulation in Wisconsin* (Madison, 1970), sheds light on the forces pressing for regulatory action. He argues that some business interests originally opposed reform but later accepted the inevitability of the regulatory trend and joined the crusade in order to moderate the regulatory legislation. He does not believe the railroads initiated the drive but they did help shape the kind of railroad commission formed. In Arkansas the railroads bucked regulation at almost every stage. Other helpful state studies include: Herbert F. Margullies, *The Decline of the Progressive Movement in Wisconsin, 1890–1920* (Madison, 1968); Lewis L. Gould, *Wyoming: A Political History, 1868–1896* (New Haven, 1968); George E. Mowry, *The California Progressives* (Chicago, 1963); Raymond H. Pulley, *Old Virginia Restored: An Interpretation of the Progressive Impulse, 1870–1930* (Charlottesville, 1968); Sheldon Hackney, *Populism to Progressivism in Alabama* (Princeton, 1969); Paul E. Isaac, *Prohibition and Politics: Turbulent Decades in Tennessee, 1885–1920* (Knoxville, 1965). The experience of Arkansas frequently compares to that of Texas and Mississippi. The parallels are evident in: Albert D. Kirwan, *Revolt of the Rednecks: Mississippi Politics, 1876–1925* (New York, 1965); Alwyn Barr, *Reconstruction to Reform: Texas Politics, 1876–1906* (Austin, 1971). See also: Lewis L. Gould, *Progressives and Prohibitionists: Texas Democrats in the Wilson Era* (Austin, 1973); Joel Williamson, *After Slavery: The Negro in South Carolina During Reconstruction 1861–1877* (Chapel Hill: 1965).

Three articles on the Wilson era in Texas are particularly helpful: Arthur S. Link, "A Letter from one of Wilson's Managers," *American Historical Review*, L (July, 1945): 768–75; Arthur S. Link, "The Wilson Movement in Texas, 1910–1912," *Southwestern Historical Quarterly*, XLVIII (Oct., 1944): 169–85; Lewis L. Gould, "Progressives and Prohibitionists: Texas Democratic Politics, 1911–1921," *Southwestern Historical Quarterly*, LXXV (July, 1971): 6–18. On the South's response to Wilsonian progressivism the following provide insights: Arthur S. Link, "The South and the 'New Freedom': An Interpretation," *The American Scholar* XX (1950–1951): 314–24; Richard M. Abrams, "Woodrow Wilson and the Southern Congressmen, 1913–1916," *Journal of Southern History*, XXII (Nov. 1956): 417–37; Anne Firor Scott, "A Progressive Wind from the South, 1906–1913," *Journal of Southern History*, XXIX (Feb., 1963): 53–70.

Rupert B. Vance, "A Karl Marx for Hill Billies, Portrait of a Southern Leader," *Social Forces*, IX (1930–1931): 180–90, and Daniel M. Robinson, "From Tillman to Long: Some Striking Leaders of the Rural South," *Journal of Southern History*, III (Aug., 1937): 289–310, illuminate the career of Jeff Davis. Other helpful articles include: Virginia Gray, "Anti-Evolution Sentiment and Behavior: The Case of Arkansas," *Journal of American History*, LVII (Sep., 1970): 352–66; Frederick W. Rathjen, "The Texas State House, A Study of the Building of the Texas Capitol Based on the Reports of the Capitol Building Commissioners," *The Southwestern Historical Quarterly,* LX (Apr., 1957): 433–62; Burton Ira Kaufman, "Virginia Politics And The Wilson Movement, 1910–1914," *The Virginia Magazine of History and Biography* LXXVII (Jan., 1969): 3–21; S. W. Moore, "State Supervision of Railroad Transportation in Arkansas," *Publications of the Arkansas Historical Association,* III (1911): 265–309; Joseph T. Robinson, "Suffrage in Arkansas," *Publications of the Arkansas Historical Association,* III (1911): 168; J. L. Charlton, "Social Aspects of Farm Ownership and Tenancy in the Arkansas Ozarks," *Bulletin,* Agricultural Experiment Station, University of Arkansas (Sep., 1947), 1–80; David Yancey Thomas, "The Land and The People," *The Nation* CX (January, 1920): 34–35; David Yancey Thomas, "Farms and the Man," *The Independent* XCI (Sept. 8, 1917): 392.

The *Arkansas Historical Quarterly* contains many valuable articles for the study of Democratic politics at the turn of the century. Those which have touched most closely upon this study include: John B. Mitchell, "An Analysis of Arkansas's Population by Race and Nativity and Residence," *Arkansas Historical Quarterly,* VIII (Summer, 1949): 115–32; Stephen E. Wood, "The Development of Arkansas Railroads," *Arkansas Historical Quarterly,* VII (Autumn, 1948): 155–93; Carolyn Blanks, "Industry in the New South: A Case History," *Arkansas Historical Quarterly,* XI (Autumn, 1952): 164–75; Corliss C. Curry, "Early Timber Operations in Southeast Arkansas," *Arkansas Historical Quarterly,* XIX (Summer, 1960): 111–18; Walter L. Brown, (editor), "Life of An Arkansas Logger in 1901," *Arkansas Historical Quarterly,* XXI (Spring, 1962): 44–74; Daniel Boone Lackey, "Cutting and Floating Red Cedar Logs in North Arkansas," *Arkansas Historical Quarterly,* XIX (Winter, 1960): 361–70; Theodore Saloutos, "The Agricultural Wheel in Arkansas," *Arkansas Historical Quarterly,* II (June, 1943): 127–40; Tom Dillard, "Scipio A. Jones," *Arkansas Historical Quarterly,* XXI (Autumn, 1972): 201–19; O. A. Rogers, Jr., "The Elaine Race Riots of 1919," *Arkansas Historical Quarterly,* XIX (Summer, 1960): 142–50; John William Graves, "Negro Disfranchisement in Arkansas," *Arkansas Historical Quarterly,* XXVI (Autumn, 1967): 199–225; Sidney Crawford, "Arkansas Suffrage Qualifications," *Arkansas Historical Quarterly,* II (Dec. 1943): 331–39; Svend Petersen, "Arkansas in Presidential Elections," *Arkansas Historical Quarterly,* VII (Autumn, 1948): 194–209; William O. Penrose, "Power Politics is Old

Hat," *Arkansas Historical Quarterly*, XI (Winter, 1952): 235–45; Paige E. Mulhollan, "The Issues of the Davis-Berry Senatorial Campaign in 1906," *Arkansas Historical Quarterly*, XX (Summer, 1961): 118–25; Thomas L. Baxley, "Prison Reforms During the Donaghey Administration," *Arkansas Historical Quarterly*, XXII (Spring, 1963): 76–84; John A. Treon, "Politics and Concrete: The Building of the Arkansas State Capitol, 1899–1917," *Arkansas Historical Quarterly*, XXXI (Summer, 1972): 99–149; Jane Zimmerman, "The Convict Lease System in Arkansas and the Fight for Abolition," *Arkansas Historical Quarterly*, VIII (Autumn, 1949): 171–88; Gilbert Richard Grant, "Joseph Taylor Robinson in Foreign Affairs," *Arkansas Historical Quarterly*, IX (Autumn, 1950): 133–71; A. Elizabeth Taylor, "The Woman Suffrage Movement in Arkansas," *Arkansas Historical Quarterly*, XV (Spring, 1956): 17–52; Charles W. Crawford, "From Classroom to State Capitol; Charles H. Brough and The Campaign of 1916," *Arkansas Historical Quarterly*, XXI (Autumn, 1962): 213–30; Foy Lisenby, "The First Meeting of the Arkansas Conference of Charities and Correction," *Arkansas Historical Quarterly*, XXVI (Summer, 1967): 155–61; Foy Lisenby, "The Arkansas Conference of Charities and Correction, 1912–1937," *Arkansas Historical Quarterly*, XXIX (Spring, 1970): 39–47; Austin L. Venable, "The Arkansas Council of Defense in the First World War," *Arkansas Historical Quarterly*, II (June, 1943): 116–26; Judith Barjenbruch, "The Greenback Political Movement: An Arkansas View," *Arkansas Historical Quarterly*, XXXVI (Summer, 1977): 107–22; F. Clark Elkins, "The Agricultural Wheel in Arkansas, 1887," *Arkansas Historical Quarterly*, XL (Autumn, 1981): 249–60; Berton E. Henningson, Jr., "Root Hog or Die: The Brothers of Freedom and the 1884 Arkansas Election," *Arkansas Historical Quarterly*, XLV (Autumn, 1986): 197–216; Richard L. Niswonger, "Arkansas and the Election of 1896," *Arkansas Historical Quarterly*, XXXIV (Spring, 1975): 41–78; Willard B. Gatewood, Jr., "Theodore Roosevelt and Arkansas, 1901–1912," *Arkansas Historical Quarterly*, XXXII (Spring, 1973): 3–24; Marvin F. Russell, "The Rise of a Republican Leader: Harmon L. Remmel," *Arkansas Historical Quarterly*, XXXVI (Autumn, 1977): 234–57; Bob Besom, "Little Rock Businessmen Invest in Coal: Harmon L. Remmel and the Arkansas Anthracite Coal Company, 1905–1923," *Arkansas Historical Quarterly*, XLVII (Autumn, 1988): 273–87; William H. Burnside, "Powell Clayton: Ambassador to

Mexico, 1897–1905," *Arkansas Historical Quarterly,* XXXVIII (Winter, 1979): 328–44; James W. Leslie, "Ferd Havis: Jefferson County's Black Republican Leader," *Arkansas Historical Quarterly,* XXXVII (Autumn, 1978): 240–51; Willard B. Gatewood, "Arkansas Negroes in the 1890s: Documents," *Arkansas Historical Quarterly,* XXXIII (Winter, 1974): 293–325; Elizabeth L. Wheeler, "Isaac Fisher: The Frustrations of a Negro Educator At Branch Normal College, 1902–1911," *Arkansas Historical Quarterly,* XLI (Spring, 1982): 3–50; Thomas Rothrock, "Joseph Carter Corbin and Negro Education in the University of Arkansas," *Arkansas Historical Quarterly,* XXX (Winter, 1971): 277–314; Tom W. Dillard, "Golden Prospects and Fraternal Amenities: Mifflin W. Gibb's Arkansas Years," *Arkansas Historical Quarterly,* XXXV (Winter, 1976): 307–33; Willard B. Gatewood, "Negro Legislators in Arkansas, 1891: A Document," *Arkansas Historical Quarterly,* XXXI (Autumn, 1972): 220–33; Richard L. Niswonger, "William F. Kirby, Arkansas' Maverick Senator," *Arkansas Historical Quarterly,* XXXVII (Autumn, 1978): 252–63; Richard L. Niswonger, "A Study in Southern Demagoguery: Jeff Davis of Arkansas," *Arkansas Historical Quarterly,* XXXIX (Summer, 1980): 114–24; Cal Ledbetter, Jr., "Jeff Davis and the Politics of Combat," *Arkansas Historical Quarterly,* XXXIII (Spring, 1974): 16–37; James F. Willis, "An Arkansan in St. Petersburg: Clifton Rodes Breckinridge, Minister to Russia, 1894–1897," *Arkansas Historical Quarterly,* XXXVIII (Spring, 1979): 3–31; Foy Lisenby, "Charles Hillman Brough As Historian," *Arkansas Historical Quarterly,* XXXV (Summer, 1976): 115–26; Ralph W. Widener, Jr., "Charles Hillman Brough," *Arkansas Historical Quarterly,* XXXIV (Summer, 1975): 99–121; Charles Orson Cook, "'Boosterism and Babbittry': Charles Hillman Brough and the 'Selling' of Arkansas," *Arkansas Historical Quarterly,* XXXVII (Spring, 1978): 74–83; Joey McCarty "The Red Scare in Arkansas: A Southern State and National Hysteria," *Arkansas Historical Quarterly,* XXXVII (Autumn, 1978): 264–77; Ralph H. Desmarais, "Military Intelligence Reports on Arkansas Riots: 1919–1920," *Arkansas Historical Quarterly,* XXXIII (Summer, 1974): 175–91; Fred H. Lang, "Two Decades of State Forestry in Arkansas," *Arkansas Historical Quarterly,* XXIV (Autumn, 1965): 208–19; Rod Farmer, "Direct Democracy in Arkansas, 1910–1918," *Arkansas Historical Quarterly,* XL (Summer, 1981): 99–118.

An examination of the recent history of the Democratic Party is available in Boyce Alexander Drummond, "Arkansas Politics: A Study of a One-Party System," unpublished Ph.D. dissertation, University of Chicago, 1957. A useful survey of the career of a prominent Arkansan is Nevin E. Neal, "A Biography of Joseph T. Robinson," unpublished Ph.D. dissertation, University of Oklahoma, 1958. Robert Bradshaw Walz, "Migration Into Arkansas, 1834–1880," unpublished Ph.D. dissertation, University of Texas, 1958 and Garland Erastus Bayliss, "Public Affairs In Arkansas, 1874–1896," unpublished Ph.D. dissertation, University of Texas, 1972, provide useful background information for the era of this study. Master's theses of value include: John E. Chiles, "The Early Public Career of Joseph Taylor Robinson," unpublished M.A. thesis, Vanderbilt University, 1953; George James Stevenson, "The Political Career of Jeff Davis: An Example of the Southern Protest," unpublished M.A. thesis, University of Arkansas, 1949; Paige E. Mulhollan, "The Public Career of James H. Berry," unpublished M.A. thesis, University of Arkansas, 1962; William Orestus Penrose, "Political Ideas in Arkansas, 1880–1907," unpublished M.A. thesis, University of Arkansas, 1945; James Edgar Howard, "Populism in Arkansas," unpublished M.A. thesis, George Peabody College for Teachers, 1931; Richard B. Dixon, "Press Opinion Toward the Populist Party in Arkansas, 1890–1896," unpublished M.A. thesis, University of Arkansas, 1953.

Other more recent dissertations and theses include: John McDaniel Wheeler, "The People's Party in Arkansas, 1891–1896," unpublished Ph.D. dissertation, University of Arkansas, 1975; Tom W. Dillard, "The Black Moses of the West: A Biography of Mifflin Wistar Gibbs, 1823–1915," unpublished M.A. thesis, University of Arkansas, 1975; William H. Burnside, "Powell Clayton; Politician and Diplomat, 1897–1905," unpublished Ph.D. dissertation, University of Arkansas, 1978; David Michael Moyers, "Arkansas Progressivism: The Legislative Record," unpublished Ph.D. dissertation, University of Arkansas, 1986; Joe Tolbert Segraves, "Arkansas Politics, 1874–1918," unpublished Ph.D. dissertation, University of Kentucky, 1974; Martha Williamson Rimmer, "Charles E. Taylor and his Administration, 1911–1919; Progressivism in Little Rock," unpublished M.A. thesis, University of Arkansas, 1977; Sharon Klug Craig, "Arkansas and Foreign Immigration: 1890–1915," unpublished M.A.

thesis, University of Arkansas, 1979; Phillip Wayne Russell, "Fort Smith City Government and the Progressive Era in Urban Reform," unpublished M.A. thesis, University of Arkansas, 1981; Ralph W. Widener, Jr., "The Political Speaking of Charles Hillman Brough," unpublished Ph.D. dissertation, Southern Illinois University, 1962.

Notes

One: The Rise of the Arkansas Democracy

1. Arkansas Writers' Project, *Arkansas: A Guide to the State* (New York, 1941), 6.

2. *The Helena Weekly World,* Jun. 1, 1898; *The Arkansas Gazette,* Jul. 16, 1899, contains Davis's Conway speech in full including his quote from *The Helena Weekly World.*

3. *Sixteenth Census of the United States Population* (Washington, D.C., 1942), Vol. I, 100; *The Arkansas Gazette,* Jan. 31, 1901.

4. Arkansas Writers' Project, *Arkansas,* 6–8.

5. Board of the St. Francis Levee District, *History of the Organization and Operations of the Board of Directors, St. Francis Levee District of Arkansas, 1893–1945* (West Memphis, Arkansas, n.d.); *The Arkansas Gazette,* Feb. 13, 1902, contains an account of progress on the construction of the St. Francis system; Robert W. Harrison, *Alluvial Empire* (Little Rock, 1961), Vol. I, 114.

6. *Fourteenth Census of the United States: 1920, Bulletin,* Department of Commerce, Bureau of the Census, 2, 19.

7. *Arkansas and Her Resources: The Official Book of the Arkansas Commission, Panama-Pacific International Exposition* (Little Rock, 1915), 11; Charles H. Brough to editor of *Country Gentleman,* July 11, 1919, Charles Hillman Brough Papers, Special Collections, University of Arkansas library, Fayetteville; Robert W. Harrison, *Alluvial Empire,* Vol. I, 18, 19; Robert Bradshaw Walz, "Migration Into Arkansas, 1834–1880" (unpublished Ph.D. dissertation, University of Texas at Austin, 1958), 35–44 contains a useful survey of the physiographic features of Arkansas.

8. C. V. Woodward, *Origins of the New South,* 305; "Inaugural Speech of Governor Charles H. Brough to the General Assembly," January, 1917, manuscript in the Brough Papers, 60.

9. John L. Ferguson and J. H. Atkinson, *Historic Arkansas* (Little Rock, 1966), 182.

10. *The State of Arkansas V. The Kansas and Texas Coal Company and The St. Louis and San Francisco Railroad Company,* United States Supreme Court Tran-

script, located in National Archives, Washington, D.C., File 17722; *The Arkansas Gazette*, Jan. 25, 1900.

11. *The Arkansas Gazette*, Oct. 3, 1899.

12. *The Arkansas Gazette*, Jul. 16, 1899.

13. Carolyn Blanks, "Industry in the New South: A Case History," *Arkansas Historical Quarterly*, XI (Autumn, 1952): 164–75; Corliss C. Curry, "Early Timber Operations in Southeast Arkansas," *Arkansas Historical Quarterly*, XIX (Summer, 1960): 111–18.

14. Walter L. Brown, editor, "Life of an Arkansas Logger in 1901," *Arkansas Historical Quarterly*, XXI (Spring, 1962): 44–74.

15. Daniel Boone Lackey, "Cutting and Floating Red Cedar Logs in North Arkansas," *Arkansas Historical Quarterly*, XIX (Winter, 1960): 361–70.

16. Thomas C. McRae to Samuel S. Barney, Mar. 7, 1902, U. L. Clark to Thomas C. McRae, Mar. 15, 1902, Thomas C. McRae Papers, Special Collections, University of Arkansas library, Fayetteville.

17. *Inaugural Message of Thomas C. McRae Delivered Before the Forty-Fourth General Assembly, January, 1923*, (n.p., n.d.), 21, Thomas C. McRae Papers.

18. *Message of Gov. Jeff Davis. Delivered Before the General Assembly, Jan. 18, 1907* (Little Rock, 1907), 13; *The Arkansas Gazette*, Nov. 18, 1896.

19. Stephen E. Wood, "The Development of Arkansas Railroads," *Arkansas Historical Quarterly*, VII (Autumn, 1948): 157, 158, 170, 178.

20. *The Arkansas Gazette*, Nov. 24, Dec. 16, 1896.

21. For a fuller analysis of the origins and operation of the Arkansas Railroad Commission, see chapter five.

22. *First Annual Report of the Railroad Commission of the State of Arkansas* (Little Rock, 1901), 13, 11–15.

23. Ibid., 26, 27.

24. Charles W. Fornoff, "The Regulation of Public Service Corporations," *Arkansas and Its People, A History, 1541–1930*, ed. David Y. Thomas (New York, 1930), Vol. I, 337–39; *First Annual Report of the Railroad Commission*, 9–16.

25. Charles W. Fornoff, "The Regulation of the Public Service Corporations," *Arkansas and Its People*, 338–40; *Message of George W. Donaghey, Governor of Arkansas, to the Extraordinary Session of the Thirty-Eighth General Assembly, May 22, 1911*, (n.p., n.d.), 10–16, 58–61; Rowland V. Boyle et al., 244 *United States Reports* 106.

26. *The Arkansas Gazette*, Jan. 23, 16, 1896.

27. *Fourteenth Census Bulletin*, 2.

28. Sharon Klug Craig, "Arkansas and Foreign Immigration: 1890–1915," (unpublished M.A. thesis, University of Arkansas, Fayetteville, 1979), 55.

29. Robert B. Walz, "Migration Into Arkansas, 1834–1880," 63–69.

30. *Fourteenth Census Bulletin*, 2; *Arkansas and Her Resources*, 12; *Sixteenth Census of the United States Population* (Washington, D.C., 1942), Vol. I, 99–100.

31. *Construction and Development: An Address Delivered by George A. Cole, President of the Arkansas Farmer's Co-operative Union of America Before the National Convention of the Farmers Educational and Co-operative Union, St. Louis, May, 1910* (n.p., n.d.), 2, Charles H. Brough Papers, University of Arkansas, Fayetteville.

32. J. L. Charlton, *Social Aspects of Farm Ownership and Tenancy in the Arkansas Ozarks*, Bulletin 471, Agricultural Experiment Station (Fayetteville, September, 1947), 1–3.

33. *Message of Governor Charles H. Brough to the 43rd General Assembly of Arkansas, January 21, 1921* (Little Rock, n.d.), 5, 6, Charles H. Brough Papers.

34. O. A. Rogers, Jr., "The Elaine Race Riots of 1919," *Arkansas Historical*

Quarterly, XIX (Summer, 1960): 142–50. Rogers concluded that the blacks did not plot an insurrection as many contemporaries erroneously reported.

35. James W. Moore to William Jennings Bryan, March 5, 1897, William Jennings Bryan Papers, Library of Congress.

36. Powell Clayton, *The Aftermath of the Civil War* (New York, 1915), 368; *The Arkansas Gazette,* Feb. 2, 1902.

37. Garland Erastus Bayliss, "Public Affairs in Arkansas, 1874–1896" (unpublished Ph.D. dissertation, University of Texas at Austin, 1972), 336.

38. The 1928 vote can be largely explained as loyalty to Arkansas Senator Joseph T. Robinson who ran for vice president that year. Support for a favorite son apparently outweighed anti-Catholic prejudice.

39. This analysis is based upon information in an article by Svend Petersen, "Arkansas in Presidential Elections," *Arkansas Historical Quarterly,* VII (Autumn, 1948): 194–209.

40. Lonnie J. White, *Politics on the Southwestern Frontier: Arkansas Territory, 1819–1836* (Memphis, 1964), 201–05.

41. David Y. Thomas, *Arkansas and Its People: A History, 1541–1930* (New York, 1930), Vol. I, 175–77; James Edgar Howard, "Populism in Arkansas" (unpublished M.A. thesis, George Peabody College for Teachers, 1931), 8; Judith Barjenbruch, "The Greenback Political Movement: An Arkansas View," *Arkansas Historical Quarterly,* XXXVI (Summer, 1977): 114–17.

42. C. Vann Woodward, *Origins of the New South, 1877–1913* (Baton Rouge, 1966), 192; J. E. Howard, "Populism in Arkansas," 10–13; Winfield Scott Morgan, *History of the Wheel and Alliance, and The Impending Revolution* (New York, 1968 reprint of the 1891 edition), 60, 62; Garland E. Bayliss, "Public Affairs in Arkansas, 1874–1896," 281–89; Robert C. McMath Jr., *The Populist Vanguard: A History of the Southern Farmer's Alliance* (Chapel Hill, 1975), 58–60; See also F. Clark Elkins, "The Agricultural Wheel in Arkansas, 1887," *Arkansas Historical Quarterly,* XLV (Autumn, 1986): 197–216.

43. Garland E. Bayliss, "Public Affairs in Arkansas, 1874–1896," 101–19; D. Y. Thomas, *Arkansas and Its People,* Vol. I, 172, 177, 187–91; C. V. Woodward, *Origins of the New South,* 89–90; Kelly Bryant, *Historical Report of the Secretary of State* (Little Rock, 1968), 184.

44. John William Graves, "Negro Disfranchisement in Arkansas," *Arkansas Historical Quarterly* XXVI (Autumn, 1967): 202; D. Y. Thomas, *Arkansas and Its People,* Vol. I, 213, 229; *Biennial Report of the Secretary of State,* (Little Rock, 1896), 84; *Biennial Report of the Secretary of State,* (Little Rock, 1890), 49; *Biennial Report of the Secretary of State,* (Little Rock, 1888), 306; Winfield Scott Morgan, *History of the Wheel,* 749.

45. Fred W. Allsop, *Little Adventures in Newspaperdom* (Little Rock, 1922), 94–95; R. B. Dixon, "Press Opinion Toward the Populist Party in Arkansas," (unpublished M.A. thesis, University of Arkansas, 1953), 55.

46. John H. Dye to Grover Cleveland, Mar. 12, 1893, G. B. Rose to James K. Jones, Feb. 4, 1893, Arkansas Appointment Papers, Justice Department, National Archives, Record Group 60. (Hereafter National Archives, Record Group will be abbreviated as NA, RG.)

47. *Biennial Report of the Secretary of State* (Little Rock, 1894), 40.

48. *Biennial Report of the Secretary of State* (Little Rock, 1894), 40, 46; *Biennial Report of the Secretary of State* (Little Rock, 1896), 281–84; *Biennial Report of the Secretary of State* (Little Rock, 1900), 421.

49. Alwyn Barr, *Reconstruction to Reform: Texas Politics, 1876–1906* (Austin, 1971), 153–60.

50. A. Z. Alexander to Grover Cleveland, April 1, 1893, Arkansas Appointment papers, Justice Department, NA, RG 60.

51. John William Graves, "Negro Disfranchisement in Arkansas," *Arkansas Historical Quarterly*, XXVI (Autumn, 1967): 199–201; John William Graves, "The Arkansas Negro and Segregation, 1890–1903," (unpublished M.A. thesis, University of Arkansas, Fayetteville, 61.)

52. Ibid., 202–04.

53. Willard B. Gatewood, Jr., "Arkansas Negroes in the 1890s: Documents," *Arkansas Historical Quarterly*, XXXIII (Winter, 1974): 296–97.

54. J. W. Graves, "Negro Disfranchisement," 205–09.

55. Ibid., 209–10.

56. P. Clayton, *The Aftermath of the Civil War*, 365–66; Garland E. Bayliss, "Public Affairs in Arkansas, 1874–1896," see 323–25 for a discussion of the 1891 law.

57. *Biennial Report of the Secretary of State* (Little Rock, 1896), 15–16.

58. *The Arkansas Gazette*, Sep. 5, 1896.

59. Ibid., Sep. 10, 11, 1986; *Biennial Report of the Secretary of State, 1899–1900* (Little Rock, n.d.), 421.

60. J. Howard, "Populism in Arkansas," 74; *The Arkansas Gazette*, Oct. 29, 1896.

61. J. W. Graves, "Negro Disfranchisement," 211–12.

62. Ibid., 219.

63. Sidney Crawford, "Arkansas Suffrage Qualifications," *Arkansas Historical Quarterly*, II (December, 1943): 336–37; J. W. Graves, "Negro Disfranchisement in Arkansas," 216–20.

64. Ibid., 221–23.

65. J. Morgan Kousser, *The Shaping of Southern Politics: Suffrage Restrictions and the Establishment of the One-Party South, 1880–1910*, (New Haven, 1974), 129.

66. *Biennial Report of the Secretary of State, 1899–1900* (Little Rock, n.d.), 421; *Biennial Report of the Secretary of State* (Little Rock, 1890), 49; *The Helena Weekly World*, Jan. 5, 1898; Joseph P. Robinson, "Suffrage in Arkansas," *Publications of The Arkansas Historical Association*, ed. John Hugh Reynolds (Fayetteville, 1911), 174.

67. C. Vann Woodward, *Origins of the New South, 1877–1933* (Baton Rouge, 1966), 342–46.

68. Dewey W. Grantham, *Southern Progressivism: The Reconciliation of Progress and Tradition* (Knoxville, 1983), 10–17.

69. Jack Temple Kirby, *Darkness at the Dawning: Race and Reform in the Progressive South* (Philadelphia, 1972), 4; See also Dewey W. Grantham, *The Regional Imagination* (Nashville, 1979), 77–115.

70. Joe Tolbert Segraves suggests that the Arkansas experience with racial segregation is in line with C. Vann Woodward's thesis that segregation during Reconstruction did not become a crystallized or rigid system until nearly the turn of the century. There were many instances of the two races mixing socially in the decades before 1890. Only the emergence of Jim Crow legislation finally set the pattern in concrete. See C. Vann Woodward, *The Strange Career of Jim Crow* (New York, 1966), 2d ed. revised, 22–35, and Joe T. Segraves, "Arkansas Politics, 1874–1918," (unpublished Ph.D. dissertation, University of Kentucky, 1974), 223. Joel Williamson in *After Slavery: The Negro in South Carolina during Reconstruction, 1861–1877* (Chapel Hill, 1965), argues that, in South Carolina at least, "well before the end of Reconstruction, separation had crystallized into a comprehensive pattern which, in its essence, remained unaltered until the middle of the twentieth century" (275). He believes that blacks had the

right by the end of Reconstruction to use public accommodations with whites, but "they seldom did so" (298).

71. Joe T. Segraves, "Arkansas Politics," 225.

72. *Arkansas Acts,* 1891, 15–17 as quoted in Segraves, "Arkansas Politics," 226.

73. C. Fred Williams, "James Philip Eagle," in Timothy P. Donovan and Willard B. Gatewood, Jr., eds., *The Governors of Arkansas* (Fayetteville, 1981), 86–90.

74. Willard B. Gatewood, "Negro Legislators in Arkansas, 1891: A Document," *Arkansas Historical Quarterly,* (Autumn, 1972): 222.

75. Joe T. Segraves, "Arkansas Politics," 225–31.

76. J. Morgan Kousser, *The Shaping of Southern Politics,* 238–39.

77. For a similar viewpoint see Dewey W. Grantham, *The Democratic South* (New York, 1963), 44–45. Grantham argues that while factionalism did not create an equivalent to the two-party system, it did in some Southern states at times provide significant competition between interests. Even without clear-cut factions, the divergent interests in Southern society contended for power and influence. The Democratic South preserved a genuine democratic heritage.

78. V. O. Key has voted an unusual degree of "consensus" in Arkansas politics. The state possessed the one-party system in its most pure form. A lack of urban centers has prevented excessive localism. Sectionalism did not play a major role in dividing the state politically. Factions have been transient, fluid, numerous, and lacking in ideological identification. Groupings of voters appeared briefly to support certain personalities and then lost their identity. But Key saw Davis's era as a brief interlude in this pattern. He admits the importance of sectional and ideological differences at the turn of the century. See V. O. Key, *Southern Politics in State and Nation* (New York, 1949), 183–204.

79. Raymond Arsenault, *The Wild Ass of the Ozarks: Jeff Davis and the Social Bases of Southern Politics* (Philadelphia, 1984), 102.

80. Ibid., 103–06.

81. Boyce A. Drummond, who has concentrated on mid-twentieth century politics, is in substantial agreement with V. O. Key. He found the same issueless shifting factionalism in Arkansas. Sectionalism affected political alliances only slightly at mid-century, although the northwest evinced a tendency toward supporting candidates of a more "progressive" character, e.g., the hill country helped send a native son, J. William Fulbright, to the United States Senate. See B. A. Drummond, "Arkansas Politics: A Study of a One-Party System," (unpublished Ph.D. dissertation, Univesity of Chicago, 1957), ii, 227–31; Albert D. Kirwan characterized Mississippi politics during the period 1876 to 1925 as "a struggle between economic classes, interspersed with the personal struggles of ambitious men." The era of Vardaman and Bilbo in Mississippi is in this respect much like the Davis period in Arkansas. Albert D. Kirwan, *Revolt of the Rednecks: Mississippi Politics, 1876–1925* (New York, 1965), 307.

82. George E. Dodge to William McKinley, July 13, 1900, Arkansas Appointment Papers, Justice Department, NA, RG 60.

83. Geoffrey Blodgett, *The Gentle Reformers: Massachusetts Democrats in the Cleveland Era* (Cambridge, 1966), vii, viii.

84. Alwyn Barr, *Reconstruction to Reform,* 243–49.

85. For a careful analysis of the effect of ethnocultural communities upon voting patterns see Paul Kleppner, *The Cross of Culture: A Social Analysis of Midwestern Politics, 1850–1900* (New York, 1970).

86. R. Arsenault, *Wild Ass,* 10–17; Laurence Goodwyn, *Democratic Promise: The Populist Movement in America* (New York, 1978), 201–11, 387–88.

87. R. Arsenault, *Wild Ass*, 8–9.

88. J. Rogers Hollingsworth, *The Whirligig of Politics, The Democracy of Cleveland and Bryan* (Chicago, 1969), 1, 2, 235–41.

89. *The Arkansas Gazette*, Jan. 12, 1902.

90. According to R. Hal Williams, localism, retrenchment, dedication to states rights, and negativism were hallmarks of the Democratic Party of Cleveland's era and contributed to the long twilight of Democratic power after 1896; see R. Hall Williams, "'Dry Bones and Dead Language:' The Democratic Party," *The Gilded Age*, ed. H. Wayne Morgan (Syracuse, 1970), 142–48.

91. Alwyn Barr in *Reconstruction to Reform*, xiii suggests that states rights and white supremacy were the basic doctrines of the Texas Democratic Party. These ideals elicited Anglo-evangelical support. As might be expected they were especially important concepts to the homogeneous society of Arkansas.

92. *The Arkansas Gazette*, Apr. 17, 1901.

93. James K. Jones to William Jennings Bryan, Jul. 30, 1897, Bryan Papers, Library of Congress.

94. H. S. Mobley to Joseph T. Robinson, May 13, 1913, J. T. Robinson to H. S. Mobley, May 20, 1913, J. T. Robinson to Woodrow Wilson, May 23, 1913. See also H. S. Mobley to James P. Clarke, May 1, 1913, which appeals to the senior senator along a similar line. A notation on the letter, probably added by an executive department official, states, "Similar letters written from Alabama, Louisiana, Texas, Georgia, and Oklahoma." All the above correspondence is located in the Woodrow Wilson Papers, Library of Congress.

95. The quotation is found in Davis's December 2, 1905, speech in Bentonville which is printed in full in L. S. Dunaway, *Jeff Davis: Governor and United States Senator, His Life and Speeches* (Little Rock, 1913), 85–86.

96. George B. Tindall, *The Emergence of the New South, 1913–1945*, Vol. X of *A History of the South*, ed. by Wendell Holmes Stephenson and E. Merton Coulter (Baton Rouge, 1967), 1–32. For a dissenting view see Richard Abrams, "Woodrow Wilson and The Southern Congressmen," *Journal of Southern History*, XXII (November, 1956): 417–37.

97. Robert H. Wiebe, *The Search for Order, 1877–1920* (New York, 1967) and Samuel P. Hays, *The Response to Industrialism, 1885–1914* (Chicago, 1957) and Gabriel Kolko, *The Triumph of Conservatism, A Reinterpretation of American History, 1900–1916* (New York, 1963); George B. Tindall, *The Emergence of the New South, 1913–1945*, 1–32.

98. Sheldon Hackney in his study of Alabama Populists and Progressives discovered that Populist voters did not flock back to the Democratic fold to become the mainstay of progressivism. Instead the Populists gave up active participation in politics or turned to the Republican Party. Populism and Progressivism were not sequential but contemporary movements representing the approach of two different social groups to the same unsettling conditions created by industrial change. Progressivism, in his view, was not an outgrowth of Populism, but the response of established social groups as opposed to the nearly simultaneous response of the socially disorganized Populists. See Sheldon Hackney, *Populism to Progressivism in Alabama* (Princeton, 1969), 324–26.

99. Charles Collins to W. J. Bryan, Nov. 24, 1900, Bryan Papers.

Two: The Election of 1896

1. Lewis L. Gould, *Wyoming: A Political History, 1868–1896* (New Haven, 1968), 195–203, 231–33.

2. Paolo E. Coletta, *William Jennings Bryan*, Vol. I: *Political Evangelist, 1860–1908* (Lincoln, 1964), 68–69, 99–102; Sheldon Hackney, *Populism to Progressivism in Alabama* (Princeton, 1969), 51–52.

3. For a fuller discussion of some of the viewpoints discussed in the above paragraphs see R. Hal Williams, "'Dry Bones and Dead Language': The Democratic Party," H. Wayne Morgan, ed., *The Gilded Age* (Syracuse, 1970), 129–48.

4. *The Helena Weekly World*, Apr. 15, 1896; *The Arkansas Gazette*, Sep. 9, 1896.

5. Alwyn Barr, *Reconstruction to Reform: Texas Politics, 1876–1906* (Austin, 1971), 108, 120–21; Sheldon Hackney, *Populism to Progressivism, 118–21*.

6. *The Arkansas Gazette*, Sep. 5, 1896; *The Brinkley Argus*, n.d., is quoted in *The Helena Weekly World*, May 6, 1896; *The Helena Weekly World*, Dec. 18, 1895.

7. James F. Willis, "An Arkansan in St. Petersburg: Clifton Rodes Breckinridge, Minister to Russia, 1894–1897," *Arkansas Historical Quarterly*, XXXVIII (Spring, 1979): 5–8.

8. *The Pine Bluff Weekly Press-Eagle*, Mar. 17, 1896; *The Arkansas Gazette*, Sep. 5, 1896, May 29, 1902; James K. Jones to Grover Cleveland, Aug. 16, 1895, James Berry to Grover Cleveland, Aug. 26, 1895, Grover Cleveland Papers; De Emmett Bradshaw, *My Story: The Autobiography of De Emmett Bradshaw* (Omaha, 1941), 96; U. M. Rose to H. L. Remmel, Jan. 21, 1906, Uriah Milton Rose Papers, University of Arkansas, Fayetteville.

9. Dr. E. G. Epler to William Jennings Bryan, May 27, 1895, William Jennings Bryan Papers, Library of Congress.

10. *The Arkansas Gazette*, Aug. 8, 1895; *The Weekly Elevator* (Fort Smith), Aug. 9, 1895.

11. D. Y. Thomas, *Arkansas and Its People*, Vol. I, 255.

12. *The Helena Weekly World*, Dec. 18, 1895; Charles Collins to W. J. Bryan, Feb. 26, 1896, Bryan Papers; Harvey's move to Arkansas came during 1900. His first letter to Bryan from Rogers, Arkansas, was dated Dec. 6, 1900 (see W. Harvey to W. J. Bryan, Dec. 6, 1900, Bryan Papers).

13. *The Helena Weekly World*, Mar. 25, 1896; *The Arkansas Gazette*, Aug. 20, Oct. 14, 15, 1896.

14. *The Arkansas Gazette*, Jan. 31, May 12, 13, 20, 1896; *The Conway Light*, n.d., quoted in *The Arkansas Gazette*, May 20, 1896; Fred W. Allsopp, *History of the Arkansas Press For a Hundred Years and More* (Little Rock, 1922), 626–27; *The Helena Weekly World*, May 20, 1896.

15. *The Weekly Elevator* (Fort Smith), May 15, 1896; *The Arkansas Gazette* does not discuss the financial transaction leading to Smithee's editorship and there is no discussion of this in Leland W. Plunkett's "The History of *The Arkansas Gazette*" (unpublished Master of Journalism thesis, University of Texas at Austin). He does record shifts in editors.

16. Allen Johnson and Dumas Malcone, eds., *Dictionary of American Biography*, Vol. V, 388–89.

17. D. Y. Thomas, *Arkansas and Its People*, Vol. I, 255.

18. E. B. Kinsworthy to Judson Harmon, Nov. 25, 1896, Arkansas Appointment Papers, Justice Department, NA, RG 60; *The Arkansas Gazette*, Mar. 11, 1896.

19. Information in this paragraph was taken primarily from "Wallace's Bryan Recollections," a manuscript in the David Yancey Thomas Papers at the University of Arkansas, Fayetteville.

20. R. Arsenault, *The Wild Ass*, 55–58; L. Goodwyn, *Democratic Promise: The Populist Movement in America* (New York, 1976), 338–401, 582–92.

21. *The Arkansas Gazette,* Jan. 9, 1896.

22. *The Arkansas Gazette,* Jan. 10, 24, 1896.

23. *The Helena Weekly World,* Feb. 2, 1896.

24. *The Arkansas Gazette,* June 29, 1894.

25. *Southern Standard* (Arkadelphia), Apr. 17, 1896; *The Pine Bluff Weekly Press-Eagle,* Apr. 14, 1896; *The Arkansas Gazette,* Feb. 22, 1896; *The Weekly Elevator* (Fort Smith), Feb. 21, 1896, gives Sebastian County to Harrod by a different margin, 1,356 to 532. The figures used above are from *The Arkansas Gazette,* Feb. 18, 1896.

26. *The Arkansas Gazette,* Jun. 2, 1908; George W. Donaghey, *Building a State Capitol* (Little Rock, 1937), 59.

27. *The Arkansas Gazette,* Sep. 23, 1896.

28. *The Arkansas Gazette,* Jan. 28, 1896.

29. *The Arkansas Gazette,* Jan. 29, 1896.

30. *The Arkansas Gazette,* Feb. 4, 1896.

31. *The Arkansas Gazette,* Feb. 21, 1896.

32. *The Weekly Elevator,* Feb. 28, 1896; *The Helena Weekly World,* Feb. 26, Mar. 25, 1896.

33. *The Pine Bluff Weekly Press-Eagle,* Apr. 14, 1896; *Morgan's Buzz-Saw,* Apr. 1, 1896.

34. *Fayetteville Democrat,* Apr. 9, 1896; *Southern Standard,* Apr. 10, 1896; *The Arkansas Gazette,* May 12, 1896; *The Helena Weekly World,* Jun. 10, 17, 1896.

35. *The Weeky Elevator,* Feb. 21, 1896; *The Arkansas Gazette,* May 14, 16, 1896.

36. *The Arkansas Gazette,* Sep. 2, 1896; Jun. 2, 1908.

37. Willis J. Abbot, *Watching the World Go By* (Boston, 1933), 179; Willis J. Abbott, "James K. Jones," *Review of Reviews,* XIV (October, 1896), 427, 428.

38. "Horace Chilton Diaries," 47, 48, University of Texas Archives, Austin, Texas.

39. Allan Nevins, *Grover Cleveland: A Study in Courage* (New York, 1932), 541–45; *The Arkansas Gazette,* Sep. 2, 1896.

40. Willis J. Abbot, "James K. Jones," *Review of Reviews,* XIV (October, 1896), 427.

41. J. Rogers Hollingsworth, *The Whirligig of Politics: The Democracy of Cleveland and Bryan* (Chicago, 1963), 236–41.

42. Willis J. Abbot, "James K. Jones," *Review of Reviews,* 427, 428.

43. Arthur Wallace Dunn, *From Harrison to Harding: A Personal Narrative Covering a Third of a Century, 1888–1921* (New York, 1922), Vol. I, 129.

44. A. Nevins, *Grover Cleveland,* 572–74.

45. John R. Lambert, *Arthur Pue Gorman* (Baton Rouge, 1953), 203–23; *The Arkansas Gazette,* Jul. 23, 1896.

46. Arthur Wallace Dunn, *From Harrison to Harding,* Vol. I, 131.

47. *The Arkansas Gazette,* Jan. 7, 1896.

48. See Richard L. Niswonger, "James Paul Clarke, 1895–1897," in *The Governors of Arkansas: Essays in Political Biography,* ed. by Timothy P. Donovan and Willard B. Gatewood, Jr., (Fayetteville, 1981), 100.

49. Board of the St. Francis Levee District, *History of the Organization and Operations of the Board of Directors St. Francis Levee District of Arkansas, 1893–1945* (West Memphis, Arkansas, n.d.), 301.

50. Charles Jacobson, *The Life Story of Jeff Davis, The Stormy Petrel of Arkansas Politics* (Little Rock, 1925), 183.

51. *Biennial Message of Gov. James P. Clarke to the Thirty-first General Assembly,* delivered Jan. 14, 1897, 45, 55.

52. *The Little Rock Times*, n.d., quoted in the Arkadelphia *Southern Standard*, Jan. 17, 1896.

53. *Southern Standard*, Jan. 31, 1896.

54. *The Helena Weekly World*, Dec. 25, 1895.

55. William Hope Harvey, *Coin's Financial School Up to Date*, II (March, 1895), 205; *The Helena Weekly World*, Dec. 25, 1895, Jan. 29, 1896, Feb. 26, 1896; *Morgan's Buzz-Saw*, Feb. 1, 1896.

56. *Congressional Record*, 54th Cong., 1st Sess. (Jan. 10, 1896), 557.

57. *Congressional Record*, 54th Cong., 1st Sess. (Jan. 10, 1896), 557–64, 557, 564.

58. *Congressional Record*, 54th Cong., 1st Sess. (Jan. 30, 1896), 1,117, (Feb. 1, 1896), 1,215.

59. *Congressional Record*, 54th Cong., 1st Sess. (Jan. 30, 1896), 1,117; *The Arkansas Gazette*, Feb. 2, 1896.

60. *The Weekly Elevator*, Jan. 24, 31, 1896.

61. *The Arkansas Gazette*, Feb. 6, 1896.

62. *The Arkansas Gazette*, Feb. 6, 1896.

63. *The Weekly Elevator*, Feb. 7, 1896; *The Yell County Republican*, n.d., quoted in the *Elevator*, Mar. 6, 1896.

64. *Southern Standard*, Mar. 13, 1896.

65. *Fayetteville Democrat*, Feb. 20, 1896.

66. Farrar Newberry, *James K. Jones, The Plumed Knight of Arkansas* (1913, n.p.), 95, 96; *The Weekly Elevator*, Feb. 21, 1896; *Fayetteville Democrat*, Mar. 19, 1896.

67. *Greensburg New Era* (Indiana), n.d., quoted in *Southern Standard*, Feb. 28, 1896.

68. William Fishback to Grover Cleveland, Mar. 31, 1896, published in *The Weekly Elevator* (Fort Smith), Apr. 17, 1896.

69. Horace Samuel Merrill, *Bourbon Leader: Grover Cleveland and the Democratic Party* (Boston, 1957), 183–84, 199–207.

70. *The Arkansas Gazette*, May 20, 1896; *The Helena Weekly World*, May 27, 1896.

71. *The Arkansas Gazette*, Aug. 25, 1896 contains a copy of the state Democratic platform.

72. *The Arkansas Gazette*, Mar. 12, Jun. 19, 1896; *The Weekly Elevator*, Jun. 19, 1896.

73. Charles M. Collins to W. J. Bryan, Feb. 4, 1896, Bryan Papers.

74. *The Arkansas Gazette*, Jun. 7, 9, 1896; William Jennings Bryan and Mary Baird Bryan, *The Memoirs of William Jennings Bryan* (Chicago, 1925), 110.

75. *The Arkansas Gazette*, Jun. 19, 1896; *The Drew County Advance*, Jul. 7, 1896.

76. Jerry Wallace, *An Arkansas Judge* (Springfield, Illinois, 1928), 37; Paolo E. Coletta, *William Jennings Bryan*, Vol. I: *Political Evangelist, 1860–1908* (Lincoln, 1964), 145.

77. Hugh R. McVeigh to W. J. Bryan, Jul. 24, 1900, Bryan Papers.

78. W. J. Bryan, "An Estimate from William Jennings Bryan," an Appendix in F. Newberry, *James K. Jones*, 327.

79. W. J. Bryan, *Memoirs*, 107–10; W. J. Bryan, "An Estimate" in F. Newberry, *James K. Jones*, 328.

80. Stanley L. Jones, *The Presidential Election of 1896* (Madison, 1964), 298, 299; J. K. Jones to J. G. Johnson, May 3, 1900, Bryan Papers.

81. *Forrest City Times*, Aug. 21, 1896, quoted in John McDaniel Wheeler,

"The People's Party in Arkansas, 1891–1896," (unpublished Ph.D. dissertation, Tulane University, 1975), 441–42.

82. J. E. Howard, "Populism in Arkansas," 98, 103; *The Arkansas Gazette,* Aug. 18, 1896.

83. *The Mena Weekly Star,* Sep. 9, 1896; *The Drew County Advance,* Jul. 28, 1896.

84. *The Drew County Advance,* Jun. 23, Jul. 14, 1896.

85. *The Arkansas Gazette,* Jan. 7, 1896.

86. *The Drew County Advance,* Jul. 21, 1896; *The Arkansas Gazette,* Jul. 16, 1896.

87. *The Arkansas Gazette,* Jul. 19, 25, 26, 1896.

88. C. Vann Woodward, *Origins of the New South,* 296; Festus P. Summers, ed., *The Cabinet Diary of William L. Wilson, 1896–1897* (Chapel Hill, 1957), 122; Arthur Wallace Dunn, *From Harrison to Harding: A Personal Narrative, Covering a Third of a Century, 1888–1921* (New York, 1922), Vol. I, 190–92; Louis W. Koenig, Bryan, *A Political Biography of William Jennings Bryan* (New York, 1971), 215, 216; Robert F. Durden in *The Climax of Populism: The Election of 1896* (Louisville, 1965), 40–43, presents convincing evidence against the "'conspiracy' interpretation."

89. *The New York World,* Aug. 3, 1896, as quoted in C. Vann Woodward, *Tom Watson: Agrarian Rebel* (New York, 1963), 310; a similar interview found in *The Chicago Tribune,* Aug. 3, 1896, is quoted in Stanley L. Jones, *The Presidential Election of 1896,* 298.

90. Stanley L. Jones, *The Presidential Election of 1896,* 322; *The Helena Weekly World,* Oct. 21, 1896; *The Arkansas Gazette,* Oct. 8, 1896.

91. *Morgan's Buzz-Saw,* Oct. 1, Nov. 1, 1896, Mar. 1, 1897.

92. Robert F. Durden, *The Climax of Populism,* 65–74.

93. *The Arkansas Gazette,* Oct. 1, 8, 10, 11, 14, 1896; C. Vann Woodward, *Tom Watson,* 326–29; Robert F. Durden, *The Climax of Populism,* 73–74.

94. "To The Voters of Sebastian Co.," Oct. 29, 1896, Bryan Papers, Box 4.

95. *The Arkansas Gazette,* Aug. 18, 21, 23, 1896.

96. *Biennial Report of the Secretary of State* (Little Rock, 1900), 421.

Three: The Triumph of the Populist Spirit in the Democratic Party

1. Dewey W. Grantham, *The Democratic South* (New York, 1963), 35, 36; Theodore Saloutos, *Farmer Movements in the South, 1865–1933* (Lincoln, Nebraska, n.d.), 142, 143.

2. Richard B. Dixon, "Press Opinion Toward the Populist Party in Arkansas," 69, 70.

3. See maps for identification of Populist centers.

4. J. L. Charlton, "Social Aspects of Farm Ownership and Tenancy in the Arkansas Ozarks." 2, has a map indicating the Census Bureau's Ozark region.

5. C. Vann Woodward, *Origins of the New South,* 246.

6. *Biennial Report of the Secretary of State, 1896,* 281–84.

7. *Morgan's Buzz-Saw,* Jul. 1, 1895, Feb. 1, 1896, Mar. 1, 1897.

8. James R. Sovereign to Marion Butler, Sep. 24, 1896, Marion Butler to James R. Sovereign, Sep. 26, 1896, Marion Butler Papers, are cited in Robert F. Durden, *The Climax of Populism: The Election of 1896* (Louisville, 1965), 63.

9. *The Drew County Advance,* Jul. 21, 1896; *The Arkansas Gazette,* Jul. 17, 23, 1896.

10. *The Arkansas Gazette,* Jul. 23, 1896.

11. *The Arkansas Gazette,* Aug. 29, 1896; Feb. 4, 1898.

13. *The Drew County Advance,* Jul. 21, 1896.

13. *The Arkansas Gazette,* Aug. 20, 1896.

14. Alwyn Barr, *Reconstruction to Reform: Texas Politics, 1876–1906* (Austin, 1971), 161; C. Vann Woodward, *Origins of the New South,* 270.

15. *The Arkansas Gazette,* Jul. 22, 29, 1896.

16. This information has been abstracted from a table in Fred A. Shannon, *The Farmer's Last Frontier* (New York, 1968), 418.

17. C. Vann Woodward, *Origins of the New South,* 276; D. V. Herndon, *Centennial History of Arkansas,* Vol. I, 346.

18. *Biennial Report of the Secretary of State, 1899–1900,* 419–21; *Biennial Report of the Secretary of State, 1896,* 281–84; Dallas T. Herndon, *Outline of Executive and Legislative History of Arkansas* (n.p., 1922), 142–55; *The Arkansas Gazette,* Oct. 7, 1896; Herndon lists the number of Populists elected to the state legislature for each biennial election, but for some reason he gives the number of Populists elected to the House of Representatives in 1896 as eight while the secretary of state's report above lists the names of eleven Populist representatives.

19. See maps for Populist strength in the counties.

20. *The Arkansas Gazette,* Sep. 7, 1898, as quoted in J. E. Howard, "Populism in Arkansas," 113.

21. John McDaniel Wheeler, "The People's Party in Arkansas, 1891–1896," (unpublished Ph.D. dissertation, Tulane University, 1975), 451–55.

22. Raymond Arsenault, *The Wild Ass of the Ozarks: Jeff Davis and the Social Bases of Southern Politics* (Philadelphia, 1984), 41–42.

23. Reuben CarlLee to Tom Watson, Sep. 13, 1907, Tom Watson Papers, as quoted in John M. Wheeler, "The People's Party in Arkansas," 486.

24. J. E. Howard argued that the vast majority of Populists returned to the Democracy. He bases his view on statements to this effect in *The Arkansas Gazette* (cf. Sep. 7, 1898) and on personal interviews with elderly leaders. See J. E. Howard, "Populism in Arkansas," 115. If this assessment is correct, it is surprising that little trace of the old Populist leadership is found in the counsels of the Democratic Party of the 1900s. J. Rogers Hollingsworth in the *Whirligig of Politics* (Chicago, 1969), 116, expresses the view that very few of the Populists ever returned to seats of power in the Democratic Party. Those few who did return were unable to bring about change for another decade. The progressive movement in the South depended more, according to Hollingsworth, on a new leadership. Evidence in Arkansas confirms this verdict.

25. *Morgan's Buzz-Saw,* March 1, 1899; James R. Green, *Grass-Roots Socialism: Radical Movements in the Southwest, 1895–1943,* 17, 136; John M. Wheeler, "The Populist Party in Arkansas," 23, 489; *The Arkansas Gazette,* June 8, 1906.

26. *The Drew County Advance,* Jul. 21, 1896, and *The Arkansas Gazette,* Feb. 19, 1896, list Prince as a member of the Populist State Central Committee; *The Helena Weekly World,* Sep. 8, 1897, Apr. 12, 1899; J. E. Howard mentions Prince as one of the Alliance leaders who founded the Arkansas Populist Party in 1892. See J. E. Howard, "Populism in Arkansas," 53.

27. *The Arkansas Gazette,* Feb. 12, 20, Mar. 25, 1898.

28. *The Arkansas Gazette,* Apr. 4, 1906; J. Wheeler, "The Populist Party in Arkansas," 487.

29. The 110 names were checked against approximately one thousand three

hundred names listed as members of the general assemblies of 1901 to 1920 in Kelly Bryant, *Historical Report of the Secretary of State (Arkansas)*, 366–90.

30. *Biennial Report of the Secretary of State, 1896,* 283–84; *The Arkansas Gazette,* Feb. 4, 1898, Apr. 5, 1906.

31. David E. Barker to Joseph T. Robinson, Nov. 25, 1907, Joseph T. Robinson Papers, Special Collections, University of Arkansas library, Fayetteville.

32. Phillip Taft, *Organized Labor in American History* (New York, 1964), 280; Charles Madison, *American Labor Leaders: Personalities and Forces in the Labor Movement* (New York, 1962), 67, 68; Robert F. Durden, *The Climax of Populism,* 55, 63; *Morgan's Buzz-Saw,* Mar. 1, Apr. 1, 1897.

33. *The Helena Weekly World,* Jun. 8, 1898; *The Arkansas Gazette,* Jun. 1, 1898.

34. J. Wheeler, "The Populist Party in Arkansas," 480.

35. James R. Sovereign to W. J. Bryan, Apr. 22, 1897, and Apr. 15, 1898, Bryan Papers.

36. J. R. Sovereign to W. J. Bryan, May 21, 1898, Aug. 7, 1899, and Jul. 13, 1900, Bryan Papers.

37. *The Arkansas Gazette,* Dec. 30, 1896; *The Helena Weekly World,* Sep. 22, 1897.

38. "Inaugural Address of Governor Dan W. Jones to the Thirty-First General Assembly," Jan. 31, 1897, manuscript located in Special Collections of the University of Arkansas library, Fayetteville.

39. *Journal of the House of Representatives of the State of Arkansas,* 31st Session, Jan. 19, 1897, 49; *Journal of the Senate of Arkansas,* 31st Session, Jan. 19, 1897, 20; *House Journal, Extraordinary Session,* Jun. 9, 1897, 99, 100; *The Arkansas Gazette,* Feb. 4, 1897.

40. *The Helena Weekly World,* Sep. 22, Nov. 3, 1897.

41. *The Arkansas Gazette,* Jul. 16, Oct. 1, 1899.

42. *The Arkansas Gazette,* Sep. 14, 1899.

43. *The Drew County Advance,* May 25, 1897; *The Pine Bluff Weekly Press-Eagle,* Jun. 22, 1897; *The Arkansas Gazette,* May 5, Jun. 1, 12, 13, 1897.

44. "Inaugural Address of Governor Dan W. Jones to the Thirty-First General Assembly," Jan. 31, 1897.

45. *Biennial Message of Gov. James P. Clarke to the 31st General Assembly, Jan. 14, 1897,* 34, a pamphlet located with "Messages to the General Assembly, Governor" in Special Collections of the University of Arkansas library, Fayetteville.

46. *Biennial Message of Gov. Clarke, Jan. 14, 1897,* 35.

47. *The Helena Weekly World,* Aug. 17, 31, 1898.

48. J. Wheeler, "The People's Party in Arkansas," 499.

49. Senator Worthen, a goldbug, was among four senators who opposed the antitrust bill of 1897; *The Arkansas Gazette,* Feb. 4, 7, 1897.

Four: One-Gallus Democracy

1. The view presented here is in basic agreement with the interpretation found in Dewey W. Grantham, *The Democratic South,* 42–51; see also Albert D. Kirwan, *Revolt of the Rednecks* for an analysis of a pattern very similar to that found in Arkansas.

2. Charles Jacobson, *The Life Story of Jeff Davis,* 43, 44; *The Arkansas Gazette,* Jan. 27, 1900.

3. Very few source materials are available which directly relate to Jeff

Davis's career. Like many Arkansas politicians, he did not preserve his letters and papers, and from indications in the papers of other Democrats of the era he did not write many letters. He liked to campaign on the hillsides rather than spending time corresponding. The University of Arkansas library at Fayetteville possesses a "Jeff Davis" microfilm which contains campaign speeches, newspaper clippings, and a brief for one of Davis's antitrust cases. The library also has a very small collection of "Political Material Concerning Jeff Davis" that contains two campaign pamphlets of Davis's opponents and a printed pamphlet of correspondence between Davis and a feuding colleague, Jephtha H. Evans. The John Herbert Page Papers, also at Fayetteville, contain only several letters of late date which have a reference to Davis, but also contain a notebook listing local Davis men in Arkansas. Also at Fayetteville in the University of Arkansas library Special Collections are a number of printed addresses to the legislature. L. Sharpe Dunaway, *Jeff Davis, Governor and United States Senator, His Life and Speeches* (Little Rock, 1913) is misnamed since it is almost totally composed of Davis's campaign speeches. Jeff Davis's personal secretary, Charles Jacobson, wrote *The Life Story of Jeff Davis: The Stormy Petrel of Arkansas Politics* (Little Rock, 1925), Davis overawed Jacobson, but his secretary eventually became a political enemy. Since Jacobson was in a position to know Davis well, his book is a major source, but much of his information does not go beyond material available in contemporary newspapers. *The Report and Testimony of the Ways and Means Committee in its investigation of the differences between the chief executive and the remaining members of the Penitentiary Board, State of Arkansas* (Little Rock, 1903) contains information on an attempt to impeach Jeff Davis. Other sources include newspapers and a few scattered letters in collections like the Theodore Roosevelt Papers at the Library of Congress.

4. George W. Donaghey, *Building a State Capitol* (Little Rock, 1937), 39–43; Richard B. Dixon in his 1953 University of Arkansas M.A. thesis, "Press Opinion Toward the Populist Party in Arkansas, 1890–1896" demonstrates the nearly solid voice of the press against agrarian movements. It was extremely difficult for the Populists to get a hearing in the newspapers. The prejudice of Arkansas's Democratic newspapers also creates difficulty for the historian who must rely upon their distorted accounts since not many of the few Populist newspapers that did exist in Arkansas are still extant.

5. Charles Jacobson, *The Life Story of Jeff Davis*, 61, 149–50.

6. Ibid., 176.

7. The Chicago *Inter-Ocean*, n.d., quoted in *The Arkansas Gazette*, Oct. 8, 1899; C. Jacobson, *The Life Story of Jeff Davis*, 22; Sam Hanna Acheson, *Joe Bailey, The Last Democrat* (New York, 1932), 48.

8. C. Jacobson, *The Life Story of Jeff Davis*, 13, 14; Jerry Wallace, *An Arkansas Judge*, 50, 51; Sam Acheson, *Joe Bailey*, 17.

9. *The Arkansas Gazette*, June 29, 1894, Feb. 2, 1896; C. Jacobson, *The Life Story of Jeff Davis*, 18–23.

10. *The Arkansas Gazette*, Feb. 2, 3, 1898; *The Helena Weekly World*, Feb. 9, 1898.

11. Albert D. Kirwan, *Revolt of the Rednecks*, 114–15, 122–35.

12. Albert D. Kirwan, *Revolt of the Rednecks*, 122–35; Francis Butler Simkins, *Pitchfork Ben Tillman, South Carolinian* (Ann Arbor, 1967), 227–30; William F. Holmes, *The White Chief, James Kimble Vardaman* (Baton Rouge, 1970), 96–97.

13. *The Arkansas Gazette*, Jun. 22, 1898, Jan. 6, 1900.

14. Alwyn Barr, *Reconstruction to Reform*, 235–36.

15. *Rules of the Democratic Party in Arkansas, Adopted March 4, 1918* (n.p.,

n.d.), contains copies of the statutes of 1909, 1911, and 1916; William F. Holmes, *The White Chief*, 96.

16. *The Arkansas Gazette*, June 18, 1904; Francis Butler Simkins, *Pitchfork Ben Tillman*, 229; Herbert F. Margulies, *The Decline of the Progressive Movement in Wisconsin, 1890–1920* (Madison, 1968) 32–40.

17. *The Arkansas Gazette*, Sep. 6, 1896; in an earlier issue, Jul. 17, 1896, the *Gazette* estimated the number of black voters at twenty thousand and charged that three-fourths of them could not properly mark their ballots.

18. *The Arkansas Gazette*, Jun. 22, 1898, Jan. 16, Feb. 8, 1902; *Digest of Rules; As Amended and Adopted by the Democratic State Central Committee, July 30, 1912, Pursuant to Resolution of the Democratic State Convention at Little Rock, Ark., June 5, 1912* (Little Rock, 1912), 3, 4; the *Digest of Rules* had been issued originally by the Democratic State Convention of June 2, 1908, and the statement quoted above is found also in the 1908 rules. See *The Arkansas Gazette*, Jun. 2, 3, 4, 1908, for the original text of the party rules.

19. *The Arkansas Gazette*, Jun. 6, 7, 1912; C. Vann Woodward, *Origins of the New South*, 321.

20. "Letter of Gov. Dan W. Jones on the Industrial Progress of the State," in *The Arkansas Gazette*, Jan. 8, 1897.

21. *The Arkansas Gazette*, Aug. 23, 1910, quoted by Joe Tolbert Segraves, "Arkansas Politics, 1874–1918," (unpublished Ph.D. dissertation, University of Kentucky, 1973), 319–20. Segraves rejects the view of Rupert Vance that Davis was a Karl Marx for the poorer classes. See Rupert Vance, "A Karl Marx for Hill Billies, Portrait of a Southern Leader," *Social Forces* IX (December, 1930): 180–90. See also R. Arsenault, *The Wild Ass of the Ozarks: Jeff Davis and the Social Bases of Southern Politics* (Philadelphia, 1984), 102–03.

22. Arsenault, 102–03.

23. The words quoted are those of *The Arkansas Gazette*, Apr. 1, 1906, and not of Davis himself.

24. *Address of Gov. Jeff Davis*, delivered Nov 5, 1903, printed speech located in "Jeff Davis" microfilm Film 121, University of Arkansas, Fayetteville.

25. *The New York Times*, Jan. 3, 1913; Chauncey M. Depew, *My Memories of Eighty Years* (New York, 1924), 184.

26. L. S. Dunaway, *Jeff Davis: Governor and United States Senator, His Life and Speeches* (Little Rock, 1913), 51; the quote is from Davis's speech at Center Point in Howard County, Feb. 12, 1900; Fred W. Allsop, *Little Adventures in Newspaperdom* (Little Rock, 1922), 102–05.

27. L. S. Dunaway, *Jeff Davis*, 85–86, from his Bentonville speech of Dec. 2, 1905.

28. R. Arsenault, *Wild Ass*, 99, 106–07; John Wheeler in "The Populist Party in Arkansas," (unpublshed Ph.D. dissertation, University of Tulane, 1975), 490, states that "An examination of available election returns at the precinct level reveals that the great majority of those boxes which returned Populist pluralities in either 1892 or 1894 went Democratic in elections thereafter." Wheeler based his argument not on the 1900 election but on available township returns for the 1906 election. He argued (494) that evidence suggests that "Davis tended to receive the support of a significant proportion of the former Populist electorate."

29. These figures are based on precinct return studies and tables found in R. Arsenault, *Wild Ass*, 153, 201. Arsenault defines a Populist precinct as any precinct that cast at least a 40 percent vote for the Populist candidate for governor in either the 1892 or 1896 election.

30. These percentages are based upon information provided in the *Biennial Reports of the Secretary of State.*

31. Reinhard H. Luthin in *American Demagogues* (Boston, 1954), 302–15, describes the pattern of the typical Southern demagogue. While Jeff Davis fits the pattern described at many points, he does not conform so closely to the charge of ignorance and anti-intellectualism. Davis had a university education, though somewhat limited, and he was an intelligent man. His wife came from a cultivated background and Davis's father was a judge; C. Vann Woodward in *Origins of the New South,* 376, expresses a common view of Davis when he speaks of his crusades as colorful but without significant results. J. R. Hollingsworth, *The Whirligig of Politics,* 193, agrees that Davis and James K. Vardaman smote the air with their angry fists, but did little to achieve significant progressive reform. But Albert D. Kirwan, *The Revolt of the Rednecks,* 310–14, views James Vardaman and Theodore Bilbo from the standpoint of weighing achievements against failings, and he suggests that the bourbons who used the epithet, "demagogue," had also practiced racial baiting. Texas Governor J. E. Ferguson, who rallied tenant farmers and suffered impeachment, compares to Davis in background. Ferguson was a Temple banker but campaigned mainly in rural areas. His rental reforms were not effective, but he did achieve many other constructive reforms. See Rupert Norval Richardson, *Texas, The Lone Star State* (Englewood Cliffs, New Jersey, 1965), 289–90.

32. Daniel Meritt Robison, *Bob Taylor and the Agrarian Revolt in Tennessee* (Chapel Hill, 1935), 32–72.

33. Cal Ledbetter, Jr., "Jeff Davis and the Politics of Combat," *Arkansas Historical Review* XXXIII (Spring, 1974): 22–23.

34. T. Harry Williams, *Huey Long* (New York, 1969), 69; R. Arsenault, *Wild Ass,* 4–10. Arsenault believes the term demagogue should be replaced with the expression, "mass leaders." The achievements of these "folk heroes" involved "catharsis and symbolic action" rather than "profound changes in the distribution of power."

35. *Address of Governor Jeff Davis,* Nov. 5, 1903, Film 121, 20, 21, 22.

36. *The Arkansas Gazette,* May 9, 10, 1902.

37. *Address of Gov. Jeff Davis,* Nov. 5, 1903, Film 121, 34, 35.

38. Pine Bluff *Graphic,* Sep. 1, 1904, quoted in Elizabeth L. Wheeler, "Isaac Fisher: The Frustrations of a Negro Educator at Branch Normal College, 1902–1911," *Arkansas Historical Quarterly* XLI (Spring, 1982): 25.

39. William F. Holmes, *The White Chief,* 78.

40. Ibid., 54–56; R. Arsenault, *Wild Ass,* 205; David Michael Moyers, "Arkansas Progressivism: The Legislative Record," (unpublished Ph.D. dissertation, University of Arkansas, Fayetteville, 1986), 129–30.

41. *Journal of the Senate of Arkansas, 1905* (Little Rock, 1905), 24–25, as quoted in R. Arsenault, *Wild Ass,* 206. For a detailed account of the struggle against Davis's proposal see D. M. Moyers, "Arkansas Progressivism," 129–35.

42. D. Moyers, "Arkansas Progressivism," 131–34; R. Arsenault, *Wild Ass,* 206.

43. Robert Cotner, *James Stephen Hogg, A Biography* (Austin, 1959), 561–63.

44. Arsenault argues that Davis's appeal to racism did not serve as a cement holding his coalition together. Race-baiting was normal for any Democratic leader, but for Davis it "was not the primary force *within* that system." See *Wild Ass,* 13–14.

45. Joe Tolbert Segraves, "Arkansas Politics, 1874–1918," (unpublished Ph.D. dissertation, University of Kentucky, 1974), 403. Segraves also believes

Davis to be less extreme in his racism than many other Southern demagogues.

46. *The Augusta Chronicle,* n.d., quoted in C. Vann Woodward, *Tom Watson, Agrarian Rebel* (New York, 1963), 168.

47. Dewey W. Grantham, Jr., *Hoke Smith and the Politics of the New South* (Ann Arbor, 1967), 143.

48. William F. Holmes, *The White Chief,* 34–39, 88–90, 132–33.

49. Speech of John S. Little at the 1906 State Democratic Convention, *The Arkansas Gazette,* June 7, 1906.

50. "After Fifty Years," a sermon on the occasion of the fiftieth anniversary of the First Christian Church of Fayetteville, Mar. 6, 1898. The sermon is found in an unidentified clipping in the Nathaniel Madison Ragland Papers, Special Collections of the University of Arkansas library, Fayetteville; Robert Neill to W. J. Bryan, Oct. 27, 1901, Bryan Papers.

51. Davis's words are quoted in an article on his tactics in *The Arkansas Gazette,* Apr. 1, 1906.

52. Daniel M. Robison, *Bob Taylor and the Agrarian Revolt in Tennessee,* 107–09; Jeff Davis to Theodore Roosevelt, Apr. 24, 1902, J. Davis to T. Roosevelt, Apr. 25, 1902; another appeal was made in J. Davis to T. Roosevelt, May 5, 1902, Theodore Roosevelt Papers, Library of Congress.

53. William N. Hill, *Story of the Arkansas Penitentiary* (n.p., 1915), 33, 68, 112–14, 131, 132.

Five: Issues of the Davis Era, 1897–1900

1. *The Arkansas Gazette,* July 16, 1899; Frances Butler Simkins in *Pitchfork Ben Tillman,* 150, 151, argues that the South Carolinian, despite his clownishness and coarse language, captured the mood and confidence of the common rural folk and as a politician championed significant principles and reforms.

2. *The Arkansas Gazette,* Jul. 16, 1899.

3. Stephen E. Wood, "The Development of Arkansas Railroads," *Arkansas Historical Quarterly,* VII (Autumn, 1948): 159–64.

4. Nevin E. Neal, "A Biograpy of Joseph T. Robinson," (unpublished Ph.D. dissertation, University of Oklahoma, Norman, 1958), 20, 21.

5. *The Arkansas Gazette,* Aug. 25, 1896; "Inaugural Address of Governor Dan W. Jones to the Thirty-First General Assembly," Jan. 31, 1897. Manuscript located in Special Collections of the University of Arkansas library, Fayetteville.

6. *The Arkansas Gazette,* Feb. 5, 1897.

7. *The Arkansas Gazette,* Feb. 5, 6, 10, 1897.

8. *The Arkansas Gazette,* Feb. 26, 1897, May 3, 1908; *The Drew County Advance,* Mar. 9, 1897.

9. *The Drew County Advance,* May 4, 1897.

10. *The Arkansas Gazette,* May 6, 1897.

11. *The Arkansas Gazette,* May 6, 1897; *The Pine Bluff Weekly Press-Eagle,* Jun. 1, 1897.

12. *The Arkansas Gazette,* Feb. 23, 1897; *The Helena Weekly World,* Feb. 10, 1897.

13. *The Arkansas Gazette,* Feb. 7, 1897.

14. The speech, delivered on February 16, is found in full in *The Pine Bluff Weekly Press-Eagle Supplement,* Feb. 23, 1897. According to one state senator,

whose reliability is doubtful, Fordyce himself wrote one of the major commission bills before the legislature. A *Gazette* reporter rejected this charge as unfounded since he, a close friend of Fordyce's, knew the latter opposed a railroad commission. See *The Arkansas Gazette,* May 9, 1897.

15. Sheldon Hackney, *Populism to Progressivism,* 237, 238.

16. *The Arkansas Gazette,* May 8, 11, 1897; Feb. 16, 1898.

17. *The Helena Weekly World,* Apr. 5, 1899; *The Arkansas Gazette,* May 3, 1908.

18. Robert C. Cotner, *James Stephen Hogg,* 236–43; Alwyn Barr, *Reconstruction to Reform,* 113–24; Dewey W. Grantham, Jr., *Hoke Smith,* 164–68; Stanley P. Caine, *The Myth of a Progressive Reform: Railroad Regulation in Wisconsin, 1903–1910* (Madison, 1970), 34–35, 117–21. Gabriel Kolko in *The Triumph of Conservatism: A Reinterpretation of American History, 1900–1916* (Chicago, 1967), 5, 6, presents the view that the large corporations themselves initiated the movement for *federal* regulation of business and that the Progressive era represents an attempt by the business community to use government to curb the increasing trend toward competition. But he concedes that this pattern does not apply to the state scene. Many state governments were more clearly radical and democratic in their regulatory movements, and railroads and other corporations opposed haphazard regulation by the states. It is clear that Arkansas was genuinely radical on the question of railroad regulation. In Arkansas, regulation did not come through railroad initiatives. Stanley P. Caine agrees with Kolko that the railroads took part in the regulatory crusade but draws back from asserting they were the primary force initiating the commission legislation. Caine does not believe reformers singlehandedly forced the commission concept on a reluctant business community but thinks various interests joined the movement in hopes of shaping the statutes to their own liking.

19. *The Arkansas Gazette,* Apr. 2, 1898, June 22, 1898. The pages of the *Gazette* during the spring and summer of 1898 reveal more about zeal for war than interest in politics.

20. *The Arkansas Gazette* contains the text of the Eureka Springs speech in its Apr. 6, 1898, edition.

21. Information in the preceding paragraphs on the debt settlement was culled from the following sources: *The Arkansas Gazette,* Feb. 2, 23, 25, 27, May 6, 1897; *The Pine Bluff Weekly Press-Eagle,* Mar. 9, 1897; *The Helena Weekly World,* Mar. 10, 17, 1897; *Debt Settlement, Senate Concurrent Resolution No. 7, The Message of Governor Dan W. Jones* (Little Rock, 1897), 5–13. The latter source is a pamphlet in the Special Collections of the University of Arkansas library, Fayetteville, and contains a technical and legal discussion of the dispute. *The Arkansas Gazette* for Feb. 23, 1897, reproduces a number of letters from Arkansas congressmen which evidence a withering of their opposition to the Meiklejohn Amendment during the winter of 1896–97.

22. *The Arkansas Gazette,* Apr. 6, 1898.

23. Ibid.

24. Ibid.; *Biennial Message of Governor James P. Clarke to the Thirty-First General Assembly,* delivered Jan. 14, 1897 (Little Rock, 1897), pamphlet in Special Collections, University of Arkansas library, 42, 43.

25. *The Arkansas Gazette,* Apr. 6, 1898.

26. *The Arkansas Gazette,* Apr. 7, Jun. 14, 17, 22, 1898.

27. Kelly Bryant, *Historical Report of the Secretary of State,* 184; *Biennial Message of the Governor of Arkansas; Daniel W. Jones, Governor.* Delivered Jan. 18, 1899 (Little Rock, 1899), 4.

28. *Morgan's Buzz-Saw*, Apr. 1, 1899; *The Helena Weekly World*, Mar. 22, 1899.

29. Edward Chase Kirkland, *Industry Comes of Age: Business, Labor, and Public Policy, 1860–1897* (Chicago, 1967), 119, 120; Stanley P. Caine, *The Myth of a Progressive Reform*, 117–19; Alwyn Barr, *Reconstruction to Reform*, 123–24.

30. Jerry Wallace, *An Arkansas Judge*, 39–41, 48. *First Annual Report of the Railroad Commission*, 1901, 5, 6.

31. *Felix M. Hanley, Jeremiah G. Wallace and Henry M. Well, Commissioners and Members of the Arkansas Railroad Commission of Arkansas V. The Kansas City Southern Railway Co.*, National Archives, Transcript of United States Supreme Court Case 187, U.S. 617, File No. 18221, Box 3161, RG 267; U.S. Supreme Court Transcript, 1–3, 9–20.

32. *Hanley V. Kansas City Southern*, NA, File 18221, Box 3161, RG 267, 63, 67, 76.

33. Exhibit B, Opinion of Felix M. Hanley, Commissioner, 46, 46–49, found with Transcript of *Hanley V. Kansas City Southern*, NA, File 18221, Box 3161, RG 267; *Hanley V. Kansas City Southern*, 187, United States Reports 617–21 (1902).

34. Interview in *St. Louis Post-Dispatch*, n.d., reproduced in *The Arkansas Gazette*, Sep. 20, 1899.

35. L. B. Leigh to Clay Sloan, Auditor and Insurance Commissioner, An Open Letter, July 22, 1899, published in *The Arkansas Gazette*, Jul. 23, 1899.

36. *In the Supreme Court of Arkansas, The State of Arkansas V. Aetna Fire Insurance Co., and The State of Arkansas V. Lancashire Fire Insurance Co., Abstract and Argument for Appellant*, 9, 2, 6, a pamphlet reproduced in "Jeff Davis" microfilm. Film 121 at University of Arkansas, Fayetteville; *State V. Lancashire Fire Insurance Company*, 66, Arkansas Reports 466–80 (1899); *State V. Aetna Fire Insurance Company*, 66, Arkansas Reports 480–85 (1899).

37. David Y. Thomas, *Arkansas and Its People*, vol. I, 205; *Address of Gov. Jeff Davis*, delivered Nov. 5, 1903, 3, in "Jeff Davis" microfilm.

38. *The Arkansas Gazette*, Jul. 6, Sep. 16, 20, 1899.

39. Robert C. Cotner, *James Stephen Hogg, A Biography* (Austin, 1959), 118–24; Gabriel Kolko, *The Triumph of Conservatism*, 89–97.

40. *The Arkansas Gazette*, Jul. 5, 1899.

41. *The Arkansas Gazette*, Jul. 16, 1899; Feb. 11, 1900.

42. Charles Jacobson, *The Life Story of Jeff Davis*, 46; *Address of Governor Jeff Davis*, delivered Nov. 5, 1903, 8, "Jeff Davis" Microfilm; The Democratic platform is found in *The Conway Democrat*, June 29, 1900.

43. *The Arkansas Gazette*, Jul. 5, 1899; in this issue of the *Gazette*, Senator John D. Kimball gives a brief history of the origins of the capitol construction project.

44. George W. Donaghey, *Building a State Capitol* (Little Rock, 1937), 37, 38; *The Arkansas Gazette*, Jul. 2, 6, 1899.

45. *The Arkansas Gazette*, Jul. 5, 16, 1899.

46. *The Arkansas Democrat*, Jun. 22, 1900.

47. George W. Donaghey, *Building A State Capitol*, 55; Charles Jacobson, *The Life Story of Jeff Davis*, 53.

48. *Inaugural Address of Governor Jefferson Davis*, Jan. 18, 1901, 13–15; George W. Donaghey, *Building a State Capitol*, 87, 88.

49. Robert C. Cotner, *James Stephen Hogg*, 134–37; Frederick W. Rathjen, "The Texas State House, A Study of the Building of the Texas Capitol Based on the Reports of the Capitol Building Commissioners," *The Southwestern Historical Quarterly* LX (April, 1957): 433–62.

50. *The Arkansas Gazette,* Jun. 24, 1898, Jul. 1, 1899; George W. Donaghey, *Building a State Capitol,* 39.

51. *The Arkansas Gazette,* Jul. 5, 23, Sep. 10, 26, 1899.

52. *The Arkansas Gazette,* Jul. 16, 21, Aug. 26, 27, 1899.

53. Paige E. Mulhollan, "The Public Career of James H. Berry," (unpublished M.A. thesis, University of Arkansas, 1962), 159, 167–68. Mulhollan made use of the Berry Papers which were not accessible at the time of this writing. The letters cited by him were: James Berry to Jeff Davis, Sep. 20, 1899, and Jeff Davis to James Berry, Dec. 25, 1899.

54. Ibid. 160.

55. *The Arkansas Gazette,* Jan. 4, Feb. 4, 1900.

56. James K. Jones to William Jennings Bryan, Jan. 17, 1899, Bryan Papers, Library of Congress.

57. J. K. Jones to W. J. Bryan, Jan. 24, 1899, J. K. Jones to W. J. Bryan, Jan. 30, 1899, Bryan Papers; *The Conway Democrat,* Jun. 29, 1900.

58. *The Arkansas Gazette,* Feb. 4, 1900; Paige Mulhollan, "The Public Career of James H. Berry," 162.

59. For discussion of the Bush Bill see *Biennial Message of the Governor of Arkansas: Daniel W. Jones, Governor.* Delivered Jan. 18, 1899 (Little Rock, 1899), 5, 6; Jeff Davis Speech at Hardy, Arkansas, is printed in *The Arkansas Gazette,* Jul. 5, 1899; *Inaugural Address of Gov. Jefferson Davis, Delivered Before the General Assembly of the State of Arkansas.* Jan. 18, 1901 (Little Rock, 1901), 9.

60. *Governor Jeff Davis, A Review of His Official Career. Some Reasons Why He Should Not Be Renominated,* a pamphlet reprinted from a *Supplement to The Forrest City Times,* Sep. 11, 1903, 2, 3, 5, 6. The pamphlet is located at the University of Texas library, Austin.

61. Some of the reforms mentioned here are discussed in later chapters. For a more complete evaluation of Davis's performance, see chapter eleven.

Six: The Davis Organization, 1900–1906

1. See Dewey Grantham, *The Democratic South,* 44–45, and his *Southern Progressivism,* 10, 412 for a discussion of Southern factionalism.

2. *The Jonesboro Tribune,* n.d., quoted in Harry L. Williams, *Behind the Scenes in Arkansas Politics,* 140; *The Arkansas Gazette,* Apr. 1, 1906; Charles Jacobson, *The Life Story of Jeff Davis,* 7.

3. *The Arkansas Democrat,* Jun. 26, 1900; *The Arkansas Gazette,* Jun. 11, 1902.

4. Charles Jacobson, *The Life Story of Jeff Davis,* 68.

5. *The Arkansas Commonweal,* n.d., is quoted in *The Arkansas Democrat,* Jun. 9, 1900; Raymond Arsenault, in *Wild Ass of the Ozarks: Jeff Davis and the Social Bases of Southern Politics* (Philadelphia, 1984), 116–17, argues that precinct returns show a Populist drift to the Republican camp. John M. Wheeler "The People's Party in Arkansas," believes that while such a drift did occur it involved only a small number of Populists. Wheeler thinks most of the former Populist voters did return to the Democratic Party.

6. *Address of Gov. Jeff Davis,* delivered Nov. 5, 1903, printed speech located in Jeff Davis microfilm, Film 121, University of Arkansas, Fayetteville, 16; *The Arkansas Gazette,* Jun. 29, 1900, May 8, 1901; Arsenault in *Wild Ass,* 111 ar-

gues that the Bourland defeat indicated that the Davis faction had not fully crystallized.

7. Tom W. Campbell, *Arkansas Lawyer,* 74; *The Arkansas Gazette,* Jan. 6, 7, 10, 13, 15, 1901.

8. *The Arkansas Gazette,* Jan. 15, 1901.

9. *The Arkansas Gazette,* Apr. 4, 5, 10, 1901; See the *Gazette* for Apr. 20, 1901, for a description of the Brick Company's operation. The contract was sometimes referred to as the "Dickinson Convict Contract" because W. W. Dickinson, the owner of a number of Little Rock firms, was president of the brick company. R. Arsenault, *Wild Ass,* 123–29.

10. George W. Donaghey, *Building a State Capitol,* 84, 85; Charles Jacobson, *The Life Story of Jeff Davis,* 153, 154; R. Arsenault, *Wild Ass,* 138.

11. *The Arkansas Gazette,* Apr. 6, 1902; Harry L. Williams, *Behind the Scenes in Arkansas Politics,* 101; Charles Jacobson, *The Life Story of Jeff Davis,* 79, 80.

12. Horace Chilton Diaries, 49, University of Texas Archives, Austin, Texas.

13. Charles S. Collins to W. J. Bryan, Apr. 7, 1902, Bryan Papers.

14. George Fred Williams to W. J. Bryan, Nov. 10, 1897, G. F. Williams to W. J. Bryan, Nov. 16, 1898, Bryan Papers.

15. *The Arkansas Gazette,* Feb. 16, 1898; James K. Jones to W. J. Bryan, Feb. 1, 1898, James K. Jones to W. J. Bryan, Feb. 16, 1898, Bryan Papers.

16. J. K. Jones, et al. to W. J. Bryan, July 1, 1900, W. J. Bryan to J. K. Jones, July 2, 1900, J. K. Jones to J. G. Johnson, May 3, 1900, J. K. Jones to W. J. Bryan, Aug. 4, 1900, Bryan Papers.

17. C. S. Collins to W. J. Bryan, Nov. 24, 1900, Bryan Papers.

18. James K. Jones to W. J. Bryan, Dec. 1, 1900, Bryan Papers; *The Arkansas Gazette,* Mar. 30, 1902.

19. John Gould Fletcher, *Arkansas* (Chapel Hill, 1947), 304; David Y. Thomas, *Arkansas and Its People,* Vol. I, 271, 272; *The Arkansas Gazette,* Jan. 12, Apr. 1, 1902.

20. *The Arkansas Gazette,* Jan. 12, 1902.

21. Charles Collins to W. J. Bryan, Apr. 7, 1902, Bryan Papers; Farrar D. Newberry, *James K. Jones,* 101–03; *The Arkansas Gazette,* Jan. 12, 28, Mar. 15, 1902; Newberry in his eulogistic work on Senator Jones argued that Davis's statements about Jones's company being a trust were ridiculous. According to Newberry, the company went bankrupt because they had a large number of round bales in their possession when the price of cotton suddenly dropped. Jones lost the few thousand dollars he had invested. Jones claimed the company ginned only 2.5 percent of all cotton baled in the country.

22. Horace Chilton Diaries, 52, University of Texas, Austin, Texas.

23. *The Arkansas Gazette,* Feb. 4, Mar. 15, 21, 1902.

24. *The Arkansas Gazette,* Feb. 6, 1900, Apr. 1, 1902; James K. Jones, Jr., to Charles H. Brough, Nov. 30, 1915, Charles H. Brough Papers, University of Arkansas at Fayetteville; James R. Grant, *The Life of Thomas C. McRae* (n.p., 1932), 77, 80, 81.

25. *The Arkansas Gazette,* Mar. 2, 23, 1902; T. C. McRae to Wood Rainwater, n.d., is found in the Mar. 2, 1902, issue.

26. *The Arkansas Gazette,* Mar. 19, Apr. 4, 1902.

27. *The Arkansas Gazette,* Jun. 11, 1902; J. K. Jones to W. J. Bryan, Apr. 4, 1902, Bryan Papers.

28. Jeff Davis to James P. Eagle, Mar. 30, 1902, Mrs. J. P. Eagle to J. Davis, Mar. 30, 1902, Jeff Davis to J. P. Eagle, Mar. 30, 1902 (second letter), J. P. Eagle to J. Davis, Apr. 1, 1902, J. Davis to J. P. Eagle, Apr. 2, 1902. These letters and others are printed in *The Arkansas Gazette,* Apr. 8, 1902.

29. J. S. Rogers, *History of Arkansas Baptists* (Little Rock, 1948), 216, 223; *The Arkansas Gazette*, May 10, 1902.

30. *The Arkansas Gazette*, Apr. 8, May 8, 1902.

31. *The Arkansas Gazette*, May 29, 1902.

32. *The Arkansas Gazette*, Jun. 11, 1902; *Address of Gov. Jeff Davis*, delivered Nov. 5, 1903, printed speech located in "Jeff Davis" microfilm, Film 121, University of Arkansas, Fayetteville, 13.

33. *The Arkansas Gazette*, Jan. 17, 21, 28, 30, Feb. 11, 12, 1903.

34. *The Arkansas Gazette*, Apr. 3, Jun. 11, 1902; Jan. 11, 17, 18, 21, 1903.

35. Jephtha Evans to Jeff Davis, Apr. 4, 1902, Jephtha Evans to Jeff Davis, Apr. 7, 1902, Jephtha Evans to Jeff Davis, Apr. 10, 1902, Jephtha Evans to Jeff Davis, May 12, 1902; all letters are printed in the pamphlet *That Correspondence! Davis vs. Evans, Evans vs. Davis, Full Text of the Correspondence Between Gov. Jeff Davis and Judge J. H. Evans* located in "Political Material Concerning Jeff Davis," Special Collections, University of Arkansas library, Fayetteville.

36. *The Arkansas Gazette*, Jan. 2, 17, 28, 1902.

37. *The Arkansas Gazette*, Jan. 28, Feb. 5, Jun. 10, 1902; *The Hazen Oracle* n.d., quoted in *The Arkansas Gazette*, Mar. 5, 1902.

38. R. Arsenault, *Wild Ass*, 150–56. Arsenault believes the 1902 election, like that of 1900, failed to show that Davis's support was a function of economic class lines. He believes the factional division was more simply an urban-rural rivalry.

39. *The Arkansas Gazette*, Jan. 3, 9, 10, 11, 13, 1903.

40. Daniel M. Robison, *Bob Taylor and the Agrarian Revolt in Tennessee,* 109–15; William F. Holmes, *The White Chief,* 150–67; Jane Zimmerman, "The Convict Lease System in Arkansas and The Fight For Abolition," *Arkansas Historical Quarterly* VIII (Autumn, 1949): 171–88.

41. *The Arkansas Gazette*, Jul. 19, 1899, Mar. 21, 1901, Jan. 31, Feb. 14, 1903; William F. Holmes, *The White Chief,* 150–51.

42. *The Arkansas Gazette*, Jan. 22, Feb. 13, 1903.

43. *The Arkansas Gazette*, Feb. 13, 1903.

44. *The Arkansas Gazette*, Feb. 13, 1903; apparently Killough's statement is the *Gazette's* paraphrase and only part of it is a direct quote.

45. *The Arkansas Gazette*, Feb. 13, 1903.

46. *The Arkansas Gazette*, Feb. 14, 15, 1903.

47. *Report and Testimony of the Ways and Means Committee in its investigation of the differences between the chief executive and the remaining members of the Penitentiary Board, State of Arkansas* (Little Rock, 1903), 104, 94, 101.

48. *Report of the Ways and Means Committee,* 4, 5; Jeff Davis to Reese B. Hogins, n.d., is published in full in Charles Jacobson's *The Life Story of Jeff Davis,* 177.

49. *Report of the Ways and Means Committee,* 5–7, 5.

50. Ibid., 6–8.

51. Ibid., 9, 11, 13, 14; *The Arkansas Gazette*, Apr. 10, 1903.

52. *Report of the Ways and Means Committee,* 13, 14; *The Arkansas Gazette,* Apr. 24, 1903; Whitley's report of brutality agrees with testimony from other sources. *The Arkansas Gazette*, Jan. 25, 1902, reported the mysterious death of a prisoner at the Cummins farm who had been convicted on a petit larceny charge. A coroners' jury ruled death resulted from causes unknown. The *Gazette* believed injuries inflicted at the farm caused the death. Governor Davis's speeches also tell of instances of inhuman treatment. See also a firsthand account by a prisoner of the time, William N. Hill, *Story of the Arkansas Penitentiary* (n.p., 1915).

53. Charles Jacobson, *The Life Story of Jeff Davis*, 71, 72; *Address of Gov. Jeff Davis*, delivered Nov. 5, 1903, printed speech located in "Jeff Davis" microfilm, Film 121, University of Arkansas, Fayetteville, 5; *Inaugural Address of Gov. Jefferson Davis Delivered Before the General Assembly of the State of Arkansas, January 18, 1901* (Little Rock, 1901), 5–7.

54. *The Arkansas Gazette*, Feb. 19, 1, 3, 1903.

55. *The Arkansas Gazette*, Feb. 19, 1903.

56. *The Arkansas Gazette*, Apr. 7, 24, 28, 29, 1903.

57. George W. Donaghey, *Building a State Capitol*, 101–03; *The Arkansas Gazette*, Apr. 9, 16, 1903, Jan. 5, 1904.

58. *Address of Gov. Jeff Davis*, delivered Nov. 5, 1903, 11, 2.

59. *The Arkansas Gazette*, Jan. 12, Mar. 24, 1904.

60. R. Arsenault, *Wild Ass*, 197–200; L. S. Dunaway, *What a Preacher saw Through a Key-Hole in Arkansas*, (Little Rock, 1975), 48.

61. Ibid., 200–03.

62. *The Arkansas Gazette*, May 3, Jun. 15, 16, 1904.

63. *The Arkansas Gazette*, Apr. 8, Jun. 17, 18, 1904.

64. *The Arkansas Gazette*, Jun. 15, 16, 1904.

65. *Message of Gov. Jefferson Davis, Delivered Before the General Assembly, January 11, 1905* (n.p., n.d.), 13; Charles Jacobson, *The Life Story of Jeff Davis*, 72.

66. Ibid., 178; Paige E. Mulhollan, "The Issues of the Davis-Berry Senatorial Campaign in 1906," *Arkansas Historical Quarterly*, XX (Summer, 1961): 119, 122; *The Arkansas Gazette*, Apr. 5, 1906.

67. *Speech of Robert L. Rogers, Candidate for Governor, Delivered at Lake City, October 16, 1905* (n.p., n.d.), pamphlet located at Library of Congress, 13; Joe P. Eagle to Joseph T. Robinson, Feb. 7, 1906, Joe P. Eagle to Joseph T. Robinson, Dec. 8, 1907, Joseph T. Robinson Papers, Special Collections, University of Arkansas library, Fayetteville.

68. *The Arkansas Gazette*, Oct. 22, 23, 1896; *Message of Gov. John S. Little, Delivered Before The General Assembly, Jan. 18, 1907* (Little Rock, 1907), 3–16; John S. Little to Charles H. Brough, Apr. 2, 1906, Charles H. Brough Papers, University of Arkansas, Fayetteville.

69. *Speech of Robert L. Rogers, October 16, 1905*, 8–10, 8.

70. *Speech of Robert L. Rogers, October 16, 1905*, 4–7.

71. James P. Clarke, *The Railroad Tax Compromise and Senator Clarke's $30,000 Fee* (Little Rock, n.d.), 1–32, pamphlet in Special Collections of University of Arkansas library, Fayetteville; the quotation is from Jeff Davis's Bentonville speech of Dec. 2, 1905, and is taken from Clarke's excerpt of the speech, 31; Clarke printed the pamphlet during his 1914 senatorial campaign to answer renewed charges. The bulk of the pamphlet is a reprint of his 1906 statement, "To the People of Arkansas."

72. Arthur Wallace Dunn, *From Harrison to Harding: A Personal Narrative, Covering a Third of a Century, 1888–1921* (New York, 1922), Vol. I, 36.

73. Paige Mulhollan, "The Public Career of James H. Berry," 140, 141.

74. Arthur Wallace Dunn, *From Harrison to Harding*, Vol. II, 47, 48.

75. Paige Mulhollan in his study of the 1906 Davis-Berry campaign saw no clash between progressive and conservative ideals in the contest. He argued that Davis's and Berry's views on trusts, the tariff, and railroad rates were closely parallel and that progressive politicians had won control in the state by 1906; Paige Mulhollan, "The Issues of the Davis-Berry Senatorial Campaign in 1906," *Arkansas Historical Quarterly*, XX (Summer, 1961): 125.

76. *Reply of Senator James H. Berry to a Speech Made by Governor Davis at Con-*

way, delivered at Bentonville, Jul. 7, 1905, 1, 2, found in the Thomas C. McRae Papers, Special Collections, University of Arkansas library, Fayetteville.

77. *The Arkansas Gazette,* Jun. 7, 1906, provides figures used above. See also *The Arkadelphia Southern Standard,* May 3, 1906, and the *Gazette* for Apr. 29, 1906, for a list of voting by counties. It is difficult to state precise figures because of disputed contests in some counties. The final result reported at the state convention omitted Lee County, and earlier returns in the *Gazette* told of two different elections held in Poinsett County. The Berry people held a second primary of their own and gave the vote to their candidate. In giving Davis fifty-one counties, I have given Poinsett to Davis and Lee to Berry although the latter contest was very close.

78. *The Arkansas Gazette,* Apr. 3, 1906; clipping from *The Record* (Russellville), Nov. 14, 1906, found in "Jeff Davis" microfilm, Film 121, University of Arkansas, Fayetteville.

79. Paige E. Mulhollan, "The Public Career of James H. Berry," 177; *The Arkansas Gazette,* Apr. 3, 1906.

Seven: The Republican Party in a One-Party State

1. Harmon L. Remmel to Powell Clayton, Apr. 7, 1911, Harmon L. Remmel Papers, Special Collections, University of Arkansas library, Fayetteville.

2. Remmel summarizes his career with the party in a letter to William R. Harr, acting attorney general, Aug. 8, 1910, File 4346, William Howard Taft Papers, Library of Congress; H. L. Remmel to Catherine R. Miles, Nov. 15, 1910, Remmel Papers; Bob Besom, "Little Rock Businessmen Invest in Coal: Harmon L. Remmel and the Arkansas Anthracite Coal Company, 1905–1923," *Arkansas Historical Quarterly* XLVII (Autumn, 1988): 273–87; for a summary of Remmel's early life and career up to 1913 see Marvin F. Russell, "The Rise of a Republican Leader: Harmon L. Remmel," *Arkansas Historical Quarterly* XXXVI (Autumn, 1977): 234–57.

3. Many of the same characteristics appeared in the Texas Republican Party. See Alwyn Barr, *Reconstruction to Reform,* 176–92, 244.

4. Tom Dillard, "To the Back of the Elephant: Racial Conflict in the Arkansas Republican Party," *Arkansas Historical Quarterly* XXXIII (Spring, 1974): 6.

5. James Harris Fain, "Political Disfranchisement of the Negro in Arkansas," (unpublished M.A. thesis, University of Arkansas, 1961), 33–34.

6. John William Graves, "The Arkansas Negro and Segregation, 1890–1903," (unpublished M.A. thesis, University of Arkansas, 1967), 70–72; M. Russell, "The Rise of a Republican Leader," 241.

7. See chapter one for more information on disfranchisement.

8. J. Graves, "The Arkansas Negro and Segregation," 7–8.

9. Ibid., 82; Tom Dillard, "Scipio A. Jones," *Arkansas Historical Quarterly,* XXXI (Autumn, 1972): 214.

10. *The Arkansas Gazette,* Sep. 3, Oct. 13, 1899; H. L. Remmel to P. Clayton, Oct. 18, 1899, Remmel Papers; William H. Burnside, "Powell Clayton: Politician and Diplomat," (unpublished Ph.D. dissertation, University of Arkansas, Fayetteville, 1978), 70–71.

11. *The Arkansas Gazette,* Mar. 8, 1900.

12. Ibid.

13. Tom Dillard, "Scipio A. Jones," *Arkansas Historical Quarterly,* XXXI (Autumn, 1972): 215.

14. H. L. Remmel to William Howard Taft, Dec. 18, 1909, George W. Wickersham to Charles D. Hilles, Sep. 15, 1911, H. L. Remmel to Charles D. Hilles, Jun. 27, 1912, H. L. Remmel to Charles D. Hilles, Jul. 18, 1912, H. L. Remmel to William Howard Taft, Sep. 16, 1912, William Howard Taft Papers, Library of Congress.

15. Scipio A. Jones to Charles J. Bonaparte, n.d., (received in Washington, Sep. 16, 1907), Durand Whipple to William Loeb, Jr., Aug. 22, 1907, William Whipple to Charles J. Bonaparte, Sep. 25, 1907, Justice Department, Arkansas Appointment Papers, NA, RG 60.

16. Mifflin Wistar Gibbs, *Shadow and Light: An Autobiography,* (New York, 1968; reprint of Washington, D.C., 1902 edition), 223; Tom W. Dillard, "Golden Prospects and Fraternal Amenities: Mifflin W. Gibbs's Arkansas Years," *Arkansas Historical Quarterly,* XXXV (Winter, 1976): 307–33; Tom W. Dillard, "The Black Moses of the West: A Biography of Mifflin Wistar Gibbs, 1823–1915," (unpublished M.A. thesis, University of Arkansas, Fayetteville).

17. James W. Leslie, "Ferd Havis: Jefferson County's Black Republican Leader," *Arkansas Historical Quarterly,* XXX (Autumn, 1978): 250; Tom Dillard, "To the Back of the Elephant: Racial Conflict in the Arkansas Republican Party," *Arkansas Historical Quarterly,* XXXIII (Spring, 1974): 10.

18. George Brown Tindall, *The Emergence of the New South,* 168–69; Tom Dillard, "Scipio A. Jones," 214–15; Tom Dillard, "To the Back of the Elephant," 11–13; Hanes Walton, Jr., *Black Republicans: The Politics of the Black and Tans* (Metuchen, N.J., 1975), 126–28; *The Arkansas Gazette,* April 29, 1920.

19. Powell Clayton to Harmon L. Remmel, June 21, 1901, Remmel Papers.

20. *The Arkansas Gazette,* Oct. 29, 1896.

21. Clipping from the Little Rock *Globe-Democrat,* Jan. 14, 1902, located in Department of the Interior, General Land Office, Arkansas Appointment Papers, NA, RG 48, Box 22, "Data" folder.

22. George E. Dodge to William McKinley, July 13, 1900, Oscar L. Miles to Theodore Roosevelt, Dec. 5, 1901, Justice Department, Arkansas Appointment Papers, NA, RG 60.

23. Marcus A. Hanna to Richard A. McCurdy, June 21, 1900, Remmel Papers; Powell Clayton to Theodore Roosevelt, Sep. 27, 1902, Powell Clayton to Theodore Roosevelt, Apr. 2, 1904, Theodore Roosevelt Papers.

24. H. S. Powell to Joseph T. Robinson, Dec. 4, 1905, Joseph T. Robinson "To Whom It May Concern," Dec. 10, 1906, Fred C. Furth to Joseph T. Robinson, Aug. 13, 1907, Fred C. Furth to Joseph T. Robinson, Sep. 11, 1907; for further examples similar to those cited above, see Joseph T. Robinson to George B. Cortelyou, Dec. 12, 1905, W. H. Martin to J. T. Robinson, Dec. 9, 1905, E. G. Trull to J. T. Robinson, Nov. 29, 1907, Joseph Taylor Robinson Papers.

25. *The Arkansas Gazette,* Jan. 12, 1902.

26. This average does not include the Republican percentage for the 1912 election since the regular Republicans lost a significant portion of their strength to the Progressive Party in that year.

27. James K. Jones to W. J. Bryan, Dec. 1, 1900, Bryan Papers.

28. Dewey W. Grantham, *The Democratic South,* 25–27.

29. Jeremiah V. Bourland to H. C. Mechem, Jan. 23, 1906, Justice Department, Arkansas Appointment Papers, NA, RG 60.

30. Powell Clayton, *The Aftermath of the Civil War,* 366–68.

31. Jeff Davis to Theodore Roosevelt, Apr. 25, 1902, Theodore Roosevelt Papers.

32. Archie Butt, *The Intimate Letters of Archie Butt, Military Aide* (Garden City, 1930), Vol. I, 229–30.

33. Congressional election returns of 1900 are analyzed in *The Arkansas Gazette,* Apr. 27, 1901.

34. Based on lists given in Dallas T. Herndon, *Outline of Executive and Legislative History of Arkansas* (n.p., 1922).

35. *The Arkansas Democrat,* Jun. 2, 1900.

36. *The Arkansas Democrat,* Jun. 2, 1900; *The Arkansas Gazette,* Apr. 12, 27, 1901.

37. Committee on Elections No. 3, Contested Election Case: George Tilles Vs. William B. Cravens, 60th Congress, NA, RG 233.

38. *The Stuttgart Free Press,* n.d., quoted in *The Fayetteville Democrat,* Mar. 19, 1896.

39. "Resolutions of the Republican Central Committee," May 6, 1902, Department of the Interior, General Land Office, Arkansas Appointment Papers, NA, RG 48; George P. Dent to William McKinley, May 6, 1897, Justice Department, Arkansas Appointment Papers, NA, RG 60.

40. "Memorandum, Matter of the Appointment of District Attorneys in Arkansas both Eastern and Western Districts," Justice Department, Arkansas Appointment Papers, NA, RG 60.

41. Charles D. Greaves, *A Few Reasons Why Claytonism Should Be Rebuked* (n.p., c. 1902), 3–6, located in Justice Department, Arkansas Appointment Papers, NA, RG 60.

42. J. A. Comer, president of the Arkansas League of Roosevelt Clubs, see *The Arkansas Gazette,* Jun. 8, 1912, for his full report.

43. *The Arkansas Gazette,* Jan. 18, 1896; John Gould Fletcher, *Arkansas,* 212–13; "General Powell Clayton," *The American Review of Reviews,* XLVII (February, 1913): 164, has a photograph of Powell Clayton.

44. *The Washington Post,* n.d., quoted in *The Arkansas Gazette,* Feb. 1, 1896; Powell Clayton to H. L. Remmel, Jan. 2, 1897, Powell Clayton to Jacob Trieber, Nov. 6, 1901, Remmel Papers; H. L. Remmel to Charles Hilles, Jan. 9, 1913, Taft Papers.

45. H. L. Remmel to P. Clayton, Oct. 27, 1898, H. L. Remmel to P. Clayton, Oct. 31, 1898, P. Clayton to H. L. Remmel, Oct. 23, 1899, Harmon L. Remmel Papers.

46. *Arkansas Democratic State Platform, 1902; Official Address of the Democratic State Central Committee* (n.p., 1902), 5, pamphlet located in Special Collections, University of Arkansas library, Fayetteville.

47. Powell Clayton to H. L. Remmel, Aug. 20, 1901, Powell Clayton to Jacob Trieber, Nov. 6, 1901, Remmel Papers. Mathews was a white Insurgent Republican.

48. Willard B. Gatewood provides two instructive case studies in Roosevelt's Southern patronage strategy in his chapters on the Indianola post office appointment and the Charleston collector's office appointment in his book, *Theodore Roosevelt and the Art of Compromise* (Baton Rouge, 1970), 62–134; C. Vann Woodward, *Origins of the New South,* 463–64.

49. C. Vann Woodward, *Origins of the New South,* 463.

50. *The Arkansas Gazette,* Jan. 24, 1902.

51. Lyman J. Gage to George B. Cortelyou, Jan. 23, 1902, Treasury Department, Collectors of Internal Revenue Appointment Papers, NA, RG 56.

52. Charles Greaves, *A Few Reasons Why Claytonism Should be Rebuked,* 7; Harmon L. Remmel to Powell Clayton, Oct. 27, 1898, Powell Clayton to Harmon L. Remmel, Feb. 2, 1902, Harmon L. Remmel Papers; Powell Clayton to Theodore Roosevelt, Sep. 27, 1902, Theodore Roosevelt Papers.

53. George B. Cortelyou to Philander C. Knox, Jan. 24, 1902, H. L. Remmel to Philander C. Knox, Mar. 13, 1902, Justice Department, Arkansas Appointment Papers, NA, RG 60; Marvin F. Russel, "The Rise of a Republican Leader," 251–52; Willard B. Gatewood, Jr., "Theodore Roosevelt and Arkansas, 1901–1902," *Arkansas Historical Quarterly* XXXII (Spring, 1973): 8; *The Arkansas Gazette,* Jan. 30, Feb. 12, Mar. 5, 20, 1902; T. Roosevelt to P. Clayton, Oct. 4, 1902, Theodore Roosevelt Papers.

54. Powell Clayton to Theodore Roosevelt, Jan. 15, 1904, T. Roosevelt to P. Clayton, Jan. 21, 1904, P. Clayton to T. Roosevelt, Apr. 2, 1904, Theodore Roosevelt Papers.

55. P. Clayton to T. Roosevelt, Jan. 15, 1904, Theodore Roosevelt Papers.

56. P. Clayton to H. L. Remmel, May 18, 1897, H. L. Remmel to P. Clayton, Oct. 18, 1899, P. Clayton to H. L. Remmel, Oct. 23, 1899, Remmel Papers. P. Clayton to T. Roosevelt, Jan. 15, 1904, Theodore Roosevelt Papers; A. S. Fowler to C. C. Long, Feb. 23, 1906, Charles Greaves to T. Roosevelt, Jan. 8, 1906, Justice Department, Arkansas Appointment Papers, NA, RG 60.

57. *The Arkansas Gazette,* Apr. 4, 1906.

58. C. B. S. to Mr. Cole, May 5, 1910, Justice Department, Arkansas Appointment Papers, NA, RG 60.

59. Henry M. Cooper to William McKinley, Dec. 25, 1897, Henry M. Cooper to Cornelius N. Bliss, Jan. 2, 1898, Samuel W. Fordyce to William McKinley, telegram, Jul. 20, 1897, "Memorandum concerning Martin A. Eisele," n.d., Interior Department, Hot Springs Reservation Appointment Papers, National Archives. W. S. Holt and others to Powell Clayton, Oct. 18, 1899; H. L. Remmel to Powell Clayton, Oct. 18, 1899, S. W. Fordyce to Powell Clayton, Nov. 24, 1899, Powell Clayton to H. L. Remmel, Nov. 30, 1899, Powell Clayton to H. L. Remmel, Nov. 11, 1901, Remmel Papers. *The Arkansas Gazette,* Jun. 24, 1898.

Eight: Decline of the Davis Faction, 1907–1912

1. Joseph T. Robinson to A. F. Yopp, May 30, 1907, Joseph T. Robinson Papers.

2. Jeff Davis's Ozark address of February 18, 1908, is quoted in H. L. Williams, *Behind the Scenes in Arkansas Politics,* 11.

3. *The Arkansas Gazette,* Jan. 6, Feb. 25, 26, 1897, Apr. 7, 1901, Apr. 26, 1903.

4. "Motion to Advance Cause," n.d., received by U.S. Supreme Court on April 10, 1907, *Hammond Packing Co. V. State of Arkansas,* National Archives, Transcript of United States Supreme Court Case, 212 U.S. 322, File No. 20649, Box 3705, RG 267; 212 *U.S. Reports* 322, 322–54.

5. "A Business Governor," *The World's Work,* XVII (December, 1908): 10965.

6. *The Malvern Times Journal,* n.d., quoted in the *Southern Standard* (Arkadelphia), Nov. 21, 1907.

7. Charles Jacobson to Joseph T. Robinson, Dec. 11, 1907, Joseph T. Robinson Papers.

8. These primary results were the official returns as compiled by the Democratic Central Committee but did not include three counties which were quite late in sending returns. The returns are found in the *Arkansas Sentinel* (Fayetteville), Apr. 16, 1908.

9. *The Arkansas Sentinel,* Apr. 2, 1908.

10. *The Arkansas Gazette,* Jun. 3, 1908.

11. Jeff Davis to George Donaghey, n.d., printed in the *Arkansas Sentinel,* Apr. 2, 1908.

12. George Donaghey to Jeff Davis, n.d., printed in the *Arkansas Sentinel,* Apr. 9, 1908; Charles Jacobson, *The Life Story of Jeff Davis,* 131; H. L. Williams, *Behind the Scenes in Arkansas Politics,* 10.

13. *The Arkansas Gazette,* Jun. 3, 1908.

14. *The Arkansas Gazette,* May 3, 5, 1908.

15. *The Arkansas Gazette,* May 3, June 2, 3, 1908.

16. *The Arkansas Gazette,* Jun. 3, 4, 1908.

17. *Proceedings of the Arkansas Bankers Association, 1908* (Little Rock, 1908), 90, 91, 96, 21.

18. *The Arkansas Gazette,* Jun. 25, 1908; William F. Kirby to Woodrow Wilson, Aug. 2, 1917, Woodrow Wilson Papers.

19. "A Businesslike Governor," *The World's Work,* XVII (December, 1908): 10966.

20. *Message of Governor George W. Donaghey to the Thirty-Seventh General Assembly, 1909* (n.p., 1909), 39, 37–41; *Message of Governor George W. Donaghey to the Members of the Thirty-Eighth General Assembly* (Little Rock, 1911), 58–61; *Message of George W. Donaghey, Governor of Arkansas, to the Extraordinary Session of the Thirty-Eighth General Assembly* (n.p., 1911), 10–14, 15; "A Businesslike Governor," *The World's Work,* XVII (December, 1908): 10965–66.

21. John A. Treon has recounted the story of the political entanglements of the capitol project. He tells of the "boodling" and improper use of influence by the firm of Caldwell & Drake, but he argues that their failings were not so serious as Jeff Davis and George Donaghey led contemporaries to believe. Vilification and reckless charges were the political coin of the day. Treon believes Donaghey, because of his desire to exploit the issue for political gain, should be remembered not as the governor who cut through all obstacles to complete the work, but as an obstructionist himself. Donaghey's course of action caused more disruption than the mistakes of Caldwell & Drake. Treon's work is a helpful corrective to Donaghey's self-adulatory work, *Building a State Capitol.* See John A. Treon, "Politics and Concrete: The Building of the Arkansas State Capitol, 1899–1917," *Arkansas Historical Quarterly,* XXXI (Summer, 1972): 99–149.

22. Dewey W. Grantham, *Hoke Smith,* 173–74; George Brown Tindall, *The Emergence of the New South,* 213; Thomas L. Baxley, "Prison Reforms During the Donaghey Administration," *Arkansas Historical Quarterly,* XXII (Spring, 1963): 76–84.

23. *Congressional Record,* 59th Congress, 1st Session, Apr. 23, 24, 1906, 5688ff.

24. *Congressional Record,* 60th Congress, 1st Session, Dec. 11, 1907, 273, 282.

25. *The New York Times,* Dec. 3, 12, 1907, Jan. 3, 1913.

26. *Congressional Record,* 60th Congress, 1st Session (May 1, 1908), 5521, 5526.

27. *The Arkansas Gazette,* May 2, 1908; *The Arkansas Democrat,* May 2, 1908.

28. *Congressional Record,* 60th Congress, 2nd Session (January 26, 1909), 1402, 1412.

29. Jerry Wallace, *An Arkansas Judge,* 51.

30. *Hearing Held Before The Committee on The Public Lands of the House of Representatives* (Washington, 1910), 20, located in the Library of Congress.

31. *Sunk Lands Hearings.*

32. *Sunk Lands Hearings,* 4–15; *Arkansas Sentinel* (Fayetteville), May 10, 1910.

33. J. L. Henson to Congressman Charles Crow, *Sunk Lands Hearings,* 383.

34. *Sunk Lands Hearings,* 9, 36.

35. Chauncey M. Depew, *My Memories of Eighty Years* (New York, 1924), 184–85; *The Arkansas Gazette,* May 2, 1908; Reinhard H. Luthin in *American Demagogues,* 308, argues that Southern demagogues tended to retreat from their early radicalism after they achieved power. Dewey W. Grantham in *The Democratic South,* 50–51, asserts that men of the Blease and Tillman type "usually became less rebellious, less representative of the poorer classes, often making their peace with the political hierarchies and the business interests" once in office.

36. *Sunk Lands Hearings,* 200–06, 205, 206.

37. *Speech of Sen. Jeff Davis, Delivered at Morrilton, Arkansas, December 4, 1911* (n.d., n.p.), 7, 5–11, printed speech located in "Jeff Davis" microfilm, Film 121, University of Arkansas, Fayetteville.

38. *The Arkansas Gazette,* Feb. 4, 1912.

39. *The Arkansas Gazette,* Feb. 15, 1912.

40. Charles Jacobson, *The Life Story of Jeff Davis,* 141–42.

41. "Jeff Davis and the 'Red-Necks,'" *The Literary Digest,* (Jan. 25, 1913): 192, 194; *Speech of Sen. Jeff Davis, Delivered at Morrilton,* 5.

42. Charles Jacobson, *The Life Story of Jeff Davis,* 146; "Jeff Davis and The 'Red-Necks,'" *The Literary Digest,* (Jan. 25, 1913), 192.

43. *The Arkansas Democrat,* Jan. 3, 1913.

Nine: Changing Patterns in the Democratic Party, 1912–1917

1. The remark of Congressman W. L. Terry and the eulogy of Joseph T. Robinson by Senator John Miller are found in *Memorial Services Held in the House of Representatives and Senate of the United States, Together With Remarks Presented in Eulogy of Joseph Taylor Robinson* (Washington, 1938), 37, 111.

2. George W. Donaghey, *Autobiography of George W. Donaghey, Governor of Arkansas, 1909–1913* (Benton, Arkansas, 1939), 215; Nevin E. Neal, "A Biography of Joseph T. Robinson," 10.

3. *The Arkansas Gazette,* Aug. 25, 1896; John E. Chiles, "The Early Public Career of Joseph Taylor Robinson," (unpublished M.A. thesis, Vanderbilt University, 1953), 1–7; Nevin Emil Neal, "A Biography of Joseph T. Robinson," (unpublished Ph.D. dissertation, University of Oklahoma, 1958), 13–20, 57–62.

4. Nevin E. Neal, "A Biography of Joseph T. Robinson," 93.

5. *Arkansas Sentinel* (Fayetteville), Apr. 21, 1910; Nevin E. Neal, "A Biography of Joseph T. Robinson," 94–98; Neal concludes that the Davis victory of

1912 came partly through the aid of Robinson. It is true that Robinson's margin of victory was much greater than Davis's.

6. A. H. France to Joseph T. Robinson, Jan. 18, 1912, Earl Hardin to Joseph T. Robinson, n.d. (This letter probably was written in January or February 1912, since it is found with correspondence of that period), Joseph T. Robinson Papers; *The Arkansas Gazette,* Jan. 18, 1912, Mar. 19, 1912.

7. *The Arkansas Gazette,* Jan. 2, 4, Feb. 9, Mar. 1, 1912.

8. Paul E. Isaac, *Prohibition and Politics: Turbulent Decades in Tennessee, 1885–1920* (Knoxville, 1965), 188, 189.

9. George B. Tindall, *The Emergence of the New South,* 18, 19.

10. *The Arkansas Gazette,* Aug. 28, 1896.

11. *The Arkansas Gazette,* Jan. 16, Feb. 7, 1912.

12. Ira D. Oglesby to Joseph T. Robinson, n.d. (apparently written between Jan. and Mar. 1912), Ira Oglesby to Joseph T. Robinson, Mar. 2, 1912, Joseph T. Robinson Papers.

13. *The Arkansas Gazette,* Mar. 17, 1912; Lewis L. Gould, "Progressives and Prohibitionists: Texas Democratic Politics, 1911–1921," *Southwestern Historical Quarterly* LXXV (July, 1971): 5–18; Paul E. Isaac, *Prohibition and Politics: Turbulent Decades In Tennessee, 1885–1920* (Knoxville, 1965), 264–65.

14. *The Arkansas Gazette,* Jan. 16, Feb. 7, Mar. 11, 1912; clipping from the Fort Smith *Southwest American,* n.d., found with letter from Ira D. Oglesby to Joseph T. Robinson, Jan. 12, 1912, Robinson Papers; *The Arkansas Sentinel* (Fayetteville), Sep. 7, 1911, contains a detailed discussion of the Turner-Jacobson Bill.

15. John E. Chiles, "The Early Public Career of Joseph Taylor Robinson," 55, 56; *The Arkansas Gazette,* Jun. 1, 6, 7, 1912.

16. John E. Chiles, "The Early Public Career of Joseph Taylor Robinson," 62–66; Reverend H. L. Winburn to Charles H. Brough, Jan. 25, 1913, L. C. Smith to Charles H. Brough, Feb. 10, 1913, Charles H. Brough Papers, Special Collections, University of Arkansas library, Fayetteville.

17. *The Arkansas Democrat,* Sep. 16, 1927, clipping found in George Washington Hays Papers; Harry Lee Williams, *Behind the Scenes in Arkansas Politics,* 15.

18. George W. Hays to Charles H. Brough, Jan. 25, 1913, Charles H. Brough Papers, *The Arkansas Gazette,* Apr. 14, 1913, clipping in Charles H. Brough Scrapbooks, University of Arkansas, Fayetteville.

19. *The Arkansas Gazette,* Apr. 29, May 2, Jun. 12, 1913.

20. R. F. Milwee to Eugene Williams, June 19, 1913, R. F. Milwee to J. M. Bush, June 10, 1913; the letters are published by Milwee as a political advertisement in *The Arkansas Gazette,* June 20, 1913; see also Williams' denial of the allegations in Eugene Williams to R. F. Milwee, Jun. 17, 1913, *The Arkansas Gazette,* Jun. 19, 1913.

21. *The Arkansas Gazette,* Jun. 24, 25, 26, 27, 1913.

22. *Digest of Rules, As Amended and Adopted by the Democratic State Central Committee,* Jul. 30, 1912 (Little Rock, n.d.), 14, 15.

23. *The Arkansas Gazette,* Jul. 2, 3, 4, 5, 1913.

24. *The Arkansas Gazette,* Jul. 2, 4, 5, 12, 22, 1913; *Biennial Report of the Secretary of State, 1913–1920* (Little Rock, 1921), 328; *The Log Cabin Democrat* (Conway), Aug. 6, 1913; The governors in 1913 were George Donaghey, Joseph T. Robinson, W. K. Oldham, J. M. Futrell, and George Hays.

25. Harry L. Williams, *Behind the Scenes in Arkansas Politics,* 12; *The Log Cabin Democrat,* Apr. 1, 3, 4, June 3, 4, 1914.

26. Charles H. Brough to Woodrow Wilson, Nov. 9, 1910, Woodrow Wilson Papers.

27. Arthur S. Link, *Wilson: The Road to the White House* (Princeton, 1947), 312; A. S. Link, "The Wilson Movement in Texas, 1910–1912," *Southwestern Historical Quarterly*, XLVIII (October, 1944): 171; Burton Ira Kaufman, "Virginia Politics and The Wilson Movement, 1910–1914," *Virginia Magazine of History and Biography*, LXXVII (January, 1969): 3–8; Lewis L. Gould, "Progressives and Prohibitionists: Texas Democratic Politics, 1911–1921," *Southwestern Historical Quarterly*, LXXV (July, 1971): 11.

28. *The Arkansas Gazette*, Jan. 5, Mar. 7, 22, 1912.

29. *The Arkansas Gazette*, Mar. 29, 1912; George W. Donaghey, *Autobiography of George W. Donaghey*, 255; William F. McCombs, *Making Wilson President* (New York, 1921), 109; Maurice F. Lyons, *William F. McCombs, The President Maker* (Cincinnati, 1922), 72.

30. *The Arkansas Gazette*, Mar. 10, 11, 14, 20, 22, 1912.

31. *The Arkansas Gazette*, Jun. 4, 5, 6, 1912.

32. *The Arkansas Gazette*, Jun. 26, 27, 1912.

33. Arthur Link, "The Wilson Movement in Texas, 1910–1912," *Southwestern Historical Quarterly*, XLVIII (October, 1944): 169–85; Arthur S. Link, "A Letter from one of Wilson's Managers," *American Historical Review*, L (July, 1945): 768–75; Arthur S. Link, *Wilson, The Road to the White House*, 333, 415, 445.

34. Edward M. House to Albert S. Burleson, Aug. 25, 1914, Albert S. Burleson to Edward M. House, Aug. 27, 1914, Albert Sidney Burleson Papers; *The Arkansas Gazette*, Apr. 25, 1916; William F. McCombs, *Making Woodrow Wilson President*, 5, 219–21; Maurice F. Lyons, *William F. McCombs, The President Maker* (Cincinnati, 1922), 132.

35. T. J. Pence to Joseph Tumulty, n.d., Woodrow Wilson to Franklin K. Lane, Aug. 7, 1913, see also Memorandum for the president, Aug. 6, 1913 (Box 226, Case file 4/400E), Woodrow Wilson Papers; clipping from the *Louisville Courier-Journal*, Mar. 19, 1913, William G. McAdoo Papers, Library of Congress, Washington, D.C.

36. William F. McCombs, *Making Woodrow Wilson President*, 212–17; Arthur S. Link, *Wilson: The Road to the White House*, 481; Arthur S. Link, *Wilson, The New Freedom* (Princeton, 1956), 4–10; Maurice F. Lyons, *William F. McCombs*, 130; Joseph P. Tumulty, *Woodrow Wilson As I Know Him* (Garden City, New York, 1921), 135; Tumulty, who had very little sympathy for McCombs, devotes a chapter to the Arkansan.

37. Arthur S. Link, *Wilson, The New Freedom*, 157–73; Oscar H. Winn to Charles B. Sornborger, May 27, 1913, Oscar H. Winn to William Jennings Bryan, Apr. 28, 1913, Justice Department, Arkansas Appointment Papers, NA, RG 60.

38. Oscar H. Winn to Woodrow Wilson, Jun. 10, 1913, Justice Department, Arkansas Appointment Papers, NA, RG 60.

39. *The Arkansas Gazette*, July 6, 12, 1913; Oscar H. Winn to W. J. Bryan, July 16, 1913, Justice Department, Arkansas Appointment Papers, NA, RG 60.

40. Andrew J. Hunter to James C. McReynolds, Jul. 19, 1913, Justice Department, Arkansas Appointment Papers, NA, RG 60.

41. Otis T. Wingo to Joseph P. Tumulty, Aug. 1, 1913, Woodrow Wilson Papers.

42. Burton I. Kaufman, "Virginia Politics and The Wilson Movement, 1910–1914," *The Virginia Magazine of History and Biography* LXXVII (January, 1969): 14–21.

43. Thomas S. Osborne to Josephus Daniels, May 13, 1913, Josephus Daniels Papers, Library of Congress.

44. Thomas S. Osborne to Josephus Daniels, May 2, 1913, see also T. S. Osborne to J. Daniels, May 26, 1913, Josephus Daniels Papers; Senator William Hughes to James C. McReynolds, May 15, 1913, Justice Department, Arkansas Appointment Papers, NA, RG 60.

45. Edwin Hines to Joseph T. Robinson, Apr. 14, 1913, Justice Department, Arkansas Appointment Papers, NA, RG 60.

46. George A. Henning to Joseph T. Robinson, Apr. 11, 1913, Justice Department, Arkansas Appointment Papers, NA, RG 60.

47. Sam R. Chew to Joseph T. Robinson, Apr. 3, 1913, Jeptha H. Evans to J. T. Robinson, Apr. 9, 1913, Justice Department, Arkansas Appointment Papers, NA, RG 60.

48. George Washington Wagner to Joseph T. Robinson, Apr. 8, 1913, Justice Department, Arkansas Appointment Papers, NA, RG 60.

49. "Memo on Conversation between Congressman Wingo and the Attorney General," May 29, 1913, James P. Clarke and Joseph T. Robinson to James C. McReynolds, May 31, 1913, Justice Department, Arkansas Appointment Papers, NA, RG 60.

50. Unidentified newspaper clipping found in Justice Department, Arkansas Appointment Papers, "Protest folder" containing items opposing reappointment of Bourland in 1917, NA, RG 60.

51. Jeremiah V. Bourland to Thomas Watt Gregory, Jun. 4, 1917, Justice Department, Arkansas Appointment Papers, NA, RG 60.

52. Webb Covington and Love Grant, General Counsel of the United Mine Workers of America to Joseph T. Robinson, n.d. (circa April, 1917), "Resolution by Democratic Central Committee of Sebastian County," Mar. 24, 1917, "Memorandum For the President concerning Emon O. Mahoney [sic], of El Dorado, Arkansas, Whose Nomination To Be United States Attorney, Western District of Arkansas, Is Recommended," Sep. 1, 1917, Justice Department, Arkansas Appointment Papers, NA, RG 60; Mahony's name is properly spelled without an e; another copy of the Memorandum is located in the Woodrow Wilson Papers, Box 226.

53. Secretary of State Tom J. Terral to Woodrow Wilson, Jan. 21, 1918, Charles Jacobson to T. W. Gregory, Apr. 19, 1917, Justice Department, Arkansas Appointment Papers, NA, RG 60.

54. Anne Firor Scott in "A Progressive Wind from the South, 1906–1913," *Journal of Southern History* XXIX (February, 1963): 53–70, concurred with the earlier view of Arthur Link that much of the impetus for the Progressive movement came from the South. Some of the most articulate supporters of the 1906 Hepburn Act were Southern Democrats. But Richard M. Abrams in "Woodrow Wilson and the Southern Congressmen, 1913–1916," *Journal of Southern History* XXII (November, 1956): 417–37, took issue with Link's view that Southern Congressmen pressured Wilson to take a more advanced reform position. Abrams believes that the Southerners were the instruments of a Wilson-initiated program. The so-called "radical progressives" did not form any consistent or cohesive group wedded to government intervention to regulate economic and social behavior. George Brown Tindall in *The Emergence of the New South,* 1–32, pictures Southern progressivism as an important influence in Washington. The major achievement of the movement in the South was the victory of the "public service concept of the state."

55. Anne Firor Scott, "A Progressive Wind from the South, 1906–1913,"

57, 68. Scott speaks of the "La Follette-style radicalism of James Clarke of Arkansas."

56. Arthur Wallace Dunn, *From Harrison to Harding,* Vol. II, 220, 267–69; "Senator Clarke," *Outlook* CXIV (October 11, 1916): 295–97; J. Roger Hollingsworth, *The Whirligig of Politics,* 204, 205; James P. Clarke to Thomas C. McRae, Aug. 18, 1913, Thomas C. McRae Papers.

57. See comments on the significance of the Adamson Act in Richard M. Abrams, "Woodrow Wilson and the Southern Congressmen, 1913–1916," 436.

58. George Donaghey, *Autobiography,* 241; Thomas R. Marshall, *Recollections of Thomas R. Marshall* (Indianapolis, 1925), 279–80.

59. *How Does Senator Clarke Stand at Washington,* a pamphlet published during the 1914 campaign and found in the David Y. Thomas Papers, Special Collections, University of Arkansas library, Fayetteville.

60. Arthur S. Link, *Wilson, The New Freedom,* 465–68; George Brown Tindall, *The Emergence of the New South,* 17–18; Lewis L. Gould, "Progressives and Prohibitionists," *Southwestern Historical Quarterly* LXXV (July, 1971): 11–13; Herbert F. Margullies, *The Decline of the Progressive Movement in Wisconsin,* 149.

61. Nevin Neal, "A Biography of Joseph T. Robinson," 125–27.

62. Joseph T. Robinson to Joseph P. Tumulty, Apr. 22, 1914, Woodrow Wilson Papers.

63. Richard M. Abrams, "Woodrow Wilson and the Southern Congressmen, 1913–1916," 431, 432; although Abrams argues that the "Progressives" were inconsistent, he lists Robinson and five other Southern senators as unfailingly loyal to child labor reform.

64. T. A. Wilson to Clara M. Beyer, Feb. 17, 1925, T. A. Wilson to Clara M. Beyer, May 13, 1925, League of Women Voters Papers, Library of Congress.

65. *The Log Cabin Democrat* (Conway), Oct. 17, Nov. 22, 25, Dec. 19, 1913, Jan. 13, 1914.

66. *The Log Cabin Democrat,* Nov. 22, 1913.

67. Arthur S. Link, *Wilson Campaigns for Progressivism and Peace, 1916–1917* (Princeton, 1965), 302 (footnote); Link considered the five men opposing the resolution to be "agrarian radicals or advanced progressives." In addition to Kirby, they included James K. Vardaman of Mississippi, Robert M. La Follette of Wisconsin, John D. Works of California, and A. J. Groma of North Dakota.

68. *Congressional Record,* 64th Cong., 2nd Sess. (Mar. 2, 1917), 4771.

69. Woodrow Wilson's statement is quoted in Walter Millis, *Road to War, America, 1914–1917* (Boston, 1935), 411; Arthur Link, *Wilson Campaigns for Progressivism and Peace,* 365; *Journal of the House of Representatives of Arkansas,* 31st Session (March 5, 1917), 989–90; *Journal of the Senate of Arkansas,* 31st Session (March 6, 1917), 64; *The Arkansas Gazette,* Mar. 6, 1917; *The New York Times,* Mar. 6, 1917; George B. Tindall, *The Emergence of the New South,* 46–48.

70. *Congressional Record,* 64th Cong., 2nd Sess. (Apr. 4, 1917), 221.

71. *The Batesville Record,* May 20, 1920, reprinted in *The Arkansas Democrat,* Jun. 9, 1920; Thaddeus H. Caraway to Newton D. Baker, Jun. 9, 1920, Newton D. Baker Papers, Library of Congress, Washington, D.C.

72. Newton D. Baker to Woodrow Wilson, Feb. 26, 1921, Joseph T. Robinson to Woodrow Wilson, Jan. 22, 1921, Joseph T. Robinson to Woodrow Wilson, Feb. 23, 1921, Woodrow Wilson to Joseph T. Robinson, Feb. 25, 1921, see also N. B. Dial and Morris Sheppard to Woodrow Wilson, Dec. 22, 1920, Woodrow Wilson Papers.

73. Thomas C. McRae to Woodrow Wilson, Mar. 12, 1913; Joseph T. Robinson to Thomas C. McRae, Jul. 28, 1913, *Shall The Banks Control the Currency or Shall the Government Control It?* Remarks of Thomas C. McRae Before

American Bankers' Association at Boston, Mass., Oct. 9, 1913, (n.d., n.p.), 3, 4, 6,~8, pamphlet located in Thomas C. McRae Papers, Special Collections, University of Arkansas library, Fayetteville.

74. *The Arkansas Gazette,* Jun. 17, 1904.

75. David Y. Thomas, *Arkansas and Its People,* Vol. IV, 509–10; *Memorial Services Held in the House of Representatives of the United States, Together with Remarks Presented in Eulogy of Otis T. Wingo* (Washington, 1931), 5, 36.

76. *Memorial Services for Otis Wingo,* 52, 36.

77. *The Arkansas Gazette,* Jul. 20, 1913; Arthur S. Link, *Wilson, The New Freedom,* 218–22.

78. Otis T. Wingo to William G. McAdoo, Jul. 17, 1913, WIlliam G. McAdoo Papers.

79. Richard M. Abrams, "Woodrow Wilson and the Southern Congressmen, 1913–1916," 421; Abrams cites Wingo's retreat as one evidence that the president held the upper hand in shaping and directing reform legislative efforts.

80. James R. Green, *Grass-Roots Socialism: Radical Movements in the Southwest, 1895–1943* (Baton Rouge, 1978), 17, 23, 30, 33, 76–77, 195, 201, 247–48, 285–86, 300–01; Robert E. Doherty, "Thomas J. Hagerty, The Church, and Socialism," *Labor History* III (Winter, 1962): 39–56.

Ten: The Woodrow Wilson of Arkansas

1. Address of Governor-elect C. H. Brough introducing W. J. Bryan at Helena, Arkansas, Jun. 4, 1916, William Jennings Bryan Papers.

2. Address by Charles H. Brough to the Silver Republican Club in Ogden, Utah, Sep. 3, 1896, Charles H. Brough Papers.

3. Franklin L. Riley, "To Whom It May Concern," Jun. 3, 1902, Brough Papers. For Brough's education and his early years as a college teacher and his interest in historical studies see Foy Lisenby, "Charles Hillman Brough As Historian," *Arkansas Historical Quarterly,* XXXV (Summer, 1976): 115–26.

4. J. S. Rogers, *History of Arkansas Baptists* (Little Rock, 1948), 227; see also Reverend C. B. Waller to C. H. Brough, Nov. 18, 1918; Speech Before Southern Baptist Convention at New Orleans, May 9, 1901, Brough Papers; Booth Lowrey, "To Whom It May Concern," Feb. 23, 1904, Brough Papers.

5. Charles Orson Cook, "'Boosterism and Babbitry': Charles Hillman Brough and the 'Selling' of Arkansas," *Arkansas Historical Quarterly,* XXXVII (Spring, 1978): 74–83. For a study of Brough's record as a public speaker see Ralph W. Widener, Jr., "Charles Hillman Brough," *Arkansas Historical Quarterly* XXXIV (Summer, 1975): 99–121; See also Widener's unpublished dissertation, "The Political Speaking of Charles Hillman Brough in 1916 and 1932," (Southern Illinois University, 1962).

6. George Brown Tindall, *The Emergence of the New South, 1913–1945,* 21–24, 229–30; Raymond H. Pulley, *Old Virginia Restored: An Interpretation of the Progressive Impulse, 1870–1930* (Charlottesville, 1968), 171–88.

7. Roy Wood to C. H. Brough, Jul. 19, 1916, Loid Rainwater to C. H. Brough, Jan. 25, 1913, Dr. F. B. Kirby to C. H. Brough, Mar. 13, 1913, Clarence J. McLellon to C. H. Brough, Mar. 10, 1913, Brough Papers.

8. Undated C. H. Brough Circular (probably January to March, 1912), Mary Lee Robinson to C. H. Brough, Mar. 12, 1916, G. T. Schrader to C. H. Brough, Mar. 28, 1916, Brough Papers.

9. An alliance seems to be implicit in a letter from Robinson aide H. S. Traylon to C. H. Brough, Jan. 12, 1913, Brough Papers.

10. *Extract from C. H. Brough Speeches in His Candidacy for Governor of Arkansas; Refusal of Mr. Hodges to Allow the People's Committee to Examine Into The Financial Condition of the Secretary of State's Office. Why?* (n.p., n.d.), pamphlet in Brough Papers.

11. "Circular Letter from Brough Headquarters to the People of Washington County," n.d., italics are in the original circular, Brough Papers.

12. C. H. Brough to G. W. Roark, Dec. 27, 1915, Brough Papers.

13. See "Speech of Dr. C. H. Brough, Candidate For Governor, Delivered at Russellville, November 29, 1915," Brough Papers.

14. Manuscript reply of C. H. Brough to Earl Hodges, n.d., Manuscript, "Copy of Announcement by Brough Denouncing Charges made by Mr. Hodges," n.d., Brough Papers; Charles W. Crawford, "From Classroom to State Capitol, Charles H. Brough and The Campaign of 1916," *Arkansas Historical Quarterly,* XXI (Autumn, 1962): 220–22.

15. C. W. Crawford, "From Classroom to State Capitol," 220–21.

16. *Extracts From C. H. Brough's Speeches In His Candidacy For Governor of Arkansas, The Hays-Hodges Combine,* (n.p., n.d.), pamphlet from Brough Papers; George Hays boasted in a speech at Newport, "I prevented from becoming a law the infamous race horse gambling bill." He expressed chagrin at criticism of his hesitation and reminded the voters that he did veto the bill. See clipping of his Newport speech in *The Newark Journal,* Aug. 17, 1916, George Washington Hays Papers.

17. St. Francis Levee Board, *History of the Organization and Operations of the Board of Directors St. Francis Levee District of Arkansas, 1893–1945* (n.p., n.d.), 1, 24, 96, 274; *Sunk Lands Hearings,* 201.

18. *The Arkansas Sentinel* (Fayetteville), Apr. 15, 22, 1909.

19. *Extracts From C. H. Brough's Speeches,* Brough Papers; *The Arkansas Gazette,* Jul. 19, 1913.

20. *History of the St. Francis Levee District,* 96; *Extracts from C. H. Brough's Speeches,* Minnie U. Rutherford-Fuller to C. H. Brough, Nov. 28, 1916, Brough Papers.

21. John Gibson to C. H. Brough, Jan. 23, 1913, T. P. Johnson to C. H. Brough, Jan. 25, 1913, Guy E. Williams to C. H. Brough, June 7, 1915, Brough Papers.

22. Ira D. Oglesby, Jr. to Joseph T. Robinson, Feb. 14, 1912, M. W. Hazel (of Marked Tree) to Joseph T. Robinson, Feb. 28, 1912, Joseph T. Robinson Papers; Harry Lee Williams, *Behind the Scenes in Arkansas Politics,* 108–10.

23. Harry Lee Williams, *Behind The Scenes in Arkansas Politics,* 19–20.

24. C. H. Brough to A. W. Sharp, Mar. 20, 1916, Brough Papers.

25. William J. Humphries to C. H. Brough, Apr. 7, 1916, Minnie U. Rutherford-Fuller to C. H. Brough, Nov. 28, 1916, Mrs. John I. Jones to C. H. Brough, Apr. 4, 1916, Brough Papers.

26. *History of the St. Francis Levee District,* 275.

27. Charles H. Brough, "The Heroic Spirit of Arkansas," *Dixie Magazine* III (June, 1927): 23, located in the George Washington Hays Papers.

28. *The Arkansas Gazette,* Jun. 1, 2, 1916.

29. *Speech of Dr. C. H. Brough, Candidate for Governor, Delivered at Russellville, November 29, 1915,* pamphlet, Brough Papers; *The Arkansas Gazette,* April 26, 1916; Allan Kennedy to C. H. Brough, Jan. 27, 1913, Brough Papers.

30. Lewis L. Gould, *The Progressive Era* (Syracuse, 1974), 142–46; Phillip Wayne Russell, "Fort Smith City Government and the Progressive Era in Urban Reform," (unpublished M.A. thesis, University of Arkansas, Fayetteville, 1981), 10, 20, 45; Ernest S. Griffith, *A History of American City Government: The*

Progressive Years and their Aftermath, 1900–1920 (New York, 1974), 57; Lewis L. Gould, *Progressives and Prohibitionists: Texas Democrats in the Wilson Era* (Austin, 1973), 51.

31. Fort Smith *Southwest American,* Feb. 19, 1913, quoted in Phillip W. Russell, "Fort Smith City Government," 33.

32. Phillip W. Russell, "Fort Smith City Government," 38–41.

33. Martha Williamson Rimmer, "Charles E. Taylor and his Administration, 1911–1919; Progressivism in Little Rock," (unpublished M.A. thesis, University of Arkansas, Fayetteville, 1977), 81–83; *Arkansas Gazette*, March 3, 1911; April 21, 1911.

34. M. W. Rimmer, "Charles E. Taylor," 3–10.

35. Ibid., 12, 29–38.

36. Ibid., 64–79.

37. *Speech of Dr. C. H. Brough, Candidate for Governor, Nov. 29, 1915,* Brough Papers.

38. *Speech of Dr. C. H. Brough, Candidate for Governor, Nov. 29, 1915,* Brough Papers.

39. "Typed Manuscript of Address to the 1918 Democratic State Convention," Brough Papers.

40. Foy Lisenby, "The First Meeting of The Arkansas Conference of Charities and Correction," *Arkansas Historical Quarterly* XXVI (Summer, 1967): 155–61.

41. Foy Lisenby, "The Arkansas Conference on Charities and Correction, 1912–1937," *Arkansas Historical Quarterly* XXIX (Spring, 1970): 41–42.

42. George Brown Tindall, *The Emergence of the New South,* 7–8; Dewey W. Grantham, *Southern Progressivism: The Reconciliation of Progress and Tradition* (Knoxville, 1983), 374–85.

43. D. W. Grantham, *Southern Progressivism,* 246.

44. Ibid., 246–74.

45. David Michael Moyers, "Arkansas Progressivism: The Legislative Record," (unpublished Ph.D. dissertation, University of Arkansas, Fayetteville, 1986), 72–73; C. Vann Woodward, *Origins of the New South, 1877–1913* (Baton Rouge, 1966), 398–99. Moyers provides a useful analysis of Arkansas educational reforms.

46. D. M. Moyers, "Arkansas Progressivism," 79–80.

47. Ibid., 77–78.

48. Ibid., 85–86.

49. Ibid., 89–98; Waddy W. Moore, "George Washington Donaghey," *Governors of Arkansas,* ed. by Timothy P. Donovan and Willard B. Gatewood, Jr., (Fayetteville, 1981), 130–31.

50. Ibid., 103–21; Foy Lisenby, "Charles Hillman Brough," in *The Governors of Arkansas,* ed. by Timothy P. Donovan and Willard B. Gatewood, Jr., (Fayetteville, 1981), 147–48.

51. For a statistical summary of educational progress of all Southern states see Dewey W. Grantham, *Southern Progressivism,* 258.

52. D. M. Moyers, "Arkansas Progressivism," 156–57.

53. Ibid., 159–60.

54. Ibid., 150–54; Thomas Rothrock, "Joseph Carter Corbin and Negro Education in the University of Arkansas," *Arkansas Historical Quarterly* XXX (Winter, 1971): 311; Elizabeth L. Wheeler, "Isaac Fisher: The Frustrations of a Negro Educator at Branch Normal College, 1902–1911," *Arkansas Historical Quarterly* XLI (Spring, 1982): 7–8, 47.

55. Thomas E. Patterson, *History of the Arkansas Teachers Association,* (Wash-

ington, D.C., 1981), 11, 21–24; See also Thomas Rothrock, "Joseph Carter Corbin and Negro Education," 277–78; The State Teachers Association of Arkansas came to be known as the Arkansas Teachers Association in 1938. In 1969 it merged with the Arkansas Education Association which had formerly been the white teachers' organization.

56. Unidentified manuscript speech of George Washington Hays, n.p., n.d., located in George Washington Hays Papers.

57. A. Elizabeth Taylor, "The Woman Suffrage Movement In Arkansas," *Arkansas Historical Quarterly* XV (Spring, 1956): 44–50; G. B. Tindall, *The Emergence of the New South,* 222–23.

58. D. W. Grantham, *Southern Progressivism,* 92–93.

59. Ibid., 34.

60. Ibid., 92–93.

61. Joe Tolbert Segraves, "Arkansas Politics, 1874–1918," (unpublished Ph.D. dissertation, University of Kentucky, 1973), 322–24; Anne Firor Scott, "A Progressive Wind from the South, 1906–13," *Journal of Southern History,* XXIX (February, 1963): 70; Howard W. Allen, "Geography and Politics: Voting on Reform Issues in the United States Senate, 1911–1916," *Journal of Southern History* XXVII (May, 1961): 220; Richard L. Niswonger, "William F. Kirby, Arkansas's Maverick Senator," *Arkansas Historical Quarterly* XXXVII (Autumn, 1978): 263.

62. Rod Farmer, "Direct Democracy in Arkansas, 1910–1918," *Arkansas Historical Quarterly,* XL (Summer, 1981): 99–102.

63. Ibid., 101–09.

64. Ibid., 103–04; *The Arkansas Gazette,* Aug. 21, Sep. 6, 1910.

65. *The Arkansas Gazette,* Jun. 4, 1912.

66. Minnie U. Rutherford-Fuller to Judson King, Nov. 5, 1916, Charles H. Brough to T. A. Wilson (telegram), n.d., David Y. Thomas to Judson King, Nov. 10, 1916, L. H. Moore to Judson King, Oct. 11, 1916, "List of Arkansas Weekly Newspapers Who Favored Amendment No. 10," manuscript, Judson King Papers, Library of Congress.

67. L. H. Moore to Judson King, Oct. 11, 1916, William S. U'Ren to Judson King (telegram), Oct. 24, 1916, William Jennings Bryan to Judson King (telegram), Nov. 4, 1916, Judson King to Rev. Charles G. Elliot, Nov. 2, 1916, Judson King to Robert L. Owen, Oct. 19, 1916, Judson King Papers, Library of Congress.

68. "Abstract of Senator Owen's Remarks on Proposed Amendment No. 13 Enlarging the Powers of the People Through the Initiative and Referendum," typed manuscript bears R. S. Owen "O.K.," Judson King Papers.

69. Robert M. La Follette to Judson King (telegram), Oct. 24, 1916, Judson King Papers; *Speech of Dr. C. H. Brough, Candidate For Governor, Nov. 29, 1915,* Brough Papers.

70. *Biennial Report of the Secretary of State, 1913–20* (Little Rock, 1920), 352.

71. Judson King to Thaddeus H. Caraway, Nov. 15, 1916, Judson King to Thaddeus H. Caraway, Nov. 17, 1916, Judson King to David Y. Thomas, Nov. 16, 1916, David Y. Thomas to Judson King, Nov. 9, 1916, Judson King Papers; Kelly Bryant, *Historical Report of the Secretary of State (Arkansas)* (Little Rock, 1968), 191; Amendment No. 13 actually became Amendment 7 in the Arkansas Constitution.

72. Virginia Gray, "Anti-Evolution Sentiment and Behavior: The Case of Arkansas," *Journal of American History* LVII (September, 1970): 352–66.

73. Willard B. Gatewood, Jr. "Theodore Roosevelt and Arkansas, 1901–

1912," Arkansas Historical *Quarterly* XXXII (Spring, 1973): 15–16; *The Arkansas Gazette,* May 7, 1909; David M. Moyers, "Arkansas Progressivism," 521–22.

74. David M. Moyers, "Arkansas Progressivism," 523–27; Fred H. Lang, "Two Decades of State Forestry in Arkansas," *Arkansas Historical Quarterly* XXIV (Autumn, 1965): 211–13; Lewis L. Gould, ed., *The Progressive Era* (Syracuse, 1974), 122–23.

75. Ibid., 549.

76. Manuscript "Speech Before the Arkansas Hotel Men's Association," n.d., Brough Papers; Dallas T. Herndon, *Centennial History of Arkansas,* Vol. I, 384; National Consumer's League, *Labor News of Twelve Southern States* (New York, 1934), no pagination.

77. "Typed Manuscript of Address to the 1918 State Democratic Convention," *Message of Governor Charles H. Brough to the Forty-First General Assembly of Arkansas* (Little Rock, 1917), 71, Brough Papers.

78. *Message of Gov. Jefferson Davis. Delivered Before the General Assembly, Jan. 18, 1907.* (Little Rock, 1907), 22, 23, 24, 25; Carroll D. Wood to Charles H. Brough, Dec. 5, 1918, Brough Papers.

79. Manuscript address, "To the Bankers of Arkansas," n.d., Brough Papers.

80. Charles H. Brough, "The Proposed New Constitution," in pamphlet, Bar Association of Arkansas, *The Proposed new constitution; modern proposals for increasing the efficiency of the various departments of government. Papers read before the meeting of the Bar Association of Arkansas held May 31st and June 1st, 1917 at Hot Springs, Arkansas* (n.p., n.d.), 28.

81. *The Arkansas Gazette,* June 19, 1918; *Address to the People of the State of Arkansas* (n.p., n.d.) pamphlet prepared by the leaders of the constitutional convention of 1918, in Special Collections, University of Arkansas library, Fayetteville; *Biennial Report of the Secretary of State for 1913–20,* 105.

82. George B. Tindall, *The Emergence of the New South, 1913–1945,* 33–69, 230; Austin L. Venable, "The Arkansas Council of Defense in First World War," *Arkansas Historical Quarterly* II (June, 1943): 116–26; Dallas T. Herndon, *Centennial History of Arkansas,* Vol. 1, 717–20; Raymond H. Pulley, *Old Virginia Restored,* 172–73.

83. David Yancey Thomas, "Farms and the Man," *The Independent* XCI (Sep. 8, 1917): 392; John Gould Fletcher, *Arkansas,* 389; Albert D. Kirwan, *Revolt of the Rednecks,* 166.

84. David Yancey Thomas, "The Land and The People," *The Nation* CX (January, 1920): 34–35; John N. Southern, "Farm Land Ownership In The Southwest," *Bulletin,* Agricultural Experiment Station, Fayetteville (December, 1905), 3.

85. Benjamin Brawley, *A Social History of the American Negro* (New York, 1921; reprinted 1970 by Macmillan), 360.

86. Ibid., 361.

87. Charles H. Brough to Newton D. Baker, October, 1919. This letter and other pertinent documents can be found in Ralph H. Desmarais, "Military Intelligence Reports on Arkansas Riots: 1919–1920," *Arkansas Historical Quarterly* XXXIII (Summer, 1974): 175–91. See also B. Boren McCool, *Union, Reaction and Riot: A Biography of a Rural Race Riot* (Memphis, 1970).

88. Joey McCarty, "The Red Scare in Arkansas: A Southern State and National Hysteria," *Arkansas Historical Quarterly* XXXVII (Autumn, 1978): 264–77.

89. *Biennial Report of the Secretary of State for 1913–20,* 104–05.

Eleven: Conclusion

1. R. Hal Williams analyzes the ills of the party in his chapter "'Dry Bones and Dead Language': The Democratic Party," H. Wayne Morgan, ed., *The Gilded Age,* 129–48. See also J. Rogers Hollingsworth, *The Whirligig of Politics,* and Horace Samuel Merrill, *Bourbon Leader: Grover Cleveland and the Democratic Party,* 190–207.

2. George B. Tindall, *The Emergence of the New South, 1913–1945,* 21–23.

3. Anne Firor Scott in "A Progressive Wind from the South, 1906–1913," *Journal of Southern History,* XXIX (February, 1963): 53–70 argued that Southern congressmen had a major impact on the national Progressive movement. George Brown Tindall, *The Emergence of the New South,* 1–32 was in basic agreement, but Richard M. Abrams in "Woodrow Wilson and the Southern Congressmen, 1913–1916," *Journal of Southern History,* XXII (November, 1956): 417–37, emphasized the inconsistency and lack of unity among the agrarians of the South. Abrams pictured Woodrow Wilson as the major force behind progressivism. To him, Southern congressmen were at their worst foot draggers and obstructionists and at best a divided and ineffective force.

4. The views presented here are generally in line with those of Dewey W. Grantham as expressed in *The Democratic South,* 44–45; V. O. Key, Jr. in *Southern Politics in State and Nation,* 183–204, agrees that factions in Arkansas displayed greater cohesiveness and strength in the Davis era, but he pictures the normal Arkansas pattern as one of fluid factionalism. Groups arose briefly to support personalities during a campaign but lost their identity once the election was over. For Key the basic characteristic of Arkansas political culture is an issueless consensus politics. Leaders usually shared similar views and raised few important questions in their campaigns.

5. Albert D. Kirwan, *Revolt of the Rednecks,* 310–14.

6. Francis Butler Simkins, *Pitchfork Ben Tillman;* T. Harry Williams, *Huey Long,* 69; George B. Tindall, *The Emergence of the New South, 1913–1945,* 27, 28.

7. Arkansas also ranked forty-ninth in the median money income of families. In 1969 the median income for Arkansas was $6,273 while the nearest rival, Alabama, had a median of $7,266 and the national median was $9,590. U.S. Bureau of the Census, *Statistical Abstract of the United States: 1971* (Washington, D.C., 1971), 319, 326.

8. For a discussion of the "booster" spirit in American see Daniel J. Boorstin, *The Americans: The National Experience* (New York, 1967), 113–68.

9. *Some Democratic Facts: 1914 Platform of the Democratic Party of Arkansas,* 5, George Washington Hays Papers.

10. Alwyn Barr, *Reconstruction to Reform,* 153–60.

11. Sheldon Hackney, *Populism to Progressivism in Alabama,* 324–26.

12. George Brown Tindall, *The Emergence of the New South, 1913–1945,* 21–24, 229–30; Raymond H. Pulley, *Old Virginia Restored,* 171–88.

13. J. L. Charlton, "Social Aspects of Farm Ownership and Tenancy in the Arkansas Ozarks," *Bulletin,* Agricultural Experiment Station, University of Arkansas (September, 1947), 3.

Index